THE COLLECTIVE DREAM IN ART

THE COLLECTIVE DREAM IN ART

A Psycho-Historical Theory of Culture Based on Relations
between the Arts, Psychology, and The Social Sciences

WALTER ABELL

HARVARD UNIVERSITY PRESS · CAMBRIDGE · 1957

Designed by Burton Jones

Library of Congress Catalog Card Number 57–9067

Printed in the United States of America

Pm 4-4-63

ACKNOWLEDGMENT

The author gratefully acknowledges permission from the following American and British publishers to quote material from their publications: American Book Company, F. A. Ogg, *A Source Book of Medieval History*; the American Psychological Association, Ruth Landes, "The Abnormal Among the Ojibwa Indians," in the *Journal of Abnormal and Social Psychology*; the American Scandinavian Foundation, *The Saga of the Volsungs* translated by Margaret Schlauch; Cambridge University Press, G. G. Coulton, *Life in the Middle Ages*; The Champlain Society, *The Works of Samuel de Champlain*, Vols. I and II; Columbia University Press, Abram Kardiner and Associates, *The Psychological Frontiers of Society*, and Gregorius, *History of the Franks* translated by Ernest Brehaut; Dodd, Mead & Company, C. G. Jung, *Psychology of the Unconscious*; E. P. Dutton & Co., Inc., Lionello Venturi, *History of Art Criticism*; Harcourt, Brace and Company, Inc., *The Indians of North America from the Jesuit Relations and Allied Documents* edited by Edna Kenton; Harcourt, Brace and Company, Inc., and the Bollingen Foundation, Inc., C. G. Jung, *Contributions to Analytical Psychology*; the Hogarth Press, Ltd., Sigmund Freud, *Collected Papers*, Vol. V; Houghton Mifflin Company, *Beowulf and the Finnesburg Fragment* translated by C. G. Child; Alfred A. Knopf, Otto Rank, *Art and Artist*; Liveright Publishing Corporation, Sigmund Freud, *A General Introduction to Psychoanalysis* and *Group Psychology and the Analysis of the Ego*; The Macmillan Company, *My Life with the Eskimos* by Vilhjamur Steffanson, and Kingsley Davis, *Human Society*; Macmillan & Co., Ltd., *Le Morte d'Arthur*; *Sir Thomas Malory's Book of King Arthur and His Noble Knights of the Round Table* edited by A. W. Pollard; W. W. Norton & Company, Inc., Sigmund Freud, *New Introductory Lectures on Psychoanalysis*; Pantheon Books, Inc., Joseph Bedier, *The Romance of Tristan and Iseult*; Princeton University Press, *Literary Sources of Art History* edited by E. G. Holt, Henri Pirenne, *Medieval Cities*; Random House, Inc., Sigmund Freud, *Leonardo da Vinci*; The Royal Historical Society, *Walter of Henley's Husbandry* edited by E. Lamond; Charles Scribner's Sons, O. Thatcher and E. McNeal, *A Source Book for Medieval History*; and Thompson, James Westfall: *An Economic and Social History of the Middle Ages*, copyright, 1928, The Century Co., Reprinted by permission of Appleton-Century Crofts, Inc. Michigan State University and the Rockefeller Foundation have helped defray expenses on the manuscript; and its publication has been aided by the Bollingen Foundation and the Ford Foundation.

CONTENTS

LIST OF ILLUSTRATIONS

PART I

Chapter **I**

INTRODUCTION

For two centuries past, archeologists, anthropologists, and art historians have been diligently at work recovering the lost art of ancient civilizations, discovering for Western man the previously ignored art of far corners of the earth, and integrating new finds with old in a historical panorama of remarkable scope and splendor. Meanwhile artists, working with equal diligence, have extended the boundaries of contemporary Western art through a series of creative revolutions each of which has added a new style to our traditions. And — as if to complete the great circle of our cultural horizons — our latest innovations have revealed a surprising kinship with the art of the most distant times and places. Modern has merged with primitive, familiar with exotic, until what had been considered contrasts and oppositions now seem to us affinities. As a result of all these developments, recent generations have gained a perspective on the world's art never before equaled in range, depth, or clarity. They have also encountered problems in the interpretation of art never before equaled in complexity.

Fortunately for the consideration of their problems, the arts have not been alone in the recent rapid expansion of their sphere of consciousness. Other fields of study, expanding with equal rapidity, have offered us new instruments of thought with which to approach the intricacies of contemporary culture. The researches of the psychoanalysts have afforded us a new and more profound comprehension of the psychic life of humanity from which all creative activity flows. The social sciences have provided new insight into the organic processes involved in the evolution of cultures. The economic interpretation of history has deepened historical awareness until it comprehends, not only military and political surfaces, but also the technological and social vitalities behind them. A new universality of historical vision, embracing the civilizations of all times and places, is enabling historians to discern, at least dimly, the underlying and recurrent patterns of human existence.

As an art historian and critic, searching the mental horizons of our time for clues to the mysteries of creative and cultural life, I have been impressed with the importance of all these aspects of recent thought. I have also felt myself hampered by their comparative ignorance of, or opposition to, each other. Art history has made only a beginning in assimilating psychoanalytical and techno-social insights. Its factual stores are rich; its interpretation of them comparatively meagre and divided by conflicting opinions which reveal the absence of any definitive frame of critical reference.

Psychoanalytical writers on culture trace their interpretations for the most part to the infantile experiences and resulting complexes of the individual. These personal sources of creative motivation are undoubtedly important, but they provide no link with the great tides of social development on which cultures rise and fall; hence they can throw little light on those common factors of style and subject which the individual artist shares with large numbers of his contemporaries.

At the other extreme, the proponents of the economic interpretation of history stress the social and technological factors in cultural evolution, but take little account of the psychic processes through which alone a technological base can find expression in an ideological superstructure. As for the universal historians and sociologists like Toynbee and Sorokin, they seem to hold themselves aloof from recent developments in both psychology and economics, making little use of psychoanalytical insights and tending to oppose the assumption that culture rests in large part upon economic foundations.

All the systems of thought referred to above throw new light upon the phenomena of culture, but no one of them provides in itself a sufficiently broad approach to cultural problems. Accordingly, I have attempted to bridge the gaps between these different systems. The result has been the gradual emergence of a synthesis which we may call the "psycho-historical" or the "psycho-technic" theory of culture. To present this theory, and to illustrate it by reference to some typical forms of art, is the aim of the present volume.

Briefly, the psycho-historical theory suggests that art can not be fully comprehended in its own intrinsic terms as artists and critics have sometimes assumed, in terms of psychic processes as most psychoanalytical writers have assumed, or in terms of technological-economic processes as the economic determinists have maintained. As it is conceived here, art — and with it culture in general — is an outcome of the interplay *between* these varied and contrasting aspects of experience. Its roots are at once immaterial *and* material, personal *and* collective, psychological *and* technological. Hence the use of the terms "psycho-historical" and "psycho-technic," which we may regard as synonymous, and which are simply condensations of the unwieldy compounds, "psychological-historical" and "psychological-technological."

Psycho-historically considered, art is one of the cultural symbols into which society projects existent states of underlying psychic tension. These states of tension, in turn, are generated by historical experiences involving the entire range of individual and social life, including technological and economic life. As imagery symbolizing underlying and often unconscious psycho-historical depths, works of art function in the mental life of society much as do dreams in the experience of an individual. Thus, we are led to conceive the higher forms of cultural expression in any society as manifestations of a "collective dream."

The reader who thinks primarily in terms of specialty, whether it is psycho-analysis, medieval history, or iconography, may look with considerable skepticism upon an effort to correlate fields of knowledge so numerous and so diversified as those which underlie the psycho-historical point of view. On the one hand, he may question the validity of some of the other specialties or points of view upon which we shall draw, especially if they contrast with or oppose his own. Conversely, where our presentation involves his particular area of intensive research, he may feel that we have lost valuable detail or have shifted emphasis from what he considers to be the major concerns or essential procedures of his field.

The author would be the first to recognize inevitable limitations in his work — despite the fact that he has devoted ten years of painstaking effort to the studies of which this volume is an outcome. No individual can hope to attain a specialist's mastery of subjects which are separately so extensive, and mutually so diversified, as the history of art, psychology in its various branches, sociology, anthropology, and general history pressed in depth to include a concern with the social, economic, and technological developments of the epochs being studied. The sweep of knowledge beyond the grasp of even its greatest and most specialized exponents is well set forth in a later remark of Freud's about psychoanalysis: "Today I no longer command a view of the whole field." [1]

If the single field of knowledge is difficult to encompass, the effort to correlate one field with another is still more difficult. The student must rely upon the secondary reports of those more familiar with a given area than himself, and he may find his problem further complicated by the fact that the experts whom he consults do not always agree with each other. He is forced to attempt hazardous passages across the gaps between one area and another, and is in danger of falling into error both with regard to fact and to correlational judgment.

Nevertheless, I believe that if we recognize these possible limitations in the work to follow, we can also advance in its favor a qualifying condition and a compensating virtue. The qualifying condition is that, because it is an essay based in part upon new directions of thought, the present work must be regarded as suggestive and exploratory rather than definitive. If the trails which it breaks between previously separate intellectual territories prove to be fruitful explorations they will be deepened and widened by future use and increasing experience. They will benefit especially by the collaboration of minds having different points of departure in one or another of the fields that we are attempting to unify. The final significance of psycho-historical thinking must therefore be judged as much in the light of its potential future development as in terms of the particular statement which is given here.

At the same time, one can presumably claim for the present study certain results which have been unattainable by the individual specialties that form its background. This we may regard as the virtue that counterbalances the limitations already recognized. The work of a specialist, while achieving remarkable sharpness of detail within a restricted area, has its own inevitable limitations with regard to range, recognition of opposing points of view, and philosophical awareness of the totality of knowledge. In various later chapters, we shall review the history of recent thought as embodied on the one hand in the cultural applications of psychoanalysis and economic determinism and, on the other, in our older traditions of the history, criticism, and philosophy of art. We shall note in some detail both the indebtedness of the present theory to its component sources of knowledge and the reasons for the author's feeling that those sources, in isolation from each other, have failed to provide an adequate basis for the interpretation of art and other forms of cultural expression. The psycho-historical approach is an effort, not to replace the intensive labors of the specialists, but to deal with comprehensive problems for which they have offered, and I believe can offer, no solutions.

Before beginning the present study, perhaps we should observe parenthetically that the part played in it by visual art is one of demonstration and illustration rather than delimitation. It is true that the visual arts offer the most extensive and complete of all records of man's cultural activity. They provide an unbroken sequence of important examples covering some forty thousand years of human life — covering the entire span of human life since the ascent of man from his subhuman ancestors. Visual artifacts in the field of the industrial arts extend our knowledge of man's cultural evolution still further back through hundreds of thousands of years of subhuman development.

In addition to this unique time range, the visual arts offer the unusually varied manifestations of cultural life comprised by such diverse fields as those of industrial and decorative art, architecture, sculpture, graphic art, and painting. Thus, they are rich in their own intrinsic significance and they are particularly well suited to broader cultural studies of the kind we are about to make.

It would be a mistake, however, to suppose that our studies will be pertinent only to the visual aspects of culture. The principles which we shall follow and the conclusions toward which we shall work our way apply to all the arts and to all the aspects of culture — literature and drama, music and dance, myth, religion, and philosophy. They involve questions of cultural dynamics that concern the anthropologist and the ethnologist, the sociologist and the general historian, no less than the critic and historian of art. While we study one form of art in particular, we shall be seeking a deeper comprehension of culture in general, and shall in fact be concerned with forces that profoundly affect the whole course of human destiny. During the 1940's, while the present studies were taking shape, seemingly uncontrollable social and economic conflicts precipitated a second world war, subjected European peoples to a ghastly ordeal, and reduced many states to the brink of ruin. As this work goes to press in the mid-1950's, the persistence of the same basic conflicts has forced large sections of humanity to realize that the destruction of their civilization is within the range of possibility. The energies involved in such conflicts are neither exclusively material nor exclusively psychological. In their identification with both these realms of being, they are psycho-historical. The further we penetrate into the insights of psycho-history, the more likely we are to discover the means of mastering its disruptive forces and of directing its course toward goals of human fulfillment.

Chapter II

PSYCHOANALYSIS AND THE
INTERPRETATION OF CULTURE

The synthesis of modern critical thought that is the goal of this book might be compared to a mountain peak which must be scaled in order to get above the divides between one mental valley and another. Our hope would be to reach an altitude from which we could perceive, in a single panorama, what was experienced below as a number of separate worlds, each hidden from the others and visible only to itself.

Fortunately, we do not have to start from the bottom of a valley. Considerable work has already been done in exploring the connections between art, psychology, history, and other subjects. It has established correlational positions which can serve us, as base camps. We shall take two of the most advanced of such positions: the psychoanalytical interpretation of culture and the economic interpretation of it.

In the total force of the impact of these intellectual movements, both psychoanalysis and economic determinism seem destined to take their places among the revolutionary advances in human understanding. They are successors to such earlier awakenings as the geographical and astronomical discoveries whereby man learned that the earth was round and could be circumnavigated, and that it was not the center of the universe, but a tiny planet of the sun. And they are successors to the doctrine of evolution whereby man gained new understanding of the unity of the biological world and new humility in recognizing that he himself had biological poor relations. Psychoanalysis is giving man access to new understanding of his mental and emotional being, economic determinism to new understanding of the relations between the material and the spiritual aspects of his culture. As was the case in earlier advances, these developments are enabling humanity to comprehend and control additional aspects of its destiny and are also demanding additional readjustments in its persistent mythical conception of itself.

The specific applications of psychonalytical thought to the cultural fields that concern us have been chiefly of two kinds. Some are psycho-biographical or "psychographic," dealing with the unconscious life of individual artists or other cultural leaders and its effect upon their work. The other is the theory that psychic dispositions such as the Oedipus complex are racial traits that have been, and indeed still are, shared by the whole of humanity. Such racial complexes are used as a basis for interpreting myths, art, and other forms of cultural expression. We will consider an outstanding example of each of these two psycho-cultural approaches.

As the prototype and one of the most interesting of psychographic studies we shall take Freud's *Leonardo da Vinci: A Study in Psychosexuality*.[1] By way of introduction to this work, we should recall the nature of the materials available to Freud for study. From the history of art, he could obtain a knowledge of Leonardo's extant works and of such related facts as the experimental technique and consequent deterioration of the *Last Supper*; also he could see the replacement of artistic by scientific activity during much of Leonardo's later life. Biography indicated that the artist was an illegitimate child who spent his first years alone with his peasant mother and who was then adopted into his father's family; that he never married; that he was fond of the society of handsome youths and was at one time accused, though acquitted, of homosexual irregularity. Leonardo's diaries and voluminous notes provided further data for study, sometimes of a personally revealing nature. Of the latter kind is the vulture "memory" or more properly fantasy, which Leonardo recorded. "It comes to my mind as a very early memory, when I was still in the cradle, a vulture came down to me, opened my mouth with his tail and struck me many times with his tail against my lips."

Most of the above was common knowledge, and all of it accessible for study, before Freud. What the pioneer of psychoanalysis did was to interpret the inherited data in psychoanalytical terms. His interpretation may be summarized as follows. The absence of a father and exclusive dependence upon the mother during the formative years of Leonardo's childhood conditioned the artist in ways which permanently affected both his personality and his work. In the first place, since there was no father present to complete the family circle, the infant was left "to the tender seduction of a mother whose only consolation he was" and was "kissed by her into sexual prematurity." The vulture fantasy, as

Freud interprets it, is a symbolical expression of the delight which the child had experienced in "being nursed at the mother's breast."

The intensity of these early emotional experiences subjected Leonardo to a "mother fixation"; he was later unable to form normal attachments to other women and never married. The seductive image of the smiling mother, later repressed but always psychically potent, became a recurrent motif in the artist's work and explains the enigmatic smiles of the *Mona Lisa,* of both the Virgin and St. Anne in the cartoon and painting (Fig. 1) which they share, and of the women represented in a number of Leonardo's drawings.[2]

Apart from the influence of the mother fixation, Freud sees further biographical significance in Leonardo's representation of the *Virgin with St. Anne.* Brought up first by his true mother, later by the foster mother who was his father's wife, the boy was successively influenced by two women whereas most children remain under the care of one. This fact, added to the reduced importance of paternity, is reflected in the artist's replacement of the more common mother, father, and child group of the Holy Family by a combination of two women and a child.

Under the necessity of repressing his real sexual attachment to his mother, Leonardo "turned away from all grossly sensual activities" and in the main "gave the impression of an asexual person." What remained of direct sexual impulse, diverted from feminine connections, expressed itself through homosexual channels, attracting Leonardo to handsome youths but remaining, in Freud's judgment, idealistic or platonic. This homosexual tendency influenced the artist's work by inspiring a number of pictures featuring nude and rather effeminate young men, notably the *John the Baptist* and the *Bacchus.* Freud does not suggest the further idea, though it seems not inconceivable, that the poignant struggle for self-mastery expressed in Leonardo's *St. Jerome* might reflect a personal experience of inner conflict and renunciation.

Another effect of Leonardo's early conditioning, according to Freud, was a precocious and permanently dominating intellectual development. The initial absence of a father not only attached the child with double force to the mother, but also afforded him unusual opportunity for the exercise of "infantile sexual investigation." Curiosity, thus allowed a relatively uninhibited growth in the child, became one of the master traits of the man. To this trait we owe the prodigious scope and frequent profundity of Leonardo's scientific investigations and philosophical speculations.

Between the three main psychic directives of Leonardo's life — mother fixation, homosexual impulse, and investigation impulse — there was internal tension. As a result of conflict between them "his activity and ability to make quick decisions began to weaken; a tendency to reflection and delay" manifested itself. A painting became for him a problem, sometimes labored on for years, sometimes left unfinished. In the execution of the *Last Supper*, the artist's incapacity for "quick decisions" led him to avoid the decisive medium of fresco and to adopt oils instead. This substitution not only permitted slow and thoughtful execution; being then a relatively new technique, it constituted in itself a research problem. But, as Leonardo used it in the *Last Supper*, it also proved to be relatively fugitive. The early deterioration of the work can thus be traced, in Freud's view, through an experimental medium to a hesitant attitude born of psychic conflicts in the artist.

In the end, the conflicts were largely resolved by a victory of the investigation impulse. The later Leonardo painted little, studied much and with "an insatiability which betrayed the activity of unconscious impulses." The artist of the earlier and middle years became the scientist and philosopher of advancing age.

Such is the gist of Freud's analysis of Leonardo da Vinci and his work. Have we reason to question that analysis? Not with regard to its positive affirmations. The individual artist is obviously the immediate agent in creative production. Although we shall later have occasion to stress other and less commonly recognized determinants, the inner depths of the individual remain important from our point of view. The questions which we must raise, however, are less concerned with what Freud says than with what he leaves unsaid. Viewed in the light of other branches of knowledge, such as the history of art and the social sciences, his interpretation appears to have its limitations.

Before considering these limitations, however, we should observe that our discussion of them implies no disparagement of Freud himself. Some of his followers take the psychographic approach so religiously that they might almost be expected to define genius as "the capacity for having been conditioned in childhood." Freud himself "did not overestimate the reliability of these results" and submitted his findings with the reservation that "the aim of pathography is not to make comprehensible the attainments of the great man." Furthermore, since Freud was a psychoanalyst rather than a historian or critic, the *Leonardo* was for him only a minor excursion into a field apart from his main contributions to knowledge.

With those of us who are primarily critics and historians of art, the situation is different. Instead of beginning with the psychoanalyst's clinical technique and exploring its possible applications to nonclinical fields, we should begin with a professional awareness of concerns vital to the field of the arts. These concerns, embrace the entire range of humanity's cultural achievement and include many of the highest and most healthful manifestations of the human spirit. The essential question for us is not whether the technique of individual analysis can be applied to artists but whether, when applied, it produces results of basic importance for our particular field of thought. In the author's opinion it does not; or rather, it does so within limits so narrow that they leave most of our main problems untouched. This is so, if our analysis of the situation is correct, because the chief determinants of an artist's work lie, not in the vicissitudes of his private experience, but in the social manifestations of epoch, cultural horizon, and period style in which he participates. Being social or suprapersonal in their origins, these main determinants are naturally inaccessible to study by a method that concentrates on the personal aspects of the artist's experience.

Two related orders of facts would seem to require the expansion of an individualistic philosophy of artistic production into one in which individual factors interplay with, and are ultimately governed by, social ones. In the first place, the totality of any given work of art involves numerous elements usually unexplained, and apparently unexplainable, by the method of individual analysis. In the second place, there are the facts of historical evolution, through which we can observe consistent developments extending from generation to generation and century to century — developments far exceeding the scope of any individual lifetime.

For an illustration of the first of these considerations, let us return to one of the Leonardo paintings involved in Freud's analysis, the *Virgin with St. Anne* (Fig. 1). Of the complex totality of this work, Freud touches only three points: the absence of the father, the presence of the two women, and the solicitous smiles which they are directing toward the child. Significant as these details may be, they are nevertheless to the work as a whole hardly more than are three leaves to the foliage of a full-blown tree. They deal exclusively with subject matter and involve only a small fraction of that. Let us note some of the other representational elements to which Freud makes no reference.

To begin with, the motif is religious. The figures are conceived as divine, not natural, beings. Since the work is a product of Western Europe, the given religion is Christian and the personages are chosen from among those permitted by Christian authority. But we have not merely a Christian religious subject, we have such a subject in the particular phase of cultural evolution which is characteristic of the transition to the High Renaissance. Humanism has so far developed as to transform the figures from pure liturgical symbols into an amalgam of religious symbolism with worldly interest in the human form and in human emotional reactions. Furthermore, the figures are shown in a natural setting which involves an illusion of atmospheric space and a preoccupation with the forms of plants, animals, and geological formations. In the background the treatment of this setting approaches the simplification and idealization typical of the High Renaissance; in the foreground it still emphasizes that newly discovered wealth of natural detail — not excluding the anatomical detail of the feet — which gave such delight to the awakening objectivity of the Early Renaissance.

When we turn from subject matter to style and design, we encounter additional elements to which Freud gives no consideration, yet which are important for a total comprehension of the work of art. Here we must note that the picture is executed in oil on a wooden panel, rather than in the earlier tempera on panel or the later oil on canvas, and that the potentialities of the oil medium are being developed by the artist in the direction of surface translucency, textural depth, controlled modeling and a general effect of material richness and softness. We must note also that the work occupies a median position in the evolution of chiaroscuro, with a wider range of light and dark than had been used in painting before this time, but with less wide a range than was to follow. And we must note a trend toward rhythmic informality as the guiding principle of design. Reminiscent stability lingers in the upright figure of St. Anne and its echo in the trees, but the general disposition is one of asymmetrical balance pervaded by a complex movement like that of waters in a shaken bowl.

Every one of the elements just mentioned is essential to the artistic identity of the *Virgin with St. Anne*, yet all are omitted from Freud's comments on the painting. A critic more intimately concerned with art could no doubt relate some of them, or at least Leonardo's particular variation of some of them, to a personal analysis. Nevertheless the fact remains — and this is the fact of special importance to us — that all these elements of the painting were characteristic of developing Renaissance art in general and were not limited to, or dependent upon, the life and work of Leonardo da Vinci or any other individual. This can be illustrated by placing the *Virgin with St. Anne* in its developmental relationship to other Madonna paintings, a few of which are shown on Plate II.

The comparisons and contrasts involved in this segment of artistic genealogy enable us to make two statements with complete assurance. The first is that had Leonardo lived in any other part of the world than he did, or had he lived more than a century earlier or later than he did, it would have been impossible for him to create the picture we are considering, even though the circumstances of his childhood had been the same. The second is that all the major elements constituting the picture he did paint were in the process of emergence in the work of other artists before him, and were shared by large numbers of his immediate predecessors, contemporaries, and immediate successors, most of whom were legitimate children and no two of whom received identical infantile conditioning.

Had Leonardo been born a Mohammedan, representation in general and the mother and child image in particular would have been prohibited in any religious art that he might have been called upon to execute. Even had his cultural affiliations differed only to the extent of his being a Florentine Jew. similar restrictions would have applied to him. By the single gesture of an iconoclastic religious proscription, culture would thus have denied existence to such a picture as the *Virgin with St. Anne* and, in so doing, would have precluded the development of most of what we think of as Leonardo's artistic individuality.

Had da Vinci, as a Christian artist, lived in the twelfth instead of in the late fifteenth century, the creation of his *Virgin with St. Anne* would have been equally impossible for other reasons. In that case, his work would perforce have shared the general characteristics of twelfth century painting (Fig. 2) and would have been impersonal in conception, archaic in representation, relatively formal in disposition and background, and restricted to the possibilities of the tempera medium.

Before the work we think of as Leonardo's could be created, and before the creative point of view we identify with Leonardo could come into being, hundreds of intervening artists had to work at long-range artistic movements which in turn were manifesting long-range psycho-cultural developments in Western society as a whole. Before oil paint, with its potentials for greater warmth of embodiment, could become available to later Italian artists like Leonardo, the medium had to be conceived by anonymous experimenters, brought to perfecttion by the Van Eycks and their Flemish contemporaries, and imported into Italy by intermediaries like Antonello da Messina. As little as a few decades prior to Leonardo's actual span of creative activity, he would have had to depend upon the older and, for his purpose, more limited medium.

Before subtle representation and intimate concern with natural detail could play a part in Leonardo's work, a still more extensive cultural foundation had to be laid. Even the archaic painting of the twelfth century had already reached a midway position in this respect. For thousands of years before its time, a slow drift toward realism had been underway in the pictorial art of Western Europe. Largely abstract during its Neolithic phase, that art had shown an increasing interest in nature that can be followed through the barbarian arts of the invasion period and through the Celtic and other illuminations of the Dark Ages. The Romanesque style of the twelfth century shown in the oldest illustration of the present series (Fig. 2) was not a beginning of the Western movement toward realism but a comparatively advanced stage of it.

Artists who were transitional from the Middle Ages to the Renaissance — such as Cimabue, Giotto (Fig. 3), and Duccio — manifested a further strong stirring of the representational tide. Their fourteenth-century successors continued the movement, laboring, for instance, to bring a greater intimacy into the pictorial relationships between the Mother and Child (Fig. 4).

In the fifteenth century the development gathered momentum and approached its climax. Artists of the time abandoned themselves with passionate intensity to the drive toward realism, often specializing on one or another of its aspects. Uccello, Masaccio, Francesca, and others developed the linear and aerial perspective without which Leonardo could not have achieved his effects of distance. Scores of artists labored at the problem of representing elusive facial expressions, studied the intricacies of anatomy, progressively abandoned the abstract background of the early pictures in favor of settings inspired by the natural world, and experimented with increasingly varied pictorial compositions.

By the time we reach the generation preceding that of Leonardo, the tide is only one swell below the level at which he utilized and, in his turn, continued it. In the work of his immediate predecessors — Fillipo Lippi, Baldovinetti, Botticelli, and Leonardo's master, Verrocchio — we find at a slightly less advanced stage of evolution all the major elements which Leonardo was to employ in the *Virgin with St. Anne*. If, for instance, we consider the Lippi *Madonna and Child with Angels* (Fig. 5), we see that by Lippi's time, the conventional symbolism of the earlier period had been replaced by figures incorporating human charm and, in the half smile of the little angel in the foreground, displaying considerable subtlety of facial expression. Formal had given way to informal composition, abstract background to a preoccupation with landscape. Even the river valley winding among rocky headlands, which Leonardo was to use with such effect in the background of our *Virgin* and that of the *Mona*

Lisa, was part of the tradition he inherited. Variations of it appear in our Lippi and in many of the paintings by Baldovinetti, Pollaiuolo, Verrocchio, and other artists — a reflection of the geographical environment surrounding Florence in the valley of the Arno and one of the major symbols of Florentine patriotism.

All this existed in art prior to the work of Leonardo; all this was taught to him by his masters, demanded of him by his cultural environment. He did not, therefore, wholly create the major features incorporated in his *Virgin with St. Anne.* He received the ideas for them from others, carried the ideas a step further along their predestined line of development, and modified them in certain ways expressive of his individual temperament and impulse. The degree to which he advanced beyond his predecessors was, in its turn, a development in no sense unique with Leonardo. Many of his leading contemporaries and immediate successors participated in it as fully as himself, as we may observe in the works of Raphael and del Sarto, Correggio (Fig. 7), Titian and Veronese.

In short, a much greater portion of the artistic identity of the *Virgin with St. Anne* is attributable to Italian Renaissance culture than to Leonardo as an individual. The only features of the painting that may be considered uniquely da Vinci's are the particular combination of personages, the haunting smile of St. Anne — both of which Freud rightly singles out — and, perhaps we should add, the suffusion of the background by a veiled expressiveness comparable to that of the smile. The choice of personages is purely a circumstantial detail of subject matter, involving no aesthetic achievement and no contribution to the religious or humanistic significance of Renaissance painting. Indeed, in its deviation from the basic tradition, it may be considered somewhat of an eccentricity.

The subtle appeal of the smile and its background, on the other hand, is a unique achievement in artistic expressiveness. Accepting Freud's analysis, we may assume that the psychic urgency which spurred Leonardo to this achievement arose from his childhood conditioning. But as the foregoing discussion has indicated, even with that urgency, the achievement would have been impossible had not cultural traditions laid the foundation for it through the cumulative efforts of hundreds of individuals during many centuries.

If we wished to press the point, we could add that in the case of our particular painting, precise analysis would require an even greater reduction of Leonardo's personal contribution. Expert connoisseurship informs us that "most of the Louvre painting was done by pupils; only the landscape, the figure of St. Anne and the right arm of the Virgin are outstanding." [3] We recognize here a practical reason for the head of St. Anne and its background possessing an intangible depth which is lacking in the remainder of the work. Freud saw the same "blissful smile of maternal happiness" on the faces of both women, but mature contemplation will show the observer that the face of the Virgin is relatively blank as compared with the mysterious reality pervading that of St. Anne. The upper head was apparently the real incarnation of Leonardo's mother image.

If the personal psychic motive explains the special achievement of one particular section of the painting, it may equally well account for a certain lack of conviction and homogeneity in the composition as a whole. Private impulse has apparently delimited and unbalanced creative impulse, concentrating the artist's effort on certain details rather than on the totality of his conception, withdrawing his inspiration from a complete formal achievement to a partial expressive one, and subjecting the final result to inequalities between the work of the artist and that of his assistants.

Further consideration will be given later to the relationship between the individual artist and the society to which he belongs as this relationship appears from the psycho-historical point of view. For the moment, we are not concerned with that point of view in itself, but with the forces that have helped motivate it. One of these forces has now been indicated. It lies in the friction that arises when we confront a biographical method like the psychographic one with either a critical analysis of the full identity of an individual work of art, or with a historical recognition of the place of the individual work in the evolutionary sequence of which it forms a part. Such critical and historical observations present us with orders of facts that must be recognized in any full interpretation of art, but which are not dealt with, and presumably cannot be dealt with, by the psychographic method. We are therefore in the presence of two groups of findings both of which appear to be true and significant, and neither of which embraces the aspects of truth and significance possessed by the other. Our problem becomes one of seeking a more inclusive frame of reference that will comprehend them both and bring them into organic relationships with each other.

Before turning to the other forms of criticism based on psychoanalysis, it will be fitting to start our correlational roots growing in two further directions suggested by the foregoing discussion. One leads from psychography to biography in general; the other from cultural traditions, as revealed by the history of art, toward the social sciences.

Biography, of course, existed long before Freud. Its connection with Western art goes at least as far back as the *Lives* written by Vasari at the end of the Renaissance. Dealing with the conscious life and daily activities of its subjects — discussing the training of the artist, his patrons, commissions, and so forth — traditional biography was on the whole broader and more fully integrated with cultural life than its psychographic variant. Nevertheless, many biographical studies, and many critical ones as well, have overemphasized individualistic factors in artistic production at the expense of cultural ones. They are thus subject to the same need for counterpoise that we have attributed to the psychographic method.

Vasari, though his actual records are broad, reveals the individualistic bias in the relative emphasis which he gives to personal factors as compared with social ones. Thus he writes with regard to Giotto.

"He alone — although born amidst incapable artists, at a time when all good methods in art had long been entombed beneath the ruins of war — yet, by the favour of Heaven, he, I say, alone succeeded in resuscitating art, and restoring her to a path that may be called the true one. And it was in truth a great marvel, that from so rude and inept an age, Giotto should have had strength to elicit so much . . . restoring art to the better path adhered to in modern times, and introducing the custom of accurately drawing living persons from nature, which had not been used for more than two hundred years." [4]

Here the individual Giotto appears as the prime mover in the whole artistic development of the Renaissance — an estimate that has recurrently echoed down our historical corridors from Vasari's day to our own. Actually, as our discussion of the examples gathered on Plate 2 has implied, Giotto like Leonardo, like all individual artists, takes a normal place in long-range developments that transcend his own lifetime. He accelerates the development as only a genius can, but he neither originates it nor deflects it from its culturally governed course. There is in fact, to the author's knowledge, no single example in the whole history of art in which the creative activity of an individual produced major artistic results unrelated to an evolving cultural tradition. The most we could say would be that certain individuals, by their precedence or their force, have carried subsequent individuals in their wake. But even this would be to deny the continued independence of individuality, and to replace it by a social force in the form of inherited cultural influence.

As an example of what seems to us the individualistic bias in pre-Freudian critical, as opposed to biographical, studies, we may quote from Lionello Venturi's *History of Art Criticism*. For Venturi, the "consideration of art as a document in the life of peoples" is to be rejected with various other "deviations from the criticism of art." [5] Art, it would seem, can properly be judged only in relation to individual creative impulse, which is regarded as spasmodic and unpredictable. This point of view Venturi emphasizes, with apparent approval, in commenting on the critical concepts of Conrad Fiedler (1841–1895).

"Genetic history sees only the historical nexus, but Fiedler notes that the artistic personality, genial and significant, appears unexpectedly and is very much more the beginning of a new series than the close of one which is past. For the essence of genius is to open the eyes of the world, so that men realize that they were blind before then; and therefore genius has no forerunners and no imitators. The so-called ideal of the painter is not nature bettered by the rules, but a way of considering and representing nature, which sinks its roots in the depths of the individual. It is an error, then, to admire the progress of art from primitive decoration to masterpieces of the great epochs, because art progresses by leaps." [6]

Or, as Venturi puts it in another passage, "all the other categories of the laws of art, of kinds, of types fall to the ground, and the only reality of art is the personality of the artist, as it is manifested in his works of art." [7]

Insofar as concerns their emphasis upon personal factors in creative motivation, it will be seen that all the approaches which we have now cited — the psychographic one, the traditional biographical one, and the more individualistically oriented aspects of traditional criticism — that all these approaches are phases of a single stream of thought. All assume as a correlative the "great man theory of history" under which cultural institutions and traditions, if they receive attention at all, are regarded in Emersonian fashion as "the shadow of one man."

Seen in this context, psychographic criticism appears less as a new approach than as a new variation of an old approach. It reveals itself — and much the same could be said of psychoanalysis in general — as one of the outgrowths of its times: post-Renaissance individualistic Western European times. The earlier more general term "depths" is replaced by the more specialized one "unconscious," and the working of the unconscious is studied by scientific means and with illuminating results, but the motivating source of creative activity is still sought within the "depths of the individual."

Conversely, our earlier observations with regard to the psychographic method can now be extended to include all other methods that depend primarily upon a study of personal qualities in the individual artist. We regard such methods as significant but one-sided, incapable of explaining all the important questions raised by the history of any of the arts, and therefore requiring the counter-balance of other and more culturally oriented approaches.

In making this statement we are only affirming, on the basis of artistic evidence, a principle already established by sociology on the basis of general human evidence. Here we may begin weaving our ties with the social sciences. To quote one sociologist:

"The paradox of human society — that it has a unity and continuity of its own and yet exists solely in the minds and actions of its members — can be resolved only by understanding how the newborn individual is molded into a social being. Without this process of molding, which we call 'socialization,' the society could not perpetuate itself beyond a single generation and culture could not exist. Nor could the individual become a person; for without the ever-repeated renewal of culture within him there could be no human mentality, no human personality. Both the person and the society are alike dependent on this unique process of psychic amalgamation whereby the sentiments and ideas of the culture are somehow joined to the capacities and needs of the organism." [8]

Studies of "wolf children" and other human offspring outcast, or largely outcast, from society, show that what we think of as our individual personalities cannot come into existence except as "the human animal is transmuted into the human being" by socialization and culturalization. The case of "Anna" provides one historical instance of a child who received from her associates merely the barest means of physical survival, deprived of practically all communicative and educational influence. At six years old, she "could not talk, walk, or do anything that showed intelligence . . . Her clothing and bedding were filthy . . . She was completely apathetic, lying in a limp, supine position and remaining immobile, expressionless, and indifferent to everything. She was believed to be deaf and possibly blind. She could not feed herself or make any move in her own behalf. Here, then, was a human organism which had missed nearly six years of socialization. Her condition shows how little her purely biological resources, when acting alone, could contribute to making her a complete person." [9]

Such is the individual when deprived of the nourishing and growth-directive influence of culture. If, by any stretch of the imagination, we can conceive of such an individual becoming an artist, such would be the individuality expressed in the resulting art. Obviously the genius who, from his purely personal depths, brings forth the culture of an epoch, is as much a myth as the Tarzan who, alone and unarmed, dominates the jungle. Factually, both are impossible.

Anna was an illegitimate child. She was subjected to her harsh fate because she was born into a puritanical culture, was therefore an object of shame and ethical condemnation and, for this reason, was hidden away from social contacts in the solitary confinement of an upstairs room. Had that other illegitimate child, Leonardo da Vinci, been born under similar cultural circumstances, the "individuality" which he was later to express in his art would never have come into being even though his physical life had occurred. That his personality did ripen and flower was due, in the first instance, to the willingness of Renaissance culture to provide illegitimate children with the same social benefits and opportunities as legitimate ones. And in the accomplishment of his socialization, family relationships during his infancy and childhood played only a minor part as compared to the cultural formation attending his youth and early maturity. We undoubtedly gain insight into some aspects of Leonardo's life and art through the recognition of the personal traits of mother fixation and tendency toward homosexuality, but full comprehension becomes possible only in the light of the artist's early education, his professional apprenticeship under Verrocchio, his exposure to the artistic heritage and stimulation by the artistic opportunities of fifteen century Florence in particular and of Renaissance Europe in general.

Thus we return, with sociological confirmation, to the conclusion already reached. Instead of accepting the psychographic or other individualistic approaches to the arts as complete interpretations, we must regard them as partial interpretations and must search elsewhere for an understanding of other equally important factors in the artistic situation.

II

According to the foregoing analysis, a first application of psychoanalysis to art — the psychographic one — though significant in itself as a specialty, is too narrow to provide a basis for dealing with the major problems of art history and criticism, and too individualistically centered to harmonize with the views on personality and culture presented to us by the social sciences. In different degrees, we may ascribe similar limitations to other types of psychoanalytical criticism. Without attempting to consider all such types, we can illustrate the point by reference to a work that lies at the opposite edge of the psychoanalytical spectrum from the psychographic one: Otto Rank's *Art and Artist*.

Here we have a psychoanalyst dealing, not with the life and work of an individual, but with the general nature of art as manifest through various periods from prehistoric times to the present day. Rank departs from some of the earlier concepts of psychonanalysts with regard to culture, takes cognizance of various findings both of anthropologists and of writers on art like Riegl and Worringer, and considers some of the collective as well as the individual motivants of culture. All this is indicative of philosophic breadth and a spirit of creative inquiry. Nevertheless, the centripetal forces pulling Rank's discussion back to its psychoanalytical base prove to be stronger than the centrifugal urge toward externality.

The main concern of the book centers around the psychic forces impelling creative activity. These forces, in Rank's view, have their source in the impulse toward immortality. The forms of art through the ages are presented as reflections of a psychological development wherein man's animal nature gives way to his spiritual one, each phase of this development being symbolically projected into art by figurative reference to some portion of the human organism.

"In conformity with this development of man from biological creature to creative and self-creative spirit, the earth's interior (corresponding to the female abdomen) was looked upon as the centre of creation and consequently was conceived as the belly of an animal. Later the whole body came to be the (earthly) underworld, and the head (consciousness, will, spirit) became heaven, which eventually became identified with man, just as the earth had been with woman (mother)." [10]

The perspective into which the history of art is thrown by this rendering can be judged from examples of one of the earlier and one of the later phases of the development. The spiral patterns used by the Cretans and other peoples are traced to labyrinthine prototypes such as "the 'palace of entrails,' which in Babylon represented a macrocosmization of the protecting womb." Here art reflects a stage of human development that was preoccupied with abdominal symbolism. Related examples cited by Rank are the concepts of the "world-navel . . . [which] counted as the entrance to the earth's belly — the underworld" and "was at the same time regarded as the starting-point of the world's creation"; and the "liver mantic" under which the liver "as the seat of life counted as a small-scale cosmos — in other words, as a copy of the whole man" and, in connection with animal sacrifices, became a basis for prophetic divination. In this view, even technology could be penetrated by the prevailing abdominal obsessions. "Indeed, for thousands of years before the wheel was invented, pots were produced by the coiling technique in which already Fuhrmann saw an imitation of the disposition of the intestines."

Typical of the later stage in which intestinal had given way to cephalic symbolism is Christian church architecture. Reducing the history of architecture to a "three-stage scheme of development, objectivized by the tomb (soul of the dead), the house (soul of the living), the temple (soul of God)," Rank comments on church building as follows:

"We cannot . . . agree with psychoanalysis in its symbolic interpretation — on biological lines — of the church as nothing but a sheltering cavity which replaces the mother's womb . . . For the cathedral represents precisely the highest architectural expression of the transformation (already discussed) of the animal conception of an underworld into a spiritual soul-concept localized in the head. If, then, the church represents rather the head of a man, with its mouth, jaws, and throat, than the whole person, Fuhrmann's ingenious idea of the bell as a 'brazen mouth' should not be taken merely as a metaphor. For this mouth (*Mund*) is also *mundus*, the whole world — according to a further linguistic indication of the same author — and it is precisely in Christianity that this has come to be a purely spiritual one (the Head), in which the *Logos* has replaced the *Pneuma*, although both originally come from the mouth . . .

"But if the church portal, through which the worshipper enters into a higher world of supernatural existence, represents the mouth, the old chthonian idea of the underworld's jaws, expressed in symbols of terrifying and dangerous animals (stylized devils' grimaces and dragons' maws), comes out as mere ornamentation of the façade or, it may be, the interior (choir-stalls) and is robbed of its alarming character by the artistic form given to it."

In the more rudimentary cases previously described, such as obvious entrail representations, there appears to be considerable evidence in support of Rank's proposals. Obvious entrail representations, however, are closer to the paraphernalia of the medicine man than to characteristic achievements of the artists. The comments just quoted on cathedral architecture seem to the present writer to illustrate the fact that when applied to mature and articulate forms of art, such an approach is grossly inadequate. Its inadequacy becomes the more apparent when we reflect that Christian church architecture enters the discussion only as a single general concept, colored by Gothic impressions, but making no distinction between styles as varied as the Early Christian, Byzantine, Romanesque, Gothic, Renaissance, Baroque, and Modern. The inadequacy is still further revealed by the fact that Rank gives no consideration to specific architectural characteristics either of structure or design, and that the iconography of cathedral sculpture and stained glass enters his discussion only in the passing mention of terrifying animals quoted above.

All phases and aspects of Christian architecture and its decorations reduce themselves in Rank's discussion to "the church," and the church reduces itself to the symbolic "head." This interpretation is too vague and general to throw much light on the evolution of Christian architectural styles, their beauties of architectural design, or the subjects of their sculpture and painting. And it is too exclusively a psychic interpretation to deal with the objective factors in architectural situations, such as the technological resources available at any given time for architectural construction or the relationship between a given style and the social circumstances that accompanied its development.

With regard to the first of these limitations — vagueness and generality — we may remark that the inclusive frame of psychoanalytical reference attempted by Rank contributes less to our understanding of art than the psychographic one as used by Freud. Within its limits, the latter does illuminate certain details of actual works of art. One doubts whether analogies as sweeping as those of Rank — analogies between racial psychic obsessions and vast heterogeneous complexes of art like Christian church architecture — can illuminate anything.

As we shall note more fully on later occasions, this limitation of generality applies in one degree or another to all conceptual interpretations of art; to all interpretations that begin with a preconceived idea, formula, or principle rather than with the observation of the complexities of artistic actuality. From the point of view that we are seeking to establish — a point of view that demands constant awareness of the horizons presented to us by the history of the arts — no approach to culture can be considered satisfactory that does not intermesh with the concrete actualities of individual works of art and with the equally important actualities of their evolutionary succession in stylistic traditions.

The second limitation that we are ascribing to Rank's presentation — unbalanced emphasis on subjective factors at the expense of objective ones — has been discussed in connection with the psychographic approach. It needs no further comment here beyond the observation that it appears to apply to all the critical efforts that have been based exclusively on psychoanalytical grounds.

If we accept ahistorical generality and extreme subjectivism as shortcomings of psychoanalytical writings on art, we are led to a first conclusion concerning the relationship of psychoanalysis to cultural studies. The actual writings of psychoanalysts about the arts do not appear to us to have made major contributions to knowledge in this field. Usually immature in their grasp of the arts themselves, these writings appear to be premature in their assimilation of cultural reality to psychic conditions discovered in the main through individual analysis.

But — and here appears our positive attitude toward this phase of our subject — existing psychoanalytical writings on the arts have hardly more than broken the ground for studies in the correlation of depth psychology with culture. The major possibilities of such correlation are still potential rather than actual ones. They have their basis not in what psychoanalysts have told us about art, but in what they have told us about their own specialty, mental life. And the chief hope of realizing these possibilities lies, not in psychoanalytical studies pursued in isolation, but in the combined operation of psychoanalytical insights with those derived from other and entirely different fields of knowledge.

Since culture is essentially a social phenomenon, the individualistic preoccupations of psychoanalysis must be balanced by contrasting contributions from social studies. And since existence is not exclusively mental, the psychic preoccupations of psychonanalysis must be balanced by adequate consideration of material ones. We must, in short, work toward a psycho-social-materialist synthesis.

Before we turn to certain other fields of knowledge for a study of their contributions to criticism, we should observe that the correlational directions just suggested are implicit in psychoanalysis itself — just as they are in any other single specialty if we examine its implications. In basic assumptions and in therapeutic practice, psychoanalysts recognize that the phenomena with which they deal cannot be explained exclusively in psychic terms, but must be referred to an interplay between psychic dispositions and forces exerted by the external world. Freud seems to have been impelled by his observations to an increasing recognition of the importance of these external factors. Thus in one of his late works he defines the ego "as that part of the id [11] which has been modified by its proximity to the external world . . . This relation to the external world is decisive for the ego. The ego has taken over the task of representing the external world for the id, and so of saving it; for the id, blindly striving to gratify its instincts in complete disregard of the superior strength of outside forces, could not otherwise escape annihilation." [12]

Again, having differentiated between "neurotic" and "objective" anxiety, Freud came to reverse an earlier concept of the relationship between them, and to recognize a fact for which, he says, "we were not prepared"; the fact that "the internal instinctual danger was only a halfway house to an external and real danger-situation." [13] And in another passage, he points out that "the problems raised by the unconscious sense of guilt" have led to a study of "its relation to morality, education, criminality and delinquency . . . Here we have quite unexpectedly emerged into the open from the mental underworld." [14]

Realities constrasting with those of the "mental underworld," a recognition of the "superior strength of outside forces," are thus implicit in Freudian and in all other systems of psychoanalysis. Therapeutically, psychoanalysis is in large part an effort to discover through and beyond certain psychic states what the "outside forces" were which caused them, and by recognizing the nature of those outside forces to allow the patient to come to terms with their psychic effects.

It would seem to be a logical extension of this program that if the psychoanalyst applies his point of view to a study of artistic and cultural phenomena, he would correspondingly relate those phenomena to the outside forces of the external world; and that since the phenomena are in this case social, the outside forces would be similarly so — would in short be historical, sociological, and economic. Freud himself envisaged the possibility of such an approach in a passage which refers to "the material of legends, traditions, and interpretations in the original history of a people. Notwithstanding all distortions and misunderstandings to the contrary . . . they show what the people formed out of the experiences of its primal past under the domination of once powerful and today still effective motives. And if these distortions could be traced back through the knowledge of all the affective forces, one would surely discover the historical truth under this legendary material." [15] Here, conceived as a potentiality beyond an "if," we have a glimpse of the psycho-historical possibility of correlating certain cultural phenomena — in this case legends and traditions — not only with psychic states but also with objective historical conditions.

In practice, as we have seen, most psychoanalytical writers on culture have followed the opposite procedure. Instead of turning to history, sociology, and economics for an understanding of the outside forces which could have generated the psychic states expressed in art, they have assumed that psychic dispositions, and usually dispositions conceived in the terms of individual psychology, offered a sufficient basis for understanding. They have interpreted the arts in ways which make the "psychic underworld" appear to be the sole determinant of cultural reality. Hence their critical practice seems to us less fundamental than the implications of either their psychological findings or their therapeutic practice. And hence, in turn, our unwillingness to stop with their critical practice and our effort to pursue directions of thought which the implications of psychoanalysis have helped to suggest.

If any single intellectual tradition of recent times can provide a balancing counterpoise to the psychoanalytical one, it would seem to be that of the economic interpretation of history. For this is an interpretation concerned with cultural dynamics but approaching them primarily from the social and the materialist points of view. What has this approach contributed to recent cultural studies? How far do its findings fill the gaps left by a purely psychological interpretation of the arts, and to what degree can the psychological and the historical points of view be correlated with each other? These questions will concern us in the chapter to follow.

Chapter I I I

HISTORICAL AND MATERIALIST
INTERPRETATIONS OF CULTURE

Theoretically, anthropology, the study of mankind, should be the mistress of the social sciences. In dictionaries, it is usually so defined, sociology and history being classed among its many subdivisions. Practically speaking, however, anthropology has been crowded into a marginal position; but history, as the study of civilizations, has acquired a central and commanding place among the social sciences. Its breadth was already forecast in the derivation of its name from the Greek ἱστορία, "learning by inquiry."

The other social sciences as we know them in practice can be regarded as sections cut through historical totality at some particular point and magnified for special study. Those who work with the section extending from the biological emergence of man to the invention of writing give us anthropology with emphasis on archaeology — which is essentially preliterate history. Those who cut sections through the sustaining structure of a civilization, give us sociology and economics. Those who cut through the structure of primitive societies give us cultural anthropology. History in its broad sense binds together all these specialties, and thus conceived as an inclusive network of social sciences, it offers what is probably our most comprehensive and most accessible approach to the social and material aspects of culture.

But while this is potentially true, the actual study of history, like psychology before Freud, was long unbalanced by overemphasis on obvious surface observations. In the case of history, these consisted in the main of political institutions, military conflicts, and commanding personalities. We had occasion to refer in the preceding chapter to one of the outgrowths of this approach: the so-called "great man theory of history" which attributed the character of epochs to the influence of leading individuals. Vasari's estimate of the personal influence of

Giotto was cited as an example of this conception as it reverberated through the minds of thinkers concerned with the history of art.

The limitations of surface history as a basis for the interpretation of art can be more fully illustrated by reference to Henry Adams' *Mont Saint Michel and Chartres*. With the sensitivity of an architectural connoisseur, the historical sense of a knowledgeable student of medieval life, and an urbanity and charm that raise his work to a high literary level, Adams envelops medieval architecture in the colorful atmosphere of its historical setting. We hear the pilgrims sing and see the people dragging cartloads of stone to the rising pile at Chartres. We learn the folk songs of the day and wrestle with its philosophy as embodied in the works of Abelard and Aquinas. We meet successive generations of French royalty and nobility, listen with William the Conqueror as Taillefer sings the *Chanson de Roland*, feel the military thrusts and counterthrusts of William's invasion of England and of the crusades.

All this reanimates the past in much the same way as a good historical novel. Its contribution to our thinking, however, goes little beyond the recognition that the various manifestations of medieval culture are all imbued with a common spirit. The basis of the demonstration is a series of parallels between one aspect of that culture and another. The *Chanson de Roland* "is in poetry what the Mount is in architecture." [1] The *Summa Theologica* of Thomas Aquinas is the consummation of the Church Intellectual as the Cathedral of Amiens is that of the Church Architectural. In the one as in the other, "every relation of parts, every disturbance of equilibrium, every detail of construction was treated with infinite labour, as a result of two hundred years of experiment and discussion among thousands of men whose minds and whose instincts were acute, and who discussed little else." The theological and social hierarchies in turn reflect each other. "The Virgin of Chartres was the greatest of all queens, but the most womanly of women . . . and her double character was sustained throughout her palace." "God the Father was the feudal seigneur, who raised Lazarus — his baron or vassal — from the grave, and freed Daniel, as an evidence of his power and loyalty; a seigneur who never lied, or was false to his word."

If one starts from any such single thought, it is broadening to realize that medieval architecture, literature, philosophy, religion, and social structure reveal certain common characteristics. But if our goal is interpretive comprehension, the recognition of these parallels can serve at best as a preliminary step. The only principle which we can derive from this descriptive procedure is that of comparing the various aspects of any given culture.

The deeper question is *why* Gothic culture should exhibit the particular characteristics which all of its manifestations share in common; *why* Gothic art, thought, and life differ in the ways they do from those of other cultural epochs. In more general terms, the question becomes one trying to discover what laws govern cultural activity and determine the nature of its products. This question Adams does not raise, nor are such questions likely to be raised in many typical presentations of surface history.[2] But they are questions generated by the study of history itself and destined sooner or later to demand the attention of historians.

The way toward a consideration of these questions had been opened long before Adams when writers like Voltaire and Montesquieu, and later Buckle, Marx, and Engels, perceived that there were significant correlations between certain types of cultural development and certain types of social and economic development. Forces which in large part has been ignored by historians, and which continued to be ignored by traditional historians, were found to have an important bearing upon historical and cultural developments. Organic history, depth history, thus emerged to become, in many respects, the social counterpart of depth psychology.

Freud made an interesting observation when he remarked that "psychoanalysis became 'depth-psychology'" at the moment when processes originally studied in their pathological deflections, and for therapeutic purposes, were recognized as extending to normal mental life and as relevant to problems in many other fields beside medicine.[3] So far as concerns the relationship between its more general and its more limited applications, depth history seems to have undergone the inverse evolution. The general conception developed first; its more specialized application to social problems — in a sense we might say to social pathology — came later.

The general development can be credited in large part to the eighteenth century, age of rationalism and rising interest in science. It can conveniently be illustrated by reference to Montesquieu's *The Spirit of Laws* (1748), but the emergence of depth history was not the work of any one man or any one book. It was itself one of those cultural trends the complex collective nature of which it began to reveal to human understanding. Many of the leading thinkers of the age participated in the movement. Jean Bodin had forecast it as early as the mid-sixteenth century in his *Method for the Easy Comprehension of History* (1566). Eighteenth-century contributors were many. In addition to Montesquieu, they included Vico with his *Principles of a New Science regarding the*

Common Nature of Nations (1725), Turgot with his *Successive Advances of the Human Mind* (1750), Hume with his *History of England* (1750–1762), Voltaire with his *Century of Louis XIV* (1751) and his *Essay on Universal History* (1756), and Condorcet with his *Outlines of an Historical View of the Progress of the Human Mind* (1795).

The development was many-sided. It abandoned the "Christian epic" as a historical bias, approaching for the first time in Western thought an objective attitude toward formerly detested "pagan" cultures like the Mohammedan. It correlated Mediterranean and Western European histories with their equivalents in Asia and elsewhere and sketched the first "universal" histories of mankind. When Voltaire wrote, not about Louis XIV but about the *century* of Louis XIV, and produced thereby the first analytical study of a modern European society, the concept of the great man as a historical symbol was balanced by a new recognition of social counterparts: counterparts dependent, in Voltaire's conception, upon the "genius of a people." And perhaps most important of all, the new movement correlated the previous concerns of history — legal and political institutions, religious systems, military powers — with factors not previously considered in connection with them. Here we may illustrate from Montesquieu.

Law, associated with divine sources in medieval thought, had subsequently been viewed in terms of rationalistic abstractions like "justice" and "reason." With an insight which caused the upholders of the *status quo* to tremble, and for which he politely but firmly asks indulgence in his preface, Montesquieu removed the law from any absolute foundation and placed it in a context of relativity to various conditioning factors. Using the laws of different societies as specimens, he investigated their relationship to the life of the peoples that had produced them. He examined the connections between the laws of those peoples and their relative military strength or weakness, their "general spirit, morals, and customs," the nature of the soil they exploited, the climate under which they lived, the number of their inhabitants, their use of money, and the state and nature of their commerce. He found that all these things had a bearing upon the evolution of legal systems, and economic factors became highly important for him in this connection. In book XIII of his first volume he discusses "the relation which the levying of taxes and the greatness of the public revenues have to liberty," and finds certain states of revenue to be economic preconditions of liberty as a political condition.

As a result of the correlations thus established by Montesquieu, the law, which had previously seemed to exist as a self-justifying entity or to be inspired from "above," was now recognized as emerging from "below." The manifest surface of legality — and correspondingly, if we view the movement as a whole, the manifest surface of culture in general — was pierced by a new perception of its underlying and motivating depths — depths as momentous for an understanding of human conduct as were the unconscious psychic ones later to be revealed by psychoanalysis. Depth history can indeed advance many claims to the title of the cultural unconscious. The self-justifying historical conceit of particular societies seems to have as many reasons to repress this cultural unconscious as individual self-esteem may have to repress the personal unconscious, with effects as false to reality in the one case as in the other.

In works like those just mentioned, the eighteenth century established depth history upon firm foundations. The ninteenth century saw more extensive formulations of the general theory and also the beginning of its more specialized application. Of the general formulations, the most comprehensive is probably Thomas Henry Buckle's projected *History of Civilization in England*. The first and only two volumes of this work, comprising an unfinished "General Introduction," appeared respectively in 1857 and 1861.[4]

Nearly a thousand pages, these volumes are a heroic effort to correlate the interpretation of history with the new knowledge that was pouring into the European mind from biology, political economy, psychology, and other scientific sources. Buckle reëxamined the resources for investigating history, the influence of climate and other material factors upon the organization of society and upon the character of individuals, the available means of discovering mental laws, and the relative importance of mental, moral, and physical factors in conditioning the progress of society. Having deduced certain principles for the interpretation of history, he then applied them in preliminary analyses of the intellectual and political life of England, Scotland, France, and Spain.

To twentieth-century readers, Buckle's work seems far from definitive. The new knowledge with which he tried so valiantly to keep abreast has increased rapidly during the century since his death, demanding new efforts at correlation. Furthermore, Buckle, always an invalid, died at the age of thirty-six before he had had time even to crystallize his own conceptions. Yet to this day, no single work seems to have replaced his as a demonstration of the intricate dynamics of depth history. The extensiveness of his frame of reference may be judged from the fact that he saw history as a process governed by evolving complemental interrelationships between material and mental forces; a process in which "from the beginning there has been no discrepancy, no disorder . . .

but that all the events that surround us, even to the farthest limits of the material creation, are but different parts of a single scheme which is permeated by one glorious principle of universal and undeviating regularity." [5] In short, Buckle saw history as controlled by natural laws and he sought for an understanding of those laws in terms of sociology, economics, and other sciences.

II

As we can see from the preceding summary, depth history was at least a century old before the agitations of the emergent industrial order led to the rise of the nineteenth-century socialism and, indirectly through it, to the promulgation of the sharper and narrower doctrine of economic determinism. Writers like Voltaire, Montesquieu, and Buckle had given economic forces an important place among the varied factors by which historical existence is conditioned. The socialists made economic factors the *basis* of historical existence. Here again, the movement was a widespread one within which many related schools of thought proposed competing, and sometimes conflicting, formulations. The formulation subsequently accepted as definitive for socialist theory was that of Karl Marx and Friedrich Engels.

Unfortunately for the history of thought, neither Marx nor Engels ever devoted a major work to the theory of economic determinism, that theory being incidental to their social concerns. As G. D. H. Cole remarks with regard to Marx and the materialist conception of history, that conception "though it underlies all his thinking, is nowhere systematically expounded in his books." [6] Destined to function culturally as a kind of spearhead for the broader movement of depth history in general, and in terms of its influence, one of the master ideas of recent times, it was a master idea without a master statement — at any rate without an exhaustive statement documented with historical examples.

What is generally regarded as the "classical" foundation for the development of the theory was set forth by Marx in the preface to his *Contribution to the Critique of Political Economy*. This work was published in 1859, two years after Buckle's first volume and one hundred and eleven years after Montesquieu's *Spirit of Laws*. The passage crystallizing the concept of economic determinism is included, almost incidentally, in an autobiographical account of Marx's studies. The main purpose of this account, its author states, was "simply to prove that my views, whatever one may think of them . . . are the result of many years of conscientious research." [7]

After reviewing the earlier phases of his work, Marx introduces the passage that concerns us accordingly: "The general conclusion at which I arrived and which, once reached, continued to serve as the leading thread in my studies, may be briefly summed up as follows." It is the ensuing "general conclusion," only two pages long, that constitutes the classical formulation of the materialist conception of history. (In later editions the propositions that succeed each other so rapidly in Marx's summary have been paragraphed and numbered for textual emphasis, but we shall quote from the block form in which they originally appeared.)

"In the social production which men carry on they enter into definite relations that are indispensable and independent of their will; these relations of production correspond to a definite stage of development of their material powers of production. The sum total of these relations of production constitutes the economic structure of society — the real foundation on which rise legal and political superstructures and to which correspond definite forms of social consciousness. The mode of production in material life determines the general character of social, political and spiritual processes of life. It is not the consciousness of men that determines their existence, but, on the contrary, their social existence determines their consciousness."

Such is the basic statement of the materialist cultural dynamic. The relative influence exerted by the contemporaries, Buckle and Marx, illustrates the complexities of the history of thought and at the same time, its deep involvement with social and economic forces. Developed purely as an exercise in learning, Buckle's monumental effort has had comparatively little effect upon subsequent historical thinking. A century has passed without major advances in the conception of depth history at which he had arrived, and with relatively little activity in applying that conception to critical ends. Many contemporary historians, like Spengler and Toynbee, and most contemporary art historians as well, still proceed from narrower foundations than those which Buckle provides.

The reasons may lie partly in the sheer intellectual difficulty of handling a frame of reference which involves, not one field of knowledge alone, but the interplay of many different fields. But there are probably subconscious reasons as well. Our dominantly individualistic philosophy of life has perhaps made us averse to exploring and applying the social implications of depth history. This is the more unfortunate since those implications are strictly democratic, indicating organic, even if distant, connections between the labors of the common man and the loftiest achievements of culture.

Quite different from the oblivion into which Buckle's work fell was the impact produced by Marx's historical formulation. Narrower and in some respects more casual than that of Buckle but supported by social movements which encouraged its development, it stimulated a wealth of philosophical and critical literature. As a result, it became the immediate vehicle for world-wide intellectual controversy, involving awareness of, and response to, the more general trend away from surface history toward depth history. Even the critics of Marx's doctrine agree to its far-reaching and constructive effect upon the conception of history.

"But with all its weakness," writes one such critic (the "weakness" resides, in this author's view, in a disproportionate emphasis on economic factors) "it remains true that Marx's interpretation of history towers as a signal contribution to social science . . . Marx's theory stimulated new investigations of the past, encouraged inquiries into human cultures, and provoked questions and posed problems that had not previously been noticed. It gave new dimensions, proportions, and coloration to old and new facts . . . It forced thinkers to restate their values and reshape their frame of reference." [8]

In some broad sense that is above dispute, depth history has established itself — and as we have seen, was in the process of establishing itself long before the advent of Marxism — as one of the important intellectual developments of recent times. Historians in increasing numbers are now aware that no period can be adequately studied exclusively in terms of its surface phenomena, and that such phenomena are related to obscure and complex processes of historical metabolism involving the whole range of man's cultural, social, and economic existence.

Lord Bryce recognized this as the prevailing historical point of view when, in his presidential address to the International Congress of Historical Studies in 1913, he stated that "We have now come to regard history as a record of every form of human effort and achievement, concerned not any more definitely with political events and institutions than with all other factors that have moulded man and all the other expressions his creative activity has found." [9] James Harvey Robinson phrased the same thought in other words when he described history as "all we know about everything man has ever done, or thought, or hoped or felt." [10]

Although non-Marxist students have long had depth history at their disposal as a means of correlating art with its social and economic backgrounds, they have shown little inclination to pursue the subject. As previously implied, contributions to the field have been made chiefly by Marxists and have therefore represented the narrower concept of economic determinism rather than the broader one of depth history in general. Consequently, it is to the work of the economic determinists that we must turn in completing this review of the historical approach to cultural dynamics. Our comments will be based upon three of the landmarks of this literature: George Plekhanov's *Art and Society*, Frederick Antal's *Florentine Painting and Its Social Background*, and Arnold Hauser's *Social History of Art*.

In *Art and Society*, Plekhanov gave new relevance to the controversy between the exponents of art for art's sake and the utilitarian view that art should express and subserve social values. Instead of seeking to disprove one of these points of view, Plekhanov suggests that each may be a natural expression of certain relations between artists and the society in which they live. The question then becomes one, not of showing that one view is right and the other wrong, but of finding out what kinds of relations between art and society give rise to each of them. The answer brought forward by Plekhanov on the basis of a number of historical examples, is summarized in the two following statements:

"The tendency of artists and those concerned with art to adopt an attitude of art for art's sake arises when a hopeless contradiction exists between them and their social environment . . .

"The so-called utilitarian conception of art, that is, the tendency to regard the function of art as a judgment on the phenomena of life and a readiness to participate in social struggles, develops and becomes established when a mutual bond of sympathy exists between a considerable section of society and those more or less actively interested in artistic creation." [11]

Plekhanov published his book in 1905, half a century ago. Its basic principles still appear to hold firm, indeed to have been reinforced by subsequent developments in both the art and the thought of the twentieth century. Broadly speaking, we may say that the contributions of the materialist conception of history to criticism are already considerable, and that its potentialities for a fuller understanding of culture appear to be great. In such respects it shares with psychoanalysis the distinction of having discovered some of the most promising frontiers now open to us for intellectual exploration. In the opinion of the present writer, however, it also shares with psychoanalysis the limitation of not providing, in and of itself, a sufficiently balanced theoretical foundation for a complete system of cultural dynamics.

The limitations of economic determinism as a basis for cultural studies appear to be three in number. The first is the danger, already alluded to in the words of a critic of the doctrine, of giving disproportionate emphasis to economic factors as cultural determinants: the danger of swinging to the opposite extreme from that which completely ignores economic factors. As M. M. Bober, the writer already quoted, observes, if the proponents of the theory "mean that the system of production and class structure explain the phenomenon under consideration, they accept a precarious guide. Fruitful in some instances, it may be misleading in others . . . Still more light and a surer orientation may be won if there is an exploration as well of such areas as politics, religion, science, literature, dominant ideas, and leading personalities," [12]

In other words, depth history in its inclusive totality, with due attention to economic factors, would seem to be a sounder basis for cultural studies than preoccupation with economic factors alone. It should be noted, however, that oversimplification on economic grounds is a temptation to which materialist writers *may* succumb, not a restriction to which they are inevitably subject. Neither Plekhanov nor Antal (we shall refer to the latter's work in a moment) give undue emphasis to economic considerations. Both relate art to inclusive social and cultural situations rather than to economic determinants in the narrow sense.

A second limitation of materialist criticism may be ascribed to its comparative youth and therefore may be regarded (to paraphrase a French aphorism) as "the defect of its value." In most of the literature thus far available for review, the concept has been only spasmodically applied to selected cultural movements. There has been little comprehensive effort to study the arts and other cultural expressions of given civilizations in close correlation with all the depth changes that went on during long consecutive spans of their history.

Instead, the tendency has been to select a given artist or movement, or to accept miscellaneously from history various artists or movements that rose to contact with the critic's thought. Plekhanov deals mainly with the French literature and art of the eighteenth and nineteenth centuries, and with Russian equivalents, but he touches on primitive, Byzantine, Renaissance, modern, and other styles. To touch is easy; to establish, difficult. Before depth history can make its maximum contribution to the philosophy of art, scholars will have to grapple with the problem of correlating, not a few attractive links between the arts and history, but the whole complex cultural and historical totalities that comprise the life of the societies involved.

The writer knows of only two works that approach the kind of program just indicated. These are the second and third of the books previously mentioned: Antal's *Florentine Painting and Its Social Background* (1947), and Hauser's *Social History of Art* (1951). The former deepens the penetration of materialist criticism intensively, the latter widens its range extensively.

Antal's study of Florentine painting bears the subtitle, *The Bourgeois Republic before Cosimo de' Medici's Advent to Power: XIV and Early XV Centuries.* The author brings several hundred specific works of Florentine painting (215 of which are reproduced for the reader) into correlation with a thoroughly documented study of Florentine life as expressed in its economic, social, religious, and other activities. Thus he comes to grips at close range with some of the more detailed problems of economic determinism as a basis for art criticism. The reader of his discussion can hardly fail to receive a new and more realistic awareness that the products of Florentine studios, and even the doctrines of Florentine churches, were intimately related with the struggle for wealth and power, and the resulting social tensions, that centered in the city's woolen mills and banking houses. Antal's book deserves recognition as one of the pioneering efforts to deal at close range with a sociological frame of critical reference. It also, we believe, leaves room for growth in certain respects.

In confining his investigation to a time span of little more than a century, Antal remains within the scope of short-range, as opposed to what we shall later call "long-range," studies. As a result, the types of art and related social backgrounds which concern him all have much in common. To see, as he does, "a vast difference" [13] between two fifteenth-century Florentine paintings of the Madonna and the Child — one by Masaccio, the other by Gentile da Fabriano — is to magnify into a bold contrast what might equally well be described as a similarity. As compared with work of decidedly earlier or later times, the two pictures mentioned resemble rather than differ from each other. Broadly speaking the two pictures mentioned involve, not two different styles, but two variations of the same style.

In making such variations the basis of his study, Antal is forced to deal in fine and often overlapping distinctions. His skill in doing so cannot but arouse our admiration. At the same time, the narrow range delimits the results of the approach. Within this range, the social and economic determinants of the various aspects of fourteenth- and fifteenth-century Florentine painting reduce themselves to class struggles between the upper and lower bourgeoisie, the waning nobility, and the workers.

Such group or class tensions, however, are not the master tensions of an epoch. The conflicting interests of the various subdivisions of fifteenth-century Florentine society may indeed influence the variations of the common pictorial style, and Antal brings convincing evidence to the support of this conclusion. But the sources of the style itself — the sources of the common vision that unites Masaccio with Gentile da Fabriano, and that differentiates both of them from a Celtic illuminator or from Rembrandt — the sources of this basic fifteenth-century Florentine vision lie deeper than class distinctions. It is misleading to assume, as Antal appears to, that such distinctions constitute the ultimate foundation for artistic style. The ultimate foundation must be sought at a more profound level, in conditions that affect all classes alike. Such conditions, and their accompanying forms of cultural expression, can be studied to advantage only in sequences of sufficient duration to show marked results of slow evolutionary change. This is rarely possible within the span of one or even two centuries.

The need for further intensive studies like that of Antal, and also for their correlation with more extensive historical developments, will no doubt be met in the course of time. The problem of extension has already been attacked with considerable energy by Hauser in his *Social History of Art*, to which we shall refer in greater detail presently. But there is one final limitation of economic determinism which, from the theoretical point of view, seems to be more serious and more permanent than those thus far considered. That is an inadequate explanation of *how* material preconditions can affect the nature of the cultural expressions which they are believed to determine.

The materialist critic, accepting economic determinism as an axiom, observes particular forms of art and accompanying types of social condition and states that the one is a result of the other. Empirically, he appears often to be right; theoretically, he can provide no demonstration that he is so. The philosophy of art for art's sake *might* conceivably be an outgrowth of forces as yet undiscovered. The same can be said of the variations of Florentine pictorial style studied by Antal. We cannot accept these cultural developments as proven to be the results of their suggested social causes until we are shown by what means such causes can produce these particular philosophical and artistic results. To the best of the author's knowledge, the economic determinists have largely ignored this problem.

In and of themselves, economic determinants cannot produce the forms of cultural expression that are attributed to them. Somewhere between the determinants and the expression of them, we must assume the existence of a transformer that converts the cultural potentials of the one into the cultural actualities of the other. This transformer, we shall maintain, is the human psyche.

It is in this connection, we believe, that the economic determinists have left a gap in their system of cultural dynamics. They have failed to make adequate use of recent psychological developments. They have sometimes recognized in a general way the existence of "intermediate links"; they have even recognized these links as primarily mental in their nature. But they have attempted no intensive study of them. This is the relatively unexplored borderland of their particular intellectual territory.

The resulting gap in the materialist interpretation of culture seems apparent in a recent work already mentioned, Hauser's *Social History of Art*. This is an ambitious two-volume effort to interpret socially the entire history of Western culture from prehistoric to modern times. It is noteworthy in its objective, stimulating in its example and of great interest in its findings. But the latter are often limited by insufficient attention to the depth and complexity of the psychic factors involved in cultural activity.

Hauser nowhere states the premises on which he bases his study, but his approach is obviously that of economic determinism. The kind of forces with which he equates the changing forms of cultural expression are those exerted by an urban economy as contrasted with an agrarian one, or by middle class stolidity as contrasted with courtly refinement. The resulting equations are based partly upon observed historical parallelisms between types of art and contemporary types of social organization, partly upon analogies drawn between the prevailing spirit of a type of art and the spirit of some contemporary aspect of life.

"The strict geometric style is connected with traditionalistic agriculture and unrestrained naturalism with a more dynamic urban economy." [14] The simplicity and directness of Giotto's work identifies it as "a simple, sober, straightforward middle class art . . . Giotto's art is austere and objective, like the character of those who commissioned his works, men who wished to be prosperous and to exercise authority, but who attached not too much importance to outward show and lavish expenditures." [15] In contrast to the sobriety of both Giotto and Masaccio, "the richness of genre traits in the art of Gozzoli and the psychological sensibility of Botticelli" represent two subsequent "stages in the historical development of the middle class as it rises from frugal circumstances to the level of a real money aristocracy." [16]

Insofar as such correspondences between art and life depend upon class distinctions, the comments previously made in connection with Antal's work would apply equally well here. But irrespective of the secondary nature of class distinctions, the equating of a type of art with a type of economy or a prevalent class mentality is too mechanistic a procedure for the adequate study of intangibles like those involved in creative and cultural experience. Abstract art did indeed synchronize with the development of agriculture in Neolithic times, and has corresponded with agrarianism in certain other periods, but the relation abstract-agrarian is still not the essential one. In our recent culture, we have seen urban artists take the lead in a shift from realism toward abstraction, while our characteristically rural art has been realistic.

Whether an economy is urban or rural is, in itself, incidental to cultural determination. There are *no fixed* relationships between specific economic or social phenomena and specific types of art. The attempt to reduce cultural analysis to such relations inevitably leads to the realization that the theory is too narrow to fit historical realities. Hauser himself indicates a number of examples which do not substantiate his assumption that agrarianism produces abstract art and urban economy, realistic art. "The real problem of Mesopotamian art consists in the fact that, despite an economy based predominately in trade and industry, finance and credit, it has a more rigidly disciplined, less changeable, less dynamic character than the art of Egypt, a country much more deeply rooted in agricultural and natural economy." [17]

Hauser is to be commended for frankly recognizing such theoretical dilemmas instead of forcing the facts to fit the theory, but the dilemmas nevertheless remain and his only observations with regard to them amount to a recognition of the inadequacy of the method. After noting that the respective types of art produced by Crete and by Greece in their turn fail to fulfill all the materialist expectancies, he observes "but this only proves that in the history of art, the same causes by no means always have the same effects or that the causes are perhaps all too numerous to be completely exhausted by scientific analysis." [18]

I believe that we have a much better chance of solving such problems if, instead of trying to establish direct relations between socio-economic conditions and cultural expressions, we recognize that there is a *third* important factor to be conjured with: the psychological one. The crucial consideration for culture is not the nature of a particular economy, whether urban or rural, but the effect produced by economic and other historical circumstances upon the psychic life of the given society. It is the activity of symbolic transformation within the psyche that constitutes the immediate matrix of the forms of art and the indispensable medium of conversion from historical conditions to cultural expressions.

The equations with which we must deal, so to speak, are not mathematical ones like $2 + 2 = 4$, but algebraic ones like $2 + x = y$. The whole mystery of psychic existence enters the sequence in the "x" of symbolic transformation, a process of such depth and complexity that scientists have only lately begun to recognize and fathom it. It is a process which works by devious ways and in an unconscious manner — a process capable of producing quite different results than those which surface interpretation might lead us to expect. Only in the light of all that is known about it, only by taking full advantage of the findings of psychology in general and of depth psychology in particular, can we hope to understand so intricate an activity, and only to the degree in which we understand it can we begin with some assurance to analyze the subtle connections between given sets of historical conditions and their assumed expressions.

III

To summarize the findings of the present chapter, and at the same time to correlate them with those of the preceding one, we may say that while psychoanalysis stops short of a complete interpretation of culture on one side, the materialist conception of history stops short of it on the other. The one is limited by its excessive subjectivity, the other by its excessive objectivity. It is as if two exploring parties were approaching the summit of a mountain range from opposite directions, each within striking distance of the top, each with scientific data on its own slope and with a vague awarenes that there must be an opposite slope, but both unable to reach the top and merge their discoveries in a comprehensive description of the whole two-sided range.

Now and then a member of one of these parties has, as it were, glimpsed the distant progress of the other. Especially in the early phases of their studies, both depth historians and depth psychologists seem to have been well disposed toward possibilities of correlation between their respective fields. Buckle among the historians, for instance, gave serious attention to the psychology of his day — although his day preceded most of what now seems to us important in psychology.

Freud, looking from the psychological direction, left us a record of his attitude toward economic determinism, and his attitude was much like the one expressed in our review of the subject. He recognized as a virtue of the materialist theory that it afforded "clear insight into the determining influence which is exerted by the economic conditions of man upon his intellectual, ethical and artistic reactions. A whole collection of correlations and causal sequences were thus discovered, which had hitherto been almost completely disregarded." [19]

At the same time, as we might expect, Freud calls for a balance of economic considerations by others of a different nature and especially by psychological ones. "It cannot be maintained that economic factors are the only ones which determine the behavior of men in society . . . It is quite impossible to understand how psychological factors can be overlooked where the reactions of living human beings are involved; for not only were such factors already concerned in the establishment of these economic conditions, but, even in obeying these conditions, men can do no more than set their original instinctual impulses in motion — their self-preservative instinct, their love of aggression, their need for love, and their impulse to attain pleasure and avoid pain."

After referring to a number of noneconomic factors in historical situations, Freud concludes: "If any one were in a position to show in detail how these different factors — the general human instinctual disposition, its racial variations, and its cultural modifications — behave under the influence of varying social organization, professional activities and methods of subsistence, how these factors inhibit or aid one another — if, I say, any one could show this, then he would not only have improved Marxism but would have made it into a true social science. For sociology can be nothing more than applied psychology."

Here, as in another passage previously quoted from Freud — and as in passages which we shall later quote from other writers — we have a representative of one of the existing disciplines recognizing potential relations between social, psychological, and cultural studies which, if pursued, would result in some form of psycho-historical conception.

Unfortunately, these early and distant glimpses of the psycho-historical horizon have been followed by no intensive efforts at correlational progress. Indeed most later psychoanalytical critics, as well as most economic determinists, seem to have receded from the exploratory attitudes toward correlation cited in connection with Buckle and Freud. Due no doubt to the tendency of once plastic ideas to crystallize into fixed forms and also to the external pressures upon intellectual life exerted by war psychology, mutual indifference or opposition has been more characteristic of the exponents of these two systems than has a coöperative search for common foundations. Of all the barriers that impede the progress of world thought today, none seems more serious than the intellectual great divide which, in thus severing our psychic from our social knowledge, lends itself to conflicts between the individualistic and the collective, the spiritual and the materialistic philosophies of life and of culture. To my knowledge our critical literature, antecedent to the present volume, has proposed no principle that might serve as a basis of unification between the two fields that concern us. To work out such a basis, if we can, becomes our main task.

Before proposing my own solution, however, I shall review a theory that has sometimes been regarded as connecting the psychic and the social worlds — the theory of the "collective unconscious" — and even in developing this solution, I shall refer back to ideas received from preëxisting disciplines like psychoanalysis. At the same time, the primary concern of this book from now on will not be with any existing concept or discipline in itself, but with the degree to which it involves, or can suggest, the means of uniting depth psychology with depth history.

THE THEORY OF THE
COLLECTIVE UNCONSCIOUS

Those who seek, whether consciously or intuitively, for connections between psychology and culture, may take hope when they first become acquainted with the theory of the "collective unconscious." Here, it seems, is a rift in the individualistic front of depth psychology, and therefore an opening through one of the main barriers that has blocked the path to a psycho-social synthesis.

The very phrase "collective unconscious" implies connection between the two main worlds of thought we have been considering. Insofar as it involves the unconscious, it has a basis in psychology and is therefore conversant with life impulse, symbolic transformation, and the other mental and emotional realities to which psychologists have devoted their research. On the other hand, insofar as the concept involves a *collective* aspect, it suggests possible connections with the social and cultural realities which have been the concern of history and the social sciences.

If such an interrelationship between the psychological and the historical aspects of experience were actually established under the concept of the collective unconscious, that concept would provide the link we are seeking between depth psychology and depth history. In point of fact, when we investigate the theory more closely, our hopes for it in this particular respect are disappointed. The actual link with history still remains to be established. Nevertheless, it will be worth our while to look more fully into the concept both to see what light it does throw on culture and why it fails to provide a basis for a true psycho-historical synthesis.

The suggestion that there is a collective unconscious resulted from an attempt to explain certain phenomena of mental imagery, some derived from the observation of individual patients, some from the study of mythology and folklore.

It became clear that such imagery is not an endless variation of separate fantasies lacking common bonds of genus and species. On the contrary, it reveals recurrent types which "present themselves in the form of mythological themes and images, appearing often in identical form and always with striking similarity among all races; they can also be easily verified in the unconscious material of modern man."[1] These recurrent forms of mental imagery were labeled "archetypes" or "primordial images." They constitute a psychic phenomenon of undoubted reality which must be explained in one way or another.

The theory of the collective unconscious explains them in terms of psychic dispositions left by the totality of past racial experience. As Jung phrases it, "If we subject these images to a closer investigation, we discover them to be the formulated resultants of countless typical experiences of our ancestors. They are, as it were, the psychic residue of numberless experiences of the same type . . . presenting a kind of picture of the psychic life distributed and projected into the manifold shapes of the mythological pandemonium."[2]

And again: "The unconscious regarded as the historical background of the psyche, contains in a concentrated form the entire succession of engrams (imprints) which from time immemorial have determined the psychic structure as it now exists. These engrams may be regarded as function-traces which typify on the average, the most frequently and intensely used functions of the human soul."[3] It is these "function-traces," inherited from the past by all individuals, which are said to express themselves in the common symbolical imagery of both individual and mythical fantasy.

The collective unconscious may thus be defined as an inherited disposition toward predetermined psychic reactions and preconditioned forms of accompanying mental imagery. A particular archetypal reaction emerges in an individual when he finds himself in circumstances corresponding to those which, on thousands of earlier occasions, left their imprint upon the psychic inheritance transmitted to him by his ancestors. In other words, the theory provides a means of interpreting certain psychological experiences and their cultural expressions in terms of a prenatal racial conditioning of the psyche; a conditioning which is presumably more profound and far-reaching in its effects than the restricted childhood conditioning of the individual.

Critics of the doctrine appear sometimes to assume that it is limited to Jung and that it is not in accord with Freudian principles of psychoanalysis. It is true that Jung did most to bring the theory to conscious formulation and to explore its implications. But the same essential facts of recurrent imagery, explained in terms of psychic inheritance, are as native to Freud as to Jung. Thus, in *The Interpretation of Dreams* Freud writes, "We begin to suspect that Friedrich Nietzche was right when he said that in a dream 'there persists a primordial part of humanity which we can no longer reach by a direct path,' and we are encouraged to expect, from the analysis of dreams, a knowledge of the archaic inheritance of man, a knowledge of psychical things in him that are innate. It would seem that dreams and neuroses have preserved for us more of the psychical antiquities than we suspected; so that psychoanalysis may claim a high rank among those sciences which endeavor to reconstruct the oldest and darkest phases of the beginnings of mankind." [4]

Elsewhere Freud states that recurrent psychic symbols "seem to be a fragment of extremely ancient inherited mental equipment," [5] and that the "primal phantasies" of the human mind "are a phylogenetic possession. In them, the individual, wherever his own experience has become insufficient, stretches out beyond it to the experience of past ages. It seems to me possible that all that today is narrated in analysis in the form of phantasy . . . was in prehistoric periods of the human family a reality; and that the child in its phantasy simply fills out the gaps in the true individual experiences with true prehistoric experiences." [6]

Karl Abraham uses a similar concept as the basis for his interpretation of myths. "The myth," he writes, "is a fragment of the repressed life of the infantile psyche of the race." It contains (in disguised form) the wishes of the childhood of the race. [7]

In such statements we have Freud and one of his followers, no less than Jung, presenting observations that coincide with the theory of the collective unconscious. The idea is, in fact, intrinsic to psychoanalytical thought. That there must inevitably be a psychological as well as a physical aspect to our biological inheritance appears axiomatic; that the common psychological inheritance may be the source of common types of mental fantasy, seems at least a reasonable hypothesis.

Jung, Freud, and other psychoanalytical writers pursued their study of the collective unconscious chiefly in terms of the literary material of dream, myth, and folklore. There is, however, no reason to suppose that the principle cannot be generalized and applied, among other things, to the plastic imagery of visual art. Primitive, archaic, and other types of artistic conception also occur with "striking similarity among all races"; they also can "easily be verified" in the experiences and productions of modern man. In terms of the theory before us, these recurrent categories of visual conception, like the literary ones of mythological subject matter, would be conceived as manifestations of archetypal experiences.

The idea that there are archetypes of cultural expression has taken a strong hold upon many artists of the twentieth century, searching as they are for forms that transcend the individual limits of both understanding and life span and will achieve thus a universal and enduring value.

> Not innovating wilfulness,
> But reverence for the archetype.[8]

The participation of many individual artists in a common collective unconscious would provide at least one possible explanation of such cultural phenomena as the unity of period styles. The realism of the late Middle Ages and the Renaissance instead of stemming from the personal influence of Giotto or any other individual, might mark the emergence into consciousness and gradual clarification of a primordial mode of vision to which all the artists of the epoch were similarly disposed. Some such nonpersonal explanation seems the more credible when we reflect that if Giotto has any influence on most artists in the twentieth century, it is an influence *away* from realism, not toward it. Contemporary vision finds its affinities among the conventions which Giotto was discarding rather than the naturalistic goals that he pursued. The work of an individual artist, it would seem, can influence the formation of a period style only to the degree in which it satisfies an emergent cultural necessity. If we ask what force, at any given time and place, determines the nature of the cultural necessity, a possible answer would be the collective unconscious.

Whether we accept or reject this explanation makes little ultimate difference so far as concerns the search for a passage from psychology to history. The hope we originally entertained for the theory of the collective unconscious was inspired by the social implications of the term "collective." We have now gone far enough with our analysis to perceive that in point of fact the meaning given to the term in the present context is *not* a social one in any exact sense.

As noted above, the collective unconscious has been conceived by the psychoanalysts as part of our racial inheritance. It is collective only in the sense that it is derived from a common ancestry and is received by all individuals. Therefore, it is still an individual phenomenon, involving no direct or necessary interraction between the members of a group in society. Actually, this so-called "collective" unconscious would be possessed by a castaway who was alone on a desert island, for his psychic inheritance would be within him as part of his individuality. If it functioned in the manner ascribed to it by psychoanalysts, it would color his fantasies with primordial imagery. In the sense here given to the word, individuality itself is "collective," since the individual is merely a small and temporary offshoot of the biological inheritance of his species.

Quite different is the significance of the term "collective" as applied to the experience shared by the players on a football team, or by the population that conceives itself to be a possible target for a hydrogen bomb. Here any involvement of inherited dispositions or "psychical antiquities" is inconsequential. The important sources of these collective experiences are objective developments, not a subjective inheritance from the past. Correspondingly, the psychic aspects of such experiences are states of group psychology that are shared by the members of a given group because all of them are jointly experiencing the same given external circumstances. In this context there can be collective experience only insofar as there is joint participation in the experience by the several members of some group.

This connotation of the term "collective" is at once more literal and more in accord with that in usage in the social sciences than with that assumed in the expression "collective unconscious." "Racial unconscious" or "congenital unconscious" would possibly be more accurate phrases for use in the latter connection, if indeed a specific phrase is needed. Since all our mental faculties are inherited; since the unconscious in its entirety, insofar as it involves dispositions, is an inheritance, one wonders whether there can be any real distinction between the "unconscious" and the "collective unconscious."

We are inclined to think that the difference between the collective and the individual aspects of experience, which Jung rightly emphasized, must be traced to other sources than our innate mental equipment; and that within the psychological sphere, the tenable distinction is not between the "unconscious" and the "collective unconscious," but between the unconscious as a congenital disposition and the particular bent given to it by any individual's life experience·

In any event, society as a currently shared phenomenon, and history as its temporal unfolding, are elements that must be brought into full organic interplay with psychic forces before we can be said to have achieved the psycho-historical synthesis that we are seeking. They are not so brought together by any concept based primarily upon psychic inheritance. Hence, we must search elsewhere for the means of integrating these different aspects of human existence.

A similar conclusion awaits us when we turn our critical scrutiny from the concept of the collective unconscious itself to the cultural effects that have been ascribed to it. Inherited mental dispositions undoubtedly exist and presumably limit the possible forms of cultural expression. On the other hand there appear to be two additional and probably more immediate sources of primordial imagery. These additional sources are the cultural inheritance and the current historical situation.

To illustrate the importance of the cultural inheritance, let us take an archetype that occurs in the myths of all nations and that will play an important part in our later studies: the theme of conflict between a monster and a hero. Some visual embodiments of this theme, as found in European medieval art, are reproduced on Plates 11, 12, 16 and 17. According to the theory of the collective unconscious, a disposition to conceive this imagery would have been imposed upon the mind by countless experiences in the past and would emerge into consciousness whenever conditions assumed a state similar to that which had conditioned the earlier development of the imagery.

With or without benefit of such biological transmission, however, we must recognize the fact that monster-hero imagery is handed down culturally from one generation to another in the form of myths, legends, fairy tales, and works of art. It is doubtful whether any human being in any of the societies known to us — primitive, ancient, or modern — has reached maturity without hundreds of times having heard and seen these transmitted forms of monster-hero imagery. Even in the recent rational and scientific Western world of the eighteenth and nineteenth centuries, which was about as far from the formative state of mythological imagery as any culture could be, children listened with awe to fairy tales involving monsters, ogres, giants, and witches.

Some of these children later went to college and studied such themes nearer to their source in literary works like *Beowulf*, the *Niebelungenlied*, and the writings based on Greek mythology. Those who studied art, or who even looked at reproductions of it, became familiar with the visual aspect of monster imagery in the painting, sculpture, and the decorative art of many civilizations. The theme is still being transmitted to the believers of many religions as part — perhaps at present a remote part — of their religious traditions. St. Michael and his conquest of the devil survive as living symbols in most versions of Christianity; there may even be reminiscent references to the battle of St. George with the dragon.

Even if the psychic inheritance included no disposition toward monster-hero imagery, the cultural one would provide a sufficient basis for its recurrent appearance. It is transmitted educationally from one generation to another, is not taken seriously when conditions give it no relevance to major cultural concerns, but persists as a latent means of expression that can be reactivated and elevated to more important functions if and when conditions so inspire.

Whether we assume a latent psychic disposition or a latent cultural inheritance, or both, a further vital factor is the historical context that generates the activation. A terrifying historical situation (to carry forward a context relevant to monster imagery) is bound to produce psychic reactions of a negative character, and these reactions will tend to symbolize themselves in equally negative mental imagery. The process by which they do so is essentially psycho-historical and will be fully discussed later in developing the grounds for our own theory. For the moment it will suffice to cite an example of the historical event as a factor in generating imagery of the kind we have been considering. One such example is provided by the Canadian anthropologist, Marius Barbeau, in connection with a figure carved on totem poles by certain Indians of British Columbia.

"The eruption of a volcano on the Nass River about 1780 left the inhabitants of the region in a state of terror. Many of them took flight. For a long time thereafter they were subject to terrifying hallucinations, which gave rise to new totems, including that of the Gnawing Squirrel. While fishing for salmon on the upper Nass, these people often saw apparitions of monstrous squirrels, large as bears; the country seemed to be infested with them. Certain hunters, taking courage, pursued them and [were supposed to have] killed the largest of them — the guardian spirit of the Squirrels. They made it their totem." [9] In this instance, the shock caused by the volcanic eruption was the immediate cause of the monster imagery. A current historical experience thus played at least as vital a part in the imagery-forming situation as the possible, but more remote, involvement of "psychical antiquities."

Our assertion is that historical circumstances of all kinds, positive as well as negative, produce psychic effects, and that these effects in turn seek symbolical expression in various forms of mental imagery. This process, which we shall later call the "tension-imagery process," is a spontaneous activity of the human mind and operates both with and without recourse to traditional imagery. The symbolical images may be drawn from current daily experience, as happens frequently in our dreams and as seemingly happened in the case of the monster squirrels referred to above. Since, however, every mind is charged with traditional imagery that has been culturally transmitted to it, a given historical impact may reactivate some aspect of the inheritance instead of, or in addition to, generating new symbols of its own.

We have frequent pseudo-activations of the monster-hero inheritance in relation to international and social conflicts. The partisans of one group or another caricature their enemies in monstrous guise as bloodthirsty Molochs, ravenous beasts, and so forth, while presenting themselves as knights in armor marching out on "crusades." These are superficial and usually calculated forms of propaganda. A true reactivation of the psycho-cultural inheritance — of which the monsters of recent surrealism would seem to offer an example — occurs when artists and writers are driven to forms of primordial imagery by their creative sensitivity, often without conscious realization of why they are so driven, and sometimes in despite of their own wills. Then it is that the larger and deeper historical situation, which engulfs both friend and enemy alike, is working its way through collective tensions into cultural imagery.

Neglect of the objective historical situation is the chief reason why the theory of the collective unconscious turns out to be disappointing from our point of view. Like the other aspects of psychoanalytical thought previously considered, the statements of this theory carry us to the borderline between psychology and history — and in this case project that borderline back into prehistoric times — but again fail to give careful attention to what happened on the other side of the border. The "countless typical experiences of our ancestors" to which Jung refers as the basis of the psychic inheritance, the "true prehistoric experiences" which Freud sees behind the "true individual experiences" of today, did not happen to psychological phantoms in some insubstantial atmosphere of mental haze. Each was a specific event involving actual men, women, and children in some actual family or tribe which lived in a given environment and was subject to particular historical circumstances.

Could we have been present when each of these events took place, we would have been vividly aware of its historical objectivity and would, it seems safe to say, have witnessed not only the sexual dramas of rivalry and incest envisaged by the psychoanalysts, but equally momentous episodes from every phase of human existence: victories and defeats in war, gluttonous feasts after a successful hunt, and death by starvation in times of famine. Like these long-past events which may once have inspired primordial imagery, the current circumstances that can still stimulate it will involve equally concrete historical situations, personal and social. All along the line, from the cavemen to their modern succes-

sors who occupy by turns the penthouse and the bombshelter, the theory of the
collective unconscious presupposes historical correlatives, but nowhere does it
accord them more than hints and passing references.

If, for instance, we turn to Jung's more exhaustive works such as the *Psychology of the Unconscious* — with the hope that since this author emphasizes
"collective" factors, he will bridge the gap between psychology and the objective
world — we find again the characteristic psychoanalytical concern with subjective states and merely inferential reference to historical realities. "The hero
battling with the dragon," writes Jung with regard to the form of imagery that
we have been considering, "has much in common with the dragon, and also he
takes over his qualities; for example in vulnerability . . . Translated psychologically, the dragon is merely the son's repressed longing, striving towards the
mother; therefore, the son is the dragon." [10]

As we read the explanation of various forms of mythical imagery proposed
in Jung's works, we find ourselves constrained in large part to the realm of
sexuality, libidinal transformations, and similar psychic figurations. Despite
the conception of the collective unconscious, we are still remote from the students of history, economics, and other social sciences with whom we have been
trying to establish contact. Jung in his turn, at least when occupied with the
primary concerns of psychoanalysis, was too exclusively a psychologist to concentrate prolonged attention upon the external world. He rightly sensed the
incompleteness of an exclusively individualistic psychoanalysis; rightly called
for more attention to collective factors, and in so doing performed an intellectual service for which he deserves more credit than he is now generally receiving. His actual grasp of the collective factors, however, appears to have been
an emergent and partial one still largely entangled with individualistic psychology.

This statement applies to the dominant concept behind Jung's major works.
Exceptions to it are not lacking. Like Freud in his more speculative moments
— like most specialists when they shift their attention from technical concerns
to philosophical horizons — Jung at times reached conclusions very much like
those we are proposing. In his more casual writings, as well as in certain
incidental references accompanying his psychological discussions, he transcends
the limitations which we have been ascribing to the standard concept of the
collective unconscious and moves in directions that forecast the psycho-historical
frame of reference. Let us note two of these marginal passages that carry us
to the growing edge of Jung's thought.

"Political, social, and religious conditions influence the unconscious, since all the factors which are suppressed in the conscious religion or philosophical attitude of human society accumulate in the unconscious. The gradual accumulation means a gradual increase in the energy of the unconscious contents. Certain individuals gifted with particularly refined intuition become aware of the change going on in the collective unconscious, and sometimes even succeed in translating their perceptions of it into communicable ideas. The new ideas spread more or less rapidly in accordance with the state of readiness in the unconscious of other people. In proportion to the more or less universal unconscious readiness, people are ready to accept new ideas, or else to show particular resistance to them." [11]

In this passage the collective unconscious is described, not as an aspect of the individual's psychic inheritance, but as a socially shared psychic condition that is subject to the impact of political and other external circumstances. It is also indicated as a potential source of "new ideas" which reflect any changes that may be taking place in the external circumstances. Organic relations are thus implied between historical circumstances, psychic states, and forms of cultural expression. Thus interpreted, the collective unconscious becomes identical with what we shall call collective psychic states and can be fully integrated with the psycho-historical point of view.

Equally significant from our point of view is a footnote accompanying a passage in the *Psychology of the Unconscious*. In his text proper, Jung explains the rise of certain ancient mystery religions as a psychic reaction against a pre-existing "state of dissoluteness." "The meaning of those cults — I speak of Christianity and Mithraism — is clear; it is a moral restraint of animal impulses. The dynamic appearance of both religions betrays something of that enormous feeling of redemption which animated the first disciples and which we today scarcely know how to appreciate, for these old truths are empty to us. Most certainly we should still understand it, had our customs even a breath of ancient brutality, for we can hardly realize in this day the whirlwinds of the unchained libido which roared through the ancient Rome of the Caesars." [12]

Thus in typically psychoanalytical terms, Jung sees Christianity and Mithraism rising from a psychological struggle to overcome unbridled sexuality. But other scholars of Jung's generation were studying the same religious developments, and some of them were working from the objective historical angle. Jung, though largely absorbed in his psychoanalytical studies, was not unaware of these other approaches nor insensitive to their value. To his own explanation of the rise of the mystery religions, he accordingly appended the following note. The references to "the religious poem" and to a "Miss Miller" involve a poem by an author of that name which Jung analyzes in the *Psychology of the Unconscious.*

"This analytic perception of the roots of the Mystery Religions is necessarily one-sided, just as is the analysis of the basis of the religious poem. In order to understand the actual causes of the repression in Miss Miller, one must delve into the moral history of the present; just as one is obliged to seek in the ancient moral and economic history the actual causes of repression which have given rise to the Mystery cults. This investigation has been brilliantly carried out by Kalthoff. (See his book, 'Die Entstehung des Christentums,' Leipzig 1904.) I also refer especially to Pohlmann's 'Geschichte des antiken Kommunismus und Sozialismus'; also to Bücher: 'Die Aufstände der unfreien Arbeiter 143 bis 129 V. Chr.,' 1874.

"The other cause [that is, the nonpsychic cause brought forward by the authors just mentioned] of the enormous introversion of the libido in antiquity is probably to be found in the fact that an unbelievably large part of the people suffered in the wretched state of slavery. It is inevitable that finally those who bask in good fortune would be infected in the mysterious manner of the unconscious, by the deep sorrow and still deeper misery of their brothers, through which some were driven into orgiastic furies. Others, however, the better ones, sank into that strange world weariness and satiety of the intellectuals of that time. Thus from two sources the great introversion was made possible." [13]

From the psycho-historical point of view, this passage is notable in several respects. In it, one of the major psychoanalysts himself recognizes that a purely psychoanalytical interpretation of cultural phenomena "is necessarily one-sided." He further indicates that the other side, necessary to equilibrium, lies in the direction of "moral and economic history." In miniature, such a passage establishes the whole psycho-historical frame of reference. If Jung had developed that frame of reference by relating myths and other cultural phenomena not only to psychic dispositions, but also to the history of the epochs that produced them, he would himself have been the originator of the psycho-historical theory. In passages like the one just quoted, he did indeed plant seeds for that theory, but we must remember that this passage is a marginal afterthought to a text the main weight of which is thrown in other, and more typically psychoanalytical directions.

We have already noted passages in which Freud likewise forecast the possibility of a psycho-historical point of view. We have also seen historians like Buckle, primarily concerned with objective cultural and historical developments, recognizing psychology as a source of illumination necessary to the full comprehension of their subject. And we could quote students of various branches of the humanities who feel that both psychology and history have an important bearing upon their subjects. An example from one of the disciplines traditionally related to art will be cited in Chapter XVII.[14]

From whichever direction one of these specialists has looked, he has, in his more philosophical moments, seen the same interdisciplinary territory that lies between his own specialty and the others involved. Each of the authors quoted has conceived, from his own angle, the same possibility of psycho-historical-cultural correlations. Such potential correlations have constituted a kind of intellectual promised land of which many have dreamed but which — if the survey given in the foregoing chapters is adequate — none has actually entered and opened up for full intellectual development.

Can we establish a base in the center of this correlational territory instead of continuing to gaze at it from one or another of its margins? To attempt to do so by formulating the theoretical basis for a psycho-historical theory of culture, will be the task to which we shall next turn our attention.

Chapter V

THE TENSION–IMAGERY PROCESS IN PSYCHO–HISTORICAL INTEGRATION

Since our objective is to bring history, psychology, and the forms of cultural expression into a single unified frame of reference, which can only be done if we find mutual interrelations between all three fields, we could start from any one of them and work our way toward the other two. In the practice of psycho-historical analysis, as we shall find later, the normal order seems to be to start with the works of art or other forms of cultural expression which we wish to interpret, then to correlate them with the historical circumstances under which they were produced, and finally to seek understanding through psychology of the mental processes that transformed the impact of the given circumstances into the given cultural imagery.

For our present purpose of establishing a theoretical foundation for the psycho-historical frame of reference, a different order seems preferable. Human mentality is the matrix upon which the forces of history impinge and from which the forms of cultural expression arise. The connecting links between them are therefore primarily psychological ones. Since our present aim is to reveal correlational agencies as fully as possible, a psychological angle of approach seems to be the most effective one for the purpose.

The basis of the following discussion lies in general psychological principles, some of them traditional, some psychoanalytical. Those derived from psychoanalysis were originally inspired in part by Jung, but have been articulated mainly by Freud. However, it would be misleading for the author to imply, or for the reader to assume, that there is an exact correspondence between any given school of psychology and the psycho-historical theory as applied to art.

The following attempt to state the psychological aspects of the theory should be taken, not as a literal derivation from a preëxisting authority, but as the result of a careful consideration of authorities in the light of a new and more extensive total situation. Insofar as this new situation seems to demand, or as our statement seems to gain in clarity or conciseness by so doing, we shall venture to extend the inherited principles or to state them in new terms.

If this exploratory rather than scriptural use of sources needs any justification, we can refer to the spirit of the men whose results we do not always follow to the letter. The authorities who rank highest in various fields often wrote tentatively, conscious that they were exploring the unknown but not exhausting it. They recognized that the intellectual ground they were able to clear was everywhere surrounded by jungles of implications which would demand further study in the future.

If, for instance, any single individual can be taken as the ultimate authority in the field of psychoanalysis, that man is undoubtedly Freud. We would do well to remember that the actual statements of Freud are often far from the definitiveness which is sometimes attributed to his system by his followers. In introducing a review of the theory of instincts in 1932, he wrote, "I cannot say that we have made any great progress or that any trouble you may take in learning about it will be amply rewarded. No; it is a field in which we are struggling hard to get some sort of orientation and understanding; you will only be witness to the efforts we are making." [1]

When Freud ventures into the fields which most directly concern us in the present study, those of mythology and art, he is at once courageous in suggesting his ideas and modest in recognizing that those ideas are only tentative. In 1919, he made a general comment on the work of Otto Rank, Hanns Sachs, and others in applying psychoanalysis to mythology, religion, and related subjects, and came to the conclusion: "No final formula has yet been found enabling us to give an appropriate place to myths in this connection." [2]   Similarly, with regard to his own interpretation of certain myths on a sexual basis, he remarks, "One has the impression that this approach might lead us quite a long way into the secrets of the myth, *but, of course, we should not carry the feeling of certainty with us very far.*" [3] And in completing his study of Leonardo da Vinci, as we noted when reviewing that work, Freud admits that he "certainly did not overestimate the reliability of these results." [4]

In the last analysis, the validity of the psycho-historical theory must be judged in terms, not of its derivation, but of its application. However great the indebtedness of our theory to psychological or other sources — or, if the reader wishes, however heretical our departure from the doctrines of such sources — the *value* of the theory will be determined neither by its indebtedness nor by its independence. Its value can be determined only by putting it to the use for which it is intended — the study of cultural phenomena — and by judging the results that follow.

Before we can apply and evaluate it in this manner, we must formulate it. This we shall now attempt to do, beginning with a summary of psychological considerations from which it seems possible to work our way toward a psycho-historical frame of reference.

II

Human beings, like other biological organisms, spontaneously seek to preserve themselves and to fulfill their needs and desires. Their success depends upon the degree to which they are able to achieve a profitable relationship with their environment. On the positive side, they must win from that environment the facilities necessary for their maintenance and satisfaction, such as food, shelter, and mate. On the negative side, they must defend themselves against whatever difficulties and dangers the environment imposes, whether these result from disease, famine, wild animals, human enemies, or other causes.

Among the internal resources employed by the organism in its interplay with the environment is psychic energy — a kind of mental-emotional drive that serves as an activating and directing force in promoting fulfillment and resisting opposition. The flow of such energy appears, as Jung puts it, "in the specific, dynamic phenomena of the mind, such as instinct, wishing, willing, affect, attention, power of work, etc." [5] For our purpose a technical term for psychic energy hardly seems necessary, but it may be noted in passing that we are here dealing with what Jung technically calls "libido." Freud uses the latter term in an equivalent but narrower sense, restricting it to the "instinctual forces of the sexual life." [6]

The normal discharge of psychic energy is in action of a kind appropriate to satisfy a given need or overcome a given difficulty. The primitive hunter pursues the game he wishes to eat and fights the enemy who attacks his camp. We today direct similar energies toward similar goals when we go to the grocery store to buy the food necessary for our survival, or when we appeal to the law for retribution in our grievances. In all such cases psychic energy has found expression in action calculated to fulfill our impulses or to protect our interests.

Only rarely and temporarily, however, is an individual's supply of psychic energy entirely absorbed into overt action. Such action is the middle term, the discharge, of a psychic dynamism which also involves its preliminary energical preparation and its subsequent energical readjustment. We not only perform a given action; in most cases of any importance, we meditate it before, and review it after, the performance. During these pre- and post-action phases, the effects of psychic energy are inward rather than outward.

Furthermore, there are circumstances in which action is temporarily or permanently impossible. The individual may not have become consciously aware of the need for it, though he is unconsciously subject to the impulse toward it. Or he may consciously desire to act but be prevented from doing so by restrictions imposed by his environment or inhibitions inherent to his own disposition. Cases in point are the hunter who is beset by hunger but who can find no game, or the individual who experiences sexual need but is unable to fulfill it because he has not found a suitable mate or because economic insecurity, social conventions, or other restrictions prevent him from consummating a sexual relationship. When, for any reason, an impulse fails to find expression in action, a certain amount of unused psychic energy accumulates in the organism and sets up what we may call *tensions*.

Tensions originating in this manner affect life in a variety of ways. In diffused form, they color our moods and influence our general well-being, exhilarating us if the tension is a positive one resulting from a delayed but anticipated fulfillment, depressing us if it is a negative result of difficulty or repression. And what particularly concerns us, these tensions stimulate our imagination to form images embodying their emotional essence. The mental activity through which psychic tensions are thus translated into equivalent forms of mental imagery, we shall call the *tension-imagery process*. This process, we suggest, is the dynamic agency behind both individual fantasies and forms of cultural expression. In terms of it we can establish all the correlations that we are seeking between things psychic and material, individual and collective. The basis for these correlations will appear as we proceed.

With a little effort all of us can detect the tension-imagery process at work in ourselves if we watch any tendencies we may have toward daydreaming. In reverie which is sometimes fully conscious, sometimes a barely perceptible substratum to other mental activities, we may find ourselves being honored for some dreamed accomplishment, meeting a wished-for lover or, if the tension is a negative one, undergoing some trial or embarrassment. If we bring our analytical faculties to bear upon these reveries, we recognize them as fantasies inspired by psychic tensions; in the first case by the desire for approval, in the second by sexual need, and in the third or negative instance, by fear or some other negative tension.

For practical purposes in normal daily living, we learn to distinguish clearly between such fantasies and objective reality, and to devote our main energies to productive action along the lines indicated by objective circumstances. To a certain extent we may indulge in daydreams of desired or anticipated pleasure, but we normally subject our fantasies to as much rational discipline as we are able to maintain. To the fantasy pleasures that are incompatible with our environment we say, "Get thee behind me Satan." The fantasy difficulties, unless they reflect problems demanding immediate attention, we banish as largely as possible from our consciousness. "Sufficient unto the day is the evil thereof."

The ability which we thus exercise to distinguish fact from fantasy and to separate the one from the other in our thoughts and conduct, is one of humanity's most hardly won and most easily lost accomplishments. It lapses whenever reason ceases to exercise a strict control over our mental operations. In varying degrees, fantasies then become illusions. Overevaluation in love is one of the commonest and most normal of such illusions. To the lover, and especially to the young and inexperienced lover, the beloved is an ideal being possessed of all perfections, free of all defects, nay even independent of the common material traits of humanity. Subsequent experience may teach him that this enraptured vision was in part an illusion, that he idealized reality by projecting upon it the fantasy inspired by his own emotional tensions.

The habitual daydreamer cultivates illusion in relative detachment from reality. Having failed to achieve sufficient satisfaction in the external world, he allows his fantasies to become a substitute world, hence a substitute outlet for his psychic tensions. In order to enjoy his substitute satisfactions as fully as possible, he must credit them with as much reality as possible. Hence he wilfully withholds his power of discrimination from them. Thus freed from rational discipline, the fantasies intensify their spell and increasingly acquire the vividness of illusions. If such a mental disposition goes beyond a certain point, as it may under the stress of powerful emotion or mental disorder, ability to distinguish fact from fantasy is completely lost and the individual then experiences hallucinations. Tension imagery, always a psychological reality, is then undifferentiated from other possible forms of reality and is simply experienced as *the* reality.

During sleep all of us lapse into a similarly undiscriminating state of mind. Our psychic tensions continue to exist and to engender mental fantasies through the tension-imagery process. But since our power of rational discrimination is dormant, all that remains possible to us is undifferentiated experience. Whatever we experience is psychologically real, since we experience it, and the question as to whether it is subjectively or objectively real is one which, for the time being, we are incapable of determining. Hence the fantasies are free to assume a hallucinatory reality. Tension imagery thus experienced during sleep as a hallucination, we call a dream.

In the dream we reach a tension-imagery product of great significance for cultural studies. Parallelisms between the dream on the one hand, and cultural products like myth and folklore on the other, have long been sensed and have been discussed by many of the writers concerned with the cultural implications of psychoanalysis. In our view such discussions have usually suffered from insufficient attention to historical factors, but the parallelism that concerned them appears to be important and worthy of continued study.

Equally significant for our purpose and less commonly emphasized, is the insight into mental processes obtainable through the analysis of dreams. The psychic activities involved in most forms of cultural expression are difficult of access for study by modern man. The historical remoteness of the experiences that gave rise to primitive and ancient myths, forces us to approach the process of myth formation somewhat in the manner of a linguist seeking to resurrect a dead language. In other cases where psychic activations lie close to us in time — those, for instance, that have motivated the twentieth-century tendency toward abstraction in art — they are submerged in depths of the unconscious even for the artist and are not a focus of recognizable experience for most individuals.

In the dream, on the other hand, we have mental activities that appear to be parallel to those involved in cultural expression but that are observable at much closer range. Here the mental dynamics operate as a living language which is vividly apprehensible to all of us as a result of repeated personal experiences. Furthermore, these dynamics have been the subject of research culminating in one of the great works of psychoanalytical literature, Freud's *The Interpretation of Dreams*. Thus in studying the dream and its cultural implications, we are in the fortunate position of being able to approach a living language of the psyche in the light of recent advances in scientific knowledge.

What are the dynamics of dream formation and how do they operate? The simplest way to answer this question is to take an actual dream for observation and analysis. Fortified by Freud's statement that "conditions are more likely to be favorable in self-observation than the observation of others."[7] I shall do as he frequently did and use a dream of my own for purposes of illustration.

With the indifference of fact and reason which characterizes much tension imagery and most other manifestations of the unconscious, I found myself high up on a mountain, the side of which fell steeply and smoothly below me like the sloping wall of a vast pyramid. Far below, at the foot of the slope, stood a white house, and beyond that a broad plain. Moved by some wayward impulse, I freed a stone from its setting and let it slide down the mountain. It sped downward with the smooth straight movement of a well-aimed ball in a bowling alley. To my surprise and disquietude it shot directly toward the front door of the house, into which it disappeared. In its descent it started other stones — two, half a dozen, a score. Then the whole side of the mountain was in movement — a vast Niagara of rock pouring downward in a steady stream and stretching, on my right and left, from one horizon to the other. A moment of panic overcame me. Surely this avalanche would sweep me away! But no, I kept my footing in the midst of it. In some miraculous way the rocky currents left me unharmed. And so I remained to watch and wonder, awed and in the end inspired by this display of cosmic forces moving around me.

Such was the dream. Now let us consider the psychological activities involved in this dream experience. One obvious though not insignificant consideration lies in the fact that, as the dreamer, I was unable to distinguish fantasy from objective fact. There was of course no actual mountain involved in the experience; no house nor plain, no avalanche. The whole thing was merely a flash of mental activity in my sleeping brain. This did not prevent me from accepting it as a world of objective reality, nor from experiencing it with as much completeness, vividness, and apparent sensory directness as if it *had* been such a world. The familiar fact that subjective dream imagery can attain full reality impact in this manner is one which we shall need to recall later in connection with culture. It prepares us to assume that equally subjective experiences like those involved in the formation of myths might, under the right circumstances, attain an equally hallucinatory reality.

Returning now to our development of thought concerning the tension-imagery process, let us consider the relation of the dream described above to motivating psychic tensions. When I reflected upon the dream after awakening, some of its elements defied my efforts at analysis and therefore presumably symbolized mental contents that were completely unconscious. Other elements were evidently inspired by impulses nearer the threshold of consciousness, for the interpretation of them appeared clear to me as soon as I awoke. This was particularly true of the rockslide and my relationship to it.

The dream occurred a month or two after I had undertaken a new work involving many problems of organization. At times this work taxed my resources and I experienced considerable anxiety lest it get completely out of my control. At the same time I clung to the conviction that these difficulties would eventually be surmounted and the situation reduced to order. My prevailing psychic state was thus a combination of, and conflict between, two opposite tensions: anxiety and confidence. Imagery generated by these tensions would in some way have to embody a negative and threatening force counter-balanced by a positive power of resistance. Is not this exactly what the dream did?

I started a rockslide that seemed capable of sweeping me away with it — a projection of the threatened danger that my work would get beyond my control. At the same time I retained my footing in the midst of the rocky currents — an expression of my faith in eventually overcoming the difficulties. Thus the mental motion picture of myself engulfed by the rockslide evidenced a perfect embodiment of the two opposing tensions of my prevailing psychic state.

Judged literally, the dream would have appeared to be a mere figment of the imagination and might have been described, in terms that have sometimes been applied to mythical and fantastic art, as "purely fanciful." Interpreted symbolically, it proved to be an extraordinarily apt image of a real psychic state resulting from real circumstances of objective experience. If my memory of the dream is accurate, even its visual composition embodied the equilibrium of the two opposing tensions, for the house was exactly below my position on top of the mountain and the line followed by the first stone in sliding from me to the house formed a central axis dividing the dream world into two equal sides. It is difficult to conceive how any form could express a meaning more completely or more vividly than this dream imagery expressed the mental and emotional experience through which I was then passing.

It will be noted that the interpretation just given involves three main levels of significance. First, there is the obvious imagery of the dream itself; in the present instance, the mountain, the rockslide, and my experience with them. Freud has provided a convenient name for this surface aspect of the dream in calling it the "manifest content" or simply the "manifest dream."

This manifest dream is a result, in the second place, of certain underlying psychic tensions: in this case, anxiety and confidence. Such tensions, if we wish to relate them to their complex Freudian equivalents, may arise either from "day residues," "latent dream thoughts," or unconscious repressed impulses.

The day residues and latent dream thoughts are effects of waking experience continued in sleep: the former recognizable to consciousness, the latter disguised from it by psychic ambiguities which Freud calls the "dream censorship." Both the residues and the latent thoughts may include, not only images derived by the mind from the external world, but also the psychic results of pressures exerted, or opportunities offered, by that world. Anxiety and envy, desire and relief, are but a few of the tensional conditions that may thus be projected into sleep from objective sources. In Freud's own words, the latent thoughts "can represent anything with which the waking life has been concerned — a reflection, a warning, an intention, a preparation for the immediate future or, once again, the satisfaction of an unfulfilled wish." [8]

Thus both the day residues and the latent dream thoughts are mental results of objective experiences during waking life. The other possible component of a tensional condition, as seen by Freud, enters the dream situation from the opposite or subjective direction. It consists of energies arising from the dreamer's unconscious psychic being; in particular, impulses toward fulfillment of repressed wishes. For our purpose it rarely seems necessary to refer separately to the day residues, the latent dream thoughts, or the unconscious repressed impulses. We may regard them as technical subdivisions of the second general level of our analytical framework: the tensions that generate the manifest imagery of dreams.

In the third place, there are the circumstances of waking life that caused the tensions. These circumstances, since they have played a part in the dreamer's objective life history, may well be said to provide a "historical" foundation for the dream experience. In the rockslide instance, the attendant historical circumstances consisted in the difficulties I was experiencing in my new position and the resistance I was making to those difficulties.

If the tensions have arisen residually from known day experiences or have been analytically traced through the latent dream thoughts to such experiences, their "historical" [9] basis is obvious. Tensions arising from unconscious repressions, on the other hand, might appear to be exclusively psychological in their origins and to have no connection with objective events. Upon closer scrutiny, even in strictly Freudian terms, the impulses from the unconscious also relate to historical sources, but in this case the events involved have been forgotten. Usually they are identified by Freud with infantile or childhood experiences — threats by parents, observation of parental intercourse, and so forth [10] — although they may also have taken place in the dreamer's later life and have been repressed from memory because of shock, unhappiness, or conflict which they occasioned.

The fact that experiences of these types have been forgotten or repressed from consciousness does not, of course, modify their historicity. We may therefore conclude that in the last analysis day residues and latent dream thoughts, on the one hand, and unconscious repressions on the other, differ from each other, not as the historical from the nonhistorical, but as the more direct effects of recent historical circumstances and the more indirect effects of remote ones. In the former case we can refer to an immediate historical basis for the dream, and in the latter to an ultimate and more diffused historical basis.

Freud does not crystallize the concept of historical circumstances into a clear-cut division of his analytical framework. Indeed, the emphasis he places on the manifest dream and the latent content, and the merely incidental way in which he treats the historical aspect of the dream situation, might lead us to regard his system as a two-level, rather than a three-level, one. In emphasis it *is* a two-level one, which is natural in the whole context of early psychoanalytical investigations. Nevertheless the third level, that of historical circumstances, is implicit in Freud's system and sometimes finds emergent expression there. Therapeutically, the chief aim of his analytical technique is to rediscover, and reintegrate with his patient's consciousness, certain objective events which originally gave rise to tensional disturbances. Occasionally he employs the terms "history" and "historical" in connection with such events. Thus in one passage he states that a patient being analyzed "is now about to bring forth phantasies in which he has shrouded the *history* of his childhood." [11] Elsewhere he remarks, after summarizing a patient's account of a certain childhood experience, "this piece of *historical* information was given, by the way, without any difficulty." [12]

To summarize our present position, we have three main factors to consider in interpreting dreams: the manifest imagery, the motivating psychological tensions, and the initiating historical circumstances. The reader who desires to study the operation of these factors in a larger number of dreams, can doubtless do so in part by analyzing the more obvious aspects of certain dreams of his own. He can also apply our three-level concept of the dream interpretations reported in psychoanalytical literature. One example from the second source may well be added here as an extension and confirmation of our discussion. As such an example, let us consider a dream reported and interpreted by Freud.

"A young woman who had already been married for a number of years dreamt as follows: *She was at the theatre with her husband, and on one side the stalls were quite empty. Her husband told her that Elsie L. and her fiancé also wanted to come, but could only get bad seats, three for a florin and a half, and of course they could not take those. She replied that in her opinion they did not lose much by that.*" [13]

Selected passages from Freud's discussion of this dream will serve to indicate the nature of his interpretation. "The first thing stated by the dreamer is that the occasion giving rise to the dream is alluded to in the manifest content: her husband had really told her that Elsie L., an acquaintance of about her own age, had become engaged, and the dream is a reaction to this piece of news . . . To what did she trace the detail of one side of the stalls being empty? It was an allusion to a real occurrence of the week before, when she had meant to go to a certain play and had therefore booked seats *early*, so early that she had to pay extra for the tickets. On entering the theatre it was evident that her anxiety had been quite superfluous, for one side of the stalls was almost empty. It would have been time enough if she had bought the tickets on the actual day of the performance and her husband did not fail to tease her about having been in *too great a hurry*. Next, what about the one florin and a half (1 fl. 50)? This was traced to quite another context, but again it refers to some news received on the previous day. Her sister-in-law had had a present of 150 florins from her husband and had rushed off *in a hurry*, like a goose . . . and spent it all on a piece of jewelry. What about the number three? She knew nothing about that unless this idea could be counted an association, that the engaged girl, Elsie L., was only three months younger than she herself who had been married ten years." [14]

On the basis of these associations, Freud arrives at this reconstruction of the latent content of the dream:

"If the strongly emphasized points: *too early, too great a hurry*, are connected with the occasion for the dream (namely, the news that her friend, only three months *younger* than herself, had now found a good husband after all) and with the criticism expressed in her asperity about her sister-in-law, that it was *folly* to be so precipitate, there occurs to us almost spontaneously the following reconstruction of the latent dream thoughts, for which the manifest dream is a highly distorted substitute.

"It was foolish of me to be in such a hurry to marry! Elsie's example shows me that I too could have found a husband later on . . . This would be the main thought; perhaps we may go on, though with less certainty for the analysis in these passages ought not to be unsupported by statements of the dreamer: 'And I might have had one a hundred times better for the money!' (150 florins is 100 times more than one florin and a half) . . . It would be still more desirable if we could see some connection between the element 'three tickets' and a husband; but our knowledge does not as yet extend to this. We have only found out that the dream expresses *depreciation* of her own husband and regret at having married so early." [15]

Thus far, Freud has provided an interpretation of the dream in terms of its latent dream thoughts, but not in terms of the repressed wishes to which, in general, he attributes so much importance. After defending himself rather vehemently against the question raised by others regarding this aspect of his theory, and after discussing symbolism and other subjects involved in his general survey of psychoanalysis, he returns to the dream in question and adds the following interpretation of the wish-fulfilling impulse which he finds in it.

"The dreamer had not always felt so dissatisfied with her premature marriage as she was on the day when she heard of her friend's engagement. She had been proud of her marriage at the time and had considered herself more highly favored than her friend. One hears that naive girls, on becoming engaged, frequently express their delight at the idea that they will now soon be able to go to all plays and see everything hitherto forbidden to them.

"The indication of curiosity and desire to 'look on' evinced here comes, without doubt, originally from the sexual 'gazing impulse,' especially regarding the parents, and this becomes a strong motive impelling the girl to marry early; in this manner going to the theatre became an obvious allusive substitute for getting married. In her vexation at the present time on account of her premature marriage she therefore reverted to the time when this same marriage fulfilled a wish, by gratifying her *skotophilia* [16]; and so, guided by this old wish impulse, she replaced the idea of marriage by that of going to the theatre." [17]

Reducing the essential of this dream and its interpretation to our extended psycho-historical frame of reference with its three main levels of signifance, we have the following summary results:

Manifest dream.	Being in a half-empty theatre with husband and learning that friend and her fiancé wanted to come but could only get bad seats, three for a florin and a half.

Psychic tensions inspiring the dream.	*Regret* at having married. *Dissatisfaction* with husband. *Satisfaction* of "gazing impulse," re-pressed in childhood but fulfilled through marriage.
Objective circumstances of case history	News of friend's engagement. Dreamer's own early marriage. Dreamer's childhood relations with parents as involving "gazing impulse."

Thus, the dream and its interpretation illustrate a sequence which proceeds from objective events (childhood experiences, marriage, etc.) to psychic tensions (regret, dissatisfaction, satisfaction) and finally emerges, in disguised symbolical form, in the manifest imagery of the dreamer and her husband in the half-empty theatre.

III

In concluding the discussion of our three-level approach to the tension imagery of dreams, we should note one further important fact concerning this concept. In *principle* it implies organic interrelationships between the two fields of knowledge that we especially desire to integrate, those of psychology and of history with all its social correlatives.

As indicated in our earlier chapters, the most difficult passage to maneuver in establishing connections between these fields is that of unifying certain pairs of opposites: the subjective as opposed to the objective; the psychic or spiritual as opposed to the material. The separation between these opposites — the intellectual "great divide" of our earlier discussion — has constituted one of the major barriers to the progress of correlational thought. It has divided philosophy into idealistic and materialistic systems, has separated arts and sciences into such seemingly intangible fields as those of religion and art and such seemingly tangible ones as those of economics and physical science. Among its other divisions, it has left psychology on the subjective immaterial side of the divide and history on the objective material one.

At least in relation to the individualistic experience of dreams — which is all we are prepared to consider for the moment — our proposed approach makes it possible to bridge this barrier and to unify the opposites that flank it. This is so because the dream, itself an immaterial mental phenomenon, is traced back through psychic tensions to historical circumstances that can include the full range of objective and material factors.

In one of his discussions of dreams, Freud quotes from Du Prel the following illustration: "Mungo Park, when nearly dying of thirst on a journey in Africa, dreamt continually of the well-watered hills and valleys of his home, So Trench, tormented with hunger in the redoubt at Magdebourg, saw himself in his dream surrounded by sumptuous meals; and George Back, who took part in Franklin's first expedition, when on the point of dying of hunger owing to their terrible privation, dreamt regularly of abundant food to eat."[18] These cases reduce to its simplest expression the sequence from material circumstances (here the absence of food and drink) to frustrated life impulses and then to their psychic expression in dreams. Such examples recapitulate a condensation of materialistic and psychic interrelationships that is normally more characteristic of primitive than of civilized life.

In complex societies, so many cultural circumstances interpose themselves between psychic experience and its material correlatives that the connection of the one with the other may easily be lost from view. The immediate pangs of hunger or thirst (to continue with the context already established) are likely to be replaced by indirect frustrations resulting, let us say, from an inadequate income. Such an inadequacy, if it does not impose stark hunger and thirst, may prevent the individual from securing properly nutritious foods, or perhaps merely prevent him from securing the rarer, more expensive, and more luxurious foods. It may thus subject him to repressed desires for sustaining staples or for unattainable delicacies.

The assumed economic incompetence may diffuse its influence over other areas of the individual's life than the one directly concerned with food and drink. His depressed circumstances may prevent him from winning the mate he desires, or may subject his marital life to so many privations and irritations that its emotional fulfillment is impossible, thus directly or indirectly frustrating his sexual needs. Many other permutations of the given elements would be possible, but in all of them the inadequate means of livelihood could be the cause of frustrations which in turn might motivate dreams.

If the dreamer were a farmer, our suggested circumstance of an inadequate income might conceivably be due to the barrenness of the soil he was attempting to cultivate. Or if he lived in a remote part of the world and his land, though barren, contained unexploited deposits of oil, his penury might be due to his lack of a technology suitable for the extraction of resources that were potentially available to him. Or if, at certain times in history, the dreamer were a serf working on the estate of a feudal lord or an underpaid miner or factory worker, his poverty might be due to social conventions that allotted a considerable part of his production to someone other than himself.

In these and countless other ways there could thus be an interdependence, an unbroken reality continuum, from material conditions (such as soil and natural resources) through cultural and social conditions (such as states of technological advancement or economic organization) to a psychic experience of life involving various degrees of fulfillment or frustration, and finally to the symbolical expression of that experience in the imagery of the dream. Within the limited personal sphere of dream psychology, this continuum spans our great divide and provides a means of correlating psychological and historical factors with each other and with one of the products of the human imagination — the dream.

TENSION IMAGERY AND CULTURE IN
PSYCHO–HISTORICAL INTEGRATION

The three-level approach to the analysis of tension imagery, which was developed in the preceding chapter in connection with dreams, constitutes the first of two basic concepts involved in the formation of the psycho-historical frame of reference. The second of these concepts — in some respects more daring and more decisive for our purpose — involves the extension of the three-level approach from the individual sphere of dream psychology to the collective one of culture.

The relations that emerge from such an extension are summarized in Diagram 1.

At the left of the diagram, our three analytical levels are indicated in general terms. In the central column, they are related to the individual imagery of dreams and daydreams; in the column at the right, to the collective imagery of culture.

ANALYTICAL LEVELS	PERSONAL IMAGERY	CULTURAL IMAGERY
MANIFEST IMAGERY	Dreams and daydreams	Myths, art forms, and other cultural manifestations
PSYCHOLOGICAL TENSIONS	Individual tensions	Collective tensions
HISTORICAL CIRCUMSTANCES	Individual circumstances	Collective circumstances

Diagram 1. Psycho-historical conception of parallelism and difference between dream imagery and cultural imagery.

Individual and collective existence are, of course, to be considered intermingling rather than separate entities, as is implied by the broken line between the second and third columns of the table. At each level of our analytical framework, the two areas of experience interplay with each other. Collective circumstances largely determine individual ones, but in lesser degree the individual also reacts upon the age and the society to which he belongs. Individual and collective tensions agitate and modify each other, and so do individual and collective forms of tension imagery. Nevertheless, individual and social life are distinguishable from each other. Their distinguishable differences form the basis of the division made between them in our theoretical framework.

In the cultural aspect of our theory, as indicated at the top of the right-hand column of the table, all the products of the creative imagination become for us types of "manifest" imagery and are conceived as parallels to the manifest imagery of dreams. Like the latter, these manifest cultural images may involve reflections of the objective world in more or less "day-residue" fashion. With or without such objective reference, they will also involve a "latent" significance of which their producers are usually unaware and an understanding which we can arrive at only by efforts of analysis and interpretation.

Descending the right-hand column of our diagram, we assume that the manifest cultural image, like the manifest dream image, emerges from and reflects an underlying state of psychic tension. The difference between the tensions involved in dream formation and in culture formation will be that the former are dominantly personal, the latter dominantly collective. In other words, the cultural tensions will be shared by various individuals comprising some social group. Examples might be a shared exaltation resulting from some social achievement, a shared fear resulting from some social shock or failure, or a shared anxiety resulting from some source of social insecurity. The exact interplay of personal and social factors in the development and expression of collective tensions involves intricacies which we shall pass over for the moment, but to which we shall return later.

The collective tensions in turn will owe their nature to the impact upon the psyche of events taking place, or conditions developing, in the external world. To understand the causes of the tensions, we must accordingly descend to the third level of our framework and study the historical and social circumstances of the group experiencing the tensions. Here we may expect to discover the nature of the achievement that generated the exaltation, of the shock that generated the fear, or of the insecurity that generated the anxiety.

On this level as on the others, the cultural context will imply a shift of emphasis from personal to collective concerns. Instead of the individual case history, we shall now be concerned with history in its most inclusive sense: all the events, institutions, states of prosperity or depression, and other circumstances that affected the destiny of the particular cultural group at the time that it produced the particular forms of cultural imagery which interest us. If we reduce our concept to a single sentence, the cultural image becomes for us a symbolic expression of collective tensions generated by the objective realities of history.

Before we consider any of the subtler questions connected with this frame of reference, perhaps it will clarify our position for the reader if we give a preliminary illustration of how the theory works when applied to specific forms of cultural imagery. (Comprehensive demonstration will be postponed to Part II. A full psycho-historical analysis of a cultural situation is a task hardly less involved than a full psychoanalysis of an individual.) For this purpose we shall use examples that can be summarized briefly either because they are relatively obvious, or because the necessary documentation has been provided for us by earlier observers.

First, let us take the detail (Fig. 8) of a totem pole (Fig. 9) carved about 1860 by the Indians of the lower Nass River valley in British Columbia. The detail (and for that matter the entire pole) presents us with a manifest cultural image. What is its latent significance? What play of forces originally inspired its conception in the minds of its carver and his associates? Had we no historical documentaton, we might seek far and perhaps never find the correct answers to these questions. Fortunately, the information necessary for an accurate interpretation is available and has already been advanced in one of our earlier chapters. The present detail is a carving of the "Gnawing Squirrel" totem reported and analyzed by Marius Barbeau.[1] As the reader will recall, Dr. Barbeau traces the origin of the totem to hallucinations caused by fright, the fear in turn having been occasioned by a volcanic eruption.

It is evident that Dr. Barbeau's explanation of the totem involves factors corresponding to each of the three levels in our psycho-historical frame of reference. At the historical level we have the volcanic eruption; at the tensional level we have the collective experience of terror; at the manifest level we have the original hallucinations, and at a later time, the projection of the mental imagery into a carved totem.

It should not, of course, be assumed that in indicating these connections we have given a complete analysis of the totem carving. Cultural analysis, like dream analysis, can be followed throughout many layers, the same images often symbolizing different contexts at different degrees of depth. The fact that the Indians were terrorized by the eruption was only in part a result of the actual volcano; it was also an index of their own stage of cultural development. A twentieth-century geologist might be delighted rather than shocked by the opportunity to observe an eruption — provided, of course, that he was sufficiently distant to be safe from physical harm. The mentality of the Indians and other such factors would have to be investigated further if we were seeking to make a complete analysis of our example. The conditions that gave rise to totemism in general, as well as the genesis of this particular totem, would have to be considered. Nevertheless, for our present purpose, we see that the illustration provides an instance of the history–tension imagery continuum in cultural life.

As a second example, let us take the evil spirits believed in by the people of the Betsileo tribe of the Island of Madagascar, off the southeast coast of Africa. Our indebtedness to the social sciences is evidenced by the fact that we owe our knowledge of the present example, like that of the previous one, to the research of an anthropologist. In the present case our information is derived from field studies made in Madagascar by Ralph Linton. The information comes to us already illuminated in certain correlational directions, for the material collected by Dr. Linton has been analyzed and discussed by a psychoanalyst, Abram Kardiner.[2]

The manifest image in this case is not described for us beyond the general status of "evil spirits." These spirits are mythological fantasies of the Betsileo people which do not seem to have been embodied in forms of visual art. We shall have further indication that such spirits are not often represented visually at that stage of their development in which they constitute a traumatic experience for those who believe in them. As in the case of the Gnawing-Squirrel totem, the monster is likely to become a subject for representation only after it has been "conquered"; which is to say, only when the collective psyche is recovering from its trauma and reëstablishing its equilibrium.

In the Betsileon evil spirits, we have a mythical concept at traumatic intensity. One of its aspects is described by our anthropological-psychoanalytical informants as "an acute hallucinatory psychosis of persecutory content. The victim hallucinates his persecutor, who makes him perform the most extraordinary feats of self-injury, against which the victim is helpless."[3]

Interestingly enough, the evil spirits which thus possessed the Betsileons were a relatively new development at the time of Linton's visit in 1927. An earlier stage of the same culture, which still survived in the neighboring Tanala tribe, involved no such malignant beings. What caused their emergence in Betsileon culture? Here is the answer as summarized by Kardiner.

"This psychological balance [of the earlier Tanala culture] could, however, be maintained only while the economic basis for subsistence was based on communal land ownership. No sooner did the subsistence economy and the social organization for it change than the whole psychological structure collapsed. The dry method of rice production became obsolete through depletion of the land suitable for this purpose. For the wet method there were only a few available valleys, and those who 'possessed' them — for this was a new concept in Tanala — held on to them, and there followed a mad scramble for valleys. This broke up the old family lineage organization; the villages had to be defended against marauders by powerful forces; slaves who were of no economic importance in the old set-up now became an economic asset . . . the tribal democracy disappeared, and a king with absolute power and a feudal hierarchy whose tenure of land was in perpetuity were instituted . . . Among the psychological changes were a rigid system of class lines difficult to move into and general all-around hostility, as shown by great increase in hysterical illnesses and in magic practices and choice of sorcery as a vocation. The individual was confronted by a long series of new anxieties which he could in no way handle . . . The anxieties confronted both those who had property and those who did not. Those who had property had to defend their title by a group of awe-inspiring ostentations . . . The property owners also had control of the weapons of coercion. Two new anxieties hitherto unknown made their appearance, fear of poverty and fear of oppression; and the general increase in crime and homosexuality were witness to this anxiety. Even religious concepts were changed and concepts denoting 'evil spirits' were invented." [4]

Thus, in the terms of our three-level approach, historical circumstances involving an economic change in methods of rice culture and consequent changes in social relations resulted on the second level in the rise of negative psychic tensions which projected themselves on the third level into mythological concepts of torturing evil spirits. This example, more complex than the previous one, is a truer indication of the kinds of factors usually involved in a fully analyzed psycho-historical situation. The specific historical event, such as the volcanic eruption, is both less frequent and less far-reaching as a psycho-historical directive than is an enduring socio-economic situation. Such a situation involves all the subtle degrees of well- or mal-being of a people as they permeate all the intricacies of its social existence.

Not to limit these preliminary examples to so-called primitive cultures, we may take our third and last one from so-called civilized life, choosing for the purpose one of the most renowned paintings of twentieth-century Western culture: Picasso's *Guernica* (Fig. 10). Like the Gnawing-Squirrel myth, this work of art was motivated in part by a specific historical event. On April 28, 1937, during the Spanish Civil War, the Basque town of Guernica was bombed out of existence by German planes flying for Franco's fascist army. Much of the world was shocked by this event, regarding it as a barbaric atrocity.

Picasso had previously been commissioned to paint a mural for the Spanish Building at a then forthcoming Paris World's Fair. As a humanist and Spaniard, he was among the most shocked by the bombing of Guernica and immediately chose it as the subject for his mural. The psycho-historical skeleton of the work is obvious: the historical event of the bombing produced psychic repercussions of abhorrence on the part of the artist and many of his contemporaries, and the artist expressed this abhorrence in images of fallen men, shrieking women, and other symbolic forms painted in the mournful colors of grey, white, and black.

In this instance, as in that of the Gnawing Squirrels, the immediate event was only a small part of the total psycho-historical situation. It functioned like the immediate cause of a war, which is often a relatively trivial incident. The war is to be understood, of course, not as a result of the incident, but as an outbreak of latent conflicts that were ready to flare up at any pretext. So the bombing of Guernica was only the immediate stimulus to Picasso's creation; the ultimate one involved the totality of his experience of life in the twentieth century. As he sensed and as we know, the bell was tolling for millions of others besides the inhabitants of Guernica. In the words of one commentator, "And if this *Ecce mundus* at the beginning was Guernica, soon afterwards it was Warsaw, Rotterdam, Nancy, Coventry . . . down to the day when all Europe was only one immense material and moral ruin . . . On that terrible day, the *Guernica* turned out ot be, of all known paintings, the most European." [5]

Although an adequate discussion of the psycho-historical correlatives of artistic style must be left for later consideration, it is evident that the distortion of human and animal forms in the painting, like the austerity of its color, is an integral part of the visual dirge with which the artist accompanies a tragic theme. This becomes increasingly evident as we study the details of the painting (Fig. 11) and is one of the marks of its greatness. What compounded associations of bleakness, of remoteness from humanity, even of torture, stir the imagination as we contemplate the almost geometrical forms of our detail. The desert, the iceberg, the pit, the spit, the vice, all have their echoes here. This detail is Picasso's representation of the mouth of the woman below the head of the bull at the left.

To emphasize the conceptual frame of reference which is still our main present concern, let us assemble our three preliminary illustrations in relation to that framework.

MANIFEST CULTURAL IMAGERY	Gnawing Squirrels in mythology of Nass River Indians, British Columbia	Evil Spirits of Betsileo tribe, Madagascar	Painting, Guernica, by Picasso
COLLECTIVE PSYCHIC TENSIONS	Terror	Insecurity, anxiety, antagonism	Horror, insecurity
MOTIVATING HISTORICAL CIRCUMSTANCES	Volcanic eruption, c. 1780, and more remote cultural circumstances	Social breakdown and conflicts caused by change in methods of rice culture	Bombing of Guernica, 1937, and related conflicts of 20th-century Europe

Diagram 2. Comparative psycho-historical digest of three preliminary examples.

When we apply it to the preceding examples from different parts of the world and from different stages of social development, our proposed principle of psycho-historical analysis appears to indicate significant relationships between history, psychic experience, and culture. It is our belief that in a similar manner this principle can contribute to the understanding of all the forms of imaginative expression which are part of man's cultural life.

II

The examples used in the preceding section have, we hope, given our scheme a preliminary justification in practice, but there is still one important question that may be raised concerning it in theory. What theoretical basis have we for assuming that the psychological processes with which we became acquainted chiefly through the study of dreams, and which inevitably take place in the individual mind, can be regarded as operating in the sphere of culture and in conjunction with psychic states that are collectively shared?

To one whose thinking has been shaped in the mold of a single discipline, particularly if that discipline is an individually based psychology, this question can be important and perplexing. But if one turns for guidance to the writings of those most concerned with collective mentality — the writings of the social scientists — the question itself soon appears questionable. Backed by data from anthropology, ethnology, sociology, and social psychology, the social scientists are emphasizing increasingly the interdependence of individual and collective mentality. In the light of this trend, the older tendency to regard individual and group psychology as separable from each other now seems untenable — a result of compartmental traditions of thought rather than of cleavages in psychic existence.

We had occasion in our second chapter [6] to quote a sociologist to the effect that the process of "socialization" is equally necessary to the development of the individual personality and of culture. Other scholars can easily be marshalled to emphasize different aspects of the personal-collective continuum.

In introducing a survey of social psychology, Otto Klineberg states that the disciplinary lines and supposed distinctions between psychological and social studies "are difficult to maintain." He continues "There is a growing recognition among psychologists of the importance of the group in determining the characteristics of the individual. In particular the discoveries of the ethnologists have revealed the extent to which personality is shaped by the cultural and social environment in which it develops. It would be difficult to point to any substantial amount of psychological description of the individual which does not reveal social influences to some degree. It may not be entirely true that 'all psychology is social psychology,' but we shall have occasion to see that this statement contains little exaggeration." [7]

Readers of Klineberg's later chapters cannot but be amazed at the extent to which seemingly self-contained experiences like tasting and smelling, perceiving and remembering, are affected by social factors of which the individual is normally unaware. Even what we think we have seen may be an illusion inspired by social expectations, as in the case of the southern American children who remembered having "seen" a Negro servant in a picture of a fine home which showed none.[8]

Relevant to our present context is a conception developed by Kardiner and his associates on the basis of detailed studies of a number of cultures in various parts of the world: the conception of different "basic personality types" for different societies. Linton, in his Foreword to *The Psychological Frontiers of Society*, one of the books on which he collaborated with Kardiner, sums up this concept as follows:

1. "That the members of any given society will have many elements of early experience in common.

2. "That as a result of this they will have many elements of personality in common.

3. "That since the early experience of individuals differs from one society to another, the personality norms for various societies will also differ.

"The *basic personality type* for any society is that personality configuration which is shared by the bulk of the society's members as a result of the early experiences which they have in common." [9]

It is evident that if psychic development was individualistically delimited, personalities would differ only as between individuals and not as between societies. That they do apparently differ as between societies is another indication of the continuity of psychic experience within the individual-social totality of life.

One more bit of testimony deserves inclusion here — again the words of Ralph Linton, but this time summing up his conclusions regarding the essential unity of psychological with social studies.

"Students of human behavior, whether at the individual or social level, have developed adequate descriptive techniques and a considerable understanding of the phenomena with which they have to deal. They have also developed an increasing awareness of the complexity of this material and of the close functional interdependence of the individual, society and culture. Following the earlier atomistic trends of scientific research, each of these has been treated as a separate field of investigation and made the subject of a distinct discipline. The individual has been assigned to Psychology, society to Sociology, and culture to Cultural Anthropology, although the last two sciences have shown a constant tendency to overlap in their investigations. It is now becoming apparent that the integration between the individual, society and culture is so close and their interaction so continuous that the investigator who tries to work with any one of them without reference to the other two soon comes to a dead end. . . it seems safe to say that the next few years will witness the emergence of a science of human behavior which will synthesize the findings of Psychology, Sociology and Anthropology." [10]

Although such emphasis on the interplay of personal and social factors in psychic life is relatively new, older psychologists — if and when they stopped to consider the matter — could not entirely overlook these connections. Thus Freud writes, in his *Group Psychology and the Analysis of the Ego:*

"The contrast between Individual Psychology and Social or Group Psychology, which at a first glance may seem to be full of significance, loses a great deal of its sharpness when it is examined more closely. It is true that Individual Psychology is concerned with the individual man and explores the paths by which he seeks to find satisfaction for his instincts; but only rarely and under certain exceptional conditions is Individual Psychology in a position to disregard the relations of this individual to others. In the individual's mental life someone else is invariably involved as a model, as an object, as a helper, as an opponent, and so from the very first Individual Psychology is at the same time Social Psychology as well. . .

"The relations of an individual to his parents and to his brothers and sisters, to the object of his love, and to his physician — in fact all the relations which have hitherto been the chief subject of psychoanalytic research — may claim to be considered as social phenomena." [11]

Freud subsequently comes to a conclusion much like the saying quoted by Klineberg that "all psychology is social psychology." "We must conclude," Freud writes at one point in his discussion, "that the psychology of the group is the oldest human psychology; what we have isolated as individual psychology, by neglecting all traces of the group, has only since come into prominence out of the old group psychology, by a gradual process which may still, perhaps, be described as incomplete." [12]

Statements like those just quoted encourage us to regard individual and collective life as a continuum which includes psychic factors, but they provide no exact analysis of the mental dynamics that may be assumed to operate within this continuum. If we search the writings of the social psychologists in an effort to determine whether they have found any new and distinctive mental processes at work in the collective sphere, the answer appears to be negative. Most of their work has consisted in coördinating social data with psychological findings originally discovered within an individualistic frame of reference. The chief result has been to show that the seemingly individualistic psychology was in fact strongly affected by social factors. Conversely, the mental operations originally studied by individualistic psychology apparently remain basic within the social sphere.

This unitary view of the psyche becomes the more inevitable when we stop to recall two equally obvious facts; first that there can be no group brain, and second that there can be no individual mind. The brain, it is true, does have an infra-individual foundation in that it has been developed through biological evolution and is received by individuals only by virtue of their racial inheritance. Nevertheless, in the practice of psychic life the brain as an organ is vested exclusively in individuals.

But as we saw earlier in connection with the case of "Anna," the individual brain, if left entirely to its internal resources, develops practically no mental capacities nor content. It remains in a ghastly state of subidiotic blankness, without means of thought or speech, and even without the ability to see or hear as we normally conceive these abilities. No inborn legacy from mental yesterdays, alas, informs it with the alertness of the noble savage or even prepares it for the ancient woes of Oedipus. Its biologically transmitted potentialities become mental actualities only to the degree, and only in accord with the manner, in which it is nourished upon the cultural accumulation of some given society. Thus we might say that the organic basis of mental life is racial-individual; its effective operation is individual-cultural, and its totality — like an ocean stirred, but not divided, by intermingling currents — is racial-individual-cultural.

In this fluid continuum, mental dynamics are to be thought of, not as individualistic *versus* collective, but as both at the same time. They are simply mental dynamics and whatever is known about them will apply, in varying degrees, throughout the entire individual-social spectrum. The subdivisions that have crept into our conception of them are accidents of the history of thought, not aspects of mental reality.

If, for instance, circumstances had led Freud to study the more inclusive mental dynamism that we are calling the tension-imagery process, instead of one of its specific products, the dream, we should have been under no later necessity of coördinating what he found out about dreams with other forms of tension-imagery. As it happened, the single manifestation of the process, rather than the totality of its varied manifestations, became the prototype for our thinking. Consequently, we are forced to try to correlate findings which were not previously connected with each other by the processes of scientific investigation.

In this present section we have questioned whether we are justified in transferring to the cultural sphere analytical concepts originally developed in connection with the individualistic phenomena of dreams. The answer appears to be not only that we are so justified in so doing, but that we should be unjustified in regarding these two spheres as separable from each other.

The general conclusion thus reached is reinforced if we study the evidence from the psychological field that particularly concerns us: that of mental imagery. The interaction of individual and cultural forces in the formation of such imagery has been richly documented by Jackson Steward Lincoln in his work, *The Dream in Primitive Cultures*.[13] This author has collected hundreds of dreams from the reports of anthropological field workers and interpreted them both in Freudian terms and in terms of their anthropological significance. He summarizes one aspect of his investigation by quoting Professor Berthold Laufer to the effect that "it is quite safe to assert now that dreams have exerted an enormous influence on the formation of human behavior and culture. Many motives of legends and fairy tales have justly been traced to dreams; many mythical concepts and motives of art and even works of art have been inspired by them." [14] In such cases the individually experienced dream serves as a point of departure for activities terminating in cultural products.

Dr. Lincoln makes equally clear the flow in the opposite direction from culture to the individual, showing that one large and important class of his examples can be classed as "culture pattern dreams." Though dreamed by individuals, dreams of this type embody religious and other concepts of the culture to which the dreamers belong, showing common traits among individuals of one culture and different traits among those of other cultures. In short, individual and collective forms of imagery continually react upon each other in a circuit that moves from the one to the other and back again.

Having, we hope, allayed any doubts as to the legitimacy of relating dream psychology to cultural psychology, we can now return to the general development of the psycho-historical theory. Our next effort will be to indicate the manner in which we believe the tension-imagery process works in the formation of the cultural image.

MYTH AND NEAR MYTH IN PSYCHO–HISTORICAL INTEGRATION

T he statement of our theory summarized in Diagram 1 at the beginning of Chapter V has permanent use in emphasizing certain relationships, but is also partly a result of the historical accidents and disciplinary segregations previously indicated. It might imply a parallelism between two separate mental processes involved respectively in dream formation and in culture formation. But we are nearer the truth if we assume that a single basic process operates in both these spheres. A more unified picture of our field, and one which also introduces some new considerations, is presented in Diagram 3.

This presentation can best be approached by giving some attention to an aspect of mental dynamics that we have not yet considered; namely, certain possible variations in the emotional character of tension-imagery experience. Although emotional life is infinitely varied and fluid, we generally conceive our experience of it as involving three main categories. These can be described, in the terms used at the bottom of our diagram, as *negative, positive*, and *neutral*.

At the historical level, whether we are concerned with personal or social history or with the common characteristics of the two, circumstances differ in their effect upon our emotions. Some of their differences in this respect are indicated in the lowest arc of the diagram. Circumstances which threaten difficulty or disaster, or which impose privation or repression, we describe as negative. Those which provide encouragement and assistance, offering opportunity for achievement and fulfillment, we describe as positive. Those which neither hamper nor assist us we regard as neutral.

In accord with these different types of circumstances, we have corresponding variations in the character of the related psychic tensions. Some of these are suggested in the second arc of the diagram. Minor negative circumstances engender the milder negative tensions of anxiety and various degrees of fear.

If the circumstances impose serious frustration or disaster, the tensions grow in intensity to the stage of melancholy or despair, and may reach a climax of agony and final collapse.

Positive tensions accompany circumstances that promise satisfaction and fulfillment. Beginning in their milder forms with states of anticipation and hope, they may expand into confidence in coming fulfillment and finally, if the fulfillment is achieved and is of a high order, to climaxes of exaltation or ecstasy.

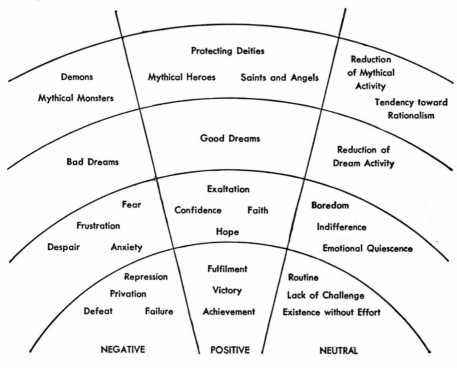

FIELD OF HUMAN EXPERIENCE

Diagram 3. Psycho-historical conception of tension imagery in relation to negative, positive, and neutral tensions.

Within the neutral zone our experience is more or less indifferent to us, involving neither negative dissatisfaction nor positive satisfaction. Tensional activity is at a minimum; we should probably speak of the comparative absence of tensions rather than of tensions specifically neutral in character. If the neutral aspect of experience can be said to involve anything in the nature of a climax, this presumably takes the form of excessive boredom.

Around this psycho-historical core of circumstance and tension is a psychic superworld: the airy realm of sympathetic mental imagery engendered by the tension-imagery process. This is represented in our diagram by the two upper arcs. And as the psychic motivations change in emotional character, so do their emanations in the realm of fantasy. If the reader will imagine our diagram to be a kind of pressure dial, with a needle pivoted at the bottom and able to swing from side to side, then he can visualize that as the needle moves through the negative, positive, and neutral segments of the dial, it will indicate not only certain underlying states of circumstance and tension, but also certain corresponding forms of tension imagery. Insofar, for instance, as the tensions motivate dreams, negative tensions will tend to induce "bad" dreams, positive tensions "good" dreams. Under the low tensional pressure of the neutral zone, dream activity will be at a minimum. We are most likely to enjoy a "deep and dreamless sleep" when we are freest from high tensions, whether positive or negative.

In suggesting direct relations between negative tensions and negative imagery, and correspondingly between positive tensions and positive imagery, we are minimizing one psychological possibility; namely, that the relation of the imagery to the tension may be compensatory rather than direct. We have seen that Freud cites examples of starving men who dreamed of banquets,[1] suggesting that a positive imagery of wish-fulfillment has resulted from negative tensions caused by hunger. The dream experience of these men is not described in detail for the entire period of their privation; hence we cannot determine to what degree it may also have included negative imagery.

Examples are not lacking from other sources to indicate connections between starvation and negative tension imagery. Ruth Landes has reported a mythological instance in the *windigo* of the Ojibwa Indians. Inhabiting a barren subarctic region of eastern Canada, these Indians are subject to hardships which include "often recurring periods of starvation . . . The neuroses . . . which flourish in such soil are . . . severe anxiety neuroses with special reference to food, and they manifest themselves in melancholia, violence, and obsessive cannibalism. For all these manifestations the Ojibwa have one term: *windigo*.

"Windigo is a mythological and supernatural figure, a giant skeleton made of ice, that flourishes in the wintertime only and is an insatiable cannibal. It epitomizes all those unhappy souls who die of starvation in winter. It is a frenzied character who howls and crashes through the land, treatening swift and horrible doom. The insane person is said to be possessed by the windigo spirit, compelled to obey its demands.

"Windigo, as we shall see, manifests itself differently in different persons, but the Ojibwa regard it as a unit. The onset is withdrawal into a melancholia. Almost universally the immediate cause is threatened starvation on the winter hunting grounds . . . the hunter . . . lies inert, said to be brooding over the possibilities of cannibalism, wanting to eat men yet afraid . . . The next stage is that of violence . . . He ceases to brood on defeat, and all his internal conflict yields to the one fixed idea: the meat to be supplied him. He kills his family quite coolly, as he does any usual food object, and eats them . . . when he has exhausted that supply, he wanders for more. Only his death can restore safety to the community, and the windigo sufferer in this stage invites his own doom." [2]

It seems evident that in this case the sufferings of hunger, the prospect of death by starvation, the struggle against impulses toward cannibalism, and the horror caused by cannibalism when practiced, all contribute to negative tensions which project themselves into the negative image of the icy cannibalistic giant. In the author's judgment, such direct relations between tensions and imagery are more frequent and more important in the cultural field than are compensatory ones. If it should be established by further study that compensation plays a more important role in the formation of cultural imagery than we are according it, this fact can easily be accepted within the psycho-historical framework.

Further examples of differing emotional character in tension imagery, and also of direct relations between tensions and imagery, will appear if we stop to consider our present thoughts in relation to the illustrations previously given. Our three "thumbnail" examples, as it happens, were all negative in character. They involved respectively the negative circumstances of volcanic eruption, economic disruption, and military destruction, with corresponding negative tensions and imagery that in each case might be described as "monstrous."

It is true that the sculpture of the Gnawing Squirrel (Fig. 8) is hardly monstrous in shocking or frightening sense, but the original hallucinations from which it descended were. Between the traumatic experience of those hallucinations and the carving of the pole, a century had intervened and had witnessed a gradual change in the emotional character of the tension-imagery experience. The negative shock had subsided; a positive reorientation toward it had emerged. The carved image represents, not the original terrifying squirrel, but the conquered squirrel that had become an emblem of pride. When the time factor is thus taken into account, the Gnawing-Squirrel myth divides itself into at least two different states, the first entirely negative, the second becoming positive in emotional character. Such evolutionary transformations of psycho-historical themes present one of the important dimensions of our subject and will receive more thorough attention later.

The examples that have been analyzed in this chapter have included none of positive imagery at a high stage of development. Without attempting such an analysis at this point, we may suggest that such a stage is represented by the Leonardo *Virgin with St. Anne* (Fig. 1). The relaxed attitudes and serene expression of the figures, and the degree of objectivity in the treatment of natural forms, all carry implications of a positive psycho-historical context. We shall have further opportunity to observe positive types of cultural imagery in the study of Gothic art in Part II. If the reader wishes to glance ahead at some of the positive Gothic examples, he will find characteristic ones on Plates 23–25.

As a type of art emanating from the neutral tensional zone, we may suggest the Vermeer, *The Little Street* (Fig. 12). Here we have a rational statement of optical experience that is aloof from pyscho-social excitements either negative or positive.

II

As the vertical dimension of Diagram 3 suggests, the imagery inspired by the tensions, whatever their character, may involve several different levels of projection. In successive imaginative strata it can rise from daydreams and dreams to myths and other forms of imagery. Doubtless it has additional spheres of emanation as well — among them neurotic symptoms and psychotic hallucinations — but daydreams, dreams, and mythico-cultural conceptions are the ones that chiefly concern us. In their increasing imaginative distance from the surface of rational experience, these three successive tension-imagery strata might be conceived, so to speak, as the atmosphere, the stratosphere, and the interstellar space of the psychic universe.

Theoretically the same original tension could give rise to any one of these forms of tension imagery, depending upon the mental conditions under which it operated. If the imagery were formed during the individual's waking hours and differentiated from outward reality by his power of rational discrimination, the result would be classed as a daydream. If the imagery were formed during sleep and achieved hallucinatory reality as a result of the temporary abeyance of rational discrimination, it would be classed as a dream. If the imagery acquired intellectual and emotional currency among a group of persons — a community, tribe, or nation — it would then achieve the status of a myth or other form of cultural expression.

For tension imagery to reach a state of complete mythical embodiment, two conditions must be operative which are not involved in the case of most dreams. In the first place, the psychic state which generates the imagery must be a *collective* rather than an individual or personal one. No doubt the inception of the imagery takes place in an individual mind, but if the tension which inspired it is a collective one, then the imagery can achieve collective validity.

Let us return to the Gnawing-Squirrel myth by way of illustration. We may assume that it was some individual Indian, hunting in the forest, who first saw the hallucinatory image of the terrifying monstrous squirrels "large as bears." He returned in fear to his village and described the apparition to his fellows. If its psychic cause had been exclusively a personal one (such as an unconscious awareness of a coming mental breakdown) then the imagery would have remained an individual matter. Others would have listened to the tale with objective detachment and would rightly have regarded it as some form of sign or symptom related to the personal experience of the teller.

But as we know in this case the traumatic condition was collectively shared, all the Indians of the region having been subjected to it by the volcanic eruption. When the hunter described the monster to others, it was as relevant to their condition as to his own. The whole community was charged with negative tensions impulsively ready to project themselves into some form of negative image. Because the psychic state that had inspired the image was collectively shared in this manner, the image itself could acquire collective validity. In acquiring such validity, it fulfilled the first condition for the birth of a myth.

But since the mythical image is a product of fantasy, subjectively meaningful but objectively nonexistent, a second condition must be fulfilled before a genuine myth can arise. Accurate and rational observation of the objective world would show that the monster or other mythical being does not exist as an outward reality, but only as a creature of the imagination. For the mental imagery to gain social acceptance as a supposed objective reality, it must therefore exist in a realm of experience within which the community is unprepared or unwilling to exercise accurate and rational observation. We have already observed in connection with dreams that when the discipline of informed intelligence relaxes in sleep, subjective imagery is no longer differentiated from objective reality. *Anything* we dream, however fantastic, *seems* objectively real to us so long as we are dreaming; that is to say, so long as our rational faculties are dormant. In this mental state the distinction between fact and fantasy does not exist.

In communities that have not as yet accumulated a large amount of factual data, or that for reasons of self-justification repress their sense of factual data, this uncritical mental state to which we return in sleep characterizes the minds of men even during their waking hours, and is collectively shared. Not having developed sufficient analytical technique to differentiate the objective from the subjective, or perhaps having done so in certain fields of experience but not in others, the community projects its tension imagery into the objective world. It accepts as equally real that which it sees imaginatively and that which it observes factually, confusing the one with the other in a general continuum of undifferentiated experience.

An amusing account of a community in this mental state is given by Vilhjarmur Stefansson in his book, *My Life with the Eskimo*. Stefansson's second arctic expedition was inspired by the belief that there might be Eskimos in the Dolphin and Union Straits region of polar Canada, a region which previous explorers had reported to be uninhabited. Since white men had never seen any such Eskimos, it was to be presumed that if they existed, they had had no contact with white civilization and would therefore still preserve their Neolithic culture intact. These assumptions proved to be correct. Stefansson found the previously unknown tribe and enjoyed among its people a remarkable opportunity to study a living exhibit of Neolithic culture.

The undifferentiated mentality of these Stone Age men was immediately demonstrated by the fact that they at first supposed Stefansson and his party to be supernatural spirits. The first of the Eskimos to be approached by a member of the exploring party was seated at a seal hole waiting for quarry. When the unexpected visitor had approached to within five paces of him:

"The sealer suddenly jumped up, grasping a long knife that had lain on the snow beside him and . . . began a monotonous noise which is neither a chant nor is it words — it is merely an effort to ward off dumbness, for if a man who is in the presence of a spirit does not make at least one sound each time he draws his breath, he will be stricken permanently dumb. This is a belief common to the Alaska and Coronation Gulf Eskimo. For several minutes . . . the sealer kept up the moaning noise, quite unable to realize, apparently, that he was being spoken to in human speech. It did not occur to him for a long time, he told us afterward, that we might be something other than spirits, for our dogs and dog harness, our sleds and clothes, were such as he had never seen in all his wanderings; besides, we had not, on approaching, used the peace sign of his people, which is holding the hands out to show that one does not carry a knife." [3] Real human beings and supernatural spirits were thus so intermingled in the minds of these people that the one could be, and in this case was, mistaken for the other.[4]

Having eventually established both their human identity and their friendly intentions, the explorers were received in the Eskimo village. Here Stefansson received further evidence of the undifferentiated mentality of his hosts when he sought to impress them with some of the inventions of the modern world. At a demonstration of the powers of the rifle, "they exhibited no surprise, but asked me if I could with my rifle kill a caribou on the other side of a mountain. When I said that I could not, they told me a great shaman in a neighboring tribe had a magic arrow by which he could kill caribou on the other side of no matter how big a mountain. In other words, much to my surprise, they considered the performance of my rifle nothing wonderful." [5]

Equally ungratifying to modern pride was the impression formed by the Eskimos of Stefansson's binoculars and of his accounts of the miracles of modern surgery.

"When they heard that my glasses could not see into the future, they were disappointed and naturally the reverse of well impressed with our powers, for they knew that their own medicine-men had charms and magic paraphernalia that enabled them to see things the morrow was to bring forth.

"At another time, in describing to them the skill of our surgeons, I told them that . . . our doctors could even transplant the organs of one man into the body of another. It was similar in their country, one of my listeners told me. He himself had a friend who suffered continually from backache until a great medicine-man undertook to treat him. The next night, while the patient slept, the medicine man removed the entire spinal column, which had become diseased, and replaced it with a complete new set of vertebrae, and — what was most wonderful — there was not a scratch on the patient's skin or anything to show that the exchange had been made . . . Another man had had his diseased heart replaced with a new and sound one . . .

"The Eskimo believed as thoroughly as I in the truth of what he told; neither of us had seen the things actually done, but that they were done was a matter of common belief among our respective countrymen; and the things he told of his medicine-men were more marvellous than the things I could tell of mine. In fact, I had to admit that the transplanting of spinal columns and hearts were beyond the skill of my countrymen; and as they had the good breeding not to openly doubt any of my stories, it would have been ill-mannered of me to question theirs. Besides, questioning them would have done no good; I could not have changed by an iota their rock-founded faith in their medicine-men and spirit-compelling charms. In spite of any arguments I could have put forth, the net result of our exchange of stories would have been just what it was anyway — that they considered they had learned from my own lips that in point of skill our doctors are not the equals of theirs." [6]

The essence of the matter, so far as concerns our inquiry, is the fact that these people accepted the imagined results of magic — a form of tension activity ultimately inspired by psychic pressures of desire or of fear — as an integral part of reality. The arrow that could shoot through the mountain, the device that could see into the future, the skill that could replace hearts and backbones, were to them as real and as significant aspects of their world as the snow houses they built or the seals they hunted. They had no basis of reference in terms of which they could distinguish the one group of experiences from the other and classify the former as fantasies and the latter as facts. And since nothing is impossible in the realm of fantasy, nothing to their minds, was impossible in the realm of fact.

The same statement could equally well be applied to the peoples who experienced the Gnawing-Squirrel hallucinations and the possessions by the Betsileo evil spirits and the Ojibwa cannibalistic giant. In all these cases, tension imagery eventuated in fully developed myths; that is, the images were confused with objective reality as a result of the double condition of collective tensions acting within and upon an undifferentiated mentality.

Such, to one degree or another, is the projective experience of all unanalytical cultures or, we might better say, of all cultures in the unanalytical phases of their experience. Through most of human history, man has fulfilled his days in this undifferentiated mental continuum of fantasy and fact. He has confused his imagery with his knowledge, inhabiting a world of which he believed whatever he imagined and imagined whatever his psychic tensions impelled. For him, the outer and the inner worlds were gloriously — and on their negative side, damnably — one. His specters and his gods, his hells and his heavens, and often his view of human groups alien to his own, were so many projections, visualized in mental imagery, of the complex movements of his own spirit. They were essentially dreams — dreams accepted and perpetuated in social tradition, collective dreams shared by society as a whole.

In applying the foregoing theory of myth formation to the analysis of specific myths, two qualifying factors must be kept in mind. Both of them arise from the fact that a myth, conceived in terms of its mental basis, is not a fixed entity. On the contrary, like the culture from which it emanates, it is a dynamism in a state of evolutionary change.

As a first result of its evolutionary nature, its emotional character — the degree to which it involves negative, positive, or neutral imagery — will change gradually if there is a causative change in the circumstances and tensions of the producing society. We have already noted one example of such change in connection with the myth of the Gnawing Squirrel. We shall later study a more complete and extended transformation of negative into positive imagery in connection with medieval mythology. The reverse transformation from positive to negative imagery would be equally implicit in historical situations involving decadence or other sources of difficulty. The emergence of the Betsileo evil spirits into a mythical cosmos from which they had previously been absent, is a case in point.

In addition to changes in emotional character, the long-range history of a myth will also involve changing relations between tensional dynamics and reason. As in the case of dreams, extraneous material may gather around the psychic core. Personal reactions of individual carriers, nontension aspects of collective mentality, may exert their intrusive influence. And since the myth is a phenomenon of the conscious as well as of the unconscious life — corresponding in this respect to the dream that is remembered and told after awakening — it is destined sooner or later to undergo a modifying process which might be called rationalistic erosion. Originally inspired by irrational tensions, the mythical material must subsequently exist in minds which also make rational observations. Although the two types of mental content may coexist for long periods without conscious conflict with each other, a time will eventually come, if rational thinking develops, when reason begins to perceive factual errors in the mythical conception. Rather than abandon the whole myth at once, rational thought is likely to modify it in whatever degree is necessary to make it congruous with the given stage of rationalistic development. In the course of such an evolution, the myth undergoes a series of transformations, each transformation weakening the traces of its emotional origin.

In this respect the history of a myth may be compared to that of a volcano. In the latter, subterranean dislocations generate powerful pressures, ejecting lava through the surface of the earth and piling it up in the form of a crater; a crater which may increase in height and impressiveness through subsequent eruptions so long as the volcano remains active. Whenever it is not active, external destructive forces attack it. Vegetation and erosion eat away its surface. If the volcano remains extinct during long periods of time, these disintegrating forces will eventually wear down the entire crater.

Similarly, a myth has not only its "active" period of psychic eruption and imaginative overflow, but also its subsequent period of "extinction" and disintegration. A late form of extinct myth will differ greatly from the earlier expressions of its active period, and may retain little of the original tension imagery.

Attention to these evolutionary factors is particularly important when we deal with myths that are available to us only in recorded form — those, for instance, of the ancient Greeks. Because the record is fixed, we may be tempted to regard the myth as equally so, assuming that throughout Greek history it was conceived by successive generations in the manner in which it appears in the record before us. What we are really dealing with is only an arrested moment of its evolutionary life: a moment comparable to the "still" photograph that is sometimes extracted from a motion picture. To grasp the myth with anything like living reality, we must secure as many versions of it as possible, must note the transformations that take place as it goes through successive versions, and must correlate the transformations with the historical development of the given society.

The cautious reader may perhaps be inclined to raise a final question. Do *all* myths owe their inception to the tension-imagery process or may some of them have originated in other manners — for instance through early speculative efforts to explain the phenomena of nature? The author does not feel that he commands sufficient data to justify a categorical answer to this question. But he is inclined to think that where the speculative element appears, it is a relatively late rationalistic intrusion, more characteristic of erosive than of formative states of mythological mentality. Somewhat as Freud presupposed an instinctive irrational pressure behind every dream, with or without additions from psychic areas closer to consciousness, we may presuppose a similar pressure as the original eruptive dynamic behind every myth. But whether we grant such a universality to the tension-imagery interpretation or not, our purpose will be served if we recognize it as a possible and frequent source of mythical imagery.

III

Picasso's *Guernica* (Figs. 10–11) was included among our preliminary examples of cultural tension imagery, but omitted from the preceding discussion of mythical projection. It was omitted because it exemplifies a variety of tension imagery in one respect different from the mythical one. Let us now consider this second variety of tension product.

In most respects the process which led to the conception of the *Guernica* was identical with that which inspired the mythical projections. Collective historical circumstances, precipitated in military destruction, produced a collective mental shock not unlike that received by the West Coast Indians from the volcano. Working within the mental dynamism of an individual, the resulting tensions sought expression in imaginative form and motivated Picasso's conception. When his work was seen by others, many of those others recognized it as an embodiment of tensions which they shared. Accordingly it acquired cultural validity, if not with every member of twentieth-century Western society, at least with a considerable group of the more thoughtful people both in Europe and in the Americas.

In all these respects the painting is cousin to the myths. But it differs from them with regard to the last of the conditions which we indicated as essential to the birth of a complete myth. It operates within a *differentiated* mentality instead of an *undifferentiated* one. The tension image remains subject to our power of rational discrimination and therefore fails to attain hallucinatory reality. Instead of confusing it with the outward world, we say that it *expresses* or *symbolizes* our reactions to certain aspects of that world. In this respect it corresponds, not to the true dream, but to the daydream as normally circumvented by reason. Cultural tension imagery which is thus circumvented might be described as near myth or, if we apply the analogy of the daydream, as day myth.

Evolutionary dynamics apply to the near myth as well as to the true myth and again involve possible transformations with regard to both emotional character and to eruptive intensity. Modification of style in the arts is one of the manifestations of changing emotional character. We have an example in the evolving visual concept of the madonna that carries the paintings on Plate II from archaic formality to a relaxed realism. According to the analysis of style which we shall undertake more fully in Chapter XIV, this increase in realism is one of the symbolical expressions of decreasingly negative, and increasingly positive, tensional character. A painting like the *Guernica* could be fitted into a sequence which would show the reverse trend away from a preceding realism toward increasing conventionality; a sequence which, in our view, would reveal an increase in negative tensional character.

The action of eruptive and erosive forces in the sphere of the near myth can be observed in the phases through which every artistic movement seems destined to pass. An exploratory or "creative" phase is eventually succeeded by a stereotyped or "academic" phase. Artists participating in the exploratory phase of a movement are the living craters of a psycho-historical eruption. Receiving powerful inspirations, they work with feverish intensity and bring forth results that are dazzling, often bewildering and seemingly unreasonable, to those who witness their cultural emergence. Such eruptive experience may persist throughout a lifetime and indeed for generations, or it may wane within a few years and leave the once creative artist adrift in search of new contacts with the motivating sources of creativity.

Soon or late, whether to the original artists or to their successors, there comes a time when the given movement loses its vitality. And as the myth is never immediately abandoned under the inroads made by reason, neither is the near myth of the art movement immediately abandoned when its eruptive vitality wanes. Those for whom it was creative may linger with it in wistful memory of the great moments which it gave them. Those who never participated in its upsurge, coming too late to do so and lacking the power to innovate the future upsurge, give the movement a quiescent old age during which it continues to repeat, as formulas, modes of construction that no longer possess the life of forms. The formulas are likely to be regarded by society as eminently reasonable because familar; the new eruptive forms, if and when they come, will again dazzle by their unexpectedness and may again produce the shock of the seemingly unreasonable.

The distinction between the myth and the near myth in any culture is neither fixed nor clear. Instead of a sharp line of demarcation between the two, we find a shifting zone of intermixture. As the daydream of the individual fluctuates from lesser to greater reality in response to changing relations between reason and emotion in the dreamer, so myth and near myth fluctuate into each other in the complicated mental atmosphere of a culture. Such fluctuation is particularly characteristic of historic civilizations with their immense populations, varied component groups and institutions, and ever widening range from the illiteracy of their least educated individuals to the higher learning of their scholars.

In such a cultural atmosphere it is impossible to classify any given tensional product as exclusively either myth or near myth; at different times and for different groups or individuals, it will be both. A given religious conception, for instance, will presumably have received complete mythical projection from those who first experienced it and will continue to receive such projection from certain persons and, officially at least, from certain institutions as a whole. The same conception will be rationally interpreted by various other persons as symbolical in its significance, and will be seen by still others through what we may call a "counter-myth." The counter-myth will deny the given religious concept all positive significance, regarding it as false or superstitious.

Furthermore the individual or group which accords full mythical reality to one particular religious conception, will probably deny a similar reality to other conceptions which are mythically projected by other individuals or groups; which others will deny the reality of the first conception. A cultural atmosphere charged with so many different attitudes might be compared to a sky pulsating with the indefinable lights and darks of the northern lights. Myth, near myth, and "superstition" play around and over each other in constantly intermingling vibrations.

When this whole process is unconscious, cultural chaos is inevitable. Myth fights myth believing on each side that truth is fighting falsehood. Psycho-historical perspective offers one of the possible paths out of such chaos toward greater cultural order. In submitting tensional products to analysis, it withholds full mythical projection from all of them, equally protects all of them from the counter-mythical criticism of being false, and accords to all the significance of symbols that express the realities of life from which they arose. Mutual respect is possible between the adherents of different sets of analyzed symbols.

In fields like the arts, fluctuation between the myth and the near myth is less evident than in ones like religion, but can still have its place. To the casual listener, music is a background of agreeable sounds and may become a nuisance if it interferes with conversation or other interests that have greater reality for him. The music lover, on the other hand, resents anything that interferes with his musical absorption. For him music is the greater reality; it may become for him, as we sometimes hear him say, a "religion." He thus projects his musical experience with an intensity, and with an impact upon his sense of objective existence, which approaches the complete projection of the myth.

In the rational aspect of our mental life, the myth is continually pulled back toward the status of the near myth just as the daydream is constantly restrained within the bounds of reason. In the *emotional* aspect of life, the reverse pressure is at work. Like the daydream striving for the unrestricted reality of the illusion, the near myth strives for the full projection of the complete myth. The mythical moment, which we may also describe as the mystical moment, is one of the climaxes of experiential reality. In it, subjective reality connects with objective reality in a single living arc through all we apprehend as being. Instead of two worlds and the constant effort to adjust the one to the other, only one world remains. Nostalgia for the complete unification of myth no doubt plays an important part in the reversal of attitude that sometimes leads the one-time rationalist to identify himself, at a later time, with one of the more dogmatic religions.

IV

Men living in civilized communities often make the complacent assumption that the myth is a phenomenon of primitive cultures which is subsequently outgrown by historic civilizations. Enough has perhaps been said, or at least implied, in previous portions of this chapter to indicate the inaccuracy of such an assumption. Before we leave the subject of the myth-forming mentality, however, it may be well to insist somewhat more fully upon the persistence of myth throughout history. What we have called an undifferentiated mentality was widely prevalent in ancient, medieval, and Renaissance civilizations, has only gradually and partially been overcome in themselves by groups of scientific thinkers at certain rare epochs, and still persists as a current mentality in large portions of the world's present population.

A study of medieval life, such as we shall undertake in Part II, is sufficient to indicate how slow was the progress of civilized communities only a few centuries earlier than our own in learning to differentiate between the various aspects of their experience. The men of Romanesque and Gothic times were little better equipped than their primitive forbears to divide their mental emanations into recognized myth and legend, on the one hand, and history and science on the other. The *Divine Comedy* records an extraordinary imaginative vision of heaven and hell which, to the medieval mind, was not merely a symbol of spiritual states but a geographically existent portion of the universe.

Chronicles like those of Geoffrey of Monmouth merge giants, sirens, and other mythical material with historical facts in so complete an amalgam that the two are practically inextricable from each other. Regarded by the majority of readers as authentic history as late as Shakespeare's time, that is to say in the full morning of the English Renaissance, Geoffrey's *Historia Regum Britanniae* was almost as completely rejected by later critical historians as conscious or unconscious fiction. How completely fact and fantasy coalesce in its pages may be judged from the circumstance that the critical historians were apparently misled by it in their turn. Some of the latest and best informed students of the subject have concluded that there is a basis of historical truth in many of the passages critically rejected as fictitious.[7]

Simple geographical facts such as the roundness of the earth were so little known at the height of the Renaissance that sailors feared to accompany explorers like Columbus lest their vessels fall over the edge of the supposedly flat world. Monsters and mythical beings of all kinds were taken for granted as a real part of the then relatively unknown real world. Many observers believed they had actually seen them. Thus Breydenbach includes a unicorn among the animals illustrated in one of the plates of his *Voyage to the Holy Land*. In the accompanying inscription he states, "These animals are accurately drawn as we saw them in the Holy Land." [8] This is a serious work of travel published at Mainz in the fifteenth century!

Large portions of the Christian world still fail to differentiate the factual from the mythical material in their sacred writings, or at best to recognize the mythological element only in such evident fantasies as the creation stories of Genesis and the mystical visions of the Apocalypse. Equally unanalytical attitudes are common among the followers of other religious persuasions. Copernicus' assertion that the earth was subordinate to the sun shocked the mentality of the seventeenth century, the doctrine of evolution that of the nineteenth century, and Freudian revelations of the unconscious that of the twentieth century because these empirical observations conflicted with the current myths of the Western world. It is quite possible that some readers may be shocked by certain of the assumptions underlying the present discussion; particularly the assumption that the world's great religions, including Christianity, involve their own mythology and in this respect, can be interpreted in terms of the tension-imagery process.

Further shocks may be expected before our view of existence is determined exclusively by facts — if indeed such a state is ever possible. The reader who takes the trouble to compare histories of recent wars as written on opposite sides of the firing line, or the accounts of modern class struggle as presented respectively by capital and labor — or even the views of themselves and of each other published respectively by the Republicans and the Democrats — will have before him an impressive demonstration of the degree to which modern man is still unable to perceive facts objectively in situations which involves his psychic tensions. He has, it is true, reduced his sphere of confusion in many directions, but he still reveals himself blood brother to the earlier myth makers in the strong subjective coloration — sometimes even the subjective domination — of his supposedly objective world.

Surprising as it appears at first glance, our own culture approaches mythical projection most often in the more intellectual and practical aspects of life which seem to be the most solidly based on fact. We differentiate the imaginative imagery of the arts from objective reality, but we frequently confuse with reality what may be called the abstract tension concept. Such confusion takes place whenever our mental products are regarded as identical with the external world instead of symbolical of our experience in it.

The world, as we are led to conceive it by John Dewey's philosophy, inspires confidence in progress. Human welfare is assured if we follow the light of knowledge and apply the power of reason. But if we turn to the works of another recent philosopher, Jean-Paul Sartres, the world presented to us is an entirely different one. It is intractable to man's control, frustrating his desires and evading his ideals; he can, at best, be the captain of his soul and cling stoically to the value of existence. Can we doubt that Dewey was projecting the optimism of the expanding phase of American industrial and scientific society? Or that Sartres was projecting the tragedy of the occupied France and the war-torn Europe in which he came to maturity? And were not both men identifying their philosophies with "reality" as fully as the West Coast hunter did his squirrels?

Even scientific concepts, it would seem, are not always free of an element of mythical projection. A hypothesis which at one time seems to be true, in the sense of corresponding with observable reality, may later fail to correspond with newly discovered aspects of reality. The first hypothesis is succeeded by a second one that fits the larger range of facts; the first is now regarded as untrue, the second as true. Evidently the "truth" originally imputed to the first hypothesis involved an element of mythical projection through which man identified a given state of his understanding with objective existence. And since man can never hope to attain a complete understanding of objective existence, it would seem that a mythical element creeps in whenever he regards scientific statements as more than theories carefully controlled up to the limits permitted by his constitution and his acquired knowledge.

If various degrees of mythical projection can thus be detected in our intellectual life, they are still more evident in what we call the "practical" aspects of our culture. Our political and international relations are viewed by many members of society through lurid imaginative lights and shadows that flicker with our national tensions as unpredictably as the flames of a wind-blown fire. Here the most common phenomenon in civilized communities is identification of the negative tension image with human opponents.

Americans of the older generation can remember a number of successive images of Germany and the German people that have been current in the American press. At the beginning of the author's recollection, the Germans appeared chiefly in the light of Europe's leading scientists, a knowledge of whose language was essential to the scientifically minded student. Successively they then became militaristic "Huns" capable of every atrocity, nascent republicans under the Weimar republic, fascist opponents of democracy whose military might must be stripped from them, and most recently of all — at least in their western territories — friends of democracy whose military might must be restored to them. Equally shifting and often equally uncomplimentary concepts of other peoples and groups have been, and are being, entertained in American consciousness. And needless to say, equally shifting and often equally uncomplimentary concepts of the American people and its leaders have been, and are being, entertained by the Germans and by other peoples in other parts of the world.

All such concepts, if delimited with sufficient exactness, involve a degree of truth, but none of them ever corresponds to the complete and exact truth. Under the stress of high tensions, such as develop during wars or other acute conflicts, some of the least true aspects of these concepts are projected with the greatest mythical intensity. The frustrations and hatreds that possess us as a result of unsolved problems and frictions in contemporary culture create their awful image upon the projective screen, much as did the somewhat equivalent frustrations and hatreds of the Betsileons.

Instead of identifying the evil spirits with the supernatural world, we identify them with the human one. But we still fail to trace them to the source in which they have their main factual basis, and in terms of which alone the difficulties that inspired them can be solved: that is to say, in problems and conflicts that are as intrinsic to our own culture as to any other. From the practical point of view in promoting our own welfare and that of the other human groups which make up with us the brotherhood of man, few things could contribute more to progress than an increasing differentiation between fact and fantasy in the realm of human relations. Here we must depend in large part upon the efforts of the social scientists.

Let us conclude the present chapter by summarizing the import of its last section. Whatever developments the future may bring forth, the discipline of informed, analytical intelligence has been a rare phenomenon in human history to date. An undifferentiated combination of fantasy and fact has governed a much larger sphere of man's ideas, and determined the forms of a much larger percentage of the world's arts, than has our recently acquired, still rare, and only partial ability to distinguish between the objective and the subjective aspects of our experience.

TENSIONAL TRANSFORMATION

W e have presented the tension-imagery process as a type of mental activity operative alike in personal and cultural life — or, better, operative in the intermingling personal and cultural experiences that make up the unity of life. If we remember that the most accurate knowledge of any aspect of this process is that derived from the interpretation of dreams, we realize that a further study of dreams offers the best means of enriching our comprehension of tension dynamics in general. Even here we can attempt only a summary treatment. The reader must depend upon the original psychoanalytical sources for a more intensive study of this component aspect of our synthesis.

It is fortunate that the mental activities involved in dream formation have been the object of detailed investigation by many psychoanalytical observers, and particularly by Freud in the studies leading to, and emergent from, his work on *The Interpretation of Dreams.*

Freud himself regarded this work as his masterpiece. Thirty-one years after its original appearance, he wrote in his Foreword to the third English edition that it "contains, even according to my present-day judgment, the most valuable of all the discoveries it has been my good fortune to make. Insight such as this falls to one's lot but once in a lifetime." [1]

Critical perspective, as it develops, seems to support this judgment. The emphasis on sex in early psychoanalysis, like that in the novels of D. H. Lawrence, may well turn out to be an index of Victorian repressions rather than a basic trait of human mentality. The early patients of psychoanalysis, the early analysts, and the early readers of psychoanalytical works, had all been conditioned by a society imposing strong sexual repression, with the result that for all of them sex acquired abnormal psychic dominance.

Ethnological and sociological evidence suggests that, in societies subject to other conditioning influence, psychic complexes center in other aspects of life. J. S. Slotkin calls attention to social situations in which compulsive pressures on the psyche were associated, not with sex, but respectively with hunger, with economic deprivation, and with a repression of the impulse to social opposition.[2] The Ojibwa *windigo*, described by Ruth Landes and cited in an earlier chapter, provides a further instance of a tensional situation dominated by hunger rather than sex.

What gives Freud's study its unique importance is that it includes the most complete presentation ever made of what we most need from psychologists, and that is an analysis of mental dynamics in their combined conscious-unconscious totality. Here, more than in any other source known to the author, we can extend our grasp of the intricate mental operations that transform historical experiences into forms of symbolic expression.

The Interpretation of Dreams was first published in 1900. When Freud later recapitulated his dream theory in his *General Introduction to Psychoanalysis* (1916), his *New Introductory Lectures* (1933), and elsewhere, he was in a position to reduce his findings to a more summary form. For our present purposes, we can turn to what appears to be the briefest of these later summaries, the section on dreams in an encyclopedia article on psychoanalysis written by Freud in 1922.

"*The Interpretation of Dreams.* — A new approach to the depths of mental life was opened when the technique of free association was applied to dreams, whether one's own or those of patients in analysis. In fact, the greater and better part of what we know of the processes in the unconscious levels of the mind is derived from the interpretation of dreams. Psychoanalysis has restored to dreams the importance which was generally ascribed to them in ancient times, but it treats them differently. It does not rely on the cleverness of the dream-interpreter but for the most part hands the task over to the dreamer himself by asking him for his associations to the separate elements of the dream. By pursuing these associations further we obtain knowledge of thoughts which coincide entirely with the dream but which can be recognized — up to a certain point — as genuine and completely intelligible portions of waking mental activity. Thus the recollected dream emerges as the *manifest dream-content*, in contrast to the *latent dream-thoughts* discovered by interpretation. The process which has transformed the latter into the former, that is to say into 'the dream,' and which is undone by the work of interpretation, may be called 'dream-work.'

"We also describe the latent dream-thoughts, on account of their connection with waking life, as 'residues of the (previous) day.' By the operation of the dream-work (to which it would be quite incorrect to ascribe any 'creative' character) the latent dream-thoughts are *condensed* in a remarkable way, they are distorted by the *displacement* of psychical intensities, they are arranged with a view to being *represented in visual pictures*; and, besides all this, before the manifest dream is arrived at, they are submitted to a process of *secondary elaboration* which seeks to give the new product something in the nature of sense and coherence. But, strictly speaking, this last process does not form part of the dream-work.

"*The Dynamic Theory of Dream-Formation.* — An understanding of the dynamics of dream-formation did not involve any very great difficulties. The motive power for the formation of dreams is not provided by the latent dream-thoughts or day's residues, but by an unconscious impulse, repressed during the day, with which the day's residues have been able to establish contact and which contrives to make a *wish-fulfilment* for itself out of the material of the latent thoughts. Thus every dream is on the one hand the fulfilment of a wish on the part of the unconscious and on the other hand (in so far as it succeeds in guarding the state of sleep against being disturbed) the fulfilment of the normal wish to sleep which set the sleep going. If we disregard the unconscious contribution to the formation of the dream and limit the dream to its latent thoughts, it can represent anything with which the waking life has been concerned — a reflection, a warning, an intention, a preparation for the immediate future or, once again, the satisfaction of an unfulfilled wish. The unrecognizability, strangeness and absurdity of the manifest dream are partly the result of the translation of the thoughts into a different, so to say *archaic*, method of expression, but partly the effect of a restrictive, critically disapproving agency in the mind, which does not entirely cease to function in sleep. It is plausible to suppose that the '*dream-censorship*,' which we regard as being responsible in the first instance for the distortion of the dream-thoughts into the manifest dream, is a manifestation of the same mental forces which during the day-time had held back or *repressed* the unconscious wishful impulse.

"It has been worth while to enter in some detail into the explanation of dreams, since analytical work has shown that the dynamics of the formation of dreams are the same as those of the formation of symptoms. In both cases we find a struggle between two trends, of which one is unconscious and ordinarily repressed and strives toward satisfaction — that is, wish-fulfilment — while the other, belonging probably to the conscious ego, is disapproving and repressive. The outcome of this conflict is a *compromise-formation* (the dream

or the symptom) in which both trends have found incomplete expression. . .
Since dreams are not pathological phenomena, the fact shows that the mental
mechanisms which produce the symptoms of illness are equally present in
normal mental life, that the same uniform law embraces both the normal and
the abnormal. . .

"*Symbolism.* — In the course of investigating the form of expression brought
about by dream-work, the surprising fact emerged that certain objects, arrange-
ments and relations are represented, in a sense indirectly, by 'symbols,' which
are used by the dreamer without his understanding them and to which as a
rule he offers no associations. Their translation has to be provided by the
analyst, who can himself discover it only empirically by experimentally fitting
it into the context. It was later found that linguistic usage, mythology and
folk-lore afford the most ample analogies to the dream-symbols. Symbols,
which raise the most interesting and hitherto unsolved problems, seem to be
a fragment of extremely ancient inherited mental equipment. The use of a
common symbolism extends far beyond the use of a common language." [3]

We need not accept all the elements of Freud's system as final or absolute.
Whether all dreams, even negative ones, involve wish fulfillment, is a question
concerning which psychoanalysts differ in opinion. Freud himself, in one of
his last commentaries on his dream theories, recognized "one genuine exception" to his wish-fulfillment principle, namely "dreams that occur in traumatic
neurosis." [4] Some students believe that there are other exceptions. Steckel writes,
"I start from the principle that a dream may be a wish-fulfillment, but is not
necessarily so." [5]

Freud's concept of symbolism as inherited rather than formative is another
point which, in our view, seems to require modification. For us the entire
dream, and similarly the entire cultural image, is symbolic of the psycho-
historical realities underlying it, regardless of whether the imagery is unique
or is relatable to forms that have occurred at other times or places. We regard
the whole process of the dream work — in more general terms, the whole
tension-imagery process — as one of symbolic transformation. Symbolism thus
becomes a more inclusive field, and one which, if studied at close range, would
probably require subdivision into a number of different categories.

Despite these or any other reservations that any particular student of the
subject may wish to make, it remains true that Freud's system offers us the
clearest vision yet obtainable of the intricate mental machinery into one end
of which, so to speak, flows the experience of life and from the other end of

which emerges the symbolic image of life. And since Freud's system permits us to peer further into this machinery than is otherwise possible, it provides our most useful references for study in connection with the psychic aspects of cultural tension imagery. What should especially enlighten and prepare us in this connection is the complexity, the infinite resourcefulness, the frequent ambiguity, of the psychic activities involved in tension-imagery formation.

In early applications of Freud's theories, the work of art was thought of as a wish fulfillment, a group of sexual symbols, or an expression of an Oedipus complex in the artist. Studies of these kinds performed a useful service in helping to establish connections between the two fields, and sometimes produced significant results, but they were partial in their grasp of psychoanalytical findings. They seized upon the simpler and more obvious psychoanalytical concepts and used them as formulas applicable to works of art.

More complete assimilation of depth psychology leads us away from such formulas toward the manipulation of a whole system of mental forces in dynamic interplay with each other. Instead of seeking certain preconceived effects, we are concerned with a partially unpredictable process that may produce *any* effects. We must conceive of cultural tension imagery as potentially reflecting the objective world in more or less "day-residue" fashion, but we must also conceive it as subject to the influence of "latent" thoughts and impulses which have a more subjective emphasis. We must be prepared for elusive transformatory processes that may involve condensation, distortion, displacement of psychic intensities, and a secondary elaboration that gives rational order to the expressions of irrational impulse. We must be alert to the possibilities of repression, unconscious censorship, and compromise formation. Only as we come to recognize such potential intricacies in the formation of the cultural image are we prepared to interpret that image with a reasonable degree of penetration. How far any one of these concepts may be necessary or useful in the analysis of cultural situations, can only be determined by practice and experiment. All of them should have a place among the instruments available for our thinking.

II

The range in dream imagery from the most literal to the most fantastic is one which we have not previously mentioned, and one which we know to have its equivalent in culture. Most readers can probably recall dreams in which familiar scenes appeared with photographic accuracy. The author remembers an anxiety dream in which he missed a train at his local railway station. All the details of the station, surroundings, baggage, and train were reproduced as they actually existed. In such cases the inspiring tension recognizes an affinity with previous real experiences, revives their images in memory, and converts them into tension images by infusing them with its own force.

A similar mental exploitation of visual fact becomes a basis for art when Vermeer paints his *Street in Delft*, when Courbet records the native valley of the Loue, and when Millet studies a peasant or Degas a ballet dancer. In such cases of artistic realism, the artist's sensitivity attaches itself to the appearance of the outward world, but it is still his sensitivity — a psychic obsession and drive — that provides the motive force for the creation of art.

This dependence of the image upon the psyche is a point which must be especially remembered in dealing with realistic cultural products. To the rational mind, realism appears self-justifying. Other modes of procedure may require apology; the realistic mode is axiomatically accepted as natural and right. This axiom, like many others, explodes as soon as our knowledge comprehends the interchange of energies between reason and the unconscious. Then we realize that literal image in art, like that in the dream, is only the *manifest* surface of the total experience and that below realistic representation are depths no less mysterious than those which inspire the most fantastic inventions. Historically, we know that realism flourishes during certain periods and wanes or disappears during others. What psycho-historical conditions correspond with its flowerings, its wanings, and its disappearances?

The literal, however, is only one, and on the whole the least frequent one, of the varieties of tension imagery. In the majority of dream cases and — if we consider the whole course of human history — in the majority of culture cases, memory images apparently prove inadequate to embody the tensions involved. Perhaps the mind disposes of no memory image corresponding in quality to the given tension, or perhaps in such cases the tension is more acute and emotionally powerful. The given mental content may also be subject to stronger repression and therefore capable of reaching consciousness only in disguised or distorted form. And, as we shall note more fully in a later chapter, a given socio-mental content becomes less capable of literal representation in proportion as it grows more inclusive in its range. What we shall call the "master tensions" of an epoch are the outcome of all the circumstances of an epoch. They are beyond the literal grasp of perception, memory, or reason, and can only be apprehended by intuition.

Under mental conditions like those just suggested, tension dynamics reject realistic images and produce fantasies conceived for the occasion. The elements are still derived from the natural world, for the psyche has no other source of elements to draw upon, but the result in this case is a new, and can be a remarkably vivid, imaginative synthesis. The astonishing power of the mind to fuse natural elements into such a synthesis must often have impressed the reader in connection with his own dreams. I can illustrate it from personal experience by referring to the rockslide dream described in an earlier chapter.

In real life I had at various times been aloft on mountains, had rolled stones down slopes, and had studies the pyramids of Egypt with their geometrically sloping sides. I had heard of avalanches without ever having seen one, but had seen and been impressed by various waterfalls, and had once forded a swift mountain stream that threatened to sweep me off my feet. Without those experiences and the impressions they had left in my memory, my mind would presumably have been incapable of formulating the imagery employed in the dream.

At the same time, that imagery was not a realistic reproduction of nature. It was a creative revision of nature. It was nature merged with, and transformed by, the psyche. The mountain with geometrically regular slopes, the symmetrical arrangement of the dream world, the vast, smoothly flowing, waterfall-like slide of rock, were creative combinations of old impressions into new forms. The total situation was one which I had never actually experienced and could never actually experience. No rockslide of that precise character and extent had, I venture to say, ever taken place in all the incalculable ages of geological history. It was a vision born of the creative power of the human imagination.

It is also easy to find examples of cultural fantasies arising from a similar flight from natural points of departure to unnatural (and supernatural) terminals. We have only to recall the concepts of angels and other good spirits that combine the more honorable attributes of humanity — head, arms, and draped torso — with such nonhuman features as the wings of the bird, the radiance of light and, for draperies, a whiteness reminiscent of snow, swan, or lily. Such beings emphasize the higher human powers while overcoming early man's only major deficiency in the face of the natural kingdom: his inability to fly. The complementary negative example greets us in the forms attributed to Satan. These remain largely human but the legs, veiled in the angel, are now fully exposed to evoke associations of the "lower" passions. If there are wings they come, not from the birds, but from the nocturnal bat. And the imagination may rove farther afield in nature, borrowing the horns of the goat and the claws of wild beasts, and bathing the whole conception in the lurid red of fire or the black of darkness.

The fantasy-building powers of the mind, only slightly illustrated by the foregoing examples, amount in fact to veritable genius. All the impressions of a lifetime — which may include cultural ingredients from the most distant times and places — are at the instant disposal of the tension-imagery process for selection, transformation, and synthesis into an infinite variety of forms. There is no shade of feeling possible to life which the creative aspect of tension-imagery formation cannot match with an image world as faithful to its psychic inspiration as is the reflection in a mirror to the form reflected. When called upon to do so by sufficiently powerful tensions, this imaginative genius of the mind compounds the attractions or the repulsions of natural things into imaginative concentrates supercharged with psychic significance. All of us recall nightmares in which any terrors we have known in reality were magnified a hundred fold, and fulfillment dreams in which reality was transfigured with a truly divine radiance and magnanimity.

Similar quintessences of tension are no less common in the fantasy world of culture. Few of us today

> Have sight of Proteus rising from the sea;
> Or hear old Triton blow his wreathèd horn,

but less differentiated cultural mentalities peopled the natural world with phantoms as vivid as those which inhabit our dreams. We have cited a number of examples of mythical hallucinations. In their eruptive stages all the world's myths and religious visions, and to a less degree its artistic and philosophical systems, dominated reality with equal obsessiveness. In them, the fantasy genius of the mind reached its cultural culminations. Heavens opened to mystical view in the heights above (Fig. 13), infernos in the depths within the earth (Fig. 22). The entire universe became a screen reflecting back to man the visions inspired by his social exaltation, his social despair, or his tranquil state of tensional neutrality.

A full analysis of tensional dynamics would direct attention to at least four aspects of the subject: the possible range in emotional character as between positive, negative, and neutral tensional states and their expressions; the possible variation of tension imagery from the literal to the fantastic; the possible range of tensions from the most individually personal to the most inclusively collective; and two different modes of expressing tensions that we may call direct or conscious, as opposed to indirect and largely unconscious, tensional projection.

Our discussion thus far has dwelt at some length upon the first three of these aspects, but has dealt little with the last. In some respects the direct and indirect modes of tensional expression can be more advantageously discussed after the more thorough application of our theory is undertaken in Part II. For the moment, therefore, we shall leave the subject of tensional dynamics at the stage to which we have now carried it, returning to round out its remaining phases in a later chapter.[6]

Chapter I X

CORRELATIONAL SUMMARY

Our attempt to define psycho-historical theory in the preceding chapters has been an effort to synthesize findings which originated in a number of different fields of intellectual endeavor. Other approaches would be possible. We shall later restate the theory in a somewhat different manner, giving less attention to its parentage and more to its organic individuality. We shall also give more thought to its relation to current traditions in the history, criticism, and philosophy of art. For the present, and from the point of view of the derivation of psycho-historical theory from the disciplines that have thus far concerned us, we can conclude our discussion with four main observations.

(1) The psycho-historical theory proposes a means of merging insights from three broad fields of learning: the arts and other forms of cultural expression, psychology, and history and the other social sciences. Each of these fields corresponds approximately with one of the three levels in the psycho-historical frame of reference, and each involves a number of specialized disciplines. The total correlational reach of our theory may be summarized by assembling all the potentially relevant disciplines and connecting them with the analytical levels to which they correspond. This is done in Diagram 4.

In promoting interchange among the disciplines listed above, the psycho-historical approach may be expected to profit by the attainments of each individual discipline while at the same time filling gaps that have existed in some of the component systems. The gap between economic foundations and cultural superstructures in historical materialism is spanned by reference to psychology. Awareness of the psychic complexities involved in tension-imagery formation should dispel any simple tendency to equate specific types of cultural expression with specific class mentalities or economic systems.

Conversely, contact with the social sciences should dispel the tendency of traditional psychology, and of idealistic criticism and philosophy, to interpret forms of cultural expression as if they depended exclusively upon subjective forces, or upon any forces explainable solely in terms of the individual personality. The inclusion in our system of social psychology and of economic considerations closes the gaps between the individual and his cultural environment, between subjective experience and the objective world, and between psychic life and the material factors which condition its survival and determine many of its fulfillments and frustrations. As an ultimate goal from the correlational point of view, our frame of reference might hope to provide a basis for the achievement of a unified field in humanistic studies.

ANALYTICAL LEVEL	RELEVANT DISCIPLINES
Manifest cultural imagery	History and criticism of: visual arts folk lore music myth dance religion literature philosophy
Psycho-social tensions	Psychology in all its branches, but with greatest relevance at present concentrated in: psychoanalysis social psychology
Historical and social circumstances	Social sciences: history ethnology sociology anthropology economics

Diagram 4. Disciplines relevant to the psycho-historical frame of reference.

(2) From the point of view of a working hypothesis, the result of our correlations is the psycho-historical theory itself. Summarized as a principle, this theory maintains that there is an organic continuum from the historical circumstances being experienced by any society to the states of psycho-social tension current in that society, and then to the symbolical expression of those states in the arts and other forms of cultural expression. Viewed critically as a problem in interpretation, any given form of cultural expression is regarded

as a type of manifest imagery which embodies an underlying latent tensional condition. Analyzing the given form psycho-historically consists in finding out what historical, social, and economic circumstances were current in the given society at the time of its production, what kinds of social tensions those circumstances were generating, and what mental operations can have transformed the tensions into the manifest imagery.

This process of analysis is parallel to, and partly derived from, the psychoanalytical process of analyzing dreams. In our theory the myth, when projected with full hallucinatory reality, is to society what a dream is to an individual. When differentiated from the objective world by the observer's power of rational discrimination, cultural imagery is to society what a rationally controlled daydream is to an individual.

The circumstance-tension-imagery continuum may be negative, positive, or neutral in emotional character, and the tension may express itself directly in realistic imagery or indirectly in fantasy. We have also suggested, as yet without adequate supporting evidence, that the motivation of the imagery toward realism or fantasy is influenced by the emotional character of tensions involved. According to our suggestion, positive and neutral tensions tend to inspire realistic imagery; negative tensions, fantastic or (as we shall later suggest) abstract imagery. This suggestion remains to be substantiated by further study.

Partial statements of the above principles in tabulated form were given in Diagram 1 and Diagram 2.

(3) In the preceding chapters, emphasis has fallen chiefly on the psychological and the historical components of our system, whereas the third component — that of the forms of cultural expression — has received only incidental reference by way of illustration. In the chapters to follow, this emphasis will be reversed. Certain forms of cultural expression will be taken as the primary subject for study; psychology and history will be used as instruments for studying them.

In view of the secondary role which we have thus far assigned to the expressive branches of the humanities, it seems well to say a word here concerning their importance for the psycho-historical field. As indicated at the top of the second column in our correlational table, Diagram 4, what we are describing as manifest cultural imagery comprehends not only all the arts of humanity, but all the forms of its myths, religion, and philosophy. This vast treasury of beauty, imaginative conception, and thought embraces many of the finest expressions of the human spirit. Its significance for those who would enjoy life fully, experience it abundantly, can be taken for granted.

What should be noted here, as we observe the place of cultural imagery in the psycho-historical field, is the importance of such imagery for those who would *understand* life as fully as possible. Problems of social relations and human behavior are now stimulating intensive efforts at the scientific study of man. If the arts and other expressions of man's imaginative life were merely sources of pleasureable recreation, they would at best have a minor relation to programs of psychological, historical, and social studies. Psycho-historically considered, they are *not* merely sources of pleasureable recreation; they are unconscious social concentrates embodying the deepest secrets of human existence. What the individual dream has been to personal analysis, the collective dream can be to social analysis. It presents, in symbolical form, through channels that are at least partly unconscious and therefore beyond the reach of rationalization, the psycho-social essence of the condition of life from which it emerged.

This being the case the psycho-historical field is not a one-sided one in which the arts alone receive benefit from psychological, historical, and social studies. It is a balanced one in which the arts, receiving such benefits, can likewise contribute to the progress of psychological, historical, and social studies. To the psychologist they present major areas of perceptive, imaginative, and other varieties of psychic activity. To the historian they provide major forms of historical record; a record produced by the given society itself and one recording, not only its conscious ideas, but all the unconscious immediacy of its existence. To the sociologist the arts offer indexes of social existence that plunge below the surface of opinion to reveal the unconscious totality of tensional experience.

These statements involve no new departure either for the psychologist or for the historian or other social scientist. Specialists in these fields have long taken an interest in the forms of cultural expression and have often included them in their studies. In this respect, the psycho-historical point of view might be expected merely to reinforce existing tendencies by promoting continued and increasing interrelationships between the humanities, psychology, and the social sciences.

(4) The psycho-historical theory is not a formula which can here be stated in any final or absolute form, nor which is fixed in terms of the present findings of any of its related disciplines. As we are presenting it, the theory is a partial indication of a correlational field that can change and grow in response to the

uses made of it and to the growth of knowledge in any or all of its component areas.

Instead of regarding the theory as a formula, the student must approach it as an exploration to be perpetually renewed. This is so for two reasons. On the one hand all the component areas are already so rich in material that no single effort nor formulation can hope to exhaust their resources for psycho-historical study. And on the other hand none of the component areas has reached a final state of completeness in which it can be accepted as an absolute authority. All the areas are developing; some of them rapidly so. In 1954, writing a preface to a new edition of a work originally published fourteen years earlier, Otto Klineberg says, "The field of social psychology is developing so actively and changing so rapidly that no writer can expect a textbook published in 1940 to be acceptable today." [1]

Thus, the student of psycho-history must continually seek to penetrate deeper into the existing funds of knowledge offered by the humanities, by psychology, and by the social sciences. And he must keep his eye on the growth horizons of all these fields for possible new contributions to the psycho-historical synthesis. The scope, the complexity, and the evolutionary movement of our area of study make it a difficult one for any single individual to master. Some of the significant results of future psycho-historical study, therefore, may come from teams of specialists each of whom has a general knowledge of his colleagues' fields, but who can also contribute a specialist's knowledge of his own field.

PART II

Chapter X

ART AND MYTH IN MEDIEVAL
WESTERN EUROPE —
WITH SUGGESTED EQUIVALENTS
FOR LOST PREDECESSORS

W e now have at our disposal a psycho-historical frame of reference in terms of which we can study cultural material, but we have thus far attempted to apply it only on a limited scale to a few examples. The aims of Part II will be twofold: to test the psycho-historical theory by making a more intensive analysis of some particular cultural situation; and to see whether we can throw any new light on the chosen situation by following the psycho-historical approach to it.

These aims could be accomplished by reference to any substantial area of human cultural activity. We could select for study one or more periods from prehistoric, ancient, medieval, renaissance, or modern times. We could use a primitive culture instead of an historic one; we could locate our context geographically in the Occident or the Orient, in Africa or the Americas. We have chosen instead the Western European Dark and Middle Ages, together with proposed equivalents for earlier material which Dark Age culture inherited but which is now lost to us in the obscurity of Western prehistory.

As a teacher of the history of art, the author had sometimes been asked by students why the medieval builders surrounded their cathedrals with grotesque chimeras and gargoyles like those shown in Figs. 14, 16 and 17. This was not an easy question to answer. Here was an illogical aspect of Gothic art as characteristic of the period as the logical one. One could expound with delight on the rational order of the structural system — as was done in the nineteenth century by Viollet-le-Duc and Charles Herbert Moore, and as has been done in the twentieth century by Erwin Panofsky — but the grotesque defies explanation on rational grounds. It presents an enigma, and its enigmatic character forces anyone concerned with it to search for meanings of a kind that heretofore have been ignored in the strictly "functional" interpretation of Gothic architecture.

The problem presented by the Gothic grotesque became thus one of the main points of departure for the series of investigations of which this book is a result. On the theoretical side, it called for principles applicable to the analysis of fantasy, thus promoting a study of depth psychology which eventually became a factor in the formation of psycho-historical synthesis. On the critical side, it led into an increasingly comprehensive effort to get at the psychological and social roots of medieval culture.

A moment's observation of the Gothic chimeras and gargoyles is sufficient to remind one that we no longer place figures of this kind on churches today — or that we do so only as eclectic imitators. Why did the Gothic builders, speaking from their hearts, complicate the spiritual exaltation of their cathedrals with hosts of these fantastic creatures?

So long as rationalistic attitudes dominated recent thought, attempts to answer this question were few and, for the most part, incidental to more factual concerns. Estheticians were content to define the grotesque in some such terms as "the fantastically misshapen" [1] and to classify it, along with the wild, the chaotic, and the gloomy, as a minor type of the sublime. Here and there we find an incidental reference to the medieval grotesque in connection with some other esthetic concept. Thus Raymond cites "grotesque gargoyles and pew carvings like those of the Middle Ages" among the exceptions to his rule that "no conception should be put into stone. . . that is not in itself sufficiently grave, serious, and dignified to correspond in character to the material in which it is presented." [2]

Among the general historians of art, Pijoan disposes of the Gothic grotesques simply as "fanciful monsters"; [3] Helen Gardner, in her widely used textbook, as "fantastic and chimerical forms of the world of imagination. . . born probably of pure fancy." [4]

Elaborate monographs on medieval art go little further in this direction, as may be illustrated by such monumental works as Arthur Kingsley Porter's *Lombard Architecture* and Emile Mâle's *Religious Art in France, XIII Century*. Porter devotes a chapter to the grotesques of the Lombard churches. His analysis of the subject is summarized in the following sentences:

"The Lombard grotesques are, therefore, fantastic creations of the imagination, quite innocent of symbolism, and designed solely for the purpose which they so admirably fill — that of amusing and delighting whoever sees them.

"The Lombard builders came into their grotesque by honest inheritance. This element was taken over from the Romans by the Early Christians, and, in fact, has never wholly disappeared from Western art. It is probable, however, that the extreme popularity of grotesques in the Lombard period was caused — at least in part — by the fact that they were easier to execute than serious figure sculptures. In the VIII century the artists found their skill hardly adequate for the representation of the human form." [5]

Porter's three explanations of the grotesque — fancifulness, stylistic influence, and technical incompetence — are typical of traditional attitudes toward such problems. While there may be partial truth in some of these explanations, they completely overlook the workings of unconscious psychological fantasy as the main source of the grotesque.

Mâle goes slightly further. "What can be the meaning," he asks, "of the long-necked gargoyles which howl there in the heights. . . ? No age has conceived more terrible spectres, partly wolf, partly caterpillar, partly bat, yet with a strange and horrible appearance of reality. . . The fact is that conceptions of this kind are essentially of popular origin. The gargoyles like churchyard vampires, or the dragons subdued by ancient bishops, came from the depths of the people's consciousness, and had grown out of ancient fireside tales." [6]

In his reference to "the depths of the people's consciousness," Mâle approaches the threshold beyond which a deeper understanding could be gained, but there he stops. What lay behind those depths, or why they engendered monster fantasies, he does not attempt to determine. Nor can we blame him. Prior to the cultural assimilation of psychoanalytical conceptions, the student of art had no instrument by means of which the products of fantasy could be successfully analyzed. The chief contributions of Mâle, and of his contemporaries and predecessors in the field of art history, had to extend in other directions.

Within the past few decades all this has changed. The psychoanalysts have recognized fantasy as one of the basic expressions of mental life, the ethnologists have discovered that myths are significantly related to the cultural conditions in which they arise, and many of the productions of contemporary writers and artists indicate that our own culture is motivating a trend toward symbolic, as contrasted with factual, modes of expression. The whole drift of our intellectual life has been such as to inspire a new interest in, and a new attitude toward, the chimerical, the fantastic, and the mythical aspects of the world's cultural heritage, including the medieval grotesque.

In view of this trend, any tendency to regard the grotesque as less signifi-cant than more rational forms of art, any dismissal of it as "merely fanciful," would no longer be possible. On the contrary, we must assume with regard to the chimeras and gargoyles, as Freud remarked with regard to dreams and neurotic symptoms, that however "confused and incomprehensible" they may at first appear, they nevertheless "have a meaning, serve a purpose, and arise from the patient's [in our case the community's] experience of life."[7] In short, we must accord to these forms of medieval art the respect and serious atten-tion due the most profound expressions of human experience — expressions which are the more significant for the very reason that they involve a revela-tion of the unconscious.

Stated in psycho-historical terms, the grotesque appears to be a symbol, unconsciously created, of collective psychic states that existed in medieval com-munities, psychic states which in turn owed their nature to the historical cir-cumstances of medieval life. Consequently, our interpretive problem becomes one of attempting to discover the nature of the underlying collective tensions and of the historical circumstances that caused them, in order that we may recognize the meaning of the symbol and the appropriateness of the place given to it in the religious architecture of the Middle Ages.

This problem can be approached better if we include in its range not only the grotesques of the cathedrals, but also the cultural context of which they are a part. Let us see, therefore, whether there are other aspects of medieval culture that merge with the carved and painted grotesque in a broader field of fan-tastic imagery. Let us also consider whether there is an evolutionary sequence of changing imagery in the Gothic grotesque that may help to reveal its mean-ing.

II

New dimensions of the problem open up before us when we turn from medieval art to medieval literature. Here, creatures akin to gargoyles and chimeras come to life, assert their presence in the world of human affairs, and reveal the spirit by which they are animated. Quotations from three typical descriptions of them will serve to give the reader a firsthand impression of their character and of their significance for the medieval mind.

The first of these quotations is chosen because it deals with a dragon, a type of creature that appears frequently in the grotesque and that is, in fact, the subject of the chimera most in evidence in our view of the apse balustrade of Amiens Cathedral (Fig. 14). Our quotation is taken from Malory's *Le Morte d'Arthur* which was not completed until 1469, a century or more after the probable date of our Amiens carvings. But *Le Morte d'Arthur* emanates from England, one of the northern European countries that clung longest to medieval traditions. Furthermore — and more important — Malory's work is based on earlier French romances of the Gothic period, and its inspirational source lies in a mentality characteristic in many respects of Gothic culture.

In the portion of Malory that concerns us — chapters V to X of book XIV — Sir Perceval, without realizing it at first, is being pursued by the devil. Tricked out of his own horse in a remote wilderness, he is offered a splendid black one by a woman who stipulates that he must fulfill her will when summoned. Perceval mounts the new horse:

"And within an hour and less he bare him four days' journey thence, until he came to a rough water the which roared, and his horse would have borne him into it.

"And when Sir Percivale came nigh the brim, and saw the water so boistous, he doubted to overpass it. And then he made a sign of the cross in his forehead. When the fiend felt him so charged he shook off Sir Percivale, and he went into the water crying and roaring, making great sorrow, and it seemed unto him that the water brent. Then Sir Percivale perceived it was a fiend, the which would have brought him into his perdition. Then he commended himself unto God. . . then he saw that he was in a wild mountain the which was closed with the sea nigh all about, that he might see no land about him which might relieve him, but wild beasts.

"And then he went into a valley, and there he saw a young serpent bring a young lion by the neck, and so he came by Sir Percivale. ["Serpent" is here to be read "dragon," as indicated by the illustration of the event, drawn about 1400, that is reproduced in Fig. 15.] With that came a great lion crying and roaring after the serpent. And as fast as Sir Percivale saw this he marvelled, and hied him thither, but anon the lion had overtaken the serpent and began battle with him. And then Sir Percivale thought to help the lion, for he was the more natural beast of the two; and therewith he drew his sword, and set his shield afore him, and there he gave the serpent such a buffet that he had a deadly wound. When the lion saw that, he made no resemblaunt to fight with him, but made him all the cheer that a beast might make a man.

Then Percivale perceived that, and cast down his shield which was broken; and then he did off his helmet for to gather wind, for he was greatly enchafed with the serpent: and the lion went alway about him fawning as a spaniel. And then he stroked him on the neck and on the shoulders. And then he thanked God of the fellowship of that beast. And about noon the lion took his little whelp and trussed him and bare him there he came from." [8]

Later the lion returned to Perceval "so all that night the lion and he slept together; and when Sir Percivale slept he dreamed a marvellous dream, that there were two ladies met with him, and that one sat upon a lion, and that the other sat upon a serpent, and that one of them was young, and the other was old." During the course of the dream the lady on the lion warned Perceval: "Make thee ready, for to-morn thou must fight the strongest champion of the world." The lady on the dragon said in part, "I have nourished in this place a great while a serpent, which served me a great while, and yesterday ye slew him as he gat his prey. . . I would, said she, for the amends of my beast that ye become my man. And then he answered: That will I not grant you. No, said she, truly ye were never but my servant sin ye received the homage of Our Lord Jesu Christ. Therefore, I ensure you in what place I may find you without keeping I shall take you, as he that sometime was my man."

On the morrow there appeared a ship bearing "an old man clothed in a surplice, in likeness of a priest," who provided the following interpretation of the dream: "She which rode upon the lion betokeneth the new law of holy church, that is to understand, faith, good hope, belief, and baptism. For she seemed younger than the other it is great reason, for she was born in the resurrection and the passion of Our Lord Jesu Christ. . . And she that rode on the serpent signifieth the old law, and that serpent betokeneth a fiend. And why she blamed thee that thou slewest her servant, it betokeneth nothing; the serpent that thou slewest betokeneth the devil that thou rodest upon to the rock."

For the moment we need comment on this passage only to the effect that the dragon, which we are likely to think of as a conception independent of religious themes, is here presented as an intrinsic part of them. It is revealed as a form of fiend: one of the actors in the conflict between good and evil which has its ultimate protagonists in Christ and the devil. In fact all the characters in the story range themselves on one side or the other of this spiritual contest. Like the dragon, the woman who offered Sir Perceval the black horse, the horse itself, the lady on the serpent, and a beautiful young woman by whom

Perceval was almost to be seduced on the day after his dream, all turn out to be fiends or disguises of the devil. Correspondingly the lion, "she that rode upon the lion," the old man "in the likeness of a priest" and, in human measure, Sir Perceval himself, all have their places in the task force of "Our Lord Jesu Christ."

Our next two quotations from medieval literature are similar to the above in assuming that fiends may appear in an almost infinite number of guises, but somewhat different and more fantastic in the particular apparitions described. The following passage is taken from the *Book of Miracles*, written by Peter the Venerable, friend of St. Bernard, in the twelfth century. It is thus contemporaneous with later Romanesque and early Gothic architecture.

"At another time another brother, who was a carpenter, lay by night in a place somewhat removed from the rest. The place was lighted with a lamp, as is customary in the dormitories of monks. While he lay on his bed, not yet asleep, he beheld a monstrous vulture, whose wings and feet were scarce able to bear the load of his vast body, labouring and panting toward him, until it stood over against his bed. While the brother beheld this in amazement, behold! two other demons in human form came and spake with that vulture — or rather, that fiend — saying, 'What doest thou here? Canst thou do any work in this place?' 'Nay,' said he; 'for they all thrust me hence by protection of the cross and by sprinkling water and by muttering psalms. I have laboured hard all this night, consuming my strength in vain; wherefore . . . tell me where ye have been and how ye have prospered.' To which the others made reply: 'We are come from Chalons, where we made one of Geoffrey of Donzy's knights fall into adultery with his host's wife. Then again we passed by a certain monastery, where we made the master of the school to fornicate with one of his boys. But thou, sluggard, why dost not thou arise, and at least cut off the foot of this monk, which he hath stretched in disorderly fashion beyond his bedclothes?' Whereupon the other seized the monk's axe which lay under the bed, and heaved it up to smite with all his force. The monk, seeing the axe thus raised aloft, withdrew his foot in fear; so that the demon's stroke fell harmlessly on the end of the bed; whereupon the evil spirits vanished forthwith. The brother who had seen this vision related it all forthwith, next morning, to the aforesaid father Hugh, who sent to Chalons and to Tournus to assure himself of the truth thereof. Here, searching narrowly into those things which the demons had asserted, he found that these ministers of lies had told the truth." [9]

Of similar significance, but with the demon appearing under different forms
and attacking his victim more malignantly, is the following passage from *Les
Grandes Chroniques de St. Denis*. The first version of these chronicles was
presented to the king of France by the monks of Saint-Denis in 1274, but the
present passage is a somewhat later addition. The incident that it records is
dated 1303, which places it in the high Gothic era shortly after the culmination of the style in cathedrals like those of Paris, Reims, and Amiens.

"This same year, on the Saturday before Christmas, a Lay-Brother of Vaux-
Cernay, of the Order of Citeaux, whose name was Adam. . . awoke before
daybreak. . . and set out on horseback with a servant on foot by his side. . .
as he rode along, saying his accustomed prayers in lieu of matins and hours,
he saw before him as it were a great tree in the road whereby he went, which
said tree (as he thought) came hastily to meet him. Then his horse fell
a-trembling and became half crazy, so that he had much ado to guide him in
the right way; and his servant, for his part, began to shudder, and the hairs
of his head stood on end, and he was smitten with so great an horror that he
could scarce stand on his feet or follow after his master. Then the same tree
began to draw near unto the Lay-Brother aforesaid; and, when it was come
nigh, it seemed dark and as it were covered with hoar-frost. Seeing this, he
would fain have ridden by without touching it; but there issued therefrom a
hideous stench of corruption. Then the Lay-Brother knew this was the Devil,
who would have done him harm; wherefore he set himself to cry upon the
Blessed Virgin Mary as devoutly as he might. So, after that he had recom-
mended himself to our Lady, he began to ride very slowly, as one in sore
dismay; then again he saw the devil riding behind him on his right side; and
the fiend seemed in human form, some two feet distant from the Brother
aforesaid; yet no word did he say. Then the Brother took heart of grace and
spake unto the Devil, saying: 'Evil one, how art thou so bold as to assail me
at this hour, when my Brethren sing their matins and lauds, praying for me
and for the other absent Brethren to God and the Blessed Virgin Mary. . .
Get thee hence, for thou has no part or lot with me, who have vowed myself a
servant of the Virgin."

The devil vanished momentarily at this admonition, but reappeared later in
a number of different forms: first, as a "man of great stature," then, "in the garb
of a black man . . . with big gleaming eyes like unto two copper cauldrons
newly furbished." Finally, he took "the shape of a strange beast, having great
ears like unto an ass." The brother now "went to meet the Devil on foot, and

began to assail him with many injurious and reviling words; and at length he spat in his face. Then the Devil changed his great ears into horns, and it seemed as though he were a horned ass: seeing which the Lay-Brother would have cut off one of his horns; but his stroke leapt back as though he had smitten upon a marble stone, for it did the Devil no harm. Then cried the servant to his master, 'Sir, make upon yourself the sign of the cross.' Then the said Brother signed himself, whereupon the Devil went suddenly thence, in the shape of a great rolling barrel, toward a town called Molières that lay hard by; and that brother saw him no more." [10]

Such passages as these — and they could be duplicated by many others — throw considerable light on the Gothic grotesque. It is evident in the first place that all the fantastic creatures described by our authors have their equivalents in the carvings which we group together as grotesque. The dragon is a common theme for writer and sculptor; "monstrous vultures" and "strange beasts, having great ears like unto an ass" can be found among the chimeras and gargoyles as well as in the chronicles — and so, for that matter, can lions, ladies riding various animals, and siren forms of womankind.

When we consider the carvings in light of the literary accounts, it seems obvious likewise that to the medieval mind the grotesque had far more than a decorative significance. We present-day observers first become acquainted with creatures like these when we see their carved or painted images. We therefore regard them primarily as forms of art. To the people of the Middle Ages the situation was reversed. Their psychic world had been haunted by such beings long before the cathedrals were built. They conceived them as living realities that any human being might personally encounter at any moment. When they eventually reduced these concepts to artistic form, they were merely recording certain facts of experience as they understood them.

It further seems apparent from the passages quoted that these creatures were conceived as forms of monster, demon, or fiend all of whom were agents of one central evil force incarnated in the Devil, and some of whom might be apparitions of the Devil in person. This being the case, it seems difficult to escape the conclusion that the grotesque is just what we originally assumed that it was not — that is to say essentially *religious* in character.

Religion, throughout most of its history, is far from being a matter of beatitude and salvation exclusively. For each of its positive elements there is a negative counterpart: for heaven, hell; for God, the Devil; for the saints, the demons. Without the latter term in each equation the former would have had no meaning, or at any rate no urgency. There can be no poignant sense of salvation if there is no danger from which to be saved. Such figures as the Virgin were "blessed" in medieval life precisely because mortals could turn to them for succor when pressed by difficulty or threatened with disaster, as did Lay Brother Adam when confronted by the Devil on the lonely road at dawn. The powers of evil are inevitable actors in the drama of religious experience and it is with these powers, it would seem, that the grotesque is associated.

This religious interpretation of the grotesque gains weight if we approach the subject from the opposite direction. Suppose that instead of beginning with the puzzling grotesque and looking for possible explanations of it, we start with the patently religious aspects of Gothic art such as the Last Judgment scenes, and that we examine their infernos and other negative imagery. Do we find a repertory of forms different from that of the grotesque? On the contrary, we find one that is indistinguishable from it.

The demons that carry off mankind (Fig. 18) are grotesque creatures. The artist knew no other way to represent them than through deformation, or unnatural combinations, of natural forms that we define as grotesque. Furthermore, as our Perceval story has already suggested, monsters that seem to us secular, like the dragon, intermingle freely with the demons in the Gothic religious context. In the carving of Potiphar's wife at Chartres (Fig. 19), the tempting devil appears not in deformed human guise but as a dragon. Dragon and devil are in fact interchangeable motifs in the Gothic imagery of evil. Both of them, along with various natural beasts, appear under the feet of saints (Fig. 20) as symbols of the powers of evil overcome by the power of goodness.

In Giotto's rendering of the Inferno in the Arena Chapel (Fig. 22), we see not only the horned Lucifer in obese human form and various demons in somewhat ape-like deformations of humanity, but five separate dragons, all striking or swallowing human beings: two at the haunches of Lucifer, two at his head, and one attacking the figure in his right hand.

Another common creature of the chimeras and gargoyles, the lion, seems in Gothic times to have emerged from a former negative status to a degree of positivism recalling man's domesticated animal friends. The Perceval story illustrates both the friendly lion and the vestiges of its negative associations. The fact that the lion "made no resemblaunt to fight with him" seems to both writer and reader a rather miraculous exception to negative expectancies. For a somewhat equivalent status in the visual arts, we may look to the column bearers of the thirteenth-century Italian churches (Fig. 21). These lions do not figure in the demonology of the period, but they occupy a marginal position in the religious context — a position akin to that of the monsters under the feet of saints. As an architectural base, their function is a positive one, but at the same time a function that is low in the scheme of things and that firmly limits them by virtue of the weight of the superstructure.

In answering the question that opened this section, we seem safe in concluding that the apparent incongruity in the use of the grotesque on religious architecture has been due to a misunderstanding, in our later and more rational minds, of the nature of the grotesque itself. It no longer seems incongruous as we come to realize that the creatures of the chimeras and gargoyles are forms of negative religious imagery, or of one-time negative religious imagery which is emerging toward a positive status. The grotesques of the eaves and parapets which we first considered (Figs. 14, 16, 17) might be regarded as demons recumbent — demons resting for a moment, as do the birds, on the upper reaches of the cathedral — while the examples subsequently examined (Figs. 15, 18, 19) show them rampant in their demonic activities. And since their identity appears in general to be demonic, their presence on the cathedrals is as natural as that of the Devil in the Christian gospels. The position at which we thus arrive had already been forecast by Emile Mâle when he compared the gargoyles to "churchyard vampires, or the dragons subdued by ancient bishops," thus identifying them with powers of evil that had been overcome by the Church.

In considering this answer to our original question concerning the grotesque, some readers may be inclined to raise two further questions. If the chimeras and gargoyles are related to demonic conceptions, how does it happen that many of them appear more humorous than terrible? And if demonic elements are intrinsic to religious impulse, why does it seem unnatural to us to incorporate similar fantasies in religious architecture today?

In addition we may well raise an even wider issue. A religious interpretation of the grotesque carries us a step further than an esthetic one in our understanding of medieval art, but only a step. Religion itself, if accepted in terms of any particular set of religious formulas, is comparatively a surface phenomenon. If we would seek ultimate answers to our questions, we must attempt to find out what lies behind and below these formulas.

Such an effort is particularly necessary for twentieth-century observers like ourselves. Living seven hundred years after the Gothic era, we are conditioned by a far less mystical and more scientific age. We still recognize dangers and evil forces in life, but we normally attribute them to germs, unbalanced economic systems, human conflicts, or other natural causes, not to dragons, "monstrous vultures," or "strange beasts, having great ears like unto an ass." To us the latter seem obviously creatures of myth or legend. Any interpretation of them which can satisfy us today must penetrate beneath the surface of their religious context and attempt to determine why the human mind during the Middle Ages evolved and credited these mythical fantasies.

All these additional questions can best be approached in terms of a dimension to which we have as yet given no careful thought: the evolutionary one. Although the grotesque in particular, and medieval religious art in general, are sometimes treated as if they were fixed entities, they are quite otherwise. Like all other cultural phenomena, they are currents in a historical flow, changing in force and character as they respond to the changing conditions of different stages of their historical course. The changes which they have undergone are as important for an understanding of their nature as is their character at any given time. In order to familiarize ourselves with these changes, let us next compare the high Gothic fantasies thus far considered with others to which they are related in an evolutionary sequence.

III

In general terms, the creatures we have been observing may be described as monster fantasies or forms of negative tension imagery. The examples thus far considered have centered around the thirteenth-century noon of the Gothic period, with some extension backward to its twelfth-century morning and forward to its fourteenth-century afternoon and fifteenth-century dusk.

We shall not attempt to cast more than a glance at the fortunes of the European monsters during the epochs that succeeded the Middle Ages. Broadly speaking, these epochs witnessed the decline and fall of monster imagery. The Renaissance occasionally used its new realism to give an air of grim factuality to traditional monster themes — Carpaccio's *St. George* comes to mind as an example — but in general the course of the monsters was a downward one. Their decadence most frequently manifested itself in one or the other of two ways. Either they were used stiffly as a conventional ornament, like the griffins of the Renaissance picture frame shown in Fig. 23, or serious monsterly ambitions were abandoned in favor of the whimsical status which appears so frequently in the sixteenth-century *misericordes*. Fig. 24 shows one of the latter in which a domesticated chimera is ridden by a monkey. This jocular attitude toward the monsters even finds expression in *mondes renverses* in which devils boil in the pot under the surveillance of the human beings who would once have been their victims (Fig. 25). By the seventeenth century, even the ornamental or the whimsical monster was a rarity. Monster fantasies had largely ceased to exist in the European mind.

If we start again with the Gothic period and move backward in time — which will be the main direction of our evolutionary study — a reverse trend shows itself. As we work our way through Romanesque art of the early Middle Ages to the pre-Romansque art of the Dark Ages, monster imagery increases in frequency, in ferocity, and in the importance of the positions given to it in religious architecture. In observing this trend, allowance must of course be made for regional advances and retardations in different parts of Europe, and for differences of skill and personal motivation among individual artists. Dates for any given stage of the trend will vary somewhat with these variable factors, but the general drift is unmistakable.

The tinge of humor that often reveals itself in Gothic demons is rarely found in Romanesque ones. The latter are more gruesome in aspect and attack their victims more malignantly, as may be seen in Figs. 26 and 27. The ghastliness of the nightmare can be felt in many of these scenes; the victims may be violently racked by swift-moving tormentors as in the capital from Vezelay (Fig. 27).

Combats between heroes and monsters become a more constant and a more absorbing subject for the artist and are instilled with a new vigor. In what we may call a transitional phase — transitional in terms of the changing tension imagery with which we are concerned — Romanesque heroes overcome their foes with a delightful athletic vigor, as in the Samson relief, Fig. 28, and to a lesser extent in the St. George, Fig. 29.

In general, as we move backward in time, the battle becomes grimmer, the monster larger in comparison with the hero, and the outcome of the combat less certain. We may see the hero standing up with doughty courage to a monster larger and stronger than himself (Fig. 30), and we may see him vanquished (Fig. 31). The heroes who experience these vicissitudes may relate to Biblical sources, as does Samson, to subsequent Christian legends like that of St. George, or to Teutonic myths which may or may not be identifiable at the present time. These literary assimilations are the verbal surface of the imagery rather than its basic character. What we have before us, fundamentally, is the Western European stream of monster-hero fantasy; a stream that sometimes drew its allusions from external sources, but always received its dynamics from the internal tensions of the Western cultures in which it flowed.

For a literary account of monster-hero combat that is close in tensional character to the plastic examples just considered, we turn to Eilhart von Oberg's metrical version of the Tristan legend, which was written in German about the year 1180. As a point of comparison, we should recall Malory's later rendering of the Perceval legend. Perceval, according to Malory, slew his dragon almost without combat, giving it but a single "buffet." Tristan, according to Eilhart, has a more formidable task to accomplish.

"Now it chanced once upon the break of day that he heard a cry so terrible that one would have called it a demon's cry; nor had he ever heard a brute bellow in such wise, so awful and strange it seemed. He called a woman who passed by the harbour, and said:

"'Tell me, lady, whence comes the voice I have heard and hide me nothing.'

"'My lord,' said she, 'I will tell you truly. It is the roar of a dragon the most terrible and dauntless upon earth. Daily it leaves its den and stands at one of the gates of the city: Nor can any come out or go in till a maiden has been given up to it; and when it has her in its claws it devours her in less time than it takes to say a Pater Noster.'

"'Lady,' said Tristan, 'make no mock of me, but tell me straight: Can a man born of woman kill this thing?'

"'Fair sir, and gentle,' she said, 'I cannot say; but this is sure: Twenty knights and tried have run the venture, because the King of Ireland has published it that he will give his daughter, Iseult the Fair, to whomsoever shall kill the beast; but it has devoured them all.'

"Tristan left the woman and returning to his ship armed himself in secret, and it was a fine sight to see so noble a charger and so good a knight come out of a merchant-hull: but the haven was empty of folk, for the dawn had barely broken and none saw him as he rode to the gate. And hardly had he passed it, when he met suddenly five men at full gallop flying towards the town. Tristan seized one by his red braided hair, as he passed, and dragged him over his mount's crupper and held him fast:

"'God save you, my lord,' said he, 'and whence does the dragon come?' And when the other had shown him by what road, he let him go.

"As the monster neared, he showed the head of a bear and red eyes like coals of fire and hairy tufted ears; lion's claws, serpent's tail, and a griffin's body.

"Tristan charged his horse at him so strongly that, though the beast's mane stood with fright yet he drove at the dragon: his lance struck its scales and shivered. Then Tristan drew his sword and struck at the dragon's head, but he did not so much as cut the hide. The beast felt the blow: with his claws he dragged at the shield and broke it from the arm; then his breast unshielded, Tristan used the sword again and struck so strongly the air rang all round about: but in vain, for he could not wound and meanwhile the dragon vomited from his nostrils two streams of loathesome flames, and Tristan's helm blackened like a cinder and his horse stumbled and fell down and died; but Tristan standing on his feet thrust his sword right into the beast's jaws, and split its heart in two. The dragon uttered his hideous scream a last time and died.

"Then he cut out the tongue and put it into his hose, but as the poison came against his flesh the hero fainted and fell in the high grass that bordered the marsh around." [11]

The examples thus far reviewed have shown power of the Romanesque monsters, the desperate encounters in which the heroes meet them, and the fact that the heroes are not always victorious. Also noteworthy are the depredations attributed to the monsters when there is no hero sufficiently strong to overcome them. Prior to Tristan's arrival, Eilhart's dragon had devoured "twenty knights and tried" and had daily blocked one of the city gates "until a maiden was given up to it." Such ravaging monsters, unchecked in their inroads upon humanity, provide a frequent theme for the sculptor of the Romanesque churches. In one Lombard carving, Fig. 32, a dragon gulps down a victim while his companion flees with arms uplifted in a gesture of futility. Fig. 33, with its helpless individual between two great rampant beasts, provides another illustration of the unhappy mythical position to which humanity could now be reduced. And when we find lions or other monsters below the feet of Romanesque saints or under Romanesque columns, they are not only larger, more independent, and more frightening than their Gothic successors; frequently, as in Fig. 34, they hold dead human victims in their claws.

These examples lead us into a world of feverish Romanesque imagery in which man is ravaged by all manner of monsters and in which all manner of monsters ravage each other. The famous trumeau at Souillac, a detail of which is shown in Fig. 35, is one of the best known examples of this nightmarish phantasmagoria. Figs. 36 and 37 provide two other examples. In the former, the sculptor has conveyed an impression of real horror in the way the shrieking victims head is jerked backward by the great bear-like monster, and in Fig. 37, monsters of primeval ferocity struggle with each other.

As compared to Gothic monsters, these Romanesque ones show a gain, not only in negative intensity, but also in position. None of the examples we have been observing come from such remote locations as the buttresses and balustrades that formed the characteristic habitat of the Gothic demons and gargoyles. Two of our Romanesque examples (Figs. 27 and 36) are capitals in the interior of churches. The remainder are, or originally were, associated with façades and in most cases with the focal points in the façades, the church portals. The Souillac trumeau originally stood in the central position between the two doors of its portal. Three of our examples (Figs. 29, 31, 33), occupy one of the dominant positions among all church sculpture: the large relief of the tympanum above the doorways. When we consider that Fig. 33, with its helpless victim and its two great beasts, occupies this position; when we consider how different is this imagery from the calm Last Judgments, with their dominant Christs, characteristic of so many Gothic tympanums, we cannot but recognize a marked change of attitude between the conceptions of the two periods.

Before we leave the demons, monsters, and heroes of the Romanesque epoch, it should be noted that although sculptured examples survive in relatively large numbers throughout Europe, many more have been lost. Erosion of exposed sculpture, destruction or alteration of buildings, and removal of images that later came to seem barbaric and uncouth, have all taken their toll.

A large relief of a human being between two immense monsters, imbedded in the façade of the church at Beaulieu, France (Fig. 38), retains only the dim outlines of what must originally have been one of the most striking Romanesque embodiments of the kind of subject that concerns us. In cases where the sculpture has been removed from its original position through the destruction of the buildings or for other reasons, it may or may not have been preserved. Museums of art give sanctuary to many capitals, plaques, and other fragments. Now and again, in some lapidary salvage yard, among the fallen stones of one-time buildings (Fig. 39), the reigning monster of some vanished portal survives to tell us a little more about the fantasies of vanished men and their society.

If we try to follow Western demon and monster-hero themes still farther back into the so-called Dark Ages, the loss increases in proportion to the distance backward in time, but the evolutionary line is clear. The trend already observed, that of increasing intensification and importance of negative imagery, continues. Representational vividness in visual art decreases, for we are moving back beyond the rise of Western realism into the era of archaic conventionality, but the artist has devices for conveying his meaning. In the ninth-century barbarian plaque (Fig. 42) the relative size of the monster, as compared to that of the hero and his horse, is many times larger than in any of the Romanesque or Gothic examples. That the fight is correspondingly fiercer may be judged from the oldest remaining literary document of the Teutonic peoples, the seventh-century poem *Beowulf*.

Monsters constitute three of the principle actors in this Old English epic, the fourth being the hero, Beowulf, who is able to meet and overcome them. In the earlier episodes of the poem the foe takes the form of two monsters, Grendel and his mother, "fell spoilers," "doers of mischief," "mighty prowlers along the borders of the homes of men." "One of these was, so far as they might most carefully judge, in form like a woman; the other misbegotten one in man's shape trod the path of exile, save that he was greater in size than any man." [12] But though manlike and capable, (as did Grendel's mother in her struggle with Beowulf,) of using implements such as a dagger, their "terrible claws" are also referred to on more than one occasion.

These creatures move with a swiftness, strike with a ferocity, and work a gruesome havoc, even greater than the dragon in Eilhart's *Tristam*. Witness the arrival of Grendel at Heorot, the mead hall of the Danes, which he had ravaged many times before and to which Beowulf has gone for the purpose of meeting him in mortal combat.

"Quickly then the fiend trod in on the shining floor, strode on, fierce of mood. An unlovely light, likest to flame, stood in his eyes. He saw in the hall many warriors sleeping, a fellowship of one blood assembled together, the throng of kinsfolk. Then his heart laughed within him. He thought, the grisly monster, ere day came, to sunder life from body of each of them, for hope of a full feasting had come to him.

". . . The monster thought not to be long about it, but for a first start seized quickly on a sleeping thane, tore him taken unawares, bit into his bone frame, drank the blood from the veins, and swallowed him down piece by piece. Soon had he bolted all the lifeless body, hand and foot."

Only in bitter hand-to-hand combat, at peril of his own life, is Beowulf able to overcome these monsters: Grendel at Heorot that night; his mother a few days later in her hall at the bottom of the sea. The intensity of the hero's struggles may be judged from the poet's comment on the first of these encounters.

"The lordly hall was clamorous with din. Panic fell on all the Danes that dwelt in the city, on every bold warrior and earl. Maddened were the raging strugglers; the building reëchoed. It was great wonder, then, that it did not fall, the fair dwelling of man's making, to the earth . . . Quaking terror lay upon the North Danes, upon those who heard the outcry, hearkened God's foe yelling out his stave of terror, his song of defeat, the thrall of hell bewailing his hurt."

In the second part of the poem evil again descends upon mankind, this time in the form of a dragon. "The old twilight-spoiler, the evil naked dragon, that flaming seeketh out the barrows and flieth by night enfolded in fire . . . Him the earth-dwellers dread exceedingly.

"A fearful thing was the feud's beginning for the people of the land. Then the stranger-one began to spew forth gledes [flames] and burn the bright homesteads; the glare of the burning struck terror into men; the loathy flyer through the air was minded to leave naught there alive. The dragon's might was seen far and wide, how the war-spoiler hated and brought low the Geat-folk. He shot back, ere daybreak, to his hoard, to his lordly hall hidden from finding. The dwellers in the land he had beset with flames, with fire and burning. The fire-drake with his flames had laid in ashes the stronghold, the people's fastness."

From the ravages of this enemy Beowulf in turn rescued the people, but this time at the cost of his own life. The narrative of the fight in which they kill each other includes the following passage: "Then the spoiler of the people, the fell fire-drake, was of mind a third time for strife, rushed, hot and battle-grim, upon the valiant one, when he gave him ground, and with his bitter fangs took in all the throat of the hero. Beowulf was bloodied with his life-blood; the blood welled forth in waves."

Relatively few visual renderings of the Dark Age monster myths have come down to us. We have already referred to the Italian plaque showing an unidentified hero in combat with an immense griffin (Fig. 42). Three other surviving examples are reproduced in Figs. 40, 41, 43. All three, like *Beowulf*, are of Norse origin. The oldest shown (Figs. 40, 41) are from a series of bronze plates ascribed by archeologists to the Vendel period of Norse art; a period that extended from the fifth through the seventh century A.D. It would be of great interest for our purpose to know precisely what these plates represent but that, to judge from the comments of Scandinavian experts, is no longer possible. "The world which we see in these images is a colorful one of legend and fantasy" writes the Swedish archeologist, Holger Arbman, ". . . but the mythological or cult representations behind these scenes are lost to us." [13] Judging by the plates themselves, and by the fact that they date from the same epoch as *Beowulf*, we would seem to be justified in assuming that they represent heroes and monsters similar to those presented by the poem. Thus, in Fig. 40, an armed and helmeted warrior is confronted by a creature which, like Grendel, is largely human and is capable of wielding sword and spear, but which also possesses certain animal features.

Fig. 43, a detail of the elaborate wood carving on a ceremonial wagon, dates from the early Viking period of about 800 A.D. In this case, authorities are able to identify the subject. It is a mythical incident later preserved for us in written form in the *Saga of the Volsungs*. It represents the death of the hero, Gunnar, in a snake pit into which he had been thrown by his enemies.[14] Like many other Dark Age myths, this one illustrates the fact that the heroes of the times are by no means always victorious. They succumb to the evil forces against them almost as frequently as they triumph.

IV

We have reviewed some typical forms of Western European demon and monster-hero imagery for a period extending back from the high Gothic Middle Ages through the earlier Romanesque era into the Teutonic Dark Ages. Our examples have dated from the fifteenth back to the fifth century and thus embrace a span of approximately a thousand years. If we now attempt to bring all this material into a single perspective, we are able to recognize that its historical relationships involve an evolutionary pattern.

The demons and monsters of the Gothic period occupy a relatively feeble and marginal position in the mythological cosmos — a position symbolized, among other ways, by the small monsters helplessly pinned beneath the feet of saints. As we have seen, the negative beings increase in importance and power as we move to the Romanseque. The positive imagery of saints and heroes undergoes an inverse destiny, decreasing from the calm dominance of the Gothic saint and savior to the grim resolution of the Dark Age hero who must fight a foe at least as strong as himself and who is killed by the monsters as often as he kills them.

These changing interrelationships between negative and positive imagery are indicated graphically by the solid lines of Diagram 5. Moving backwards in time, the demon-monster line rises from a low position to a higher one, the hero-savior line descends from a high position to a lower one, until in Dark Age mythology the two meet on the common level of equally matched hero and monster. Historically, the actual evolution was, of course, in a forward temporal direction. From a Dark Age phase in which hero and monster were equally matched, there was a gradual rise of the hero-savior line, a gradual decline of the monster line, until by Gothic times, the savior had become all-powerful and the demons and monsters subservient.

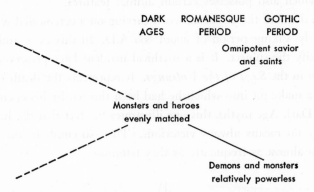

DARK   ROMANESQUE   GOTHIC
AGES   PERIOD   PERIOD

Omnipotent savior
and saints

Monsters and heroes
evenly matched

Demons and monsters
relatively powerless

Diagram 5. Graphic summary of evolutionary relationships between negative and positive mythical imagery during the Western European Dark and Middle Ages.

If these evolutionary lines were to be projected farther back in their established directions, as is done in the broken portion of the lines in the diagram, they would eventually suggest a reversal of the Gothic interrelationships. The continued decline of the hero-savior line, and the complementary rise of the monster line, would lead us to conceive of a primeval mythology in which the monsters were transcendent, the positive beings relatively powerless. Is there any evidence that this theoretical possibility was ever extant in actual myths?

So far as concerns the Western European sequence that we have been studying, we cannot answer this question either affirmatively or negatively, for the reason that no real evidence of a direct nature remains to us. Assuredly the Teutonic, Celtic, and other Western peoples of pre-fifth-century Europe had their myths, but of the nature of those myths we know practically nothing. Literary embodiments of them end with *Beowulf*. Beyond that stretches the silence of Western prehistory. It was a time that once rang with the songs, cries, and declamations of ritual and legend. Could those sounds have been recorded, as we today record the rituals of the Bantu and the Maori, and could we interpret the languages being used, we would have before us a mythology of surpassing interest. Since the sounds were not recorded, only the silence remains.

Visual art has come down to us from the early Western periods in question, but it gives us little help from the mythological point of view since it becomes increasingly abstract as we penetrate back beyond the Dark Ages. We have already had incidental occasion to note that realism decreases along the line of our investigation, Dark Age representations showing an archaic conventionality in style. If the reader will look again at our two oldest representations — the bronze plates of the Vendel period — he will find that in one of them (Fig. 41) the hair is dotted and the bodies hatched in a manner which amounts to a number of geometric patterns. These patterns are persistences of earlier traditions of geometric art which become increasingly dominant as we move through the Bronze Age and into Neolithic times. In European Neolithic art, representation of any kind is rare, monsters do not seem to figure in what little there is, and the most typical figurative expression of the period is geometrical patterns such as we find inscribed on so much Neolithic pottery (Fig. 44).

This absence of monster-hero themes in pre-Dark Age Western art might tempt us to assume that these earlier peoples were not exercised by tensional fantasies. But the same facts might also be explained by the contrary assumption — which would fit with the theoretical projection of our evolutionary lines — the assumption, namely, that in these earlier times the fantasies were negative ones experienced with hallucinatory and traumatic force. Fantasies of this kind are profoundly terrifying. Their terrifying character presumably leads men to banish them as largely as possible from consciousness rather than to create permanent images of them for contemplation. Conceivably both the absence of monster representations in pre-Dark Age art and its tendency to abstraction, are related to a traumatic psycho-social situation.

Such indirect evidence as we can bring to bear upon the question appears to support the latter view. This indirect evidence is of two main kinds: the comments on the Western barbarians left by Roman observers like Caesar and Tacitus, and the more recent anthropological studies of Neolithic and early metal cultures in other parts of the world.

The Roman commentators, unfortunately, were soldiers and administrators rather than priests or anthropologists. Their accounts were inevitably based upon external observation rather than upon subjective psychological experiences. Hence, the Roman accounts deal chiefly with the material rather than the psychic life of the barbarians. Tacitus, however, does make one reference of considerable interest to us. Certain Germanic tribes known as the Suebi, he says, "worship in common Nerthus, or Mother Earth," whose shrine is a holy grove "in an island of the ocean." During festivals in her honor she is described as riding away in a consecrated chariot drawn by cows. "After this the chariot and the robes, and, if you are willing to credit it, the deity in person, are washed in a sequestered lake: slaves are her ministrants and are straight-way swallowed up by the same lake: hence a mysterious terror and an ignorance full of piety as to what that may be which men only behold to die." [15]

The "mysterious terror" with which the Suebi regarded Nerthus and the "swallowing up" of men associated with her, strongly suggest that she may have been related to a type of monster of which we have fuller accounts from Neolithic societies in other parts of the world, and of which examples will be considered below.

This is about all we can say with regard to the mythology of Western Europe before the Dark Ages. Perhaps we should stop here, and accept the myths of the Dark and Middle Ages as all the material that is necessary for our psycho-historical interpretation. But there is one other source of indirect evidence pertinent to our problem which should be considered. That is the evidence of comparative mythology available in the accounts of explorers, anthropologists, and ethnologists.

When, in the fifteenth and sixteenth centuries, the world circle of racial migrations completed itself and civilized European man established contact with his primitive contemporaries on other continents, he discovered among them, as it were, living records of his own past. Many of these other races were still living under the conditions of the Stone Age. Among them, the Neolithic cultural patterns and mentality which had once characterized Europe, but which had faded from recollection during centuries of civilization, were still active realities. A vast store of information on these surviving prehistoric cultures has been accumulating during recent centuries; a store of information which is of great interest both in its own right and in relation to the lost myths of early Western Europe.

Material available to us from this source appears to support the theoretically projected portion of our evolutionary diagram. Examples are not lacking to substantiate all three of the theoretical suggestions advanced: First, that there is an early mythology of omnipotent monsters; second, that such monsters are not likely to be represented in art so long as a community's experience of them is traumatic; third, that the geometrical art frequently contemporaneous with transcendent monster myths may be in part a recoil from overwhelmingly negative imagery but may also, at least in some cases, refer to such imagery in a guarded indirect manner.

As an instance of the transcendent monster in a Neolithic culture, we may take the giant "Gougou" described to Samuel de Champlain by the Indians of northeastern Canada. Champlain's account of this monster, written in 1603, is as follows:

"There is another strange thing worthy of narration which many of the savages have assured me is true; this is, that near Chaleur Bay, toward the south, lies an island where makes his abode a dreadful monster, which the savages call Gougou. They told me it had the form of a woman, but most hideous, and of such size that according to them the tops of the masts of our vessel would not reach above his waist, so big do they represent him; and they say that he has often devoured and still devours many savages; these he puts, when he can catch them, into a great pocket, and afterwards eats them; and those who had escaped the danger of this ill-omened beast said that his pocket was so large he could put our vessel into it. This monster which the savages call Gougou makes horrible noises in that island, and when they speak of him it is with unutterably strange terror, and many have assured me that they have seen him. Even the above-mentioned Sieur Prevert from St. Malo told me that, while going in search of mines . . . he passed so near the haunts of this frightful beast, that he and all those on board his vessel heard strange hissings from the noise it made, and that the savages with him told him it was the same creature, and were so afraid they hid themselves wherever they could, for fear it should carry them off. And what makes me believe what they say, is the fact that all the savages in general fear it, and tell such strange stories of it that, if I were to record all they say, it would be considered untrue; but I hold that this is the dwelling place of some devil that torments them in the manner described. This is what I have learned about this Gougou." [16]

Another example of a gigantic man-eating monster and, as it happens, one that has survived to the present day in a part of the world north of the territory of Champlain's Indians, is the *windigo* of the Ojibwa Indians. We have had earlier occasion to quote Ruth Landes' description of this "giant skeleton made of ice . . . who howls and crashes through the land, threatening swift and horrible doom." [17]

Neither Gougou nor the *windigo*, it appears, were used by those who believed in them as subjects for visual representation in art. The same is apparently true in the case of another traumatic, or near traumatic, situation referred to in Part I: that of the Betsileo evil spirits. These instances demonstrate the fact that absence of monsters in the art of a given culture *can* signify the exact opposite of what we might at first suppose. Instead of coinciding with a parallel absence of monsters from the related mythology, it may coincide with mythical monsters so terrible that the artist and his society shrink from the contemplation of them. Psychic *re*pression of the traumatic image, it would seem, results in creative *sup*pression of the image from art.

Only when psychic readjustment has so far progressed as to counteract the negative tensions with emergent positive ones — only when the fears associated with the trauma are modified by a sense of recovery — does a will arise to contemplate the monsters through representations of them in the arts. Stated in terms of tension-imagery, the fantasies become a subject for art only when the dominance of the negative monster-image is offset by the rise of the positive imagery of a hero or other champion of humanity.

Our Gnawing-Squirrel totem provided an ethnological example of this kind of readjustment. The volcanic eruption that caused the original hallucinations took place in 1780; the carving of the totem was not made until approximately 1860. During the eighty years that separated the original trauma from its expression in art, the terror that caused the hallucinations had subsided. Recovery from the shock permitted certain individuals to conceive the fantasy of having "killed" the guardian of the monsters. What had once been a symbol of fear now became one of conquest and pride. It was the latter association that led to the adoption of the squirrel as a totem and to its visual representation on the pole.

The obverse of the same tensional dynamics might well help to motivate a tendency toward geometrical abstraction in the art of cultures ridden by fears of omnipotent monsters. When negative imagery is overpowering, positive imagery is so weak as to be negligible. If the negative mythological themes are suppressed from art and positive ones are not available to it, the resulting art is left without mythological subject matter. Only two resources remain to it. It can turn to the real objects of the external world for subject matter, or it can have recourse to abstraction through some form of nonrepresentational design. Abstraction seems to be its most frequent and characteristic response. Specific art objects are not available to substantiate this assertion with regard to the traumatic monster complexes cited above. We do know, however, that the pre-Columbian art of the Indians of northeastern Canada tended in general toward geometric abstraction. The same can be said of much of the art produced elsewhere by societies that survived on or near Neolithic cultural horizons.

The possibility still remains that some or all of this abstract art retains an indirect symbolic connection with the suppressed negative imagery. It would, in this case, act as a compromise formation that avoids the full contemplation of the monsters yet permits them indirect recognition. How frequently there is such a connection between monster concepts and abstract design will have to be determined by a wider study of comparative ethnology than has yet been made. One instance of such a connection that has come to the author's attention, is reported by André Gide in his account of a visit to the Massa tribes of equatorial Africa.

"Here and there," Gide writes, "sometimes in the country, sometimes at the edge of a village, or in the village itself; at the foot of a tree, anywhere in fact, one is surprised to see a small mound of earth, usually painted white, about the size and shape of a beehive. One asks for information — 'It is the devil,' one is told. I did not succeed in understanding whether they thought that the devil was actually inside the mound, whether it was a propitiary altar, a devil-trap, a protection or defense against devils. What is certain is that if you see one of these little monuments, a devil is involved." [18]

The form of these mounds being abstract, visual examination of them reveals only their abstraction and provides no clue to their symbolic meaning. Only a member of the society that produces the mounds, conversant with their motivation can reveal to us the fact that they are associated with a concept of the devil. We may presume that there are other known instances of such connections between an abstract form and a negative tension concept. Even more important, we may assume that the geometric art of cultures no longer extant may have involved such connections. Without surviving interpreters to indicate its symbolical meaning, that meaning is lost to us, though it may have been more important to the creators of the art than the formal effect which we now see.

V

The ethnological material reviewed in the preceding section can be related to our main context in one or both of two ways. In its own right as a sampling of mythological horizons dominated by transcendent monsters, it presents material of interest for psycho-historical analysis. When related to the Western

European myths that are our main concern at present, this ethnological material takes on a further significance. It appears in many respects to substantiate our theoretical assumptions regarding lost European material.

By following the Western myths as far back as we can trace them, we were led to assume a previous phase of transcendent monsters and nonexistent or impotent champions of mankind. Our ethnological examples have demonstrated the actual existence of such a phase in various parts of the world and the identification of that phase with Neolithic and post-Neolithic cultural horizons. These examples have also indicated, at least in a general way, that the dominant monster occurs in cultural complexes which tend toward geometrical forms of art, and that the geometrical forms sometimes involve symbolic references to nonrepresented monsters or devils.

With regard to our Western European sequence we are aware, not only that the monsters gained in dominance as far back as we can trace them, but also that the art became increasingly geometrical (Fig. 41). We also have surviving evidence of what seems to be one example of the transcendent monster in early European mythology: the account of Nerthus preserved for us by Tacitus. The island home of this goddess, the way she "swallows up" those who look upon her, and the "mysterious terror" with which she is regarded by the Suebi people, all suggest that we are looking — indirectly through the eyes of a sceptical Roman — at a being related in kind to Gougou and the *windigo*.

These correspondences seem, to the author at least, to justify us in hypothetically reconstructing the pre-Dark Age phase of our Western European mythical sequence. We shall postulate a Neolithic and early metal stage of transcendent monsters as an accompaniment to the abstract art and other material remains of these cultures that have come down to us. If this is done, we can now establish the full extent of the mythological sequence which is to be our immediate subject for psycho-historical analysis.

This sequence, so far as concerns the known myths of the Dark and Middle Ages, was already summarized in Diagram 5. We can put our concept of it into final form (Diagram 6) by repeating the former graph and filling in the blanks which we previously left with regard to its conjectural beginnings. We shall now assume that the parity of hero and monster in the Dark Ages was historically preceded by a stage of stronger monsters and weaker heroes emanating eventually from a time when the monster was all-powerful and the hero powerless if indeed he existed at all. We shall further assume that the cultural horizons associated with this phase were the same in Europe as elsewhere, and that therefore this type of European myth occurred during the Neolithic and early metal ages — which are, in fact, the periods preceding the Dark Ages that left us our oldest known myths.

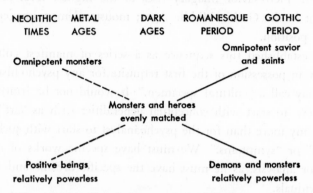

Diagram 6. Graphic summary of evolutionary relationships between negative and positive mythical imagery from Neolithic times to the European Middle Ages.

We shall still use broken lines on the left side of our diagram to indicate that, although a dominant monster phase is a known historical reality on Neolithic horizons, its connection with the later European material is that of a conjectured restoration. If the reader wishes to maintain his caution to the extent of doubting the justice of the restoration, he is free to do so. This should modify his attitude toward the remaining chapters of Part II only in one respect. He will regard our discussion of Neolithic psycho-history as an independent subject, preferring not to connect it with our subsequent analysis of the Dark and Middle Ages. He can still presumably accept all three of our main phases as historical realities, though he prefers not to connect the first with the second and third.

Assuming, as the author will do, that our three phases can occur and have occurred — probably at many different times and places — as successive stages of a single development, it seems clear that the negative and positive aspects of this development maintain a consistent and apparently meaningful relationship to each other. This relationship, graphically indicated by the lines of the diagram, may be described as an evolutionary complemental one. That is to say that the negative and positive mythical themes, in their passage through time, maintain continually inverse and gradually reversed positions with regard to each other. In Neolithic times, monster consciousness is at its highest point, hero consciousness at its lowest. Starting with these high and low points, the monster consciousness gradually decreases, the hero consciousness gradually increases until, in the Dark Ages, the two have reached a common level. Following this phase, the developmental lines cross and reverse their former relationships. Hero-savior imagery rises to the highest level of its Western embodiment in the Gothic Middle Ages; monster-demon imagery sinks to a subservient position.

Having established this sequence as a series of manifest cultural images, we are now in possession of the first requisite for any psycho-historical study: what we may call a "cultural specimen." It would not be fruitful, from our point of view, to start with conceptual generalities such as "art" or "poetry" or "myth," any more than for the psychoanalyst to start with such generalities as "dreams" or "symptoms." We must have specific works of art or poems or myths for analysis, as he must have the specific dreams and symptoms of actual individuals.

Furthermore, significant results are more likely to follow in both cases if the material available for study is sufficiently comprehensive to involve a developmental dimension. The psychoanalyst would ordinarily have difficulty in discovering the essential facts of his patient's experience from such a limited expression of them as, let us say, a single dream. Give him a series of dreams over a period of time and he begins to detect significance both in their recurring elements and in the changes which they gradually undergo. So with the forms of cultural expression that concern us. If a number of them from different but related periods are observed comparatively, they are likely to reveal meanings that could not be detected at any single stage of their development.

Our mythical sequence, which embraces all the forms of art, literature, and religion embodying the myths, satisfies both these requirements for psycho-historical study just mentioned. It is concrete in its character and long enough in its range to involve clearly recognizable evolutionary developments.

Chapter XI

MYTH AND HISTORY IN
SOME NEOLITHIC CULTURES

We now have a cultural specimen for analysis in our sequence of myths. We also have an analytical principle in the psycho-history theory developed in Part I. By confronting the specimen with the principle, we can next establish the general lines to be followed in the psycho-historical investigation of our material.

First, we recognize that the medieval works of art representing monsters and heroes are material embodiments, permanent arrestations, of mental images that had their origin in the tension-imagery process. The Neolithic monsters, which had not been reduced to art in most of the examples we considered, showed us tension imagery still at the quick of psychic experience. In both cases, the imagery, regarded in our terms, appears as a form of "manifest content" projected onto the mythological plane by an undifferentiated collective mentality. We must therefore presume, in terms already quoted from Freud, that however "confused and incomprehensible" these mythical themes may at first appear, they nevertheless "have a meaning, serve a purpose, and arise from the. . . experience of life." [1]

Second, since we regard these forms of myth and art as tension images, we assume that the producing societies experienced tensions capable of inspiring the images, and historical circumstances capable of generating the tensions. Further, we assume that the general character of the tensions and of the historical conditions — whether positive or negative — can be inferred from the character of the images. The negative imagery of monster and demon implies negative tensions such as those of fear and insecurity, which in turn we can interpret as an effect of negative circumstances: poverty of natural resources, inadequate technology, or overpowering enemies. Conversely, from the positive imagery of hero and savior, we infer positive tensions — resolution, hope, triumph — made possible by sustaining positive circumstances: advanced technology, economic abundance, social and military expansion, or similar attainments in social power and well-being.

Third and last, we are able to relate these assumed tensions and circumstances, whether positive or negative, to a pattern of evolutionary development. The medieval myths with which we are concerned involve a time span of approximately a thousand years. If we credit the proposed reconstruction back to Neolithic times, the reconstructed portion of the sequence extends through several additional millenia. During this long historical unfolding, the mythical imagery underwent what we have called a complemental evolutionary development. At the time of its Neolithic beginnings negative images were strongest, positive ones weakest. During its subsequent development, the relationship between negative and positive imagery gradually reversed itself until, at the height of the Gothic epoch, positive images were strongest, negative weakest.

From this sequential change in the imagery, we can now infer corresponding changes in the nature of the underlying tensions and historical circumstances. If our interpretive principle is sound, these in turn must have undergone evolutionary and, in due course, revolutionary developments in order to produce such developments in the imagery engendered by them. Historical conditions must have been painfully difficult for Neolithic man, charging his social mentality with powerful negative tensions. With the passage of time through the Dark Ages to the Middle Ages, the historical circumstances must have improved and must have occasioned a corresponding shift from negative toward positive tensions. By the Gothic period, society must presumably have achieved a masterful equilibrium between the demands of life and possibilities of environment and must accordingly have been imbued with a spirit of triumph and exaltation.

If these inferences are to be granted a reasonable degree of probability, we must, of course, test them as fully as possible in the light of observable facts. The principal way to do so is to examine the evidence provided by recorded history. History deals with the events and conditions of life, the "historical circumstances," operative during the epochs of which it treats. Not infrequently it supplements its accounts of these events and conditions by describing the states of collective emotion to which they gave rise. In order to submit our interpretation of the mythical imagery to this test, and at the same time to enrich it with historical meaning, let us ask ourselves the following questions. Insofar as written records indicate, were the communities which originated our mythical monsters actually haunted by collective fears? If so, what circumstances caused those fears? And — taking into account our total evolutionary progression — did the fears diminish and did satisfactions increase as man evolved from the Neolithic stage of culture to medieval horizons? If so, we establish a corresponding change of historical circumstances to explain this psychological progress? In seeking answers to these questions we shall be paralleling, on a collective level, that part of a psychoanalytical investigation which examines the circumstances of the patient's life in order to discover among them the possible causes of his psychic condition.

II

The psycho-historical interpretation of Neolithic monster imagery has already been anticipated by several of the thumbnail examples cited in Part I. We found that the Gnawing-Squirrel monsters were originally inspired by terror and that the terror was caused by a volcanic eruption. The Betsileo evil spirits emerged from psychic insecurtiy due to disruptive changes in the economic basis of Betsileo life. The Ojibwa *windigo* appeared in a culture in which the survival was so uncertain that an individual could find himself confronted by two alternatives: cannibalism or death by starvation. In all these cases, the cultural context of the negative imagery appears to fulfil psycho-historical expectations: a negative psychological condition arising from negative historical circumstances.

What about the Canadian Indians who cringed at the thought of the monster, Gougou? Does Champlain throw any light on the psychic states and conditions of life of the people who described this monster to him? Indeed so; we cannot read far in his chronicles, or in those of other early observers, without coming upon passages that are highly significant for our investigation. According to these reports the Indians in question, in addition to suffering the strain and discomfort attendant upon primitive life in a severe climate, were subject to at least three frequent and terrible dangers: famine, attack from human enemies, and the possibility of torture if taken captive.

In the early seventeenth century, when Champlain observed them, the Indians of eastern Canada were just at the point of transition from a hunting to an agricultural economy. Some tribes were developing a rude agriculture, others still depended entirely on wild foods for their sustenance. Among all of them, but particularly among the latter group, life was precarious and famine frequent. "All these tribes suffer so much from hunger," Champlain reports, "that sometimes they are obliged to live on certain shellfish, and to eat their dogs and the skins with which they clothe themselves against the cold." [2] And in another passage, "All these people sometimes suffer so great extremity, on account of the great cold and snow, that they are almost constrained to eat one another; for the animals and fowl on which they live migrate to warmer countries." [3]

The terrible reality of the situation, both with regard to hunger and to the general dangers and hardships of primitive life, comes home to us when we read of specific incidents such as the one witnessed by Champlain at Quebec in February 1609. "On the twentieth of the month some Indians made their appearance on the other side of the river, and shouted to us to go to their aid, but this was out of our power, on account of the large amount of ice which was floating down the river. So hungry were these poor wretches that being at their wits' end, they, men, women and children, resolved to die or cross the river, in the hope that I would succor them in their dire need. Accordingly having taken this resolution, the men and women seized their children and got into their canoes, thinking they would reach our shore by an opening in the ice which the wind had made; but no sooner were they in the middle of the river, than their canoes were caught between the ice floes and broken into a thousand pieces. They manoeuvred so well that they jumped with their children, whom the women were carrying on their backs, upon a large block of ice. While they were on it, we could hear them screaming so much that it was pitiful; for they expected nothing less than death. But fortune favoured these poor wretches so much that a large ice floe struck the side of the one upon which they stood with such force that it threw them upon the land. They, seeing such a favorable turn of events, went ashore with as great joy as they ever experienced in spite of the famine they had endured. They came to our settlement so thin and emaciated that they looked like skeletons, most of them being unable to stand. I was astonished at their appearance, and at the way they had crossed the river, seeing them so weak and faint. I ordered bread and beans to be given to them. They could not wait for these to be cooked before eating them." [4]

On subsequent pages, Champlain tells how these starving people discovered and devoured the putrid carcasses of a sow and two dogs which he had set out months before to attract foxes and birds of prey. One of these carcasses was suspended in a tree top. "These savages went to the tree, and not being able to climb it on account of their weakness, they felled it, and carried off the dog, which was now only skin and bones, with the head stinking and rotten, and immediately devoured it." [5]

Accounts of similar extremities, and of death from starvation as a result of them, are frequent in the reports of all early observers. The *Relations* written by the Jesuit missionaries contain numerous accounts of famine. To quote but one example, Father Paul le Jeune's *Relation* of 1634 contains a graphic description of the hardships of Indian life; a description which the author entitles "What One Must Suffer in Wintering with the Savages." One of the trials to be suffered was famine. "The snow not being deep in comparison with that of other years, they could not take the Elk, and so brought back only some Beavers and Porcupines, but in so small a number and so seldom that they kept us from dying rather than helped us to live . . . When I could have, toward the end of our supply of food, the skin of an eel for my day's fare, I considered that I had breakfasted, dined, and supped well.

"At first, I had used one of these skins to patch the cloth gown that I wore, as I forgot to bring some pieces with me; but, when I was so sorely pressed with hunger, I ate my pieces; and, if my gown had been made of the same stuff, I assure you that I would have brought it back home much shorter than it was. Indeed I ate old Moose skins, which are much tougher than those of the eel; I went about through the woods biting the ends of the branches, and gnawing the more tender bark, as I shall relate in the journal. Our neighboring Savages suffered still more than we did, some of them coming to see us, and telling us that their comrades had died of hunger. I saw some who had eaten only once in five days. . . When a young Savage of our cabin was dying of hunger, . . . they often asked me if I was not afraid, if I had no fear of death; and seeing me quite firm, they were astonished, on one occasion in particular when I saw them almost falling into a state of despair. When they reach this point, they play, so to speak at 'save himself who can'; throwing away their bark and baggage, deserting each other, and abandoning all interest in the common welfare, each one strives to find something for himself. Then the children, the women, and for that matter all those who cannot hunt, die of cold and hunger. If they had reached this extremity, I would have been among the first to die." [6]

Added to the stress of famine, and no doubt often related to it through competition for hunting and fishing grounds, was the devastation of war. The effect of the latter on Indian communities is vividly portrayed in Father Paul Ragueneau's *Relation* of 1650. Prior to the passages to be quoted, the author has devoted several pages to a description of the way in which the Huron tribes were being decimated, first by famine, "which was rendering their existence a living death" and which forced them to scatter widely in search of food, and secondly by "the fire and flame of the Iroquois, who were continually seeking their lives. . . They split up into bands, so that, if some fell into the hands of the enemy, others might escape." [7]

After telling how band after band had been tracked and destroyed by the Iroquois, Ragueneau gives an account of the Huron encampment in which he himself was staying — an encampment which in its turn was breaking up to scatter in search of food. The majority of the Indians, he says, "parted from us, leaving in our care all their little property — the greater number publicly declaring that they made us their heirs, perceiving clearly that their death was not far away, and that they carried it within. Indeed, but a few days had slipped by when news reached us of the misfortune we had anticipated. That poor scattered band fell into the snares of our enemies, the Iroquois."

"Eight days afterward a similar misfortune assailed yet another band. Withersoever they go, massacre awaits them. Famine follows them everywhere, in which they meet an enemy more cruel than cruelty itself; and to fill up the measure of misery without hope, they learned that two powerful war-parties were on the way, who were coming to exterminate them; that the first designed to make havoc of their fields, to pluck up their Indian corn, and to lay waste the country, while the second party was to cut down everything that might have escaped the fury of the first. Despair reigns everywhere." [8]

Two striking instances of the manner in which fear affected the dreams of the Indians are recorded by Champlain. With regard to the natives who were encamped near the French settlement at Quebec at the time of its foundation in 1608, the explorer writes: "The whole time they were in such constant dread of their enemies, that they often took fright at night in their dreams, and would send their wives and children to our fort, the gates of which I used to have opened for them, but let their men remain about the fort, not permitting them to enter; for they were as safe there as to their persons as if they had been inside. And I used to send out five or six of our men to give them courage, and to go and search the woods whether they could see anything, which used to satisfy them." [9]

A similar passage forms part of Champlain's account of an expedition to the rapids of the Richelieu River, then known as the "River of the Iroquois," which he made in company with some members of the Montagnais tribe. "When we reached the mouth of the river of the Iroquois, there were some of the Indians who dreamed that their enemies were pursuing them. This dream made them at once shift their camp, although the weather that night was bad on account of wind and rain; and they went and spent the whole night in the high bulrushes which are in the lake St. Peter, for fear of their enemies." [10]

III

The foregoing account of the dangers and difficulties of Neolithic life in eastern Canada could easily be extended. Enough has now been quoted, however, to indicate that these peoples were exposed to objective dangers and difficulties of the most severe nature, that these dangers and difficulties subjected them to intense psychic strains, and that these strains affected their tension imagery. Indeed, the chroniclers of New France provide factual evidence for our whole case, although they do not themselves perceive the connection between the fears experienced by the Indians and the mythical monsters in which the latter believed. Such a perception was impossible on the part of the seventeenth-century Europeans owing to the fact that they themselves were still in a mythological stage of human mental evolution; that is to say they were as incapable as their Indian associates of distinguishing clearly between fact and fantasy in the realm of supernatural concepts. Time and again, these writers state that the dreams and monsters of the Indians "are visions of the devil who deceives them and leads them astray," which is merely explaining an Indian myth in terms of a European one.

Armed with deeper insight into psychological processes, we today can interpret the psychic aspects of the seventeenth-century chronicles better than could the chroniclers themselves. In the preceding pages we have already followed the sequence of developments from objective dangers and difficulties to subjective psychic tensions and to the expressions of those tensions in the tension imagery of dreams. In the case of the dreams reported by Champlain, the imagery may have been either realistic or symbolical, employing actual memory images of the dreaded human enemies or embodying the fears which they inspired in fear fantasies. Certainly we cannot doubt that in many instances the tension-imagery process activated the creative powers of the imagination in the Indian mind, as it still does in us today, and that in such cases the fears expressed themselves in imaginative rather than literal imagery.

Now let the reader ask himself what kind of imaginative conception would be capable of symbolizing fears that were overpowering, fears capable of driving men to hide themselves in a swamp on a rainy night, fears inspired by conditions which, to the particular groups of Indians experiencing them, were insurmountable. Would not the resulting imagery inevitably take the form of some force or being bent on the destruction of Indian life, and so powerful that resistance to it was impossible? Try to conceive such a being and you arrive exactly where our hypothesis would indicate that you should: at a Gougou. This great malicious man beast who catches Indians and eats them and whose gigantic size and strength makes resistance unthinkable, is a perfect imaginative embodiment of the kind of negative tensions to which the Indians were subject. It is not the only possible symbol of such tensions — the number of possible fear symbols, like that of other forms of creative imagery, is legion — but certainly no other form could more perfectly express tensions of the kind we are considering.

Once the terrifying vision of the monster was experienced, whether in daydream, dream, traumatic hallucination, or other psychic manifestation, the steps which led to its mythological acceptance are easy to imagine. Lacking the power to differentiate subjective from objective reality, he who first saw this nightmarish apparition projected it into the outward world and accepted its existence as an objective fact. He communicated his vision to others. They were as unanalytical and as fear-ridden as himself. They too accepted the creature as a reality. From time to time others, subject to the same tensions, had similar imaginative experiences. They would naturally identify their visions with the evil being whom they had already come to dread from general report, thus confirming the report by reference to "reality" — undifferentiated psychic reality. Eventually, after different accounts had been compared and merged, a more or less standarized version of the evil creature would come into being. Gougou would then have taken form as a mythological entity.

Marquette provides another instance of the man-eating mythical monster in Neolithic North America and — what is rarer for his day — gives an explanation of it that is essentially psycho-historical. His account concerns one of the demons reported to him by the Indians whom he met on his first voyage down the Mississippi. "At a river called Ouaboukigou . . . we passed by a place that is dreaded by the Savages, because they believe that a manitou is there, — that is to say, a demon, — that devours travelers: and the Savages, who wished to divert us from our undertaking, warned us against it. This is the demon: there is a small cove, surrounded by rocks 20 feet high, into which The whole Current of the river rushes; and, being pushed back against the waters following It, and checked by an Island near by, the Current is Compelled to pass through a narrow Channel. This is not done without violent Struggle between all these waters, which force one another back, or without great din, which inspires terror in the savages, who fear everything." [11]

No doubt in other instances, as in the one just considered, the objective basis for a particular demon, and especially for its particular location, was a specific awe-inspiring or fear-inspiring phenomenon of nature. The "strange hissings" ascribed by Champlain to Gougou may well have been caused by air pockets compressed by the high tides of the Bay of Fundy into fissures in the rocky coast — a phenomenon which can still occasionally be heard in that region today. But unless the objective occasion is sufficiently powerful to produce profound psychic repercussions of its own accord, as was the case with our volcanic eruption, it merely provides the signal for the release of previously existing fears. It is unlikely that either Marquette's whirlpool or our conjectural Fundy hissings would have inspired demonic imagery had the Indians had no other evils to contend with. The key to their negative mythological impulsiveness lay in the overflowing reservoir of repressed fears which Marquette implies when he says that they "fear everything" and which Champlain had abundantly revealed to us.

IV

Was belief in the monster myths a useless though spontaneous result of the tensions of Neolithic life, or did it perform some positive psychic function? Presumably what Freud remarked about dreams and neurotic symptoms — that they not only "have meaning" and "arise from the patient's experience of life," but that they also "serve a purpose" — applies with equal force to mythological experiences. Among his comments on the possible functions of dreams, Freud observes that "the dream relieves the mind, like a safety valve, and that, as Robert has put it, all kinds of harmful material are rendered harmless by representation in the dream." [12] No doubt the same could be said with regard to negative myths.

Subject to conditions imposing powerful negative tensions, the members of our Neolithic communities were placed in a difficult psychic position. If they retained full and continuous consciousness of their fears, those fears would tend to induce a state of chronic melancholia and to incapacitate them for the demands of life. Such melancholia was, in fact, one of the responses to the situation that actually occurred in certain instances. We have noted Le Clerc's reference to the "fits of profound melancholoy" suffered by the Indians of the Gaspé Peninsula.

At the other extreme from continuous awareness of the fears would be complete repression of them. Assuming that such repression had been possible to the peoples we have been considering, it would have charged the unconscious levels of their mental life with negative energies dangerous to psychic equilibrium. The ultimate result in this case would presumably have been insanity.

Mythical activity, it would seem, intuitively resolved this psychic dilemma through a "compromise formation." On the one hand the conscious acceptance of monsters precluded the dangerous contingency that the fears would be completely repressed. On the other, it detached the fears to some extent from the real but too often uncontrollable circumstances to which they were due. In the case of Gougou and of Marquette's whirlpool manitou, projection of negative tensions had progressed to the point of associating their symbol with a particular spot, thus detaching them to that extent from the remainder of the tribal world. Furthermore, the myth centered tribal fears in a being so formidable that no man could be condemned for fearing him: an indirect way of granting the fears social sanction.

With at least a portion of their negative tensions thus projected, localized, socially recognized, and socially justified, men could better steel themselves against the actual dangers which they must resist and the tortures which, if necessary, they must endure. In short it seems likely that the belief in mythical monsters permitted a more balanced mental adjustment than would have been possible without it.

V

Before leaving our Neolithic examples from other parts of the world than Europe, it remains to substantiate a further fact assumed in our general mythical sequence: the fact that Neolithic mythology is extremely low in positive imagery. If we recall for a moment the possible range of tensions and tension imagery between what may be called the positive and the negative poles, it is evident that creatures like Gougou occupy a position close to the negative pole. For Neolithic man the positive pole, collectively speaking, seems to have lain in unknown psychic territory, as remote from human reach at those geographical poles of the earth which so long defied the efforts of their would-be human discoverers. All observers confirm the impression that under Neolithic conditions, humanity's vision of beneficent beings was as vague and shadowy, its sense of religious faith and exaltation as little developed, as its conception of tormenting devils was vivid and its fear of them universal.

The Jesuit relations and Champlain's chronicles both give a wealth of detail concerning the religious conceptions of the eastern Canadian Indians. "They honor a deity," says Father Joseph Jouvency, "who has no definite character or regular code of worship. They perceive, however, through the twilight, as it were, that some deity does exist."[13] "They believe that there is One who made all," reports another commentator, Father Charles l'Allemant, "but they do not render him any homage."[14]

Champlain gives a long account of a theological discussion which he had with Anadbijou, a grand sagamore of the Montagnais. "I asked him also," we read in this account, "whether he did not believe that there was more than one God. He replied that their belief was, that there was one God, one Son, one Mother, and the Sun, which were four; that God was above them all; but that the Son and the Sun were good, because of the benefit they receive from them, but that the Mother was of no value, and ate them up, and that the Father was not very good."[15]

The Indian conception of the future life matches this emergent theology in its indeterminate character and neutral coloring. Belief in immortality was universal, burial customs were well defined and rigorously observed, but no thought of heavenly splendor attached to the Indian's concept of the afterworld. From a long account given by le Jeune, we may select a few leading sentences. "They represent the soul of man as a dark and sombre image, or as a shadow of the man himself . . ." Except for those of the children and the infirm, who cannot endure the hardships of the journey, the souls go on foot "to a large village situated where the sun sets . . ." On the way "they eat bark and old wood which they find in the forests." After their arrival, "during the daytime, they are seated with their two elbows upon their two knees, and their heads between their two hands, the usual position of sick Savages; during the night, they go and come, they work, they go to the chase."[16]

André Gide reports a comparable negative weighting of religious outlook among the African Massa tribes, to whose abstract, symbolical devil mounds we have already referred. "I could find no evidence that this belief in an evil power was balanced, in the minds of these poor people, by the belief in some protecting power. The most they can hope for is the absence of enmity . . .

These natives believe in the devil, in devils — and believe nothing else. No other supernatural force aids man in his struggle against them . . . Correspondingly after death, there is nothing. 'Among these peoples,' I was told . . . 'when a man is dead it is like a wind which has passed." [17]

It seems evident from the records that the positive aspects of Neolithic tension imagery were relatively little developed, offering nothing comparable in vividness or intensity to the monsters which swarmed around the negative pole. God and his heaven were, so to speak, crushed beneath the feet of all-powerful demonic forces; the exact opposite of the relationship which was to exist between them during the High Middle Ages.

The psycho-technic reasons for this negatively weighted mythology should be evident from our examination of Neolithic conditions of life and can be further illustrated by an interpretation of the theological concepts recorded by Champlain and quoted above. The sun was revered by Neolithic peoples for its obvious beneficial effect on mankind. In this instance an objective source of well-being was endowed with mythological status by the unconscious projection into it of the gratifying reactions which it stirred in human beings. Were a man dying of heat and thirst in a desert, the sun would soon shift its position to the negative pole in his psychic experience, and would become in fact, as it might also well appear in his fevered imagination, a destructive monster.

The "mother" who ate the Indians, a kind of death goddess among them, is obviously a fear symbol akin to Gougou. Psychoanalysts would doubtless find here an expression of conflicts due to repressed desire to "return to the mother"; in other words a symbol of incest impulse or nostalgia for prenatal security. If conceived in narrowly sexual terms, this explanation would differ from the present but would not necessarily contradict it. Both views might be, and presumably are, true at different levels of experience. In our "Mother's" as well as in our Father's house "are many mansions."

If, however, the author correctly understands the psychoanalytical concept of incest as a mythical symbol — a different matter from incest as a thing in itself — the symbol is not conceived primarily as an expression of desire for sexual relations with the mother. Rather it implies an impulse to escape from painful tensions by abandoning the effort at mental adjustment and retreating into a psychic underworld or "womb" of the unconscious. The imagery of sexual incest, secondary in itself, becomes a symbol of psychological "incest" — a more far-reaching and potentially more disastrous contingency which involves the danger of a complete "swallowing up" and disappearance of rational consciousness.

In this broader, more figurative sense, the psychoanalytical interpretation of incest symbols is in perfect accord, is in fact identical, with our psycho-historical one. The danger of psychic withdrawal into the unconscious is greatest when negative tensions are strongest, and they are strongest when objective circumstances are most difficult. In this respect the psycho-technic theory merely reinforces and amplifies the psychoanalytical one by emphasizing its collective implications and by relating collective tensions to their objective causes in historical experience.

The "son" to whom, in various myths, the Indians gave credit for teaching them the use of fire, for rendering animals susceptible to the chase, and for other advantages, evidently represents the emergence of positive imagery in Neolithic mythology. Despite the severe handicaps under which it labored, Neolithic life did receive its measure of support from nature and had achieved its measure of cultural advance. Its satisfaction in these positive aspects of its experience found symbolical expression in the conception of a friendly even if still secondary being.

The "father," apparently identified with an emergent sense of some ultimate universal control, is conceived by the Indians as a wavering and uncertain factor — and naturally so. If he indeed possessed the power to provide the fulfillments for which the Indians longed, he cannot have been wholly good since he so often took them away. One of the myths associated with him is particularly revealing in this connection. According to this myth, the Father gave a certain grand sagamore of the tribe a tobacco pipe with the admonition to guard it carefully and the promise that the tribe would lack nothing so long as the pipe remained in its possession. "And as long as he kept it the savages wanted for nothing in the world; but afterward the said Sagamore lost his pipe, and this is the reason for the great famine which sometimes comes among them." [18] This myth, a parallel of the biblical earthly paradise and of man's expulsion from it, reflects the Indians' dependence upon the fluctuations of an environment which fulfilled his wants in seasons of peace and plenty only to withdraw these blessings later and desolate his land with famine and invasion.

Neither in cultural and political unity nor in military and economic security had Neolithic society reached a stage of development capable of reflecting itself in a single all-powerful deity and an attendant heaven vibrant with exaltation.

Champlain in his reply to the grand sagamore's statement that "God is not very good," made one of the many unconscious inversions found in the writings of the chroniclers. "I replied and told him that God was wholly good . . . and that if they believed in God as we do, they should lack nothing of which they stood in need." [19] Expressed objectively the last statement would read, "If they lacked nothing of which they stood in need, they would believe in God as we do." That is to say that if the Indians had reached an equivalent stage of economic and social well-being, their conceptions of life would have been parallel to those formed by Europeans under similar conditions.

The Indian view of this matter held closer to reality than the European one. A Montagnais said to le Jeune, "Thy God has not come to our country, and that is why we do not believe in him." [20] To render this an objective statement, we need only modify it to the extent of saying, "The conditions which gave rise to thy conception of God have not come to our country, and that is why we do not believe in him."

In the light of the preceding discussion, does it not appear that the records confirm our psycho-historical assumptions with regard to Neolithic mythology? The negative psychic tensions and severe historical circumstances which we inferred from the mythological monsters, prove to have been historical realities. Hence we seem to be justified in concluding that the monster imagery was a result of those realities and that it is capable of interpretation by reference to them. Conversely, the undeveloped state of positive imagery on these cultural horizons may be attributed to the fact that the adverse circumstances rendered impossible any sustained collective experience of positive tensions, and thus limited the development of positive tension imagery to minor and wavering forms.

VI

We assumed in relation to our total mythical sequence that pre-Dark Age mythology in Western Europe had passed through stages equivalent to those of Neolithic societies in other parts of the world. One slight surviving evidence of mythological parallelism was cited from Tacitus in his description of the goddess Nerthus who lived "in an island of the ocean" swallowed up her ministrants, and was regarded by the Suebi people with "a mysterious terror and an ignorance full of piety as to what that may be which men only behold to die."

Equally slight, but equally indicative of parallelism, is the evidence that the early Western European barbarians had made little progress in developing the positive aspects of their mythology. "They count among the number of the gods," says Caesar of the German tribes, "only those which they can see, and whose benign influence is manifest, namely the Sun, Vulcan, and the Moon. Of the others they have never even heard." [21] The basic objects of Teutonic worship, as Caesar indicates, were the sun, fire, and the moon. The gods of whom these peoples had "never even heard" would include most of the personifications of the more friendly and humane forces that were to emerge in the religions of later stages of society.

What little we know of this early Western European mythology thus appears to support assumption that it was similar in nature to that of better known Neolithic cultures in other parts of the world. Let us turn now to the psychological and historical foundations of pre-Dark Age European life. As in the case of the related myths, the historical evidence is indirect and relatively slight. The general conditions of life in Neolithic and Bronze Age Europe have been inferred from surviving artifacts, but were historically recorded only to a limited extent and by external and casual observers like the Roman commentators.

For our present purpose, the scanty documentation provided by the Roman writers is chiefly useful as a connecting link. It establishes beyond doubt the close parallelism between Neolithic conditions in Europe and in those other parts of the world concerning which we have the reports of more intimate observers. Tacitus, for instance, makes it clear that in the first century A.D. certain Teutonic tribes were still living under social and economic conditions strikingly similar to those later found by Champlain among the more northern American aborigines. "The Fenni," says the Roman historian, "live in astonishing barbarism and disgusting misery; no arms, no horses, no fixed homes; herbs for their food, skins for their clothing, earth for their bed; arrows are all their wealth; for want of iron they tip them with bone. This same hunting is the support of the women as well as the men, for they accompany the men freely and claim a share of the spoil; nor have their infants any shelter against wild beasts and rain, except the covering afforded by a few intertwined branches." [22]

"Their whole life is made up of hunting and thoughts of war," Caesar had written of the Teutonic tribes a century earlier. "It is a matter of the greatest pride to the tribes to lay waste the borders of their territory as great a distance as possible and to make them uninhabitable." [23] "You will not so readily per-

suade them," adds Tacitus along the same line, "to plough the land and wait
for the year's returns as to challenge the enemy and earn wounds; besides, it
seems limp and slack to get with sweating of your brow what you can gain
with shedding of your blood." But Tacitus also notes the emergence of agriculture among certain tribes. Of the Aestii he remarks, "Grain and other products
of the earth they cultivate with a patience out of keeping with the lethargy of
the Germans." [24]

To cite but a few other traits common both to European, American, and
other peoples at the cultural level we are considering, we may mention the
division of the population into tribes among which, as Tacitus puts it, "powerful kingdoms" had not yet emerged; the holding of land as a common possession of the tribe and not as individual property; scrupulous observance of the
laws of hospitality based upon a tradition of communal sharing of food and
shelter; loose political organization dependent for the most part upon voluntary
rather than obligatory loyalties; menial labor by women, body painting, fond-
ness for dancing, susceptibility to drunkenness, and reckless abandon in
gambling.

Visual art in turn offers strong evidence of common cultural horizons. Three
of the examples of Neolithic pottery shown on Plate 18 are European, one
comes from the Algonquian and Iroquoian Indians about whom Champlain
wrote. In general effect, and in their use of geometric ornament, the European
and the Canadian examples are hardly distinguishable from each other.

The available information thus appears to indicate common levels of material and social development, as well as common mythical conceptions, in pre-
Dark Age Western Europe and in those communities elsewhere which we have
been roughly classifying as Neolithic. As already suggested, the reader who
doubts the validity or the usefulness of this parallelism, can regard our discussion of non-European myths and their cultural backgrounds as an independent phase of our subject, unrelated to its European phases. The author
believes that the parallelism is sufficiently well established to merit scholarly
consideration. He also believes that our understanding of the European myths
of the Dark and Middles Ages is increased by the realization that those myths
emerged from a lost background of life and thought similar in its general
nature to that which we have observed in Neolithic cultures in other parts of
the world.

MYTH AND HISTORY IN THE DARK AGES

It goes without saying that the circumstances prevailing in Neolithic times were by no means the earliest conditions of human existence. Long ages had passed during the preceding Paleolithic epoch and had involved a whole cycle of cultural evolution and decline based on a hunting economy. Neolithic culture was, however, the point of departure for the subsequent development of agricultural society, one branch of which, in Western Europe, led through the Dark Ages to the Middle Ages. Hence for our present purpose, we may regard Neolithic mentality as our ultimate point of reference. Having observed some of its characteristic mythological expressions, and having suggested a psycho-historical interpretation of them, we can now move forward in our sequence and attempt a corresponding interpretation of the mythology of the Dark Ages.

We have taken the monster-hero conflicts of *Beowulf* as a typical myth of the period and have illustrated through it the approximate equilibrium of negative and positive imagery in the mythical cosmos of the Dark Ages. A similar equilibrium — the evolutionary result of declining negative and rising positive imagery — can be observed in many other mythical and religious conceptions of the age. Before proceeding to our historical analysis, we would do well to broaden our perspective on Dark Age mythology by a glance at some of these other manifestations. They fall under three general headings: some further reference to monster-hero conceptions; the rising major gods of the Teutonic world such as Thor, Loki, and Odin; and the amalgamated heathen-Christian conceptions typical of Dark Age Christianity.

The precise balance of negative and positive imagery found in *Beowulf* was, of course, only the middle phase of the slow millennium-long drift of Western mythology away from the gloomy negativism of Neolithic times toward the triumphant positivism of the High Middle Ages. Study of Dark Age mythology reveals examples characteristic of most of the other points along this line of development. During the earlier centuries of the epoch and — even during later ones in less favored geographical areas — the old negative weighting persists. During the later centuries and especially in more fortunate regions, the new positive growth is marked.

Negative weighting seems to have survived longest in the northern portions of Europe. The Icelandic sagas provide cases in point. Thus the *Saga of the Volsungs*, though committed to writing in the thirteenth century — six centuries after *Beowulf* had been similarly transcribed — is nevertheless much less advanced than *Beowulf* in the growth of positive imagery. The saga comes to an unhappy ending; nowhere in it do we find more than a brief and passing triumph. Its imagery, its psychic revelation, reminds one of a stormy sky: often dramatically lowering, sometimes pierced by brief flashes of sunshine, but usually a sullen grey. The death of the hero, Gunnar, in a snake pit, bound and incapable of defending himself is typical of this Icelandic tension imagery. As described in the *Saga of the Volsungs*, the incident is as follows:

"Then Gunnar was put in a snake-pit full of many worms, and his hands were fast bound. Gudrun sent him a harp, and he played upon it by reason of his great skill, for he plucked the strings with his toes so excellently well that few men have heard the like, even when hands were needed. So skillfully did he play that all the snakes fell asleep, save for a large and ugly adder which crept up and stung him to the very heart. And there he died, right bravely."[1]

Two sculptural renderings of this incident are reproduced among our illustrations. One received attention when we were establishing the Dark Age phase of our mythical sequence (Fig. 43). The other appears in Fig. 48.

In the Gunnar story we observe mythical imagery in transition between the stage represented by Neolithic monsters like Gougou and that personified by fully developed Dark Age heroes like Beowulf. In the Neolithic instance there was no hero even to challenge the monster. In *Beowulf*, the hero is sufficiently powerful to overcome all the monsters he faces and to succumb to the last only in a valiant battle. Gunnar dies a helpless captive. Heroism at this stage consists, not in conquering the evil fate — that is still impossible — but in dying with fortitude instead of fleeing in terror. We are witness to the birth and first tottering steps of collective courage in a world still uncontrollable, but no longer quite so devastating.

The unconquering, yet at the same time spiritually unconquered, status of these northern Dark Age heroes is well summarized by Margaret Schlauch. " 'The thrall is fit to die, for no matter how long he lives he will ever be wretched.' A hero, on the other hand, knows that life is not worth cherishing, and therefore he ceases to be wretched. It is a sort of philosophical pessimism which makes him a hero . . . the so-called sensationalism of many of the sagas seems to have been used deliberately to bring out the superiority of the heroic will to horrible circumstances. When Hogni laughs as his heart is being cut out; when Gunnar plays his harp in the pit of snakes; when warriors in other sagas summon their last strength and breath before dying of ghastly wounds in order to utter a humorous epigram; they are proving their invincibility even to defeat. The more harrowing the circumstances, the more triumphant their vindication." [2]

Between these forlorn nascent heroes and vigorously combative ones of the Beowulfian type, Dark Age mythology spreads an unbroken monster-hero spectrum. Since we have now examined the upper and the lower edges of this spectrum, however, we would advance little were we to dwell upon the types between these two extremes. Instead, let us turn to the conceptions of great gods that were slowly emerging through the shifting mists of lesser Dark Age imagery. Here again we meet evidence of the trend toward a balancing of old negative by new positive imagery. Gods are becoming more positive and, to humanity, more helpful beings, yet they have not attained final superiority over challenging and sometimes victorious enemies.

Thus we read of Thor, "He is properly the Teutonic god of the upper regions, who manifests himself in the thunder . . . In all the Norse countries, he is the friend of man, succoring him in his conflict with demonic powers. The latter being represented mainly as giants, Thor's battles with giants form the theme of numerous myths." [3] Battles between gods and giants are merely another and more monumental expression of the conflict theme involved in the struggles between heroes and monsters. In the one as in the other, the high-water mark of Dark Age consciousness is an approach to balanced tension between the antagonists. Sometimes one triumphs, sometimes the other. Thor's hammer gives him thunderous power; the giants rob him of it and carry it off to their domain; Thor and some fellow gods organize an expedition to the giant land and wrest the hammer back again. So the fortunes of the gods, unsteadied by omnipotence, fluctuate between victory and defeat.

Equally revealing is the dual nature of many of the gods themselves. Humanity projects the negative and the positive tensions of its divided consciousness into one and the same being and finds that being at times friendly, at times inimical, and therefore always uncertain. This negative-positive vacillation is perhaps most strikingly illustrated in the Norse deity, Loki. "He is the Asa [type of god] who sometimes succors, sometimes works injury; he is sometimes an ally of Odin and Thor, and their comrade in travel, while, again, he seeks to over-reach and deceive them. His double character makes him a favorite theme of poetic legend, and he became the nucleus of mythical incidents and Christian stories about Satan . . . Loki joins with Odin and Hoenir in the creation of man . . . he brings the apples of Iðun to the giants, and in the form of an eagle takes them away again . . . he cuts off Sif's hair, and then brings hair of gold for her from the dwarfs; he accompanies Thor upon the expedition in which the latter recovered his hammer from the land of the giants . . . But Loki also brings about the death of Balder, and it was on this account that Norse poetry fastened upon him the saga of the chained monster, telling how he was fettered by the Asas."

A step in advance of the Indian Father who was "not very good," Loki is, so to speak, a Father who is sometimes good, sometimes bad, and who — as if exhausted by his effort in the direction of goodness — falls to a final state of evil.

In lesser degree, many of the other Teutonic gods have this ambiguous character. Odin (Woden or Wotan) rose from leader of departed souls to become lord of the dead, lord of life and death, and god of war. He was approaching the status of supreme deity in which he possessed invincible powers of magic and healing, hence embodied "all higher wisdom." Yet at some times and places he was believed to require human sacrifice. In common with various deities from other parts of the world who did become supreme for their followers, Odin "is depicted as an old man with a long grey beard," yet — with a dark background startling to later minds — "he is one-eyed, like the man-eating demons of other myths."

In Teutonic theology, it would seem, an exclusively positive character was possible only to figures who arrived late upon the mythological scene and who remained relatively obscure. One such, among the gods, was Balder; and two among the goddesses, Hlin and Eir. Balder's name "signifies 'light,' 'the bright one.' . . . The Snorra Edda says that he was noted for his luminous appearance and his gentleness of nature." Characteristically enough, this gentle luminous being had no established cult of worship as did major gods like Thor and Odin, and the myths relating to him centered chiefly around the death inflicted upon him by Loki. As to the goddesses mentioned, Hlin was "protectress in times of danger" and Eir, "the special goddess of healing . . . of relatively late origin, she was the personification of the gentle hand of woman in nursing the sick (Old Norse *eira*, 'to care for,' 'nurse')."

Views of the future life held by the Teutonic peoples during the Dark Ages show the same character and the same trends as the other aspects of their mythology. At one extreme were conceptions largely or wholly negative. "If, as has been suggested, Jötunheim, the world of giants, was originally a realm of the dead, and the word jötunn really means 'devourer,' it seems as if Teutonic thought had contemplated a world in which the dead were nothing but corpses, devoured by ogres." Or again, "The realm of Hel, goddess of the dead, seems to have been somewhat shadow-like, since its guardian chides the living Hermod for making more noise than five battalions of the dead."

These somber pictures, black or colorless grey, recall the gloomy view of the afterlife that we encountered on Neolithic horizons. More typical of emergent Dark-Age attitudes are visions offering some hope for the future. There is as yet no universal heaven, no fixed connection (unless late and under Christian influence) between ethical behavior and future rewards or punishments; and no certainty that any man, righteous or unrighteous, will enjoy future happiness. But there are various halls of the gods, some hospitable, some dangerous, into which individuals may stray after death. "Many abodes are there then good, and many bad; best is it to be in Gimle in heaven with Surtr; and great store of good drink is there for them who drink with joy in the hall called Brimir; it stands also in heaven. That is also a good hall which stands on Nithra-fells wrought of red gold; it is called Sindri."

Valhöll, the hall of Odin, was reserved for fallen soldiers. "There the dead warriors dwelt with Odin, who welcomed them; ordered the benches got ready, the goblets prepared, and the wine brought by the Valkyries." It is interesting to note that in early Teutonic society the only human beings assured of a favorable reception among the gods were, not the righteous, but the militaristically aggressive. And even they did not enjoy eternal satisfaction nor, it would seem, even eternal life. They feasted of nights, but during the day they fought and in this fighting they were "doomed to fall again, with no further hope of renewed life, in the battle between gods and giants."

From this brief survey of Teutonic theology we may conclude that, as compared with Neolithic precedents, Dark Age conceptions of the gods and of the future life had moved a considerable distance in a positive direction, but that they had as yet achieved no decisive supremacy of positive over negative elements. Further mythological growth would have been required to produce supreme deities of an exclusively beneficent character, and an opportunity open to all to achieve eternal bliss on the basis of ethical behavior. Such growth was under way in Western Europe and would presumably have continued to its logical conclusion if the Western peoples had been left to pursue their own cultural evolution without influence from abroad.

Such cultural independence they were not destined to preserve. Missionaries from the Christian cultures of the Mediterranean world penetrated their territory and began by persuasion a religious conversion which kings and military conquerers often finished with the point of the sword. Starting in the fourth century, when Ulfilas converted some of the Goths, the movement spread gradually from tribe to tribe and later from kingdom to kindgom. By the tenth century it had effected most of Western Europe, though the Norse peoples were still in the process of debating, and in part resisting, the new faith at that time.

The conversion of the West to Christianity concerns us at present only in one respect. To make our survey of Dark Age mythology complete, we must note that the gradual transposition of that mythology from "heathen" into Christian imagery in no sense changed its basic character or its previously established evolutionary direction. On the one hand the stage reached by Teutonic imagery, and by the experiences and ideas underlying it, was such as to make the transition to Christianity relatively natural and easy. The rise of a high religion and of universal gods was imminent in the West and would undoubtedly have occurred there — as it had occurred or was to occur in some other parts of the world — even without Christian influence.

Conversely, Christian conceptions, however exalted they may have been at certain other times and places, could enter Western experience only in the degree to which Western life and mentality were prepared to receive and sustain them. The "Christianity" that resulted from the conversion was neither that of the original Early Christian communities in the East nor that of subsequent Roman church fathers like Augustine; it was not the Christianity to be evolved in the West during the High Middle Ages nor that conceived by Christians today. It was a typical manifestation of Dark Age culture, substituting Christian names and rites for Teutonic ones, but carrying from one into the other the same dark background of the evolutionary past and the same slow movement toward a brighter evolutionary future. In the picturesque phrasing of one historian, "Catholicism sat upon the Franks like an ill-fitting garment patched all over with relics of heathenism."[4]

The hordes of Western evil spirits transformed themselves, with only a mocking grimace at human simplicity, into the Christian devil and his demonic hosts. Dragons and other monsters continued to be feared. As we have observed in connection with our early medieval carvings (Plate 16), these negative beings formed one of the major themes of Christian sculpture during the postconversion period. Heroes continued to combat them. The legend of pagan heroes like Beowulf was gradually surrounded by a Christian frame of reference, and the hero tradition eventually crystallized for Christianity in the combats of St. George with the dragon and St. Michael with the devil.

Teutonic gods slowly gave place to Christian ones, but the Christian deities, to the Dark Age mind, inevitably appeared as modified and sometimes clarified and rationalized versions of Teutonic ones. The near-supreme "old man with the long grey beard" could easily become the supreme Jehovah, perhaps gaining a second eye in the process, but perhaps already endowed with two eyes in some of the later Teutonic conceptions of Odin. The gentle luminous Balder, done to death in the Norse myths, could easily merge with the conception of the beneficent Christ and his crucifixion. "It is clear," says one of our authorities on Teutonic religion, "that in the latest form of the myth, Balder has been endowed with certain attributes of Christ." Hlin, "protectress in times of danger," could merge insensibly into the image of the protecting Virgin Mary.

The basic unity of Dark Age conceptions, regardless of whether they were Teutonic or Christian, can be indicated visually by a comparison of the two Viking founts shown in Figs. 48 and 49. One represents the Teutonic theme of Gunnar in the snake pit; the other the Christian one of the temptation of Adam and Eve. However we consider them, any supposed gulf between heathen and Christian conceptions melts away in a common manifestation of Dark Age mental and technical horizons.

Mythologically, both examples involve the defeat or damnation of humanity by serpentine monsters. Although the Hebrew myth originated at a more advanced cultural level and was correspondingly more intellectualized, the Norse conception of it pulls it back to the more instinctive fear-charged plane of Dark Age culture. Technically and artistically, both carvings reflect the same level of sculptural development. Their common style is intrinsically neither pagan nor Christian. It is archaic; that is to say representative of a particular stage of cultural evolution, and it inevitably reveals that stage of evolution in whatever it touches.

Speaking realistically, rather than theoretically or mythically, we are safe in asserting that Western Dark Age Christianity was a manifestation similar in kind to the native religion of the same period; that the two were parallel expressions of the same underlying psycho-historical circumstances, differing in their degree of relative advancement. The immense gulf which, in Christian feeling, existing between things "heathen" and things "Christian," was a mental construction rather than a historical fact. It was the gulf between the ego and the nonego; between that with which the subject identified himself and that from which he differentiated himself.

The conclusion is that *all* the mythical and religious conceptions of the Dark Ages, Teutonic *and* Christian, can be grouped together as typical expressions of their epoch; that they occupy an evolutionary position between those of Neolithic times and those of the High Middle Ages; and that, while they vary from a persistent negative weighting to a nascent positive weighting, they are most comprehensively typified by an approximate balance of negative and positive forces.

What, now, is the relation of all this to our psycho-technic theory? Finding Dark Age myths less negative and more positive then their Neolithic predecessors, finding that they tend toward a balance of negative-positive relations, we can draw certain inferences with regard to the mental and cultural evolution of humanity during the passage of time from the Neolithic epoch to the Dark Ages. On the mental plane, we assume a decrease in negative tensions and an increase in positive ones, resulting in a collective mentality divided between fear and hope, insecurity and confidence. And to explain this psychic duality we presume that there must have been an equivalent division of historical circumstances. Destructive or frustrating situations, it would seem, were still common collective experience, but at the same time there had apparently been a great increase in constructive mastery over environment and a corresponding growth of opportunity for human fulfillment. Again we must now ask ourselves, does history justify these assumptions?

II

The period to be considered is that of Western Europe during, let us say, the first millennium A.D. *Beowulf* dates from almost the exact middle of the millennium, having been written in the seventh century but containing mythological material that goes back at least to the fifth century. Teutonic religious conceptions are more difficult to date, but those we have considered were certainly active or emergent during the first millennium. And, as already noted, it was that millennium which saw the conversion of most of the Teutonic peoples to Christianity. Thus if we take the first millennium for our historical study, we shall cover a time span centered around our typical Dark Age mythological material and involving the historical circumstances most closely related to it.

No general historical name for the first millennium seems to exist. The second half of it, from 500 to 1000 A.D., is commonly referred to as the Dark Ages. Although, as we shall see, this terminology is partly misleading, we shall use it for want of a better one, and shall extend its accepted duration, but not in any degree its accepted connotation, to make it cover the millennium to which it belongs. Were we to choose another name for that millennium we should have to call it the Migration Period, the Period of the Barbarian Invasions, or simply the Barbarian Period, but each of these alternatives would need at least as much qualification for our purpose as does the more widely used phrase, the Dark Ages.

No elaborate argument is necessary to establish historical grounds for negative tensions during the period in question. One-sided though the name "Dark Ages" undoubtedly is, it nevertheless embodies at least the negative aspect of the historical truth. At one time or another during the first millennium, practically the whole population of Western Europe was displaced. Warfare was constant between the various barbarian tribes, between the barbarians and their former Roman conquerors, between the barbarians and new Asiatic assailants like the Huns in the northeast and the Moslems in the south. Victorious peoples entered new domains; defeated ones sank from freedom to serfdom or fled in vast shifts of population, often dying in large numbers along the way.

The annals of the times abound in descriptions of what the sixth-century bishop, Gregory of Tours, well characterizes in his *History of the Franks* as "the slaughters of the nations." A century earlier, St. Jerome had mournfully lamented the fact that "Nations innumerable and most savage have invaded all Gaul." Centuries later chroniclers were recording, with almost mathematical regularity, the yearly attacks of the Norsemen who "pillaged, destroyed, and burned all the regions along the coast." Not until after the middle of the eleventh century, in the Norman conquest of England, do we reach the last major convulsion of Western Europe's age of invasions.

How far to support these general statements by specific contemporary accounts reduces itself to the question of how long to detain the reader with historical quotations. In an effort at comparative brevity, it seems well to limit ourselves to brief glimpses of the flight of a dispossessed people, the devastation of rural areas, the siege and destruction of cities, and the brutality, famine, and plague by which such events were frequently accompanied or followed.

Ammianus Marcellinus, last of the Roman historians, gives us a glimpse of the trials of forced migration when he describes how the fleeing Visigoths, driven from their former homes by fear of the Huns, struggled without adequate facilities to cross the flooded Danube. "They crossed the stream day and night, without ceasing, embarking in troops on board ships and rafts, and canoes made of the hollow trunks of trees. In this enterprise, since the Danube is the most difficult of all rivers to navigate, and was at that time swollen with continual rains, a great many were drowned, who, because they were too numerous for the vessels, tried to swim across, and in spite of all their exertions were swept away by the stream." [5]

Wastage of the countryside is repeatedly described in the annals of the time. Here are three brief examples from Gregory's *History of the Franks*. "They robbed the huts of the poor, wasted vineyards, cutting off the vines and carrying them away grapes and all, taking domestic animals and whatever they could come upon and leaving nothing along their road. . . . They burned their houses and crops and whatever they could not carry away conveniently, and they plundered flocks and herds and carried all that was not fast. . . . The besiegers of Bourges, on receiving orders to return home, took wth them so much plunder that all the district they left was believed to be empty of men and domestic animals. The army of Desiderius and Bladast went through the land of Tours and burned, plundered, and slew . . . . There followed upon this disaster a disease among domestic animals so that scarcely enough remained to make a start with, and it was strange if any one saw an ox or a heifer." [6]

What such conditions meant to common country folk is well suggested by a passage in the *Geste Abbatum S. Albani,* a passage descriptive of conditions in England following the Norman conquest. "Scarce any man could go safely abroad in his own neighborhood; the houses of the peaceful folk were armed like a besieged city with bows and arrows, bills and axes, clubs and daggers and iron forks; the doors were barred with locks and bolts. The master of the house would say prayers as if on a tempest-tost bark; as doors and windows were closed, men said *Benedicite* and *Dominus* echoed reverently in response . . ." [7]

Parallel with the devastation of rural areas ran the siege, sack, and destruction of cities. The kind of fighting involved in the attack and defense of a city is well described by the poet-chronicler, Abbo, a monk of Saint-Denis, in his *Wars of Count Odo with the Northmen in the Reign of Charles the Fat*. We quote but a short passage from a long account of repeated attack and repeated repulse. The occasion is the siege of Paris by the Danes in 885. "Once more the latter [the Danes] engaged with the Christians in violent combat. On every side arrows sped and blood flowed. With the arrows mingled the stone hurled by slings and war-machines, the air was filled with them. The tower which had been built during the night groaned with the strokes of the darts, the city shook with struggle, the people ran hither and thither, the bells jangled. The warriors rushed together to defend the tottering tower and repel the assault . . ." Count Odo, military chief of the besieged city, "never admitted defeat and continually revived the spirits of the worn-out defenders. He ran along the ramparts and hurled back the enemy. On those who were secreting themselves so as to undermine the tower he poured oil, wax, and pitch, which, being mixed and heated, burned the Danes and tore off their scalps. Some of them died, others threw themselves into the river to escape the awful substance." [8]

When a city was carried, either by assault or — as occurred not infrequently — through treachery within the walls, carnage followed. Gregory tells what happened when the Frankish town of Comminges, successful in withstanding a siege, was betrayed by its self-seeking rulers. "The next night the leaders secretly carried off all the treasure they could find in the city, together with the church utensils. And in the morning they opened the gates and admitted the army and gave the common folk to the edge of the sword; butchering also the bishops of the Lord with their attendants at the very altars of the churches. And after they had killed all so that not one remained, they burned the whole city, both churches and other buildings, and left nothing but bare ground." [9]

Events like these, times like these, were naturally attended by every manner of personal violence and brutality. Rival kings and lords frequently murdered each other — often their own sons or fathers — in their lust for power and treasure. Shakespeare's *Macbeth* though written much later, is based on the legend of an eleventh-century king and reflects conditions of the kind we have been considering. Even the secession of a rebellious faction of nuns from a monastery could end in bloody feud and give rise to scenes like those described by Gregory in his chapter, "Scandal at the Convent of Poitiers." The leader of the rebellious faction, having ordered her armed male retainers "to break into the monastery at night and drag the abbess from it . . . the men came with drawn swords and spears and tore the nuns clothes and almost crushed their hands and seized the prioress instead of the abbess, since it was dark, and pulled her robes off and tore her hair down and dragged her off to place her under guard in St. Hilary's church."

After various attacks and counter attacks of this kind, the kings of the region decided to bring the affair to an issue by appointing a court of bishops to judge the case. First, however, they had to send soldiers to subdue the rebel faction by force. In accomplishing this mission, the soldiers rushed "upon those who were resisting and bound them and dragged them from the monastery and tied them to stakes and beat them fiercely and cut off the hair of some, the hands of others, and in a good many cases the ears and noses, and the rebellion was crushed and there was peace." [10]

As one reads the chronicles of the millennium under consideration, one is frequently forced to reflect how close, in certain respects, Western European man still was to savagery; how close to many of the more cruel practices and devastating conditions which explorers like Champlain found among the North American Indians. We have just noted an example of bodily mutilation of enemies, and torture was a common means of forcing confessions and of humiliating enemies. The dungeon, the rack, and other such infernal inventions added their threat to the terror of the times.

Abetted by so much social disruption, famine could still raise its gruesome head and, with increasing density of population, plague was becoming a menace of previously unknown proportions. Gregory tells frequently of both. "In this year [he does not give the exact date, but the time is the later sixth century] a severe famine oppressed almost all the Gauls. Many dried and ground into powder grape seeds and oat chaff and fern roots and mixed a little flour with it and made bread; many cut straw and did the same. Many who had no flour ate different herbs which they gathered, and in consequence swelled up and died. Many too wasted away and died of starvation. At that time the traders plundered the people greatly, selling scarcely a peck of grain or a half measure of wine for the third of a gold piece. They subjected the poor to slavery in return for a little food." [11]

The Venerable Bede also gives us a moving glimpse of famine, this time in seventh-century England. "For three years . . . no rain had fallen in those quarters, whereby too a very sore famine came upon the common people and overthrew them with pitiless destruction. In short it is reported that ofttimes 40 to 50 men being famished from hunger would go together to some cliff or bank of the sea, and there joining hands in miserable sort would cast themselves all down together, either to be killed with the fall or drowned in the waves." [12]

As to plague, here is Gregory's description of one of its attacks on central France. "And presently the plague came and such a carnage of the people took place through the whole district [of Clermont] that the legions that fell could not be counted. For when sepulchers and gravestones failed, ten or more would be buried in a single trench. Three hundred dead bodies were counted one Sunday in the church of the blessed Peter alone. Death was sudden. A wound the shape of a serpent would appear on groin or armpit and the man would be so overpowered by the poison as to die on the second or third day. Moreover the power of the poison rendered the victim insensible . . . At that time Lyons, Bourges, Cahors and Dijon were seriously depopulated from this plague." [13]

Accounts like these are more than sufficient to establish the point which concerns us, namely that during the Dark Ages, even as in Neolithic times, the inroads ascribed to the monsters of fantasy in no whit exceeded the dangers and difficulties suffered by men as sober facts of history. A thousand times during these turbulent centuries had flames as all-consuming as those of the dragon "burned the bright homesteads," "struck terror into men," and "laid in ashes the stronghold, the people's fastness." A thousand times had assault, famine, and plague attacked whole populations and "sundered life from body" with a force as overbearing and gruesome as that of the most "grisly monsters."

Nor must we imagine that the tribulations of the age were exclusively military, material, or physical. Intellectual and spiritual conflicts were likewise rampant and were often the cause of, or the excuse for, physical violence. Pagan and Christian religious concepts, orthodox and heretical versions of Christianity, the conflicting ideals of roving warrior groups and newly settled populations, all glowed with the heat of their mutual frictions. European ideology was as divided and as passionately contested as European territory and European military control. It was in short the "melting pot" stage of Western European agricultural civilization; the stage of antithesis — of almost innumerable antithesis — out of which was later to emerge the medieval synthesis.

Taken as a whole the historical circumstances of the first millennium provided every ground for the experience of negative tensions, hence abundant motivation for negative tension imagery. We seem, therefore, to be amply justified in explaining the Dark Age monsters as a mythological expression of this psycho-historical background.

III

The difficulty in interpreting Dark Age mythology lies not in finding grounds for the negative imagery of the monsters, but in explaining the positive imagery of the hero. In view of the chaotic aspects of life already considered, can there have been at the same time favorable circumstances sufficient to counterbalance the negative psychic states with positive ones and through the latter to generate the resolute and conquering symbol of heroes such as Beowulf? Surprising as it may seem at first glance, the answer is unquestionably in the affirmative.

Barbarism, in the sequence of cultural evolution, is the state of transition between savagery and civilization. Despite the military and ideological chaos of the Dark Ages — indeed one might say partly by means of that chaos — the Western European peoples were then laying the foundations of their civilization-to-be. In the technological and psychic gains already achieved and, we may suppose, in a stirring if still confused intuition of the goal before them, those peoples stood upon the frontiers of a richer, more fulfilling, and more stable world.

The developments of a dawning civilization have everywhere been approximately the same, whether, as in Egypt and Mesopotamia, they took place four or five millenniums before Christ, in Western Europe during the first millennium after Christ, or elsewhere at other times. These developments include the evolution of primitive agriculture to a point at which it provides an economic foundation for an expanding society; the diversification of that society into specialized groups, including skilled craftsmen, who achieve new wonders in technology and the arts, and priestly scholars who cultivate new learning; the amalgamation of tribes into kingdoms some of which, in time, are destined to absorb others and become empires; the formulation of law as a means of regulating increasingly complex social relationships; the invention or adoption of writing and consequent further acceleration of the whole process through the accumulation of knowledge in written records.

In Western Europe this evolution — a growth from the primitive agricultural beginnings of the preceding Neolithic epoch and Bronze Age — reached full momentum during the millennium before us. The Western peoples entered that millennium as the prehistoric roving tribes known to the Romans; they left it as historic nations with written languages, literatures already rich, economic and social systems already highly developed. The varied and rapid cultural advances involved in the change from the first to the second of these conditions comprise the positive aspects of life during the Dark Ages.

The taproot of the emergent Western civilization, like that of others, was agriculture. We have already noted that at the time of Christ most of the Teutonic tribes, as described by Caesar and Tacitus, still clung to a life of hunting and warfare, while a few of the more advanced had become regular, if still primitive, cultivators. Agricultural techniques, limited in Neolithic times to digging sticks and hoes worked by human hands, progressed during the Bronze Age (immediately preceding our millennium) to rude ploughs drawn by draft animals. Roman conquest and example stimulated the development.

Early Dark Age farm implements included the plough, the harrow, and the two-wheeled cart. The use of animal traction was an immense boon to humanity, though limited at first by poor stock, inefficient methods of harnessing, and the absence of any means of protecting the comparatively tender hoofs of the draught animals. Improvement of stock began early in the period we are considering. "The old Frankish horses were of the native race — small, ill-favored but hardy. But by the end of the Fifth Century the breed had been much improved, and when Charles Martel captured many horses from the Arabs, he used them for crossing, and so laid the foundation of the excellent Limousin breed." [14]

By the fifth century, in the Frankish kingdom under Clovis, says H. St.L. B. Moss, "Agriculture had made progress. Besides hand-querns, big ox-driven mills were used and the Roman water-mill was becoming known." The general state of agriculture among the Franks at this time, and some of its benefits in food resources, are well summed up by the same writer. "One may picture this country as dotted with villages and farmsteads, groups of low thatched houses and barns, of wood or wattle-and-daub, separated by a palisade from the gardens, orchards, meadow and ploughland. Practically all our modern meats, fruits, and vegetables were known, as we see from the treatise on diet which Anthimus, a Byzantine doctor, composed for Clovis, to whom he had been sent by Theodoric the Great. Bacon and hard boiled eggs are favorite dishes . . . Fresh cheese . . . fish, poultry, game, meat garnished with vegetables, sauces of wine and honey, preparations of milk, beer, and mead are mentioned." [15]

Some further details concerning Dark Age agriculture are provided by J. W. Thompson. "Cattle-raising played a great part in the life of the Franks, and herds were numerous, though wolves were a pest. Sheep abounded in Champagne, swine in Germany . . . The most expert, intensive, and lucrative form of agriculture was wine-growing. The Goths had learned the use of wine from the Romans in the fourth century, and developed the taste during their occupation of Spain and Italy. The Franks, when they entered Gaul, found the land covered with vineyards . . ." [16]

Toward the end of the millennium, in the eighth, ninth, and tenth centuries respectively, agricultural progress was accelerated by three of the most important inventions in its history: the iron horseshoe, the "modern" type of horse collar, and the "three-field system." The full effect of these inventions was not felt until the opening centuries of the second millennium — hence we shall postpone discussion of them until we reach the technology of the Gothic period — but the inventions themselves were achieved as part of the cumulative agricultural advance of the Dark Ages.

Supplementary to, and interrelated with, agricultural progress came technological developments in many other fields. Metal, at the beginning of the millennium a comparatively recent addition to Western European resources, now became the basis of highly developed crafts, both utilitarian and artistic. The Bronze Age had led, during the last millennium B.C. to the Iron Age. The first millennium A.D. was, in general, for this part of Europe, characterized by an Iron Age culture. Swords, daggers, and other weapons of bronze and iron replaced the earlier wooden or stone ones, as did metal implements for productive purposes. The metal weapons played an important part in the rise of the barbarian peoples to new military power. The metal implements gave them new potentials of economic production and artistic achievement.

On the artistic side, metal crafts, employing silver, gold, and colored enamel inlays, reached heights never to be surpassed. As Homer, at an equivalent stage in the evolution of Greek culture, had delighted in singing the glorious achievements of the craftsmen, and especially the craftsmen in metal, so was it with the bards of Western Europe during the Dark Ages.

Praise of metal "treasures" recurs like a refrain throughout *Beowulf*. We read of "shields covered with gold," "bridles heavy with gold," a "saddle fashioned with cunning art and well-dight with treasure." Many swords are enthusiastically described. Of one we are told that "Its edge was of iron, dyed with poison twigs, hardened with blood," but such stark functionalism in the blade did not prevent, indeed found triumphant emotional expression in, mountings of the greatest splendor. Sculptured images were "duly lined in rimed staves on the guard of gleaming gold, set down and told for them for whom the sword was wrought, choicest of blades, with twisted hilt and decked with dragon-shapes." Helmets added to the array of splendid armor. Frequently they were enriched with encircling figure plaques; in fact, the type of bronze plate considered among our illustrations of monster-hero art (Figs. 40 and 41) are believed to have served as a matrix for making helmet decorations. And quite apart from the armor and horse trappings thus far indicated, there were "deckings of gold" and "arm-jewells" for personal adornment, "gemmed beakers" for serving wine, and many other objects which the poet might well vaunt as among "the hoarded treasures of heroes." [17]

These descriptions, however enthusiastic, by no means exaggerate reality. Dark Age metal craft remains today among the "hoarded treasures" of human accomplishment. Displayed with pride in museums fortunate enough to possess examples, it is an eternal source of wonder and admiration to all who see it. As illustrated in Plate 20, Fig. 50, its crowning achievements are superb works of art both technically and esthetically.

Other crafts had also reached, or were reaching, high states of development during the first millennium. "The skill of the artisans and cloth makers of Britain," says Langer, "was already famous on the continent in the fourth century." [18] Decorative textiles enriched the setting of *Beowulf* and help to reveal its times. "Gleaming with gold shone the hangings on the wall" when the Danes celebrated Beowulf's success against Grendel; "a broidered war banner" went with arms and armor to reward the hero for his victory.

Carving in wood and stone added to the number of techniques through which the ornamental passion of the age expressed itself. The examples thus far considered were chosen for the mythological subjects they represent. Only incidentally do they illustrate the other aspects of the Dark Age carver's art. For a full realization of the technical proficiency and ornamental genius of that art, we must turn to the decorative borders that enrich all kinds of objects from the Wendel and Viking periods in Scandinavia (Plate 20, Fig. 52) and that, during the following centuries, encircle so many Romanesque doorways.

At about the same time as the Norse cultures just mentioned — that is to say during the second half of the millennium — Celtic monks produced some of the world's most beautiful calligraphy and decorative page design (Fig. 51). Indeed so far as concerns decorative arts and crafts, Western Europe reached during our period a summit of achievement which it was never to surpass and which, subsequent to the Middle Ages, it rarely if ever equalled.

Before leaving the material accomplishments of the Dark Ages, we must take note of ship building and of accelerated architectural advance. Ocean-going vessels became the pride, as they were one of the main means of military conquest and economic gain, of many coastal peoples and especially of the Viking Norsemen. "The good sea-goer . . . the foamy-necked ship, likest to a bird," is among the fairest objects to the Old English poet and has remained a fair object to all of us ever since. In Western Europe, it was one of the technological developments of the Dark Ages.

On land it was matched by "the hall . . . lofty and broad-gabled," "the fair dwelling of man's making . . . shrewd care had bound it fast with iron bands within and without" and its door was "fastened with iron forged in the fire." Defensive towers, elaborate manorial and monastic buildings (Fig. 53), the churches of Merovingian and Carolingian times (Fig. 54), were among the many manifestations of an architectural development that was to reach its climax in the great Gothic cathedrals only two centuries after the close of the millennium.

This brief review of the material arts of the Dark Ages should be sufficient to establish the fact that the period was one of momentous technological progress in Western Europe; progress involving revolutionary advances in agriculture, in metallurgy, and in fact in the whole technological basis of Teutonic life.

IV

While the agricultural and technological roots of Western culture were vigorously entrenching themselves, other aspects of cultural growth were quick to respond. What may be considered the armature that supported and at the same time shaped the social form of the growing cultural organism lay in its military power, its governmental organization, and its legal order. All these contributed a rapid and constructive growth to the positive aspects of life during the Dark Ages. Since we have already observed the devastating negative effects of military conflict during this period, the reader may be surprised that we should now grant a positive significance to the growth of Western military power. Nevertheless, it was in certain respects a positive achievement, inextricably linked with other such achievements and, in its own way, a part of the upward drive of the Teutonic peoples toward civilization.

Motivated at least in part by the lure of newly developed wealth and wealth-producing land, Dark Age military expansion was also in part an outcome of newly developed technical resources. We have noted that it profited by the development of metallurgy and the replacement of primitive weapons by metal arms and armor. It profited also by agricultural progress in the field of stock raising. A military outcome of the domestication of animals, apparently first exploited by the Teutonic peoples, was the development of cavalry. In 378 the Visigoths overcame the Romans in the battle of Adrianople, a battle concerning which Langer remarks, "This defeat of Roman infantry by mounted warriors forecasts the revolution in the art of war which determined the military, social, and political development of Europe throughout the Middle Ages." [19]

Wealth and land, arms and war horses, were among the positive *sources* of the new Teutonic military power; its positive *effects* included important developments in both the political and the psychological spheres. Politically it resulted indirectly in the emergence of larger states and more fully organized systems of government. Psychologically, devastating as were its results upon the vanquished, it offered the victors an exhilarating career of individual opportunity and collective achievement. Feverish but purposeful and triumphant activity brought in its train new wealth, new power, new glory. Under such circumstances, for those who were in a position to profit by them, psychic impulse could flow directly into successful action to a degree rarely possible in more settled states of society.

The positive value of the resulting psychic freedom, linked with positive developments of many other kinds already considered or to be considered, indicates how one-sided an impression of the period has been perpetuated by the term "Dark Ages." It is a term expressive of the mentality of the defeated, not of the victorious. For Rome, which had had its own day of expansion and conquest and was now sinking into decline, the times were indeed dark. But for the Western people, the situation was reversed. At an earlier time many of them had been conquered by the then superior Roman strength; others had been driven from their homes by stronger Asiatic forces. Now the tide was turning in their favor. They were becoming conquerors. As the world knows, they ultimately overcame the fabled power of Rome, at the same time in many cases supporting the tradition of that power by themselves becoming governors, kings, and even emperors of the persistent "Roman empire" — an empire which in reality had by this time become Teutonic.

In some respects this was the barbarian's "grandest hour." These centuries were to them, not "dark ages," but ages of steadily increasing light; "dawn ages" transfused with all the radiance of new hope and new achievement. Looked at intrinsically rather than externally or theoretically, there is no more reason for calling the formative stages of Western civilization "Dark Ages" than there would be to apply that name to the equally barbaric and equally pregnant formative epochs of civilization in other parts of the world. We associate no concept of darkness with the opening dynasties in Egypt or the archaic period in Greece. Instead we conceive these epochs as times of vigorous growth, which laid the foundations for their respective civilizations and produced the first fresh flowering of their arts. Terminology notwithstanding, what we are really dealing with in the later centuries of the first millennium is the equally vigorous archaic period of Western Europe.

Outwardly, the most immediate positive effects of the new Teutonic military power lay in the emergence of larger social units and their necessary by-product, codified law. Tacitus had remarked the absence of "powerful kingdoms" among the Teutonic tribes of his day. By the middle of the first millennium, such kingdoms had been established or were being established, in most parts of Western Europe. Stronger kingdoms in turn were overcoming and absorbing weaker ones, as Lower Egypt had once overcome and absorbed Upper Egypt and as Rome had overcome and absorbed her rival city states in archaic Italy. At the end of the eighth century, as a result of the conquests of Pepin and Charlemagne, the kingdom of the Franks had been progressively extended until it included the territories of modern France, Belgium, Holland, and Switzerland, much of Germany, Austria-Hungary to a point about as far east as Vienna, Italy to a point farther south than Rome, and a portion of northern Spain. Such a vast expanse of territory under a single rule provided a wider basis of political unity than had ever existed in Western Europe prior to that time, or than has ever existed since the disintegration of Charlemagne's empire — far wider, of course, than exists at the present day.

When Charlemagne, a hero of true Beowulfian stature, was crowned emperor at Rome in the year 800, the stability of the Roman Empire appeared at last to have been restored and a new western Pax Germanum to be within reach of the Teutonic peoples. To many men then alive it must have seemed that troubled Europe was about to enter upon an age of unity and peace such as the north had never known before, and such as the Mediterranean south could remember only through the dust of nearly five centuries of disintegration and conflict. The enthusiasm of the moment can be gathered from a contemporary account in the *Liber Pontificalies.*

"After this, on Christmas day, all gathered together in the aforesaid church of St. Peter and the venerable pope crowned Karl with his own hands with a magnificent crown. Then all the Romans, inspired by God and by St. Peter, keeper of the keys of Heaven, and recognizing the value of Karl's protection and the love he bore the holy Roman church and the pope, shouted in a loud voice: 'Long life and victory to Karl, the pious Augustus crowned of God, the great and peace-bringing emperor.' " [20]

"Peace-bringing" in an underlying and ultimate sense, the conquerors and rulers of the Dark Ages were, even though their reign was extended by force and all too often by treachery; even indeed though wars did not cease in their day nor have yet ceased in ours. Their function was not only to conquer but also to defend what they possessed, and above all to rule. The states which grew up under their leadership could survive only if they succeeded in establishing an internal unity of law and order. Despite an intractable human heritage that resisted it, the slow growth of such law and order can be followed throughout the Dark Ages.

Each new kingdom in due course produced a law-giving king who was the first, for his territory and people, to organize tribal customs and surviving Roman traditions into a code of written law. This legal development apparently began with Euric (466–484), ruler of the Visigothic kingdom of Toulouse, who first codified Visigothic law, but the *Breviary of Alaric* (506), "a codification of Roman law for Visigothic use, had tremendous influence among the Visigoths and among many other barbarian peoples." A short time later "King Gundibald (died 516) codified the Burgundian law in the *Lex Gundobada.*" [21] So, from people to people and century to century, the establishment of written law proceeded throughout Western Europe.

Typical of the early stages of this legal evolution is the so-called "Salic Law," the law established in the kingdom of the Salic Franks. It was, say Thatcher and McNeal, "probably written about the year 500, in the reign of Choldovech (481–511)." Some characteristic excerpts will illustrate the social trends of the times.

"XVII WOUNDS

"6. If a freeman strike another freeman with a club, so that the blood does not flow, he shall pay 120 denarii, which make 3 solidi,[22] for each blow, up to three.

"7. If the blood does flow, he shall pay as much for each blow as if he had wounded him with a sword.

"8. If anyone strikes another with the closed fist, he shall pay 360 denarii, which make 9 solidi; that is, 3 solidi for each blow up to three.

"9. If anyone is convicted of trying to rob another on the highroad, even though he fails, he shall pay 2,500 denarii, which make 63 solidi."

"XLI MANSLAUGHTER

"1. If anyone is convicted of killing a free Frank or a barbarian living by the Salic law, he shall pay 8,000 denarii, which make 200 solidi.

"3. If anyone kills a man in the king's trust, or a free woman, he shall pay 24,000 denarii, which make 600 solidi." [23]

These are but a few selections from hundreds of clauses dealing with wounds, injuries, and manslaughter. Every type of personal injury is described and the monetary reparation for it indicated. Men and women of every walk of life are listed and provision made for a specific *wergild* (literally 'man-payment') appropriate to them; that is, for a specific amount of money that must be paid by the slayer and that must be accepted by the family of the slain in retribution for his death.

Although one author has characterized these early laws as little more than "lists of compensations for crimes among savages," [24] their social significance is evident. Traditionally, conduct among the barbarians had been governed to a large extent by instinctive impulse. Disagreement flared readily into assault. In a flash of anger, a man might be wounded or killed. If killed, his relatives regarded themselves as responsible to avenge his death and the long protracted curse of a blood feud began. Social progress at this stage of group life required the replacement of private revenge by collective control. So the state prescribed penalties for damage done and substituted legal sanctions for personal resentment as a means of exacting those penalties.

It seems clear from such considerations that even in the supposedly darkest phase of the Dark Ages, at the end of the fifth and the beginning of the sixth centuries, strong forces of social cohesion were at work to combat the destructive forces of the times and to promote growing collective stability and security. The increasingly humane results of three centuries of further social growth are evident in the laws and administrative institutions of Charlemagne. Further legal quotations would unnecessarily lengthen our discussion, but we may note in passing that the *General Capitulary about the Missi*,[25] an edict issued by Charlemagne in 802, is an impressive statement of the will to order in Carolingian society. Nor must we forget that the law-building impulse of the Dark Ages manifested itself, not only in civil developments like those just considered, but in the religious sphere as well. The Papacy rivaled the secular courts in taking upon itself a law-giving prerogative, and each of the monastic orders, as it came into being, established a set of laws for the conduct of its members as one of the prerequisites to its existence.

V

With vigorous economic roots, sturdy social trunk, and branches pressing out in many directions, it was but natural that Western culture should produce its blossoms. And it did — in the arts, in learning, and in religion. We have already noted that technical excellence in the crafts of the period was matched by superlative qualities of decorative design. We may conclude our survey of the positive aspects of Dark Age life with some reference to developments in the fields of learning and religion.

By the middle of the first millennium the royal courts enjoyed economic independence, sometimes originally attained through conquest, but always in the long run maintained by royal estates or through tribute and taxation drawn ultimately from the productiveness of the soil. The other chief centers of Dark Age culture, the monasteries, had usually obtained, as part of their foundation, large grants of land. They applied the labor of the monks to the cultivation of this land with a thoroughness that soon established them as the leading "model farms" of their epoch. Thus, they in turn achieved, through agriculture, an independent and self-sustaining economic position. Having thus attained a favorable economic balance, both courts and monasteries devoted a portion of their means to intellectual pursuits. Native talent was given the leisure and the training necessary for its development. Foreign talent was attracted to these rising new communities from older but less dynamic cultures, somewhat as European talent was to flock to America during the first half of the twentieth century.

One of the results of these conditions was a whole series of Dark Age

"renaissances." Best known among them are the Celtic Golden Age center-
ing in Ireland between the sixth and ninth centuries, the Carolingian Renaissance of the late eighth and early ninth centuries, the English flowering in the
ninth century at the court of Alfred, and the tenth century Ottonian Renaissance in Germany. (Strictly speaking these cultural flowerings were not "renaissances" but "naissances"; not "rebirths," but births.) In them, for the first time,
Western European peoples were entering upon the stage of literate culture,
and were experiencing all the intellectual stimulus that results from the development of writing and the consequent ability both to create records and
to use the records of the past. As abundant stores of food were first becoming
potential to an agriculturalized Western Europe, so abundant stores of knowledge were first becoming potential to a literate Western Europe.

This scholarly aspect of evolving Dark Age culture seems to have born
its first fruit in the fourth century when "Ulfilas (311–381), a Gothic bishop
of Arian conviction, invented the Gothic alphabet for his translation of the
Bible." This translation, "the first literary monument of the Germanic in-
vaders, had enormous influence." [26] Gregory of Tours, as we have seen, wrote
his *History of the Franks* in the sixth century, using the Latin which for
many centuries was to remain the language of Western European erudition and
which was to divide literary production with the various Western vernaculars.
In the eighth century, Paul the Deacon wrote a *History of the Lombards*. Another early monument of continental literature, the Old French *Chanson de
Roland*, though not known to us in written versions antedating the eleventh
century, was based upon an eighth century incident of one of Charlemagne's
campaigns in Spain and was undoubtedly composed before the end of the first
millennium. In England the Venerable Bede, "father of English literature,"
wrote his ecclesiastical histories in Latin at the end of the seventh century —
about the same time that *Beowulf* became a written epic in Old English. By the
eighth century, it would appear, the monks of Winchester were at work on
the Anglo-Saxon Chronicle; in the ninth century King Alfred translated Bede
and other writers from Latin into the vernacular.

The intellectual vigor of many Dark Age leaders, and the scholarly circles
with which they surrounded themselves, can be judged by the example of
Charlemagne as recorded by Einhardt. Einhardt, himself one of the scholars
gathered by the emperor at his court, wrote a *Life of Charlemagne* in which we
find the following description of the emperor's intellectual activities and attainments.

"He spoke foreign languages besides his own tongue, and was so proficient in Latin that he used it as easily as his own language. Greek he could understand better than he could speak . . . He was devoted to the study of the liberal arts and was a munificent patron of learned men. Grammar he learned from Peter, an aged deacon of Pisa; in the other studies his chief instructor was Alcuin, a Saxon from England, also a deacon, and the most learned man of his time. With him he studied rhetoric, dialectic, and especially astronomy . . . He tried also to learn to write, keeping tablets under the pillow of his couch to practice on in his leisure hours. But he never succeeded very well, because he began too late in life.

"After he became emperor he undertook a revision of the laws of the empire . . . He also wrote down for preservation the ancient German songs, in which the wars and adventures of old heroes are celebrated. He also began to make a grammar of his native tongue." [27]

Equally revealing is the even more scholarly Alfred's exposition of the importance of education and learning to his people, and the consequent need of translating Latin texts into current Anglo-Saxon. In the introduction to his own translation of the *Pastoral Charge* by Pope Gregory the Great, Alfred discourses at some length on this subject. We quote but a paragraph.

"Therefore it seems better to me, if you agree [he is addressing one Bishop Waerferth] for us also to translate some of the books which are most needful for all men to know into the language which we can all understand; and for you to see to it, as can easily be done if we have tranquility enough, that all the free-born youth now in England, who are rich enough to be able to devote themselves to it, be set to learn as long as they are not fit for any other occupation, until that they are well able to read English writing; and let those afterwards be taught more in the Latin language who are to continue learning, and be promoted to a higher rank." [28] Alfred concludes the passage by saying that he is sending a copy of his translation of the *Pastoral Charge* to every bishopric in his kingdom and that — linking his literary work to the rich decorative craftsmanship of the period — "on each copy there shall be a clasp worth fifty mancuses."

Thus Western learning, though not yet in full flower, was certainly in vigorous bud during the later Dark Ages, and was adding new practical knowledge and new intellectual discernment to the resources of Western culture. Sustained in the last analysis by technological and economic advances and thus, in the main, a result rather than a cause of Western progress, this new learning in turn became a means to further progress and a positive factor in historical growth.

When we turn from learning to the religion with which, in the Dark Ages, it was closely allied, the embracing context of cultural relations is similar. Basically, the slow movement away from a negative toward a positive religion was a reflection of improving psycho-historical circumstances, rather than a means by which those circumstances were improved. At the same time, evolving religious conceptions and institutions, as they assumed more positive form, encouraged and strengthened the forces that gave rise to them and thus became sustaining historical circumstances in their own right.

In the sphere of mythical and theological imagery, heroes like Beowulf, gods like Thor, Woden, and their Christian successors, were symbols which fixed and focused the growing positive consciousness of the age and which, by so doing, stabilized that consciousness and furthered its growth. The same is true of the more sociological aspects of religion — the natural contrabass to the supernatural imagery — such as the advance in ethical standards, the development of more positive religious institutions and ceremonies, and the pursuit of educational and charitable activities under religious supervision.

The crueler practices of earlier terrorized religions, such as human sacrifice, seem to have reached the Dark Ages only as dying vestiges of traditions that had outlived their time; much as they reached the earlier sections of the Judaic-Christian scriptures in the account of Abraham's intention to sacrifice Isaac. Even the pre-Christian West was far advanced in positive religious practices, as we learn from the accounts of its native priests, the Druids.

"The Druids were philosophers and teachers of youth. They taught not only theology and mythology, but also much of the course of the stars, of the nature of all things, and the magnitude of the universe. Of all the moral teachings of the Druids only a single sentence is preserved (Diogenes Laertius, proemium 5): 'To be pious toward the gods, to do wrong to no man, and to practice fortitude.' But their chief doctrine was that the souls do not die, but pass after death to another body . . ." [29]

"To be pious toward the gods, to do wrong to no man, and to practice fortitude." Could the Christians of that age have recognized prophets other than the Hebrew ones, they would have seen here a Western equivalent of what is often regarded as one of the noblest summations of their own gospels: "Thou shalt love the Lord they God with all thy heart and with all thy soul . . . and thy neighbor as thyself." Whether we take the Celtic version of the early Dark Ages or the Christian one adopted by the West during the later Dark Ages, the development of a devotional-ethical religious tradition in the West was bound to stabilize the flickering impulses of man's spiritual life and to promote social growth by progressively raising standards of moral judgment and goals of spiritual aspiration.

This spiritual growth of the West was to find its highest and most permanent embodiment in the acceptance of the New Testament as the religious corner stone of Western civilization. Rarely and poorly as the gospels may be applied in social living, they are nevertheless an inspirational directive for any society that meditates upon them. They became such a directive for the West during the Dark Ages.

In fact the Christian scriptures, and the commentaries of the Latin church fathers by which they were followed, might not inappropriately be considered forms of Dark Age literature. They were composed during the early and middle centuries of the first millennium, contemporaneously with Teutonic works like *Beowulf*. It is true that they emanated from the Greco-Roman south. It is also true that during the centuries in question the south had much in common, psycho-historically speaking, with the north and west. In both spheres of Europe, collective hope and despair struggled with each other for ascendancy. In the south it was a desperate hope of survival struggling with the despair of a disintegrating civilization. In the north the elated hope of an emergent civilization had come to grips with the inheritance from a desperate past. The evolutionary directions were opposite; the temporary conjunction of negative and positive circumstances similar.

The Christian spiritual documents adopted by the Teutonic peoples during the Dark Ages were matched by others of their own production. As concluding examples of the religio-ethical ideals of the times, let us glance briefly at two of these Christianized pronouncements of the West: the *Regula* or *Rule* of St. Benedict and the *General Capitulary about the Missi* issued by Charlemagne.

Benedict's *Rule*, written in the sixth century, was a response to the crying need for order in the chaotic world of early Western monasticism; a strange world of individual vagaries in which the monk was bound by no permanent vows or social responsibilities and not infrequently degenerated into a begging tramp. In the decaying East, the asceticism of individual hermits had had its psychological function as an escape from social corruption and disillusionment. In the emergent West the situation was different. Here monasticism had a future only to the degree in which it could become a vehicle of social purpose, organized energy, and constructive vision. Benedict had the genius to recognize these demands of the times and to satisfy them by providing, in the *Rule*, a program for positive social monasticism. As a result, his work remained for centuries the organizing principle of the monastic movement in the West.

The *Rule* deals with many things besides spiritual matters: with institutional government, with the manual labor to which the monks were to give seven hours a day; with the technological bases of community life in agriculture and the trades through which the monastery was to "contain within its walls every-thing necessary to the life and labor of the monks, such as wells, a mill, bake-oven, gardens, etc. . . ." But through it all, not detached from but permeating these material necessities of existence, runs an ethical ideal. This is perhaps best summarized in Chapter 4 of the *Rule, The Instruments of Good Works*, which sets forth the ethical code and conduct of the ideal monk.

"First to love the Lord God with all the heart, and with all the soul, and with all the strength, and then his neighbor as himself. Then not to kill, nor to commit adultery, not to steal, not to covet, not to bear false witness, to honor all men, and not to do to another what he would not have another do to him. To deny himself that he may follow Christ, to chasten the body, to renounce luxuries, to love fasting. To feed the poor, to clothe the naked, to visit the sick, to bury the dead, to offer help in trouble, to comfort the sorrowing." The passage continues to three times the above length and contains, near its close, the summarizing phrase, "Lo these are the implements of the spiritual pro-fession." [30]

These were ideals hard to reach, easy to fall from, and only partially realized even at the crest of monastic vitality. Yet they *were* ideals — ideals of Dark Age humanity — and they were among the lights that helped to counterbalance the darks of the Dark Ages and to give those ages a sense of movement from darkness toward light. That, as ideals, they permeated the social as well as the religious institutions of the epoch, is indicated by the degree to which Charle-magne incorporates them in his statements of civil law. His *General Capitulary about the Missi* provides a case in point. The "missi" were officials charged with the oversight of governmental affairs and acting more or less as liaison officers between the emperor and the various departments of his administration through-out the empire.

"He ordered these men to investigate and report to him any inequality or injustice that might appear in the law as then constituted, that he might under-take its correction. He ordered that no one should dare to change the prescribed law by trickery or fraud, or to pervert the course of justice for his own ends, as many were wont to do, or to deal unjustly with the churches of God, with the poor or the widows and orphans, or with any Christian man. But he commanded all men to live righteously according to the precepts of God, and to remain each in his own station and calling; the regular clergy to observe the rules of monastic life without thought of gain, nuns to keep diligent watch over their lives, laymen to keep the law justly without fraud, and all, finally, to live together in perfect peace and charity . . ." Similar admonitions are several times repeated and on one occasion the command is addressed to "every man in his kingdom, clergyman and layman . . . that each shall strive with all his mind and strength on his own account to serve God according to the commandments and according to his own promise, for the emperor is not able to give the necessary care and oversight to all his people." [31]

Through the formulation and propagation of such ideals, religion took its place, along with art and learning, among the flowers of Dark Age culture — dependent upon the material roots and stems below them, but at the same time setting forth the life principles essential to the vitality and perpetuation of the cultural organism.

VI

If we think back over the developments of the first millennium — in agriculture, metal crafts, and other phases of material technology, in growing political organization and legal order, in written language, learning, and religion — it seems evident that the historical circumstances of the period included many positive elements. The emergence of these elements as historical realities would inevitably be attended by corresponding gains in positive psychic experience. And with this gathering reservoir of positive energy in the Western soul, the symbolical figures of its conquering heroes and its increasingly beneficent gods are readily understandable as tension-imagery projections.

We have previously seen that the negative aspects of life during the Dark Ages were also marked and far-reaching, providing ample instigation for the imagery of monster and demon. The period was in fact psycho-technically dualistic to an extraordinary degree. When we consider its history as a whole, we can observe some resistant or destructive force at work against every positive development; some constructive development emerging to oppose every negative influence. It would be difficult to conceive historical circumstances more likely to inspire a state of soul divided between hope and despair, confidence and fear, security and insecurity. And given these divided and conflicting tensions, it would be difficult to imagine a more accurate imagery expression of them than Dark Age mythology: a mythology powerful alike in its negative and in its positive fantasies and vivid in its presentation of conflict between the two. Thus the facts, the feelings, and the myths of the Dark Ages fall into place as interwoven aspects of an organic cultural relationship.

It is even possible that in some cases we have linguistic or other circumstantial links between the historical realities and their symbolical expressions. The name "Beowulf," for instance, is related to the Old English word *beow* (grain), which at an earlier time had also been used as the name of a grain god, Beow.[32] As in dreaming we sometimes retain enough consciousness to penetrate the dream imagery with a fleeting recognition of objective reality, so here we seem to see through the hero myth to the harvests that played so decisive a part in combatting human misery and in bringing a new era of life to Western European peoples.

Another name that stands midway between symbol and reality was noted earlier in this chapter: that of Eir, one of the later and kindlier Norse goddesses whose special province was healing. Her name was derived from the Old Norse *eira* (to care for, nurse), and her mythical existence was evidently a projection of the benefits of human care and nursing.

Frey was one of the greatest and most positive of the Norse gods. It can hardly be a coincidence that we read of him he "was regarded as the dispenser of wealth and prosperity" and that his "principal sphere of worship was in the fertile plains of Sweden." Geographical fertility, human prosperity, and a prosperity-giving god make a logical psycho-technic equation. And if the Icelandic sagas persist in negativism so much longer than continental myths, can we doubt that this is so in large part because the Icelandic environment, isolated and inclement, resisted much longer the development of a prosperous agricultural society?

Sudhoof, in his study of diseases and medicine, has suggested interesting links between states of physical suffering and negative mythical imagery; among them the link from smoke to suffocation to strangling demon. "What mysterious power was it that . . . caused hale and hearty youths to perish by suffocation . . . ? The inmates of the smoky turf-cabin had often felt this malign power at work, as it squatted — crushing and squeezing — on the breast and throat, and had awakened with screams of terror and bathed in perspiration: it was the dreaded *alp* (incubus, nightmare), who had all but strangled them to death." [33] Only with the subsequent medieval invention of the chimney could northern humanity escape the menace of suffocation from smoke, and only when it had escaped that menace could its fears of the strangling alp, like smoke itself, slowly dissolve in a healthier atmosphere.

Chapter XIII

MYTH AND HISTORY IN THE MIDDLE AGES

We return at last to the Gothic imagery of the High Middle Ages which formed the point of departure for our historical excursions, and which is the third and last of the three periods under consideration. Gothic iconography brings to completion our evolutionary sequence of mythico-religious conceptions. In it, the relationship between negative and positive components becomes the exact opposite of what it had been at the beginning of the sequence. Instead of omnipotent monsters dominating shadowy and helpless gods, we now have an omnipotent God and his attendant hosts dominating comparatively helpless demons.

Negative beings still inhabit the mythological cosmos — even the Gothic period is unable to banish them entirely — but they are reduced to a subservient role. Monster-slaying heroes, Christianized in figures like St. Michael and St. George, retain an honorable place in the new order. Along with a partly natural, partly supernatural multitude of other saints and angels, they continue to radiate a diffused aura of blessing for mankind, but they are now as foothills to more recent and loftier conceptions. Above them rise the noble figures of the Virgin Mother and of Christ, and these in turn form connecting links with the dominating summit of the whole mythico-religious range of Western Europe: the conception of an omnipotent and omniscient God. The Father has evolved from the uncertain status of being "not very good" to a position of power and majesty which renders him the source and symbol of all good.

Expressions of this positive emphasis in imagery are manifold in Gothic art; in fact they constitute its major and recurrent theme. We meet them in a variety of embodiments ranging in scope from the microcosmic to the macrocosmic. Four examples, illustrating three different degrees of extension in their range, are shown in Plates 22–24. In the *Beau Dieu* at Amiens (Fig. 55) as in thousands of other representations of Christ, the Virgin, and the saints, the theme is expressed through a single figure. Deified humanity stands before us majestic and serene, with no suggestion of struggle or even of effort, unless it be the quiet masterful effort of a concentrated will. We hardly notice the diminutive monsters pinned helplessly, inconsequentially, beneath the savior's feet. Yet the monsters are there, and are reduced to such a sorry station in the mythical universe of the thirteenth century. This relationship of the masterfully controlling deity to the discomfited demon is as far from Beowulfian pitched battles as were the latter from the unchallenged reign of Neolithic monsters.

More inclusively, the same relationship of positive to negative appears in the Last Judgment scenes that were carved in one of the portals of practically every Gothic cathedral (Plate 26, Fig. 66), and that formed a climax to many of the more ambitious schemes of Gothic mural painting. We observed among our earlier examples of Gothic negative imagery, the rendering of Hell in Giotto's *Last Judgment* at Padua (Fig. 22). If this scene existed in isolation, as we then reproduced it, it would comprise a chamber of horrors not unlike the Neolithic monster myths in subject, though softened in intensity. Giotto's man-crunching Lucifer, like Dante's,[1] seems in fact to perpetuate traditions of man-eating giants descended from Gougou and his like. The difference of attitude between the two periods only becomes apparent when we observe the Giotto detail in the totality of which it forms a part (Fig. 56). Then we recognize that the evil being who stood on the mythological zenith in Neolithic times has been reduced to a low and relatively minor position in the Gothic context. He has been conquered by God and has dominion only by the will of God and over those who have offended God. Hell as a whole occupies only about a quarter of the Giotto painting. Three quarters of it are given to the imagery of heaven, with the savior and his saving cross as the central and dominant features.

As Neolithic men found every renewed occasion for fearing their monsters, so Gothic men found every renewed occasion for exalting their saviors. The most inclusive of their expressions of this impulse — springing from the soul and demanding the creative energy of their entire society — was the Gothic cathedral in all its sublime architectural and iconographical totality. Amiens (Plate 23) provides one of the greatest, but only one among scores of great examples. The whole vast organism is inspired by a sense of the transcendent glory and efficacy of the heavenly hierarchy and, in particular, of the Virgin Mother to whom this and many other such cathedrals were dedicated. The positive nature of this inspiration reveals itself architecturally in the serene exaltation of Gothic interiors: an exaltation blended of noble spaciousness and lofty height, daring yet secure and elegant structure, shadowy calm and radiant color (Plate 24). Today still, as we enter one of these buildings, we feel ourselves to be in a sanctuary governed by a benign power; a sanctuary within which positive faith becomes easier and negative tensions subside.

What the architecture of the cathedral thus implies, its figured decorations explicitly state. The multitudinous representations, whether in the sculpture of the exterior or the stained glass of the interior, are all but exclusively given to the positive imagery of divinities, saints, and sacred legends. Whatever negative imagery survives, does so by divine ordinance and in the negligible proportions and positions noticed in our previous examples, and the observer finds in these vestiges of evil little occasion for fear.

Nor is the transcendence of positive imagery in Gothic art manifest only in the subjects chosen for representation; it is also evident in the quality of emotional expressiveness achieved in the representations. The Gothic artist has a unique capacity for feeling and communicating positive states of consciousness. Typical achievements of this sort — all of them familiar — appear on Plate 25.

What other period has left us with faces so aglow with tranquil light such as those in Fig. 59, or has so engagingly revealed, through an angel's smile (Fig. 60), the blessed character of the Annunciation? Could we find a more touching image of protective providence than the group at Reims (Fig. 61) in which solicitous angels carry newly resurrected souls to Abraham's bosom? And what later painter ever equaled Giotto in portraying states of spiritual grace such as the tender concern shared by Joachim and Anna at the Golden Gate? (Fig. 62). Many more examples could be mentioned. In short, the felicity with which the Gothic artist handles positive emotions is as much an indication of the emphasis on the positive in Gothic imagery as is the predominance of positive themes in subject matter.

The only surviving demonic powers to retain a quasi-independent existence on the cathedral are the gargoyles and chimeras in the upper reaches of the exterior and these are detached from the immediate context of divine control. These prove indirectly the dominance of the positive through their displacement, their marginal locations, and also through the transformation of their character from the once terrible to the now half-humorous grotesque.

Surviving example of the earliest Romanesque art, such as the Lombard carvings of the eighth, ninth, and tenth centuries, indicate that at that time the monster still contested the focal points of consciousness and, therefore, those of religious representation. Our previous Romanesque examples included several in which the important space above the church doorway was given to carvings of monster-hero combats (Figs. 29 and 31). For the sake of present comparison, a further instance is reproduced on Plate 26 (Fig. 63). Here we have approximately Beowulfian equality between hero and monster. The rapid upswing of positive imagery, and corresponding displacement of negative imagery, during the first three centuries of the new millennium can be interestingly followed in the tympani of the later Romanesque and Gothic churches.

A transitional conception introduces Christ as the central motif of an Apocalyptic Vision or Last Judgment, while at the same time retaining monsters among the figures that surround him. At Neuillyen Deujeu (Fig. 64), the two lower zones of the tympanum surge with chimerical beasts, several of which are tearing human figures limb from limb.

In the most characteristic late Romanesque, and in many early Gothic tympani (Fig. 65), the monsters are gone; the Apocalyptic Vision alone remains. Christ dominates calmly, surrounded by the apostles on the lintel below and by heavenly hosts on the encircling archivolts. Chimerical fantasies linger in two of the four apocalyptic symbols of the evangelists — the winged lion of St. Mark and the winged bull of St. Luke — but they are not destructive monsters. The chimera has been positivized as part of an exclusively positive conception.

The most important High Gothic tympani (Fig. 66) carry forward the image of the dominant Christ, usually replacing the chimerical symbols by more humanistic attendants in the form of saints or angels, and expanding the general theme from the Apocalyptic Vision to the more cosmic and universal Last Judgment. Negative imagery remains only in the few demons who herd the damned to Hell and they, as we have seen, are present only as ministers of divine justice.

Thus by the thirteenth century — to summarize the effects of this positive development upon negative imagery — the monsters had been reduced to minor roles in the paintings and stained glass of the church interiors and in the carvings of the doorways; which is to say that they no longer dominated, or even threatened, any of the central areas and prominent aspects of the cathedral.

There still remained the remote and exposed intricacies of the upper exterior — encircling buttresses, balustrades crowning the walls, galleries around the base of the towers. Here, in the gargoyles and chimeras (examples of which we observed in Figs. 14, 16, and 17), the degraded and comparatively powerless monsters made a last inglorious stand. In the gargoyles they were even subjected to the menial function of drains, and on rainy days could be seen spouting water from their unwilling mouths — an object of derision and amusement to those who passed below.

Nevertheless, although displaced and discomfited, the monsters were not quite banished from the religious edifice nor from human consciousness. Brooding from their inaccessible heights, they seemed to remember better days and to wait resentfully for the time when their empire may be restored. And days may come when they will press upon human consciousness with a resurgence — witness the recrudescence of the monstrous in twentieth-century surrealism — but in the thirteenth century theirs was a lost cause. Gothic imagery so exalted the positive and subordinated the negative that the latter was little more than a final proof of positiveness.

II

In the terms of our psycho-historical theory, the clear dominance of positive imagery in Gothic myth and art implies a corresponding dominance of positive psychic states in the collective mentality of Gothic Europe. Such states in turn presuppose a generating basis in historical circumstances that were humanly fulfilling to a degree previously unknown among the peoples who experienced them and rare among peoples anywhere. The question to which we must now turn our attention is whether history supports this interpretation.

Our period, if we establish its limits so that they will synchronize narrowly with Gothic art, would begin about the middle of the twelfth century and would extend, according to the portion of Europe involved, into the fourteenth, fifteenth, or even the sixteenth century. It is universally recognized, however, that thirteenth century marked the crest of Gothic achievement; also that this achievement was the consummation of developments already under way during the eleventh and twelfth centuries. Hence, for our present purpose, the eleventh, twelfth, and thirteenth centuries are the primary ones to be considered. These three centuries saw the rise and culmination of the major types of medieval art which we are attempting to interpret and therefore comprised the historical matrix from which those types of art emerged.

The interpretative problem before us is only a little less beclouded by inherited concepts than was our effort to discern the conditions of life during the Dark Ages. The mental atmosphere surrounding the terms "Gothic," "Middle Ages," and "medieval," permits somewhat better visibility. Even that visibility, however, has varied enormously during successive cultural epochs, and still varies greatly from one mind to another according to the cultural tradition which each has inherited.

The Renaissance, looking back upon its ancestry, saw nothing but darkness between itself and its self-chosen totemic progenitors in ancient Rome. Even a cathedral like that of Amiens was crude and barbaric. Therefore, the Renaissance dubbed such buildings "Gothic" in the same condemnatory sense in which we use such words as "Huns" or "Vandals." In this conception, there were no Middle Ages, only Dark Ages, and the term "medieval" implied all that was barbarous and benighted.

By the nineteenth century there was a reaction, which exhibited itself in a phase of Romanticism and which, as is the case with most reactions, was in danger of pressing to the opposite extreme. "Middle Ages" became synonymous with "golden age." "Gothic" now implied all that was sublime and exalted; "medieval" all that was chivalrous, spiritual, and creatively vital.

Traces of both these attitudes still complicate any effort to view medieval history objectively. "Middle Ages" and "medieval" (though they continue to mean "golden age" to certain architects, theologians, and other specialists) have in general a decidely mixed, if not a preponderantly negative, connotation. They do indeed presume certain glories — cathedrals, knighthood, and the crusades, and chivalry and courts of love — but they also denote superstition and fanaticism, the Inquisition, Jeanne d'Arc and others burned at the stake, serfdom, the turbulence of feudal or "private" warfare, recurrent famines, and plagues.

Were these negative circumstances actually so predominant a part of medieval history and, if so, how can we justify our assumption of a historical basis for dominantly positive states of collective mentality? If we sift historical evidence and historical opinion, we discover that a number of the negative circumstances mentioned above, and commonly attributed to the Middle Ages in general, were at their worst either before or after the particular centuries that concern us. Serfdom, for instance, imposed its heaviest burdens at the end of the Dark Ages in the ninth and tenth centuries and again, with the reaction that set in during the late Middle Ages and the Renaissance, in the fourteenth and fifteenth centuries. The eleventh, twelfth, and thirteenth centuries, for reasons which we shall consider more fully below, saw a rapid and widespread improvement in the condition of the peasantry; so much so that by the end of the thirteenth century, in the words of James Westfall Thompson, "the serfs, or at least several million of them, had ascended to freedom." [2]

Religious persecution did indeed exist throughout the Middle Ages — the "crusade" against the Albigensians was one such incident — but many of its worst phases occurred subsequent to, not during, our period. Jeanne d'Arc was burned in the fifteenth century; the infamous Spanish Inquisition began about the same time and extended through the sixteenth, seventeenth, and eighteenth centuries. These notorious deeds of the church, and many like them, are thus phenomena of late medieval, Renaissance, and Baroque times. Even Coulton, who makes a militant point of combatting idealized conceptions of the Middle Ages, refers to "that comparative freedom of thought which, especially in Italy, makes the thirteenth century so living a period in the history of the pre-reformation church." Coulton also goes on to point out that "the rigid frame-work and inexorable discipline of the modern Roman church" — which contrast so forcibly with the thirteenth century "freedom of thought" — "are mainly the work of the Counter-Reformation." [3]

Of the two most devastating cycles of European pestilence one occurred before, the other after, the period which concerns us. The first had taken place during the sixth and seventh centuries and figured in our discussion of negative historical circumstances during the Dark Ages. The second began with the Black Death in the mid-fourteenth century and continued intermittently through the fifteenth, sixteenth, and seventeenth centuries.

Thus, the opening centuries of the second millennium can be thought of as a relatively positive divide between what preceded and what followed them. They rise triumphantly above many of the negative circumstances that had formed the darker aspects of the preceding Dark Ages. And in certain respects, they maintain this rise above the sequence of European catastrophes and social disorders which occurred soon after them and which, as Pirenne says, "makes the fourteenth century so violent a contrast to the thirteenth." [4]

In their own measure and manner, of course, the Romanesque-Gothic centuries underwent trials and tribulations and revealed their degree of human frailty, cruelty, and error. Their history was by no means completely free of negative circumstances. Nevertheless, they enjoyed a comparative immunity from collective dislocations and disasters and in addition the rare conflux of positive developments which will be discussed shortly. All things considered, what seems to emerge as the psycho-historical key to the epoch is a relation of positive to negative experiences in such proportions to each other, and in such relations to prior historical conditioning, that the sense of growth, progress, present achievement, and future promise vividly permeated large sections of society and generated a "boom" psychology on a heroic scale.

Some such interpretation certainly accords with the consensus of recent historical opinion. It is easy to assemble an almost lyrical chorus of praise for the eleventh, twelfth, and thirteenth centuries. The opening of the second millennium writes the eminent Belgian scholar, Henri Pirenne, "is characterized . . . by a recrudescence of activity so marked that it could pass for the vigorous and joyful awakening of a society long repressed by a nightmare of anguish. In every demesne was to be seen the same burst of energy and . . . optimism." Professor Pirenne then enumerates some of the developments and concludes, "Such undertakings testify not only to energy and vigor of spirit; they testify also to the health and vigor of society. They would obviously have been impossible without that native strength which is one of the characteristics of the eleventh century." [5] And, we may interpolate, if the eleventh century had the "native strength" to inaugurate this "joyful awakening," the twelfth and thirteenth centuries, with sustained vigor, carried it forward to triumphant fulfillment. "The Renaissance of the Twelfth Century" is a common historical phrase; Charles Homer Haskins uses it as the title of one of his volumes of historical studies. James J. Walsh, revealing Catholic predilections, goes even further and writes a volume entitled, *The Thirteenth, Greatest of Centuries.*

"The deeper we penetrate into the details of the history of these two centuries," (twelfth and thirteenth) writes James Westfall Thompson, "the more we discover that this was an epoch fertile in social origins, in the adjustment of society to new conditions, the evolution of new institutions." The construction of the Gothic cathedrals, he later goes on to say, "coincided with this social awakening and this new consciousness of power in Europe expressed in the establishment of better government, better laws, and the formation of new religious and social ideals. The phenomena all hang together as parts of one whole." [6]

One more historian, E. B. Osborn writes, "The Middle Ages exhibited the spectacle of a new order of society, a new outlook on the world within and the world without, which had struggled to birth in chaotic centuries and for a long period (from 1100 to 1400 A.D. perhaps) had an appearance of majestic finality and glowing self-sufficiency." [7]

In short, the centuries whose history we are to study are widely recognized by historians as a period of expansion, stabilization, and integration resulting in the first fresh maturity, and a number of the consummate achievements, of Western European civilization. The long night of Neolithic preparation, the Dark Age dawn, give way in early Gothic history to radiant morning.

The types of evidence which lead students of history to conclusions like the above are numerous and varied. In the basic sphere of agriculture, they include the exploitation of important new technological developments, the clearing and cultivation of large areas of previously barren land, and widespread improvement in the condition of the largest class in agricultural society — the peasantry. Related economic expansion brought the "revival of commerce," the rise of a merchant middle class, and the development of an economic superstructure involving monetary systems, credit, banking, and capital investment — the development in short, of the fundamental economic framework of subsequent Western civilization.

Civil life saw the growth of mercantile cities and the acquirement by them of liberties that became the cornerstone of Western democracy, the continued progress of law, beginnings of what were to become the permanent nations of subsequent Europe, and beginnings of national government by representative assemblies. All these sources of new strength contributed in turn to the final check by Western Europe of the long sequence of invasions that had shaken it for more than a thousand years, and the beginning of the counter-tide of European expansion in foreign conquest and colonization.

Higher cultural aspects of the historical situation included religious, intellectual and artistic developments of impressive range and calibre. Western Christendom reached its many-starred zenith in waves of popular religious fervor, in religio-social movements for the improvement of law and order such as the "Peace of God" and the "Truce of God," in the apex of the moral and political ascendancy of the papacy, in the lives of many of the West's most beloved saints — Saint Bernard, Saint Dominic, Saint Francis — and the ardent following of such spiritual leaders in new monastic orders like the Cistercian, the Dominican, and the Franciscan.

Henry Osborn Taylor speaks of "the enormous intellectual advance that took place in the last half of the twelfth and the first half of the thirteenth century." [8] That advance involved the founding of the first Western European universities, the use of Latin as an international language, and increasing knowledge of Greek, Arabic, and other earlier languages and literatures. The West was now able to acquire and assimilate previously unknown works of Aristotle which completed its knowledge of Greek philosophy, and to achieve a final integration of classical and Christian thought in such intellectual master-pieces as the *Summa Theologia* of Thomas Aquinas. Works like the *Summa* were at once the crowning achievements of Western theology, and through their development of logical processes of thought, the foundations of subsequent Western philosophy. The same epoch saw the birth and at least the infancy of Western experimental science with its will, as Roger Bacon put it in the thirteenth century, "to test, by observation and experiment," every aspect of human experience.

In the field of literature we find variety and abundance: a rich folk pro-duction of animal fables, humorous and satirical short stories (*fabliaux*), and ballads sung by wandering minstrels; the courtly love lyrics of the trouba-dours; a vast panorama of epic poetry that included the cycles dealing with King Arthur, the knights of the Round Table, and the Holy Grail, and the *Nibelungenlied*. In miracle and mystery plays, the Western theatre was born. In Dante, the West produced one of its half dozen culminating poets. Artis-tically, apart from the culmination of Western architecture in the Gothic cathe-drals, and the magnificent accompanying production of architectural sculpture, stained glass, and other decorative arts, these same centuries carried the evo-lution of painting to a point at which it could produce, in Giotto, the first of the culminating Western painters.

III

Volumes could be and have been written on every one of the topics included in the foregoing section. But most of these works discuss only the conscious level — the manifest surface of Gothic culture when it is viewed in a psycho-historical perspective. Our chief concern in the remainder of this chapter is to penetrate below the manifest imagery of Gothic art, religion and philosophy, and to seek the motivating sources of that imagery on the underlying levels of historical circumstance and psychic tension. What we hope to achieve is a deeper sense of the cultural metabolism that transformed the vitalities of the Gothic community into the flowers of Gothic culture. To accomplish these aims we will limit our discussion to three chief aspects of Gothic life: the extension and solidification of its economic and technological base; the expansion of its political liberties and military power; and the evidence of overflowing positive spirits which we find in many accounts of collective Gothic undertakings and their accompanying mass emotions.

As has already been implied, the whole historical development of the centuries under consideration is simply a more mature phase, in Western Europe, of that general cultural sequence which began with the Neolithic invention of agriculture, and which, in various parts of the world, led through economic and technological developments to richer cultural productions.

One of the links between the expanding economic base and the growing cultural superstructure is discussed by Pirenne: "From the middle of the tenth century the population of Western Europe, delivered at last from the pillages of the Saracens, the Northmen and the Hungarians, began an upward movement concerning which we have no precise details, but the results of which appear clearly in the following century. It is plain that manorial organization no longer harmonized with the excess of births over deaths, and a growing number of individuals, compelled to leave the paternal holding, had to seek fresh means of subsistence." [9]

Pirenne regards this increase in population, which he says "was still more striking at the beginning of the twelfth century and continued without interruption to the end of the thirteenth," as the prime mover in the social progress of the period. Since there were now more people than could profitably work the existing amount of arable land, the way was open for a further, and in part superagricultural, evolution. The clearing of new land, the colonizing of new territories, the emergence of a new mercantile middle class, and a whole concatenation of other developments, inevitably followed.

The freedom from invasion cited by Pirenne, however, can hardly have been the sole or even the main cause of Europe's expanding population. Large numbers of men were still lost in persistent feudal and interurban warfare, and especially in new foreign wars like the crusades. The basic reason for the increase would seem to lie in the growing abundance of food resulting from technological progress in agriculture. Neolithic food resources were insufficient to provide security even for the small and scattered Neolithic populations, which gave economic sanction to such practices as infanticide and cannibalism in many Neolithic communities. The archaic agriculture of the Dark Ages progressed steadily, but was still incapable of preventing recurrent famine or of supporting more than a basically agricultural population with its related military and clerical minorities.

Because the growth of population during this period was such that agricultural labor could no longer absorb it, increasing numbers of people were forced to seek a livelihood in other fields of economic activity such as commerce and industry. But since merchants, craftsmen, and industrial workers must eat if they are to live, what this situation really meant was that agriculture had now reached a point of efficiency at which it could supply food for an entire society while requiring the labor of only one portion of that society. The arrival of Western agriculture at this turning point at which its support for life overbalanced its demands upon life seems to the author to be the key factor in the rapid cultural expansion and diversification that marked the opening of the new millennium.

Students of medieval architecture are aware that the perfected structural system used in the Gothic cathedrals was not primarily an invention of the Gothic architects, but an outcome of cumulative experiments carried on by their Romanesque predecessors. The new productiveness of medieval agriculture appears to have a similar history. It resulted less from new technological inventions at its beginning than from the diffusion and general application of inventions made immediately prior. It was accelerated by two sociological developments that *were* in the main new: a highly organized and efficient system of farm labor and management, and the new incentive to agricultural effort which accompanied the release of the peasants from serfdom and the consequent opportunity to profit by their own initiative.

In discussing Dark Age agriculture we saw that during the eighth, ninth, and tenth centuries, European agricultural progress was quickened by three inventions which were to remain basic until the twentieth century, and which in part still remain basic today. These inventions were the iron horseshoe, an efficient form of horse collar, and the "three-field" system of cultivation. These developments, though they originated prior to the centuries under consideration, required time for their general diffusion and assimilation. Not until the opening centuries of the new millennium do they seem to have received regular and widespread application; not until then, in consequence, did they enrich Europe with their full benefits.

Lefebvre des Noëttes performed one of the most curious, original, and influential pieces of recent historical research when he examined large numbers of medieval illuminations for light on medieval methods of shoeing and harnessing draft animals.[10] As a result of his investigations, he concludes that prior to the ninth century, horses were harnessed with a type of collar which tended to choke them when they pulled and which therefore prevented the application of their full strength in traction; also that they were further hampered on stony or slippery ground by the absence of shoes. Oxen were efficiently attached for pulling, but they in turn suffered from unshod feet. The first known representations of the iron horseshoe appear in the ninth century, those of efficient or "modern" harnessing in the tenth century. Both types of representation become general during the eleventh, twelfth, and thirteenth centuries. During the twelfth century the swinglebar appears as a further technical innovation in harnessing.

These developments greatly increased the amount of animal power obtainable from a given number of draft animals. More land could be ploughed, more products hauled, without increasing the number either of animals or their human attendants. The wagon drawn by a single horse, which had previously been too weak for most purposes, now became widely practicable, while the use of several horses in single file multiplied the possible applications of the improved traction.

These new power potentials resulted in an increase in the size of wagons and their loads and, as Lefebvre des Noëttes points out,[11] had even more far-reaching consequences. Since the transportation of larger loads over greater distances was now possible, it was no longer necessary to depend so exclusively on local milling facilities. Hence, the many small and comparatively inefficient hand mills were replaced more and more by water and windmills that could be fewer, larger, more efficient and more strategically located to exploit water and wind power. Water wheels, as previously noted, were known to the West during the Dark Ages, but the introduction of the windmill was one of the technological developments of the new millennium. Though invented earlier in the East, the first known Western use of the windmill, according to Thompson, occured in 1105, thus synchronizing with the rising tide of Gothic cultural achievement.

The new power potentials did more than increase productiveness; they likewise *de*creased the burdens of human toil and in so doing were an immense technological boon to the peasantry. One commentator on Lefebvre des Noëttes goes so far as to say that "the discovery of means by which animal power could be used to its fullest extent divided the history of the Western world into two distinct periods, the period of hand labor and slavery before the tenth century and the period after the tenth century when better animals, with better harness and vehicles, relieved men of their hardest work, initiating the movement which substituted serfage for slavery and, with the use of modern tools, ended by abolishing serfage. In this way, M. des Noëttes remarks, the brilliant invention of the modern harness by some unknown person or persons, made during the night of the Dark Ages, changed the face of the world and, by changing the means of production, affected a profound change in our social organization." [12]

Perhaps there is some exaggeration in these statements, and there seems also to be some inaccuracy with regard to the history of serfdom, but there is at the same time an underlying and significant truth.

Further gains to agricultural productiveness resulted from the progressive extension of the "three-field" system. In the earlier "two-field" system (the only one known to the Romans), there was an annual rotation of the land in two major divisions: one fallow, the other planted in spring grain. In the three-field system, these two divisions were both reduced in order to make room for a third, the latter being sown with winter grain. What Thompson calls the "revolutionary change" involved in this development was less a matter of field division as such than of the fact that winter planting was now added to spring planting. "We can have no doubt of the enormous economic gain implicit in this change. The discovery that wheat and rye might be sown in autumn as well as spring, thus giving two yields where one had been before, is undoubtedly one of the most beneficial discoveries in the progress of man." [13]

Hardly less important than the increase in the amount of grain harvested under the new system was the reduction in the danger of famine. There were now two sources of staple cereals instead of one. So long as there had been only one, famine was an almost inevitable consequence if that failed. But with the new system, one might fail and the other succeed. And the new system had still another advantage. For a given amount of land, it resulted in and enlarged crop-bearing area while at the same time it required less ploughing. How this took place is explained by Professor N. S. B. Gras.

"Let us compare the two systems on a manor containing 1800 acres of arable land. In the two-field system we would have:

900 acres (arable ploughed once)	900
900 acres (fallow ploughed twice)	1800
Total acres of ploughing	2700

In the three-field system we would have:

600 acres (winter grain ploughed once)	600

600 acres (spring grain ploughed once)	600
600 acres (fallow ploughed twice)	1200
Total acres of ploughing	2400

"Thus in the two-field system we get only 900 acres of crops for 2700 acres of ploughing, whilst in the three-field system we get 1200 acres of crops for 2400 acres of ploughing." [14]

Added to these gains — and no doubt stimulated both by them and other conditions favorable to increasing profit from agriculture — was the development of extraordinary efficiency in the organization and management of manorial estates. To set forth systematic methods of attaining such efficiency was one of the main objectives of the treatises on agriculture that have come down to us from the thirteenth century — treatises such as Walter of Henley's *Husbandry* and the anonymous *Seneschaucie* or *Book of the Seneschal*. These writings discuss a thousand details of farm practice. One learns from them that it "is a good thing for swine to lie long in the morning, and to lie dry"; also that shepherds ought to obtain due leave before they go "to fairs, or markets, or wrestling matches, or wakes, or to the tavern . . ." [15] But all the details in the medieval treastises are subservient to a governing plan aimed at the efficient exploitation of agricultural resources, and requiring an amazing degree of specialization and functional adaptation.

The organization of an estate as described in the *Seneschaucie* differs little, in principle, from that of a modern industrial corporation. In place of stockholders and bondholders substitute landholders; the rest follows in the style of the methodical hierarchy of a company organization. At the head of the agricultural enterprise is the seneschal who, may be the chief executive for all the manors under one ownership. Next in descending order come: the bailiff or superintendent of the individual manor; the provost, a kind of combined foreman and union leader "who ought to be elected and presented by the common consent of the township, as the best husbandman and the best approver among them"; [16] the hayward, the ploughman, the wagonner, the cowherd, the swineherd, the shepherd; and the dairymaid who "ought to be faithful and of good repute, and keep herself clean, and ought to know her business and all that belongs to it." [17] The above are all, in varying degrees, superiors or officers. The responsibilities attaching to each office, and the ways and means of fulfilling them, are discussed at length in the *Seneschaucie*. Under the officers, in turn, came the larger number of assistants, servants, and general laborers.

No less carefully planned than the organization of personnel is the managerial procedure. On assuming office, the seneschal is to make a survey of all the properties under his supervision and to estimate their potential annual productiveness. Careful accounts are then to be kept both of production and of all business transacted. At the end of the year the seneschal is to compare the results obtained with the estimates previously made and take such action as the situation may call for.

It is no exaggeration to say that in this phase of his duties the seneschal rendered services akin to those which we today associate with an "efficiency expert." In addition to evaluating returns in relation to estimated potentials, he was required to inspect the work of each manorial officer in order to see "what care he takes, what improvement he makes, and what increase and profit there is in the manor in his office, because of his being there . . . and thereby he [the seneschal] can be more sure who makes profit and who harm. Also he ought to provide that there be no waste or destruction on any manor, or overcharge of anything belonging to the manor. He ought to remove all those that are not necessary . . . and all the servants who do nothing . . . and other profitless and unreasonable offices that are called wrong outlays, without profit." [18]

Even the seneschal is answerable for his results in this elaborate managerial system. He and the entire internal organization under him, together with the manorial accounts, are subject to annual inspection and approval by external auditors. These auditors "ought to be faithful and prudent, knowing their business and all the points and articles of the account in rents, in outlays, in return of the grange and stock, and other things belonging thereto. And the accounts ought to be heard at each manor, and then one can know the profit and loss, the doings and approvements of the seneschal, bailiff, provost, and others, for as much as they have done of profit or loss can be seen by the account in a day or two, and then can soon be seen the sense of the folly of these said seneschals, bailiffs, and provosts; and then can the auditors take inquest of the doings which are doubtful and hear the plaints of each plaintiff and make the fines." [19]

All this careful planning of organization and management, all this exacting concern with profit and loss, is an index of the fact that by Gothic times agriculture had become a major field for economic exploitation; a field rich in potentials, not only for the support and expansion of society, but also for the accumulation of private wealth.

No analysis of the new productiveness and efficiency of Western agriculture would be complete without reference to one other contributory factor: the new incentives to peasant labor. Labor at any time is likely to be efficient in direct proportion to the degree in which it shares in the profits of its own exertions. During the Dark Ages, the serf could hope for little more than his keep whether he worked hard or slackly. By the turn of the millennium, altered technological and social circumstances were providing agricultural labor with a new and much more favorable frame of reference. The new potentials of animal, wind, and water power relieved the peasant of the more brutish strain imposed by earlier and cruder methods of cultivation. Widespread release from serfdom made him more the master of his own destiny. And at the same time, through the rise of city markets for agricultural products, there came into being a means of converting crops into currency and manufactured goods and, through them, of attaining a better life and a higher standard of living. These rewards would naturally increase in direct proportion to the industry and efficiency of the peasant himself. There was thus a much greater incentive to personal effort than there had been before.

The substantial character of many peasants of the period is reflected in the thirteenth-century German poems, *Meier Helmbrecht* and *Der Arme Heinrich*.[20] Both involve peasant families of solid worth and comfortable means, one capable of acquiring embroideries from a nearby nunnery in return for some of the fat of the land, the other of providing a refuge for the lord of the region when he is in distress. That the younger generation sometimes suffered from the besetting weakness of the *nouveau riches* is suggested by *Meier Helmbrecht*. The son of the family, fopped up in the embroidered fineries received from the nuns, scorns the labor of his father's calling, joins a robber baron, and bows to poetic justice by coming to an untimely end.

One more fact remains to be noted in concluding this discussion of Gothic agriculture. The gains already considered were accompanied by, and were among the causes of, a vast expansion of agricultural enterprise through the clearing, settling, and cultivation of new land. Prior to the eleventh century, according to Pirenne, the amount of land under cultivation in Western Europe had changed little since Roman times.[21] Much of the land in most feudal holdings had remained in a virgin state of forest and marsh. Two-thirds of

Europe was still a wilderness, for the clearing of which Dark Age economy had offered neither opportunity nor purpose.

The circumstances of these centuries we are studying revolutionized Europe's attitude toward its waste lands. The new technological conditions permitted and favored the cultivation of land in larger units. The growing population, at first made possible by agricultural progress, in turn hastened that progress by creating an ever-growing demand for food and an ever-increasing supply of human labor. The new municipal and commercial developments opened up new markets for farm products. The result of these combined forces of the times was a European pioneer movement comparable, as many historians have pointed out, to the westward expansion of American society during the nineteenth century. This movement, in which the peasantry, the landowning nobility, and the monastic orders all participated, involved two distinct phases. Within Western Europe itself, the amount of arable land was multiplied many times over by clearing forests, draining swamps, and diking coastal marshes. On the northeastern fringe of Western Europe the clearing and settling process merged with a tide of colonial expansion, pressing the frontiers of the West further into territories formerly held by its eastern enemies.

A thirteenth-century chronicler, Caesarius of Prüm, provides an interesting glimpse of the land-clearance movement in the West. "During this long space of time," he writes with reference to the twelfth and early thirteenth centuries, "many forests were felled, villages founded, mills erected, taxes ordained, vines planted, and an infinite amount of land reduced to agriculture." [22]

In the Netherlands, land had been in prey to the sea rather than the forests. Here the "land-making" movement took the form of elaborate and technically difficult diking operations destined to withstand the tides and convert the widespread coastal marshes into fertile alluvial plains. It was, in fact, the labors of the Gothic centuries which gave the Low Countries of Europe the physical appearance and dairy economy which they have retained since that time. Under Baldwin V, Count of Flanders from 1035 to 1067, the progress in this direction "was already considerable enough for the Archbishop of Reims to be able to congratulate the Count on having transformed regions, until then unproductive, into fertile lands, rich with grazing herds. From that time, the whole maritime region was dotted with vaccaries [23] and sheepfolds (*vacarriae, bercariae*), and, at the end of the century, their revenues were sufficiently large to be the subject of elaborate accounts drawn up by professional notaries." [24]

On the eastern frontier, Gothic life hummed with the vitality characteristic of all epochs of pioneer settlement. Reinforced by its growing military power, the Germanic West pressed its eastern frontiers back through the wilderness which had been thinly populated by hostile Saxons and Slavs until the boundaries of the Christian West reached approximately the extent which they have since retained. German territory was more than doubled by this colonial expansion and the territory, once possessed, was cleared, settled, and carried through a swift pioneer evolution "from cattle-raising and swine-raising, to farming, to commerce, to manufacturing." [25]

Feudal promoters of the new East sent messengers through the West "to proclaim that all who were in want of land might come with their families and receive the best soil." Informed advisors of the younger generation might well have counseled youth, "Go East, young man, go East." Pioneer towns grew rapidly to become the lusty Chicagoes of their epoch, and profited by their fresh start to apply advanced conceptions of city planning. "Nowhere in Europe was town-planning so energetic as in trans- Elbean Germany in the twelfth and thirteenth centuries . . . Breslau, Berlin, Dresden, Leipzig . . . are examples. These new towns were not like older medieval towns, which had narrow, torturous and crooked streets, but were carefully laid out with rectangular streets and wide-open squares." [26]

These civic developments anticipate considerations to be dealt with in the section to follow. What concerns us now is that the Eastern pioneer movement added hundreds of thousands of square miles of newly developed arable land to the agricultural foundations of Gothic culture. Add to these in turn the large amounts of land newly cleared in the West itself, the new incentives to labor, management, and landowners, the new efficiency of organization and exploitation, the new technological developments and power potentials, and it should be evident that Gothic agriculture provided a broad and solid economic base for the superstructure of Gothic culture — a base which gave both a new degree of security and a new degree of expansive vitality to the society that profited by it.

IV

With food to support the rapid multiplication of human life and to permit and even require its employment in a variety of nonagricultural pursuits, the expansion of Gothic culture in other directions was spontaneous and many-sided. Two of the most striking consequences, and two which lead directly to the climax of Gothic art in the cathedrals, were the "revival of commerce" and the accompanying growth and enfranchisement of cities.

To the present writer the term "revival" like other "re" terms such as "renaissance," seems misleading when applied to the historic unfolding of Western European civilization. To say that trade "revived" in the eleventh century is to assume that an earlier commercial structure, the Roman one, had merely hibernated for a period and now awoke once more to its former activity. Any truth involved in such an assumption seems to me secondary compared to the greater truth that a new culture, to a large extent that of new races, had reached the point in its evolution at which its expanding energies found commercial expression. This would inevitably have happened, has happened in every civilization, regardless of its previous occurrence in earlier civilizations and regardless of any influence which its earlier occurrences may have had upon its later ones. Hence it would seem more fitting to speak of what happened in Western Europe in the eleventh, twelfth, and thirteenth centuries as the birth of Western commerce rather than its "revival."

All authorities, however, agree that the centuries under consideration witnessed the development of a new and imposing commercial superstructure upon the expanding agricultural base of Western economy. The new surplus population, ejected from the manors as an unnecessary drain on profit, lived at first by alms and temporary employment and was frequently reduced to vagabondage and beachcombing. As Henri Pirenne recounts in picturesque detail, [27] the people exposed to these conditions developed an adventurous spirit and a quick-witted ability to seize every opportunity for gain, lawful or unlawful. Free from agricultural ties to the land, they displayed a mobility previously unknown in feudal society, and through that mobility soon discovered the gains to be made by transporting goods from a territory in which they were common to one in which they were rare. Under favorable conditions capable men built up fortunes in a comparatively few years. Even a few sacks of wheat, if carried to an area suffering from local shortage, might result in gains sufficient to launch larger mercantile operations.

A twelfth-century success story of rapid rise from poverty to riches through trade is the *Biography of St. Godric of Finchale*.[28] Offshoot of peasant stock, Godric rose from beachcomber to peddler, associated himself with others in more ambitious trading, developed the business until the associates were able to load an entire ship with merchandise, and emerged from the venture a rich

man — whereupon, moved by the religious concerns that were as characteristic
of his age as the opportunity for rapid gain, Godric distributed his wealth to
the poor and became a hermit.

From the multiplication of such careers, usually without so extreme a religious ending, arose a new social class: a merchant class soon to augment itself
by association with the growing number of craftsmen, conveyors, accountants,
and other specialists necessary to produce and transport the goods circulated in
trade and to record the transactions involved.

Linked with the rise of the merchant-craftsman middle class was the growth
and enfranchisement of cities and the shift of cultural emphasis from manorial
to civic centers. The earlier merchants, when they settled from their wanderings — which occurred only during the inclement seasons of the year — sought
the protection of existing towns or feudal castles. As the commercial class
grew in size, neither the towns nor the castles were able to contain it. As a
result, merchant quarters were commonly adjacent to the older settlements — a
fact which has left interesting relics in modern languages. The older towns
had been known in Latin as *urbes*; the new adjacent merchant quarters were
accordingly called *sub-urbs*, and the "suburb" is still a residential area adjacent
to a city and still, interestingly enough, one of the main seats of dwelling for
the middle class. The equivalent French term, *faubourg*, had a similar origin.

The first small suburbs and faubourgs were hardly more than squatter communities clinging to the older settlements for protection, and frequently adding
to their own security by surrounding themselves with wooden palisades. But
the future lay with the suburbs rather than with the *urbes* themselves; which is
to say that the future lay with the mercantile middle class that was increasing
so rapidly in size, in wealth, and consequently, in power. By the beginning of
the twelfth century many of the new settlements had completely encircled the
old ones. Furthermore, as their prosperity increased, the suburbs replaced their
primitive palisades by stone walls possessing all the protective strength and
monumental beauty of twelfth- and thirteenth-century military architecture;
walls like those impress us so vividly today in Carcassonne and other surviving
examples.

As a result of these developments, it frequently happened that an original
castle fortress was rendered useless. The castle then moldered, a relic of the
feudal, precommercial past, or it was razed to make room for city buildings or
market squares. A social equivalent of these architectural signs of the times
(Italy excepted) was the withdrawal of the nobility from the press of the new

urban centers to country seats. Economically, the city was left primarily to commerce and industry; socially, it was left primarily to the middle class.

To recount in detail the evolution of medieval city life is unnecessary for our present purpose and has in any case been well and briefly done by Pirenne in his *Medieval Cities*. Suffice it to note that by the thirteenth century this evolution had resulted in large numbers of "municipal republics" equivalent to the ancient Greek city states, and these were undoubtedly among the most thrivingly prosperous, the most stirringly hopeful, and the most socially unified communities ever produced by the Western world.

Pirenne, after summarizing the government and fiscal accomplishments of medieval cities, turns to the commercial sphere and finds there "a system of regulation so marvellously adapted to its purpose that it may be considered a masterpiece of its kind. The city economy was worthy of the Gothic architecture with which it was contemporary. It created with complete thoroughness — and, it may well be said, it created *ex nihilo* — a social legislation more complete than that of any other period in history, including our own. In doing away with the middlemen between buyer and seller, it assured to the burgher the benefit of a low cost of living; it ruthlessly pursued fraud, protected the worker from competition and exploitation, regulated his labor and his wage, watched over his health, provided for apprenticeship, forbade woman- and child-labor, and at the same time succeeded in keeping in its own hands the monopoly of furnishing the neighboring country with its products and in opening up distant markets for its trade.

"All this would have been impossible if the civic spirit of the burghers had not been equal to the tasks that were laid upon them. It is necessary, in fact, to go back to antiquity to find as much devotion to the public good as that which they had given proof. *Unus subveniet alteri tamquam fratri suo* — Let each help the other like a brother — says a Flemish character of the twelfth century, and these words were actually a reality. As early as the twelfth century the merchants were expending a good part of their profits for the benefit of their fellow citizens — building churches, founding hospitals, buying off the market tolls. The love of gain was allied, in them, with local patriotism. Every man was proud of his city and spontaneously devoted himself to its prosperity. This was because, in reality, each individual life depended directly upon the collective life of the municipal association. The commune of the Middle Ages had, in fact, all the essential attributes which the State exercises today. It guaranteed to all its members the security of his person and of his chattels.

Outside of it he was in a hostile world, surrounded by perils and exposed to every risk. In it alone did he have a shelter, and for it he felt a gratitude which bordered upon love. He was ready to devote himself to its defense just as he was always ready to bedeck it and make it more beautiful than its neighbors. Those magnificent cathedrals which the thirteenth century saw erected would not have been conceivable without the joyous alacrity with which the burgher contributed, by gifts, to their construction. They not only were houses of God; they also glorified the city of which they were the greatest ornament and which their majestic towers advertised afar. They were for the cities of the Middle Ages what temples were for those of antiquity." [29]

The culmination of Gothic art in cathedrals like those of Chartres, Paris, Reims, and Amiens was the achievement of just such city republics as Pirenne describes. When we consider the prosperity, the social cohesion, the patriotic ardor of those republics, and when we consider the many-sided progress and expansion that were transforming the entire world around them, are we not justified in concluding that Gothic myth and art did indeed synchronize with a remarkable confluence of positive historical circumstances? If this be granted, the first and main objective of the present chapter has been attained.

Further evidence pointing to the same conclusion could be marshalled from many other fields of Gothic activity. It would be tempting to enlarge upon the new intellectual maturity through which the twelfth and thirteenth centuries harmonized the conflicts between Teutonic, Christian, and Classical thought and achieved a new Western synthesis in *summae* — intellectual summations — like that of Thomas Aquinas. As if from a mountaintop, these monumental works provided a unified panorama of a mental universe that was the outcome of thousands of years of growth in three successive cultures.

It would be tempting to trace the military expansion that transformed the West from a basin for successive invasions into a power summit hurling forth the forces of foreign conquest. We could dwell long over the Crusades and could still allow them their glory — a glory less of principle than of vitality. In the reckless abandon with which they cast surplus wealth and surplus population into the crucible of foreign war, and in the gains which they achieve for Western commerce and colonization, they were another and a grandiose demonstration of the triumphant dynamism of Gothic Europe.

It would be tempting, too, to follow the advance of Gothic technology into other spheres beside that of agriculture. Let us content ourselves, however, with brief mention of one further type of technological advance that did much to move Gothic experience closer to the positive pole: the progress of architecture and the benefits it conveyed in new comfort, new security, and new esthetic exaltation.

The homes of Gothic burghers (Fig. 68) were substantial, many-storied edifices compared to which the finest baronial halls of the Dark Ages had been primitive in their appointments. The then modern invention of the fireplace and chimney gave increased warmth while at the same time liberating eyes and lungs from the age-old danger and discomfort of smoke. This advance was reinforced by extension of glass manufacture and the introduction of glazed windows. Conservation of the new warmth, adequate control of draughts, and greatly improved illumination all became possible as a result.

Military and eccesiastical architecture made even more striking advances. As late as the tenth century, fortifications had consisted almost entirely of earthworks surmounted by stockades and blockhouses of logs. By the eleventh century, Western architecture was entering upon its age of monumental construction in stone. The twelfth and thirteenth centuries saw the erection of large numbers of stone castles and city walls — the latter often twice or thrice expanded as cities grew in size (Fig. 67). These imposing constructions were at once invaluable aids to collective defense and impressive, ever-present symbols of collective unity and security.

In the evolution of medieval church building to the fully developed Gothic cathedral of the thirteenth century, European technology reached one of the crowning achievements of its genius. So organic is the integration of religious, civic, esthetic, and technical elements in these buildings that, in our ordinary converse with them, we are rarely aware of their supremacy when considered as sheer engineering. The surprise of an unaccustomed angle (Plates 28, 29, Figs. 69, 70) shocks us into a realization of the breath-taking skill involved in poising hundreds of tons of stone a hundred feet in the air upon slender clusters of supporting shafts — steadied externally, of course, by that unique invention of Gothic engineering, the flying buttress. Leaving aside all other considerations, these buildings are prodigious technical achievements. Any society capable of providing the economic resources, the engineering skill, the subsidiary decorative techniques, and the advanced concepts of design necessary for such achievements marks itself at once as a society of the highest and, in its own way, of the most technologically advanced order. To participate in such consummate creative achievements, to feel those achievements as expressions of their own collective power and aspiration, could not but afford the members of that society a positive experience of such richness and intensity as is rarely vouchsafed to mankind.

V

Before taking leave of Gothic history, let us ask ourselves one final question. Do medieval sources provide any direct evidence that Gothic communities actually experienced those accumulations of positive feeling which we are assuming as the psychic link between their fortunate historical circumstances and the positive imagery of their myth and art? The answer is that the sources do provide such direct evidence and provide it abundantly. Accounts of overflowing positive emotionality — of communal fervor and religious exaltation, of pageantry, processions, and public rejoicings — appear and reappear in medieval writings like a recurrent refrain.

From thirteenth-century Italy comes Salimbene's account of the "Alleluia" that transfigured North Italian life in 1233. "This Alleluia, which endured for a certain season, was a time of peace and quiet, wherein all weapons of war were laid aside; a time of merriment and gladness, of joy and exultation, of praise and rejoicing. And men sang songs of praise to God; gentle and simple, burghers and country folk, young men and maidens, old and young with one accord. This devotion was held in all the cities of Italy; and they came from the villages to the town with banners; a great multitude of people, men and women, boys and girls together, to hear the preaching and to praise God. And they sang God's songs, not man's; and all walked in the way of salvation. And they bare branches of trees and lighted tapers . . . And men held stations in the churches and the open places, and lifted up their hands to God, to praise and bless Him forever and ever; and they might not cease from the praises of God, so drunken were they with His love . . ." [30]

This popular conviction of "walking in the way of salvation," this communal experience of being "drunken with the love of God" — in other words, this intoxication with positive collective emotions — is one of the characteristic traits of Gothic humanity. Abbot Suger of Saint-Denis gives us numerous glimpses of its occurrence in twelfth-century France. The consecration of the enlarged choir of the abbey church in 1144 was accomplished with such splendor and exaltation that those present "believed themselves to behold a chorus celestial rather than terrestrial." When the proceedings reached the point at which the remains of the abbey's patron saints were to be transferred to their new resting places, the excitement rose to hysterical intensity. The king (St.

Louis), the nobility, and the clergy "chanted and wept with immeasurable joy." Then they carried the sacred relics in a procession which Suger can only describe in terms of an earlier and equally ecstatic occasion "when [those in the procession] proceeded through the cloisters with candlesticks, crosses and other festive ornaments and with many odes and hymns; when they carried their Patrons amicably yet, for joy, weepingly. No greater joy in the world could ever have exalted them." [31]

Scenes of zealous communal participation in the building of churches are numerous in medieval records. Leo of Ostia describes "the fervor and loyalty of the faithful citizens" who carried up the mountain on their shoulders the first column for the "new" church of Monte Casino. Suger records similar popular enthusiasm at Saint-Denis. But the best known as well as the most striking of such accounts are those concerning the construction of the cathedral of Chartres. In this case we have reports from two separate observers, Abbot Haimon of Tutbury and Archbishop Hugo of Rouen. The former writes of nobility and common folk alike harnessing themselves "like beasts of burden" to the carts bearing materials for the cathedral:

"A thousand persons and more attached are to the chariots — so great is the difficulty — yet they march in such silence that not a murmur is heard . . . When they halt on the road, nothing is heard but the confession of sins, and pure and suppliant prayer to God to obtain pardon. At the voice of the priests who exhort their hearts to peace, they forget all hatred, discord is thrown far aside, debts are remitted, the unity of hearts is established.

". . . There one sees old people, young people, little children, calling on the Lord with a suppliant voice, and uttering to Him, from the depth of the heart, sobs and sighs with words of glory and praise! After the people, warned by the sound of trumpets and the sight of banners, have resumed their road, the march is made with such ease that no obstacle can retard it . . . . When they have reached the church they arrange the waggons about it like a spiritual camp, and during the whole night they celebrate the watch by hymns and canticles." [32]

What the populace thus exhibited in overflowing fellowship and fervent activity, theology expressed through the intellectual intricacies of philosophic thought. The highest object of religious worship can be conceived by the greatest of medieval theologians only in terms of the greatest human happiness. "God," says Thomas Aquinas in his *Summa Theologica*, "is man's beatitude." [33] "Beatitude" is one of the key words in Gothic experience, as "terror" had been a key word in Neolithic experience.

How are we to explain this positive emotionality or, in the traditional phrase, this "religious fervor," of Gothic humanity? We can hardly suppose that it was an act of God, He, during those centuries, having been disposed to shine forth upon humanity with radiant affection whereas, before and after, He withdrew to more hidden distances and to a sterner indifference. Neither can we suppose that it was simply a matter of chance and that, had luck so disposed, the emotional orientations of Neolithic and Gothic men might equally well have been reversed. Adequate understanding of any aspect of nature or experience seems always to show that law rather than chance underlies its operation. We have no reason to suppose that the present case is an exception.

Furthermore, our studies thus far, by indicating a gradual change from dominantly negative to dominantly positive conditions as humanity moved from Neolithic times through the Dark Ages to the Middle Ages, have already suggested that the positive emphasis in Gothic mentality was not a sudden interpolation or unexpected effusion in psychic history. Like the culminating architecture, philosophy, and other aspects of Gothic culture, it was an outcome of evolutionary processes which had long been at work and which now rose to a climax with the accumulated momentum of a breaking wave.

Viewed psycho-historically, the positive emotionality and religious fervor of Gothic man, together with the positive imagery of his art, appear as a natural outcome of the positive historical circumstances which he was enjoying — circumstances under which, as we have seen, technological, economic, vital, social, intellectual, and other advances were all contributing to a strong flow of human progress and well-being. As an individual experiences elation when he achieves a long-sought success; as he sighs with relief when he escapes from long-feared dangers, so Gothic society experienced elation and relief in the degree to which it had attained well-being and security, had emerged from inherited mental conflicts, and had bulwarked itself against existing dangers.

Not a few of the medieval records give us circumstantial glimpses of the connection between Gothic achievement and Gothic emotion. About the year 1200, the Count of Guisnes and Ardres in France surrounded the latter town with imposing fortifications and "a mighty moat . . . such as no hand had conceived hitherto in the land of Guisnes, nor no eye had seen." The parish priest of Ardres, in recording the progress of the work, tells how "many oftimes came together to see these great earthworks; for such poor folk as were not hired laborers forgot their penury in the joy of beholding this work; while rich, both knights and burgesses and oftimes priests or monks, came not daily only, but again and again every day, to refresh their bodies and see so marvelous a sight. For who but a man stupefied and deadened by age or cares could have failed to rejoice in the sight of . . ." [34] and the chronicler goes into a long description of the feverish activities involved in this great enterprise in public works. New town walls, at Ardres as elsewhere throughout Europe, meant constructive coöperative activity during the period of their erection, and permanently increased civic security and prestige thereafter. Who indeed among the inhabitants of the community "could have failed to rejoice" in such an enterprise? And conversely, who can doubt that the impulse to rejoicing common in Gothic Europe was the natural concomitant of an age in which all sorts of similar enterprises, spiritual, intellectual, and artistic as well as material, were under way?

That Gothic communities themselves sensed a link between their dominantly positive religious symbols and the varied circumstances that contributed to their daily well-being, is suggested by their practice of recording those circumstances upon or within the fabric of the cathedrals. Town charters, as they were obtained, were often blazoned upon the church doors. "The 'Privileges of Speyer,' which Henry V granted in 1111, were set in gold letters in the great door of the cathedral. The same was done at Mainz in 1135 . . ." [35] Human freedom sought the protecting sanction of divine law; inevitably, as a result, the community's conception of divine law was permeated by the sweetness of experiencing freedom.

"Reims had a curious building law forbidding any structure for residence purposes to be erected higher than the eaves of the cathedral, and it is recorded that whenever a building was going up the archdeacon was enjoined to look out daily from the portholes in the eaves and see that the walls of no structure rose higher than the level of his eyes." [36] Here the divine order, as symbolized by the cathedral, became the expression of the social principle that no community can long enjoy the benefits of cohesion unless individual and private enterprises remain subservient to civic or, as in this case, religio-civic ones.

The eight monumental statues of oxen upon the towers of Laon Cathedral (Fig. 70) are not unworthy of note as another example of the Gothic practice that linked things worldly with things divine. Tradition has it that they were placed there in grateful recognition of the part played by such beasts of burden in hauling stone and other materials to the cathedral. If this was the rational motive, it may well have been supported and deepened by extensions which were perhaps unconsciously sensed. The cathedral was, as it were, the pinnacle of Gothic culture, standing upon a summit which sloped down, through various grades of social and economic organization, to the agricultural base upon which depended the survival of the entire system. The significance of domestic animals to the total cultural organism was not delimited by their use in dragging stone for church building. Their strength ploughed the fields and hauled in the harvests; their flesh, sacrificed to humanity, provided meat. Well might they symbolize the indispensable service of agriculture to Gothic life; well might their images, though realistic, mingle on the cathedral with the more patently symbolical religious imagery. It seems as if the men of Laon had sensed through their myths the outward realities which the myths expressed, much as their forebears had done in naming a hero and a grain god with the name of grain.

We have many other, and sometimes more precise, indications that social and economic satisfactions were closely related to Gothic religious fervor. The cathedral of Amiens provides some interesting examples. Below the Last Judgment, the *Beau Dieu*, and the other grand religious sculpture of the west front, in the quatrefoils that decorate the lowest zone of the portals, are more than a hundred small reliefs. In them the human and natural reveal their presence at the borders of the divine and supernatural. Here, in personifications of the virtues and vices, we see the human reality of ethics. Here, in the signs of the zodiac, (as in the floral capitals and string course of the interior) we recognize a growing interest in nature. And here, in a "calendar" typifying each month of the year through scenes of the activities associated with it, we find representations of the whole annual cycle of agriculture. Cutting hay and harvesting grain (Fig. 71), picking fruit and tramping out the wine, threshing and fall sowing — these and other phases of agrarian husbandry assert their significance to, and receive their recognition from, the cathedral.

Many of the crafts and commercial occupations similarly recorded their own special skills, pride, and economic importance in stained glass windows dedicated to their patron saints and expressive of themselves. Most pertinent of all, the façade of the south transept includes a sculptured group of *waidiers* (Fig. 72). These were cultivators and merchants of *waide*, a plant used for dye, which was one of the chief products and exports of Amiens from the twelfth to the fifteenth century. The realism, one might almost say the air of smug satisfaction, of this peasant and dealer with the sack of *waide* pulp between them, is in strange contrast to the impersonal grandeur of the *Beau*

Dieu. Yet the one like the other is a true reflection of Gothic life and honestly earned its right to be represented on the cathedral.

Had Amiens developed no commerce in *waide* or some equivalent source of abundant revenue, and had its citizens not possessed the agricultural techniques necessary for raising the *waide* plant, the craft skills necessary for its conversion into dyes, and the commercial organization necessary for its wholesale distribution, the city could never have accumulated the surplus wealth necessary for the erection of such a vast and elaborate building as the cathedral. In fact, without these or similar technological foundations, the whole cosmic dream reality of thirteenth-century Amiens could never have come into existence. The populous and prosperous city-state would have been impossible for want of economic sustenance; the cathedral would have been impossible for want of a community capable of building it, and the positive religious experience of the age would have been impossible for want of a sustaining sense of human welfare and also for want of the magnificent formulations made possible by the training and patronage of theologians, sculptors, stained-glass designers, architects, and other creative specialists.

In taking leave of Gothic history, we should perhaps recognize an objection that may have arisen in the minds of some of our readers. They may possibly feel that in the foregoing discussion, if we have not overemphasized the positive aspects of Gothic life, we have at least minimized the negative ones. In one sense this is true. There are original sources, such as Salimbene's chronicle, which contain decidedly negative admixtures along with their positive material. There are also retrospective commentaries from subsequent periods which take a negative, sometimes a militantly negative, view of medieval history. The author has read his share of both these types of reference. It still seems to him that while the existence of negative elements in Gothic life is not to be denied, the relative dominance of positive over negative elements remains a fact — and for our purpose the decisive fact.

Let us grant that the eleventh, twelfth, and thirteenth centuries were free neither of human imperfections nor of the inevitable buffetings of fate. Their high religious conception of their destiny was a myth which not only expressed their power and inspired them to noble deeds, but also led them, not infrequently, into bigotry and persecution. They, like other centuries before and after, reeled at times under the shock of catastrophe. The essential point for us is that, with the strength of a champion, they could reel and conquer. Their accumulated material and human resources, their potentials of energy and effort, were such as to transcend whatever difficulties they faced and still leave a positive balance. After describing the destruction frequently involved in the wars between the Italian commercial cities of the thirteenth century, Thompson remarks, "But Europe in the thirteenth century could bear such terrific losses because her wealth was far greater than before, and because the profits of trade were so great that they canceled all losses, however disastrous, and still left a balance of profit." [37]

This irreducible triumph of profit over loss is symbolic of every aspect of European life during the centuries under consideration. We have another illuminating manifestation of it in the recovery of the Languedoc region of southern France after the devastation of the Albigensian crusade. "The ruined cities were rebuilt. The destruction of the old, cramped, unhygienic towns with crooked narrow streets proved a blessing in disguise. For the new *bastides*, as they were called, were laid out in geometrical form . . . with straight streets crossing each other, and a broad plaza in the middle of the town." [38] Like Athens rising to her glory from the ruins left by the Persians, Gothic Europe rose in glory from whatever blows "outrageous fortune" could still fling upon her. Her own sense of this glory remains to us in the exultingly positive imagery of her myth and art.

VI

We have seen that Gothic culture synchronizes historically with the emergence of Western Europe from the conflicting and experimental adjustments of a nascent civilization to the integrated and masterful ones of a civilization in its first full bloom. Now at last Western society was achieving victory in its millennium-long struggle for existence, integration, and fulfillment. With victory comes the psychology of victory; a psychology of triumph and exaltation, of relief from one-time dangers, of rejoicing in new-found power and security. All the major characteristics of Gothic art become intelligible, become inevitable, in the light of this glowing dynamic. Its radiance illuminates a thousand forms of cultural expression as a single sun, shining upon a meadow, stirs the response of a thousand flowers.

The exaltation of victory shows itself in the soaring reach of nave and spire; in the radiant color of window walls, jewell-studded metal crafts, and pictures keyed to brilliant hues of the illuminator. The relief, and accompanying energical release, of victory shows itself in the inexhaustible creative power that enabled communities of only moderate size to undertake the vast building projects of the cathedrals and to carry those projects beyond architecture to a superb integration of architecture with an almost inconceivable wealth of sculpture and other decorative arts. The poise that follows victory shows itself in the serene expression of individual saints and angels, in the quiet sense of lawful order that permeates the Last Judgments, the Ascensions, the Coronation, in the ease with which the buttresses retain the vaults, in the tranquil equilibrium that permeates the cathedral interiors despite the complexity of their structure and decoration. And the same psycho-dynamic, far from being exhausted by its expression in art, reveals itself in the processions that advanced triumphantly, in the masses that were exultingly chanted, and in many other manifestations of Gothic society that took place within and around the cathedrals. All can be viewed as expressions of a collective soul intoxicated, at times hysterical and delirious, with the effects of cultural mastery long struggled for in vain and now at last attained.

If this be so, how are we to explain the presence of the grotesque as a constant, albeit secondary, theme in Gothic art? Here we return to a question raised at the outset of our discussions — a question to which we are now prepared to offer a psycho-historical answer. The answer, as we conceive it, is that the grotesques were lingering vestiges of negative symbolism in a mythical universe which came close to, but did not quite attain, exclusive positivism. Their vestigial and negative character bears significant relations both to the Gothic past and to the then Gothic present.

Seen in evolutionary perspective, against the background of the Gothic past, they become one of the minor variations on the theme of victory, for the psychology of victory is two fold. Insofar as it involves escape from danger and relief from fear, it induces thankfulness, rejoicing, and new assurance, in the manner already cited to explain the dominant characteristics of Gothic culture. Insofar, on the other hand, as the victorious mentality returns to contemplate the sources of its former terror, now disarmed of their once sinister power, the reaction is to find ridiculous or amusing what had once been experienced as terrible. In ordinary life, we laugh at past mishaps however much they may have disconcerted us at the time of the occurrence. In the security and conviviality of some postwar reunion, we may laugh at miseries suffered on the battlefield. Laughter — not the completely carefree laughter of pure humor, but a laughter alloy conditioned by various negative admixtures — is one of the spontaneous expressions of the relief of negative tension.

This transformation of negative tensions into semipositive discharges would seem to have taken place in Gothic mentality as it contemplated the monsters by which it had traditionally been terrorized. Its psychic composition in this respect was one of vestigial fear linked with the disdain and amusement born of newly acquired confidence. If such a psychic compound were to be projected into art, it would result in forms combining the diminished traits of the terrible with the emergent ones of the ridiculous and amusing. Such are the forms, half sinister, half humorous, of the high Gothic grotesque (Figs. 14, 16, and 17).

Nor was the transformation of the one-time monstrous confined exclusively to changes in its character. As we have seen, it was also displaced from its earlier and more central locations, withdrawing to the margins of Gothic art in precisely the same measure as inherited collective fears, calmed by the new ambiance of collective well-being, were withdrawing to the margins of the local and contemporary mental universe. The demons, the chimeras, and the gargoyles could occupy only underlying or outlying stations in the positively ruled dominion of the cathedral.

If we consider the grotesque in relation to the present rather than the past of the Gothic era, we arrive at similar conclusions from a slightly different angle. Then we may see the grotesque as a reflection of that intractable residue of experience which resists even the surest system, lurking on the periphery of order as a warning that man is, after all, not the final master of the universe. Gothic life, however dominantly positive, was not without its negative admixtures and they, being elements of the underlying psycho-social reality, would inevitably rise to the symbolical surface of that reality in forms of cultural expression. But in doing so they would be both subordinated and transformed by the positive context in which they found themselves. Like underlings masking humiliation behind forced smiles, they could manifest their negativism only in disguised form, since they were confronted by positive powers too strong for them to oppose. Thus again, in the characteristics to be expected of vestigial symbols of negative tension, we have all the features of the Gothic grotesque: subordination, marginal location, a character half sinister yet disarmed by mockery.

Students of esthetics will perceive that our analysis confirms the traditional definition of the grotesque as an intermingling of the terrible with the comic. But in doing so it also indicates that this esthetic category is not — at any rate that its more profound expressions are not — the result of an inclination to combine, more or less recipe-like, two specifically esthetic ingredients. Rather we find that when the grotesque is one of the characteristic expressions of an epoch, as it was in Gothic times, it results from the convergence of powerful forces within the psycho-historical dynamism of collective life. It is one of those compound forms of expression in which positive and negative tensions, neither escaping each other's influence nor overcoming each other's resistance, meet tangentially and intermingle their effects.

The proportions in which the intermingled elements may appear vary all the way from the first slight relaxation from the exclusively terrible, at one extreme, to the last vestige of the terrible in the almost exclusively humorous at the other. Most high Gothic grotesque lies somewhat beyond the central point of this progression. Much later Gothic and Renaissance grotesque (Figs. 24–25) lies at the end of the progression and may even leave the category of the grotesque to enter that of pure humor. There is thus an element of truth in the traditional tendency to explain the grotesque in terms of the humorous, but that truth is falsified when it is extended to cover all grotesque and doubly so when it is applied to the earlier forms of the grotesque. It is also falsified if either humor or fancifulness is regarded as the sole, or even the main, formative impulse at work in the creation of the grotesque.

If the foregoing discussion has achieved its aim, it has revealed an organic relationship between Gothic art and the psycho-historical experience of the communities from which it emanated. Ruskin coined a memorable description of the cathedrals when he called them "Bibles in stone." Today we can go further. We can see them as "dreams in stone." With the marvelous power of symbolic expression that enters into dream formation, the creative intuition of Gothic theologians and artists — sustained by the vitality of Gothic merchants, agronomists, and peasants — manifested in the cathedral all the complex stirrings of a collective soul at one of the culminating moments of its cultural evolution.

Chapter XIV

REALISM, ABSTRACTION, AND PSYCHO-HISTORY

In the terms of art criticism, mythological, and religious themes, when represented in art, become types of "subject matter." We have seen that these particular types of subject, far from being chance inspirations of the artist, far indeed from originating in esthetic preoccupations as such, owe their presence in art to profound connections with the conscious and unconscious life of society. By implication, this principle applies to *all* types of subject matter in art: to the portraits, figure studies, and historical scenes, the landscape and still lifes, of the later stages of a civilization as well as the monsters, heroes, and saviors of the earlier ones; and naturally to the subjects in other representational arts such as literature, drama, and the mimetic dance.

Art, even distinctively representational art, however, is a complex totality of which subject matter is only one component. Other components include its medium or physical basis in stone, paint, or other materials, its effects of color and design, its possible relationship to buildings or other ornamented objects in a decorative capacity, and its possible range of "style." We shall use the latter term in its commonly accepted sense to mean "those characteristics of form which are peculiar to a certain work or group of works, and which at the same time distinguish it or them from other works."[1]

In recent critical thinking these other aspects of art have frequently been given a higher importance than subject matter. In view of this attitude, and in view of the primary place which subject matter has held thus far in our discussions, some readers may have wondered whether the psycho-historical theory does not involve a one-sided emphasis on representation and a corresponding inadequacy in other respects. The author, of course, conceives the theory as applying to all the aspects of the arts and to all the manifestations of culture. The present chapter, therefore, will be devoted to a more thorough discussion of the relations between psycho-historical factors and the nonsubject aspects of art than has been done in previous chapters. In so doing we can reëxamine medieval art in terms of its more formal characteristics, and at the same time extend the discussion to some examples from other periods.

Let us begin by applying the psycho-historical point of view to the analysis of artistic style — or more particularly, to an analysis of the historical fluctuation of style between those polar opposites that are commonly termed "realism" and "abstraction."

During the same epochs of Western European culture which produced the development from the transcendent monster to the transcendent god, and indeed in the same works of art which represented this evolving sequence of subjcts, there occurred also an evolution in style. This evolution is summarized visually in the sculptural examples shown on Plate 30.

In tracing the history of the monsters from Gothic times back through earlier epochs, we have already had occasion to note that the representation of such subjects virtually ceases when we reach the Neolithic period. Earlier expressions of the theme, if they existed at all, appear to have been symbolically associated with abstract forms like those of the African devil mounds. From the point of view of style, the tendency toward abstraction thus illustrated is the most striking characteristic of Neolithic art. Figs. 73 and 74 of our Plate provide examples.

The great menhirs like that reproduced in Fig. 73 are completely "nonobjective" — that is to say, completely devoid of represented subject matter. In some respects we might be inclined to classify such menhirs as architecture rather than as sculpture. When aligned in avenues they were certainly submitted to an architectural order, but so for that matter were the alignments of sculptured sphynxes that formed an approach to many Egyptian temples. Utilitarian functions such as shelter or defense play no part in the conception of the menhirs. Architecture in the narrower sense, therefore, they are not. Their function is psychological: to express and to impress; to symbolize certain experiences important to the societies which produced them. In this sense we may regard them as abstract sculpture, a classification which gains weight from the fact that an occasional "statue menhir" introduces rudimentary representation as a means of elucidating the ideas symbolized.

Most of the menhirs are nonobjective and so is most of the graphic art of the period, as we have seen in the countless geometrical decorations on Neolithic pottery (Plate 18). Nonobjective design is, then, a characteristic phenomenon of style during the Neolithic epoch.

Either contemporaneous with, or subsequent to, these nonobjective works, and still in Neolithic times, we find a nascent impulse toward representation resulting in a modified but closely related style. To distinguish between these two styles, we need an exact terminology. Recent criticism provides us with one in differentiating the meaning of the term "abstract" and from that of "nonobjective." "Nonobjective," as already suggested, applies to artistic forms conceived by the artist without references to external or objective stimulus — in other words without reference to nature, hence completely devoid of representation.

"Abstract," on the other hand, implies a point of departure in nature and at least a minimal degree of representation. But whereas realistic art reproduces nature more or less completely and literally, the artist working in an abstract style selects, extracts, or "abstracts" only certain elements from nature, perhaps no more than certain design suggestions. These elements or suggestions he weaves into a new formal context dictated by his own creative impulse.

The degree to which the resulting art form resembles the natural objects from which it took its point of departure depends upon how far the artist has carried the abstracting process. If he has not pressed far in that direction, his work may show a considerable resemblance to nature and in that case might be described as "semirealistic." If he has abstracted radically, he may have eliminated practically all vestiges of nature, producing a result that borders on the nonobjective. The terms "abstract" and "abstraction" thus cover a broad zone of related effects, ranging from the near-nonobjective at one extreme to the near-realistic at the other.

While we are discussing terms, it might further be noted that although the words "nonobjective" and "abstract" have the meanings indicated above when contrasted with each other for the purpose of fine distinction, "abstract" is also used in a broader sense to cover both these categories of effect when non-realistic art in general is being distinguished from more definitely representational art. It is in this broader sense that we referred to the African devil mounds as "abstract" although they have no point of departure in nature and are therefore, literally, nonobjective.

Returning to Neolithic art and to its two closely related styles, we have already observed an example of its nonobjective style in the menhirs. The second or "abstract" style can be seen in the rare statue menhirs, in the more numerous statuettes, and in mural carvings like the one shown in Fig. 74. In the latter, nose, eyes, and mouth are easily distinguishable, but the four concentric curves below them have been so far abstracted that the observer may fail to identify them with the collar or necklace by which they were undoubtedly inspired. The remaining features of the human form and of its dress have either been entirely omitted or have been radically transformed in proportion, surface treatment, and in other ways.

Of far greater concern to the sculptor than literal representation have been the material impact upon him of massive stone, the quality of his technical execution, and the appeal of his formal organization. With a "respect for his material" akin to that felt by direct carvers at the present day, he has added a representational element to stone without disturbing its basic solidity and repose. With an execution worthy of a twentieth-century Brancusi, he has polished his lines and surfaces into a smooth-flowing, one might well say "streamlined," continuity. And with an organizational emphasis comparable to that of a cubist, he has accepted from nature only those suggestions which would fall into place in his particular concept of design. Note how the lines derived from the necklace repeat and at the same time invert the broad curves of the head and eyebrows, and how the verticality and angularity of the nose provide invigorating opposition to the dominant curvelinear motif. Harmony and contrast could not be more directly achieved nor made to offset each other more effectively.

If we take the nonobjective and the abstract types of Neolithic art as two points on an imaginary line of development beginning nonobjectively and then introducing a minimal representation, and if we project that line through the periods that were to follow Neolithic times, we should expect it to lead through various degrees of increasing representational emphasis to a point at which complete realism eventually appears. That is exactly what happens in the various civilizations that have their point of departure in Neolithic art, including the Western European civilization, a portion of which we have been studying.

Dark Age art presents a midway stage in this respect as well as in the balanced tensions of its monster-hero imagery. Fig. 75 typifies its sculptural style. As compared with the preceding example, concern with representation has manifestly increased. The general appearance of the human form and of a garment enclosing it have now been incorporated in the work. Facial features are all present in approximately their natural relationships, and there is even an indication of details such as locks of hair and the fingers of the remaining hand.

Hardly less determinant than the suggestions of nature in the conception of this work, however, is a persistent preoccupation with formal order. Proportions are only seminatural, the hand of the main figure being much too large for the body. Symmetry and rhythmic placement govern the arrangement of the forms. Surfaces perpetuate the spell of nonobjective order in their display of geometrical ornament. In short, the opposing impulses toward realism and toward abstraction here reach a point close to pivotal equilibrium. Each is important; neither dominates the other. Hence the style of such work might equally well be characterized as "semiabstract" or "semirealistic."

In the later Romanesque and Gothic art of the Middle Ages (Figs. 76 and 77), the scales gradually descend on the side of realism. Formalizing traditions still persist in Romanesque sculpture, as Fig. 76 illustrates through the geometrical parallelisms of its drapery folds and hair, the conventionalized ringlets of the beard, and the harmonizing of the uplifted arm with the motif of verticality so many times repeated in other elements of the figure. At the same time we perceive that another wave has pressed forward the advancing tide of realism. Proportions are now approximately natural. There is even a suggestion of informal stance in the position of the feet and the bent head. Details have reached the point of including the pupils of the eyes, the bone structure of the hand at the right, and a thumbnail on the one at the left. We are still not far from the point of equilibrium between organization and representation, but we sense that representation is now the controlling force. Organization has become its accompaniment or, we might say, its handmaid, adjusting with careful scrutiny the finishing touches of a conception based primarily upon the human form.

By the height of the Gothic epoch, still another stage in stylistic evolution is apparent. It is not quite fully realistic — maximum emphasis on factual representation does not occur in Western Europe until the end of the sixteenth century — but thirteenth-century Gothic Europe is not far from it. The most characteristic Gothic art might be described as "near-realistic."

In our example (Fig. 77), proportions and features faithfully reflect natural appearance. The drapery, though still semiformal, has assumed a freer, more varied, and seemingly more spontaneous disposition. Traces of archaic formality linger in the face and hair, but the hands are executed with freedom, elegance, and complete fidelity to natural detail. The Bible is a stone facsimile of a medieval book. The right hand, with its broken fingers, indicates that we have already passed the turning point at which the sculptor's desire for naturalistic representation overbalances his respect for his medium and results in a partial loss of permanence.

The evolution of style in Western European art, like that of subject matter, continues through later phases, but we have now traced it as far as our present historical context permits or our present purpose demands. It is evident that the cultural progression from Neolithic to Gothic times involves changes of style no less unmistakable and no less consistent than those of subject matter — changes which lead from the nonobjective to the near-objective or near-realistic.

If, now, we correlate these changes of style with the aspects of their respective periods which we previously studied, as is done in Diagram 7, a surprising observation results. The more abstract styles are dominant at the same time as the negative imagery of the dominant monsters. Emergent realism synchronizes with the emergence of the mythical heroes and increases with the increase of positive mythical imagery. Realism becomes the dominant style during the

ANALYTICAL LEVELS		HISTORICAL PERIODS		
		Neolithic and Early Metal Ages	Dark Ages	Gothic Middle Ages
Cultural Imagery	Style	Nonobjectivism and abstraction	Balance of abstract and realistic tendencies	Near-realism
	Mythical Subjects	Omnipotent monsters	Balance of monsters and heroes	Omnipotent gods
Tensional Climate		Dominant negative tensions, frequently at traumatic intensity	Balance of negative and positive tensions	Dominant positive tensions, frequently at hysterical intensity
Historical Circumstances		Difficult conditions due to primitive technology, etc.	Conditions greatly improved by agricultural and other progress, but still subject to strong negative circumstances	Highly favorable conditions in technically and socially advanced municipal republics

Diagram 7. Correlation of stylistic changes in early Western European art with other cultural factors.

same Gothic epoch in which the gods come to dominate the monsters. This suggests that an abstract style, like negative mythical imagery, is a manifestation of negative tensions and of untoward historical circumstances; it suggests also that a trend toward realism, like one toward positive mythical imagery, reflects increasingly positive psychological adjustments resulting from increasingly favorable historical circumstances.

Are these correspondences mere coincidence or do they involve principles applicable to artistic style in general — principles through an understanding of which we may hope to penetrate more deeply into the symbolic meaning of style?

II

The particular conjunction noted above between style and other aspects of early Western European culture may be accidental or it may be meaningful. In principle, psycho-historical thinking would lead us to assume that it must be meaningful. Since we regard all the manifestations of culture as outgrowths of psycho-historical forces, we can hardly suppose that style will be an exception in this respect. Instead, we are inclined to view it as another facet of the embracing cultural totality; a facet inevitably and organically linked with the prevailing mythical, religious, and philsophical attitudes, and with the underlying psychological and historical conditions. Thus considered the style will, in fact, appear as a component aspect of the manifest imagery of its period and will be no less significant as a manifestation than are the types of subject matter with which it is merged.

If these general assumptions are to be substantiated, we must have supporting evidence for them. Such evidence can be sought in two main directions. We can observe equivalent types of art from other times and places to determine whether they involve similar conjunctions of style, subject, and cultural background; and we can resort to psychological analysis to discover, if possible, whether there are psychic reasons why any given style should synchronize with its accompanying types of subject and background.

The first of these avenues of investigation involves the comparative study of various historical periods and their arts, and is in itself so vast a field of study that we can do little more here than cast a glance at it. Even a general acquaintance with the history of art is sufficient, however, to indicate that the style trend from the nonobjective toward the realistic is characteristic of the formative stages of all the civilizations that emerged from Neolithic cultural foundations. Greek art, for instance, offers a close parallel to what we have observed in Western Europe. It began with the abstract emphasis of its so-called "geometrical" period; featured monster-hero themes linked with increasing realism during its archaic stage, and reached the near-realism of the early fifth century at the same time that the great gods assumed their calm command of the culminating temples.

Even the relegation of negative imagery to subservient positions and outlying stations, which we found in Gothic art, had its Greek equivalents. The only reminiscences of conflict inside the Parthenon occurred as minor foils to the repose of the Athena Parthenos and, like the minor monsters under the feet of the *Beau Dieu*, occurred in lowly stations. On the sandals of the goddess were embossed the battles of Lapiths and Centaurs; on the shield that stood at her feet those of gods and giants, and of Greeks and Amazons. The main surviving representations of conflict myths were found in the upper reaches of the exterior. On the metopes of the outer frieze the same battles were shown on a larger scale, but they were shown under the cornice, far from the observer, and they were shown within the firm controlling order of the Doric entablature.

Equivalent trends from abstraction toward realism, and from myths of struggle toward those of supremacy, occur in other post-Neolithic cultures. The relations of style, subject, and historical nexus which might be coincidental if found only once, can hardly be so when they recur in a considerable number of instances. There must be governing laws at work and those laws, though cultural and historical in their broad operation, must be psychological in their immediate nature. Artistic style is an outcome of feeling, thinking, seeing, reacting to materials and technical processes, and these are psychological operations. Assuming, then, that psychological laws are at work in the formation and evolutionary direction of artistic styles, let us turn back to psychology for possible insight into reasons why an abstract style might result from negative tensions and a realistic style from positive ones?

The tension-imagery process, which we have thus far invoked as our chief psychological principle, is presumably again involved, but it is now involved in much more complex and less obvious ways. Style does enter into the formation of tension imagery, and even dreams reveal what might be considered stylistic differences to the extent that some are more realistic, some more fantastic. The deformation or elimination of various aspects of reality in certain dream images seems to correspond to the more antirealistic trends in art and to suggest that similar psychological forces may be at work in both cases.

If this is true, nonrealistic styles in art, like nonrealistic images in dreams, presumably result from some inner force of psychological "resistance." This resistance, acting as an unconscious "censor," may be assumed to oppose the emergence of realistic images and to replace them by "substitute formations" removed in various degrees from objectivity. Are there any psychological data which might help to confirm this assumption and to explain the presumed activity of censorship in connection with abstract and nonobjective art?

One possible key to the situation can be found in a mental process recognized by all schools of psychoanalysis. This is the tendency of the mind to repress from consciousness whatever is unpleasant to it. This tendency is well described by Freud in a passage from his *Psychology of Errors* in which he is considering why people frequently find it impossible to recall the name of a person or place which is nevertheless quite familiar to them. The reason given is a "counter-tendency," an active "will to forget," caused by some unpleasant association with the place or person involved or, if not directly with them, with experiences which they indirectly suggest or recall. "As a motive of the tendency opposing the recollection of the name, we here for the first time encounter a principle which will later reveal itself to be of quite prodigious importance in the causation of neurotic symptoms; namely, the aversion on the part of memory against recalling anything connected with painful feelings that would revive the pain if it were recalled. In this tendency towards *avoidance of pain* from recollection or other mental processes, this flight of the mind from that which is unpleasant, we may perceive the ultimate purpose at work behind not merely the forgetting of names, but also many other errors, omissions, and mistakes." [2]

Is it not possible that the absence of representation from abstract art is one of the "omissions" due to the mental principle just indicated? Such an explanation gains plausibility from our earlier analysis of the whole cultural context in which Neolithic abstraction occurred. Not only the details of experience such as particular places or persons, but in a certain sense the whole objective world was inimical to Neolithic man. The central reality of his collective experience was a difficult struggle to survive in a world which threatened him with extermination and which, for tribe after tribe, resulted in extermination.

Consider, then, what Neolithic man might represent in his art. The world around him was full of negative associations, the related mythical superworld equally so. If he represented the one, he forced himself to contemplate the scene of monstrous practical problems. If he represented the other, a reflection of those problems still assailed him in monster fantasies. His psychological position was certainly one which might be expected to generate a powerful "counter-tendency", a will to forget painful contingencies and to cultivate a stoical detachment in their half-forgotten shadow. So, as our individual minds blot out the name with unpleasant associations, the collective mind of Neolithic society may well have blotted out, as far as it was able, a whole world of unpleasant associations. Such a blotting-out process, if applied to art, could only result in one stylistic direction: the direction of reducing or eliminating representation — the direction leading to abstraction and nonobjectivity.

This, as we know, was precisely the direction followed by the Neolithic artist. To be exact, we should say this was precisely the direction that had been followed by the immediate cultural ancestor of the Neolithic artist, the late Paleolithic artist — and here we meet one of the strongest confirmations of the present interpretation of style. If there had been no previous realism we might assume that Neolithic abstraction was simply a primitive stage of art beyond which civilized man was later to evolve — an assumption that has had its exponents. In point of fact there *had* been a previous realism. As a result of an earlier evolution of hundreds of thousands of years, Paleolithic hunting man, during the Aurignacian and Magdalenian periods, had attained a refined, one might well say "classic," representation of the animals that were the basis of his economy and the chief factor in his security and well being. As illustrated in Fig. 78, the style of Magdalenian art was a sensitive selective realism which conveyed an extraordinarily complete impression of both the form and the spirit of its animal subjects.

Those whose conception of style takes no account of changing psychological attitudes are likely to assume that, once having reached this stage of artistic development, humanity would thenceforth retain a realistic style in its art. Historically, quite the opposite is true. The concluding post-Magdalenian periods of the Paleolithic epoch reveal in their art a progressive abandonment of the inherited realism. Two midway stages of this trend can be seen in Fig. 79. The larger animals, though stereotyped in comparison with our earlier reindeer painting, retain the approximate contours and proportions of the animal forms. The deer and hunter in the upper left corner of the illustration are little more than "stick figures" or barely recognizable pictographs. In the terms commonly used to describe the later stages of a cultural cycle, the traditional realism has entered its decadent phase, undergoing progressive deterioration. But this deterioration, viewed psycho-dynamically, would also involve an unconscious counter-tendency: a positive antirealistic or abstractionist will which leads eventually to completely nonobjective art.

One of the leading students of Paleolithic culture, the anthropologist Hugo Obermaier, has traced the final stages of this process. In the plate which we reproduced from one of his works (Plate 32) he has assembled late Paleolithic pictographs in the sequences of increasing abstraction that led finally to the end in nonobjectivity. Some of the resulting nonobjective designs of the Azillian period are reproduced on a larger scale in Fig. 80.

If we submit these stylistic developments to a psycho-historical examination, coördinating them with the attendant historical circumstances, we find that the return to abstraction in late Paleolithic art synchronized historically with a recession in hunting economy. At the end of the Old Stone Age, the glacial epoch was passing. Climate, flora, and fauna were changing. Most of the key forces to which man had adapted himself, and upon which he depended for survival, were disappearing from his world. As a result his hunting technology, including his hunting ritual and art, increasingly revealed their incapacity to nourish further social growth or even to maintain existing social standards. Late Paleolithic societies were thus faced with the double problem of extricating themselves from an habitual way of life and of making painful efforts of readaptation.

We can only deduce from the total correlation of Paleolithic art with Paleolithic culture that so long as hunting prospered, Paleolithic men gave increasingly realistic attention to the animal forms that were the chief symbols of their social well-being; conversely that when hunting ceased to function positively as a basis for collective life, the will to realistic representation of the animals receded.

The experiences that would motivate these changing attitudes seem evident enough. When the Magdalenian reindeer of Fig. 78 was painted, the creation of the painting and the performance of the related ritual were likely to be followed by a successful hunting season and the prosperity of the group. Success and prosperity inspired confidence in the efficacy of the whole system, attended by a will to perfect it. Improvement of the animal image through more accurate resemblance to the quarry would be one of the natural expressions of these attitudes.

When animal abundance began to fail — the reindeer, for instance, was leaving southern Europe for the arctic as the glaciers receded — consider what would probably happen. Painting and ritual would be carried out as before, but now would be increasingly followed by unsuccessful hunting seasons, the pinch of hunger, the sense of bewilderment and insecurity. The men who actually lived in those late glacial times had none of the knowledge that we have today concerning the long-range changes that were going on in their environment. For centuries, no doubt, they persisted in their former ways, but they did so with decreasing success and therefore with decreasing conviction. What had been to their fathers a social and artistic vitality was becoming for them a social and artistic convention. The growing conventionality of their artistic style was one of the manifestations of this attitude.

Eventually there came a time when men realized that dependence on the hunted animal must go; a realization reflected in the disappearance of the animal image from art. There were as yet no symbols of a new order, for the new order was to be based on agriculture, which at that time was still unborn. For the time being the ties of the old order with the objective world had passed; the ties to be established by the new order had not been determined. What remained to art was nonobjectivity. Late Paleolithic abstraction thus symbolized, for the communities that produced it, a mentality of withdrawal from an old way of life and consequent striving for reorientation. The slate, so to speak, was wiped clean of the past for whatever the future might hold in store. And the wiping clean was culturally important as a means of insuring open-mindedness toward future possibilities.

It was this terminal abstraction of late Paleolithic cultures which Neolithic cultures inherited, and which they continued to use because it possessed continuing relevancy to continuing collective problems of an insecure way of life. In due course necessity became the mother of invention. Agriculture was developed to eke out, and later to wipe out, the penury of late hunting culture. We have already seen that the growth of agricultural technology and of its cultural superstructure, from Neolithic to Gothic times, was accompanied by the growth of a new realism. Intensification of the latter continued through the Renaissance, reached its zenith in the sixteenth and seventeenth centuries, entrenched itself as the dominant European style until the later nineteenth century and then, to the bewilderment of the Western World, gave way once more to a retreat from realism.

The manifestation of this recent reversal appeared in the progressive distortion and abandonment of nature by large numbers of the more creative European and American artists. First becoming evident as a general trend in the later works of the Impressionists, the movement gained momentum in Post-Impressionism, and reached its logical conclusions in twentieth-century non-objectivism, on the one hand, and surrealism on the other. Plate 31, Figs. 81–83 reproduce typical examples of three stages of this recent stylistic reversal as it led from the realism to the nonobjectivism. Comparison with the Paleolithic works on the same plate will indicate how similar was the general style will of late Paleolithic times and of the past century.

And there can hardly be room to doubt that the current will to abstraction again synchronizes historically with a period of cultural uncertainty and insecurity. The very foundations of agrarian economy and of its cultural super-structure have been shaken by the expanding effects of the Industrial Revolution and the concomitant scientific advances. Western societies are again forced to make their dangerous and painful progress through the cultural no man's land that lies between the distintegrating faiths and securities of a passing order and the reintegrating ones of a new order that presumably lies beyond the mists of chaos.

To summarize the foregoing discussion, psychology has made known to us a mental tendency to withdraw consciousness from subjects involving painful associations; history reveals that the epochs that produced our examples of abstract art were times of social stress. Thus there seems to be considerable evidence to support the assumption that the psychic motive force leading to abstract art is a recoil from painful collective experience.

Other motives, more evident and less disturbing to contemporary consciousness, are more frequently cited. Contemporary abstraction is said to reflect the mechanical forms of the industrial world. It is also said to reflect the scientific realization that conceptions of reality can no longer be limited to optical appearance. In the latter view the nonobjective painting is an outcome of the same mental climate that has produced our conception of cosmic rays, of stellar systems beyond human observation, of invisible neutrons and electrons whirling inside the atom.

No doubt there is a truth in such interpretations, but from the psycho-historical point of view it appears to be a relatively superficial layer of truth, based largely on conscious analogies. The best proof of its failure to reach the heart of the matter is the fact that abstraction has existed in ages that were neither industrial nor scientific, as shown by our late Paleolithic and Neolithic examples. We should presumably be closer to the real motivations if we could show causes that seem to have operated in all the known cases, prehistoric as well as recent. Such causes we have already suggested.

The "flight of the mind from that which is unpleasant," which we took from Freud as a psychological point of departure for the present inquiry, emphasizes only the negative aspect of our subject. The cultural processes related to abstract styles in art are more involved than a simple flight from pain and involve their positive as well as their negative aspects. The positive aspect of such situations deserve more careful consideration than we have yet given them.

Psychologically, the retreat from realism to abstraction corresponds to a swing from objectivity to subjectivity, from extraversion to introversion. Both these modes of psychic orientation have their functional value in the interplay between life and environment. Although the equilibrium between the two, which Jung calls "ambiversion," constitutes an ideal adjustment, there are circumstances under which the dominance of one or the other may become fruitful and even essential.

The daily alternation between waking activities and sleep provides a demonstration of the normal succession of the two extremes. Success in waking activities calls for a large measure of extravert adaptation to, and management of, the objective world. After a certain number of hours, the energies available for such adaptation and management are exhausted. The individual than lets go the outer world and withdraws his being into the subjective realm of unconscious vital processes, there to relax tensions and restore energies for a fresh attack on the outer world next day.

When an individual meets outer difficulties that exceed his ability to cope with them, the recuperation provided by a normal amount of sleep proves insufficient to support continued objectivity. Such a hard-pressed or frustrated individual is forced to call more at length and more deeply upon his inner resources. More prolonged and more complete introversion may then become a necessary basis for compensation, recuperation, and reorientation.

Similarly, it would appear, the hard-pressed society not only withdraws as much of its consciousness as possible from a hostile and in some cases hopeless world, but at the same time steeps itself in the inner depths from which all adjustments arise and, perhaps without consciously realizing it, prepares itself for a renewed and more effective assault on its objective problems. In the terms of one of Jung's archetypes of mental experience, society thus "returns to the mother." It withdraws into the psychic matrix of life in order that it may call upon the primal forces of regeneration and from them receive, in due course, the strength and, above all, the vision necessary to its rebirth. More precisely, the driven society withdraws its faith from an order of life to which it no longer dares to trust its destiny, reëntering the collective indeterminateness which is without faith or system yet which contains the basic constants from which all faiths and systems are born.

As one of the cultural manifestations of this return to the maternal sub-jectivity, abstract art ministers to the hard-pressed spirit of the times in two related ways. We may call them the esthetic, and the organizational or direc-tional. Esthetically, abstract design can embody all the basic laws of visual composition — rhythm, harmony, proportion, balance, and so forth — laws from the control of which the creative spirit receives some of its most rewarding experiences, and from the perception of which in created things the sense of beauty receives much of its keenest delight. Having given up the world, as it were, man can still find in abstract beauty one realm in harmony with his soul, one realm where things are as he enjoys making and seeing them. Esthetic satisfaction in design remains to him as a sanctuary within which, with a kind of esthetic mysticism, he may refresh his tired spirit and keep unbroken a last thread of faith that something at the heart of things is still with him.

Linked with the intrinsic value and restorative virtue provided by abstract art through esthetic experience, is another positive function which we shall call organizational or directional. The refuge into which the creative spirit has withdrawn from a frustrating world, imbued with the metamorphic impulse of psychic extremity, turns out to be an observatory from which paths to a more fulfilling world can be discerned.

For what, actually, has broken down in the traditional world to leave man in the difficult cultural position that coincides with periods of abstract art? In the broadest and simplest terms, can we not say that it is a system of cultural relationships? Technological relationships between certain human needs, cer-tain natural resources, and certain methods of exploiting those resources; social relationships between competing groups, classes, or societies; mental relation-ships between habitual ways of thought and results once attained but no longer attainable by those ways of thought.

And how can a more fulfilling order of things again be achieved? By estab-lishing new and more effective relationships, by connecting the needs with new resources or new technological potentials, by aligning the conflicting social entities in new and more harmonious configurations, by establishing contact between the problem-solving power of human intelligence and the particular problems imposed by the new cultural circumstances.

To achieve these results society must cease its habitual repetition of inherited culture patterns, must revert to the basic principles which underlie such patterns and, by observing and applying these principles, must evolve new culture patterns. As collective attitudes grope their way through the obscurities and anxieties of this period of change, what they need from art — or perhaps we should say, what they reflect through art — are symbols of the laws of relationships, patterns of pattern, visualizations and vivifications of the principles of order and organization in which lie their hope of reorganizing their chaotic world. Artistic abstraction is of precisely this nature. It is the simplest and clearest manifestation possible in art of a satisfying order obtained through organized relations.

Nowhere do we find a more striking demonstration of the fact that the universe is really a universe, a oneness. In retreating from the outer world into the depths of his own bruised soul, man finds there the principles by means of which he can emerge to triumph again over the outer world. Outer and inner may be opposite poles of experience, but poles are merely the extremities of a connecting continuum. Order resulting from relational laws, relationality or relativity, appears to be a universal manifestation of existence. It reveals itself in the revolution of planets around their suns, in the revolution of the atomic electrons around their protons; it reveals itself equally in man's inner being, manifesting itself creatively in his power to organize, esthetically in his enjoyment of organization.

In the light of all these considerations, it seems reasonable to interpret the emergence and development of an abstract style in art as indicating a negative withdrawal from an unfulfilling cultural order but also, positively, as conserving the benefits of esthetic experience and, above all, as directing cultural awareness toward the organizational laws essential to the development of a new cultural order.

III

We have remarked that an abstract style in art implies extreme subjectivity or introversion, and that under certain curcumstances such an extreme is inevitable and indeed fruitful. Nevertheless, being an extreme, it is a one-sided rather than a balanced adjustment. Developmentally it must either be temporary, balance being restored by a return to greater objectivity, or it becomes pathological, balance being permanently lost through incapacity for objective adjustments.

In the long run, psychic stability can be maintained only through responsiveness to both the objective and the subjective factors of experience and through an integration of their opposite demands. As Jung has put it, man "can only meet the demands of outer necessity in an ideal way if he is also adapted to his own inner world, that is to say, if he is in harmony with himself. Conversely, he can only adapt to his inner world and achieve unity with himself when he is adapted to the environmental conditions. As experience shows, the one or the other function can be neglected for a time only. If, for example, only a one-sided adaptation to the outer world is attained while the inner is neglected, the value of the inner conditions is gradually increased, and the fact becomes manifest through the eruption of personal elements into the external adaptation." [3] The converse, of course, is equally true; when the inner or subjective is given a one-sided predominance, the neglected value of outer conditions accumulates repressed energy and eventually forces a swing to, or "eruption of," objective considerations.

Psychological considerations would therefore indicate that periods of extreme introversion, whether individual or collective, would be succeeded by a reorientation toward extraversion: by the psychic reëmergence or rebirth of interest in the objective world. As we have seen, the psyche's meditations within the subjective sanctuary would already have revealed to it, in a renewed consciousness of the importance of the laws of relationship, the principle essential to its reconquest of outer circumstances.

Technologically, the result of returning extraversion would be a renewed and more intelligent attack on the problems imposed by the physical and social environments, and the gradual development of new culture patterns capable of affording a new or renewed state of collective well-being. Artistically the result would be, among other things, a re-sensitizing of the artist to the attractions of the natural world, a shift of creative impulse toward representation, and the beginnings of a movement that would lead to an eventual return of realism.

As we have seen in the segment of history of which we made our special study, these implied directions, both technological and artistic, actually constitute the grand lines of development in Western culture during the periods extending from Neolithic to Gothic times. Technological readjustment to the outer world took the form of the substitution of agriculture for the no-longer adequate hunting, the gradual attainment of renewed and indeed previously unattained economic abundance, and the growth of a new and elaborate cultural superstructure upon this agricultural base. The mythological and artistic reflection of this cultural regeneration showed itself, on the one hand, in the gradual swing from negatively weighted to positively weighted imagery and, on the other hand, in a gradual reversal of style.

When, it would seem, the imagery had become sufficiently positive that its associations for the collective mind were no longer predominantly painful, it was accepted into art as subject matter. Nonobjective forms gave way to representation, though as it were cautiously, in the firmly controlled, geometrical manner of a "primitive" style. Gradually objective confidence increased. More elements of the outer world, and more complete representation of them, were creatively accepted. In due course, as we have seen, stylistic evolution led to the semirealistic archaism of the Dark Ages and then onward to the near-realistic early maturity of Gothic art. The movement subsequently continued to the point of complete realism which implies the one-sided extreme of objectivity and forecasts the eventual necessity of a return toward greater subjectivity to restore balance.

If there are indeed psycho-historical laws at work in the determination of style trends in the arts, then those laws must be expected to operate in the future as they already have in the past. It should therefore be possible to forecast long-range style trends in advance of their appearance. If we assume that the recent trend toward abstraction is one of the manifestations of the need for cultural reorientation in emergent industrial society — and if, as we might also assume, recent surrealism is another such manifestation, revealing in this case the negative pressures of an age of transition through more or less monstrous negative imagery — then we may further assume that these styles will remain vital only so long as the present negative psycho-historical pressures continue to strain our world.

If and when positive tensions begin to dominate our cultural mentality as a result of favorable historical developments and the maturing of a humanly fulfilling industrial order — if and when the hundreds of millions of men living in industrial societies begin to sense a relief from conflicts like those between capital and labor and between capitalistic and communistic states, if and when, as a result of such harmonizing trends, men no longer feel so acutely the threat of seering wars, then in those times we may expect the more sensitive artists to find their sensitivity impelling them to a renewed excitement in the forms of the outer world. As the new cultural integration proceeds, harmonizing intellectual tensions like the present imbalance between the sciences and the humanities as well as economic and social ones, we may expect the emergence of a new realism as the most vital artistic manifestation of its period.

What will be chosen as the major themes for representation, we cannot say, any more than the reindeer artist could have foreseen that Christ and the Virgin Mary would have been to his successors in the Middle Ages what the reindeer was to him, but we can assume that the new integration will in time give rise to symbols of itself and that men will desire to integrate those symbols as fully as possible with their objective experience of the universe through realistic representation. We can also assume that they will weep in beholding those symbols as Suger's generation wept in beholding the relics of its saints, so great will be the exaltation of release from inherited negative tensions.

The probable alternative to such a positive development seems equally clear. If cultural integration is *not* achieved by the industrial world, then the destructive waste and fury of its conflicts will gradually sap its vital energies. The evolution of the new will give way to efforts to salvage what can survive of the old. In that case we can predict a gradual petrification of art as the re-flection of a petrifying society. Inherited symbols, permeated by various degrees of the abstractionist impulse but resisting it, will harden into formulas as they did in the Byzantine art of the terminal periods of ancient Greek society. Motivating the growth neither of new thematic symbols nor of a new realism in style, the accepted symbols will prolong their existence as more or less static conventions.

It is not to be expected that the author or any of the members of his genera-tion will live to see the historical demonstration of the truth or falsity of the forecasts just hazarded. But if these pages should be fortunate enough to come into the hands of any reader in the twenty-first century or, better in the twenty-fifth or the thirtieth, it will eventually be clear that our assumptions did foresee future trends or that they failed to do so. The evidence received in this manner should be one of the strongest confirmations or disprovals of the concepts set forth in the present chapter.

Our discussion of style has by no means covered, or attempted to cover, all the problems involved in a psycho-historical analysis of art forms. Our present objective will have been attained if the reader is prepared to recognize stylistic trends toward or away from realism as integral aspects of the psycho-historical development of the cultures that give rise to them. If our discussion has justified itself, the style as well as the subject matter of the arts reflects collective men-tality and this mentality in turn reflects historical experience.

THE PSYCHO-HISTORICAL THEORY;
RECAPITULATION AND EXPANSION

The chapters comprising Part II were undertaken with two aims in view. The first was to test the psycho-historical theory by applying it in a more intensive and comprehensive manner than had been possible with the slight examples of Part I. As material for study in conducting this test, we took a sequence of art forms and related myths to which we were first attracted by the enigma of the Gothic grotesque but which, as we pursued it, led us to consider evolutionary connections extending from Neolithic to Gothic times and organic connections binding the art and myths to many other aspects of the cultures from which they emerged.

Our second, and in a sense secondary, aim was to obtain any new light that our analysis might shed upon the particular forms of myth and art, the particular periods and cultural situations, that served as specimens for our more general and theoretical study. Our immediate findings included the indication of psycho-historical reasons for the appearance of various forms of cultural expression such as the monster myths and abstract style of Neolithic times, the rise of mythical heroes and of archaic representation during the Dark Ages, and the flowering of a triumphant religion, culminating religious architecture, and a near-realistic style at the height of the Gothic Middle Ages. Our immediate findings also included the discovery of organic relations between the seemingly aberrant grotesque and the context of Gothic religious art and architecture in which it appears.

These immediate findings, though we shall not discuss them further, involve various implications for the fields of study to which they relate, particularly the fields of esthetics and the history of art. Implications of this kind, extensions of the psycho-historical point of view to some topics of current scholarly or general interest, will form the subject of Part III. What remains for discussion here is the outcome of the first and broader aim of Part II: that of testing the psycho-historical theory itself by applying it to some substantial segment of cultural actuality. What are the results of our test on this more general plane?

If the facts and conclusions brought forward in the preceding chapters are accurate, the theory seems to have validated itself in each of the cultural contexts to which we have applied it. It has enabled us to make analytical assumptions which, upon examination, appeared to be in accord with the preponderant mass of historical data and opinion and to be comprehensible in terms of psychological principles. The relationships which we assumed to exist between historical circumstances, collective tensions, and cultural products appeared in fact to have acted as dynamic forces in the experience of cultures studied. The given forms of expression in each case seemed logical for their times when considered as projections of existing tensional states and those states in turn seemed to be natural results of prevailing historical conditions.

As a result of these studies, the psycho-historical theory, which could originally be conceived and proposed only on a conjectural basis, has now been reinforced with a certain amount of supporting evidence. The measure of confirmation thus obtained should carry the theory some steps further along the line of development from its initial state of an hypothesis toward the position of a working principle that has given at least a preliminary demonstration of its possibilities and that seems worthy of further application and development.

The remainder of the present chapter will be given to a recapitulation of our theoretical frame of reference for cultural studies. As compared to the derivational and therefore somewhat conglomerate approach followed in Part I, we shall now state the theory in its own intrinsic terms and thus give to it a more independent and organic form. We will also add to the conception of it a number of considerations which are important from our point of view but which were not involved in its derivational sources.

In earlier diagrams (pages 78 and 233), we summarized our theory in terms of the three levels of existence which we have been calling historical circumstances, collective tensional states, and manifest cultural imagery. These were presented in vertical relations to each other, like superimposed strata through which energy progressed upward from the circumstance to tension and emerged at the top in the form of cultural imagery. Although these relations are in the main basic to psycho-historical thinking, there are two respects in which we can now refine our conception of them. Both are incorporated in the somewhat more comprehensive Diagram 8.

A first modification results from the fact that the psyche is not exclusively a product of a given set of historical circumstances. Its tensional condition at any given time and place will largely be so, as we have been assuming, but human needs, drives, and capacities exist before history in the usual sense of the term and become one of the major determinants of history. It therefore seems necessary to recognize their claim to priority in this respect, as is done in 1–A in Diagram 8.

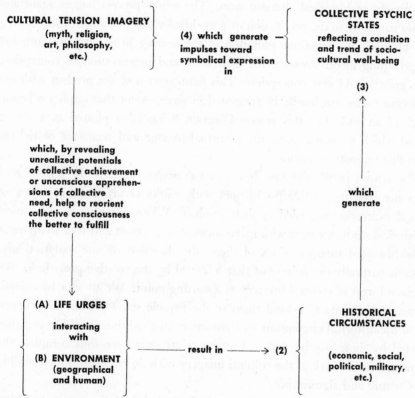

CULTURAL TENSION IMAGERY
(myth, religion, art, philosophy, etc.)

(4) which generate — impulses toward symbolical expression in

COLLECTIVE PSYCHIC STATES
reflecting a condition and trend of socio-cultural well-being

(3)

which, by revealing unrealized potentials of collective achievement or unconscious apprehensions of collective need, help to reorient collective consciousness the better to fulfill

which generate

(A) LIFE URGES
interacting with
(B) ENVIRONMENT
(geographical and human)

————— result in —————→ (2)

HISTORICAL CIRCUMSTANCES
(economic, social, political, military, etc.)

Diagram 8. Graphic summary of the psycho-historical conception of cultural dynamics.

A second modification of our earlier schema seems desirable in view of the fact that a purely vertical movement from circumstance to tension to cultural expression might lead us to regard resulting cultural objects — works of art, religious concepts, or philosophical systems — as terminals. The whole process could then be graphed as a straight line beginning with circumstance and ending with object, and would involve no recognition of the continuing vitality and future effects of the object.

This terminal view of the cultural product is relatively adequate if we are merely concerned with interpreting a given object or type of object. But in the creative experience of life from which the object emerges, there is and can be no terminal. The object, after its creation, remains within the culture and becomes thenceforth an aspect of environment and an element in history. It satisfies, resists, or otherwise modifies life urges, participating with other factors in the interaction between life and environment which in turn results in a modification of historical circumstances. The whole process begins again and follows its course to the production of a modified variety of object, thus sharing with life itself the repetitive pulsation of the beating heart and the outgoing and returning blood stream — the generation and regeneration of conception, birth, growth, and new conception. This reintegration of the product with the producing forces can hardly be suggested in any concept that implies a beginning and an end. For this reason Diagram 8 has been plotted as a circuit around which we can assume the perpetual passage and repassage of the energies that animate a culture.

The arrows in the diagram have been drawn to indicate the sequence of forces involved in creative production, with works of art or other forms of cultural expression regarded as their product. When, for purposes of critical or historical study, we start with given forms of expression and seek to arrive at psycho-historical interpretations of them, the direction of our analytical procedure is naturally the reverse of that followed by the creative procedure. We are given forms of cultural imagery as a starting point. We attempt by analytical means to penetrate behind them to the psychic states which they express and to the historical circumstances, environmental conditions, and life impulses reflected by those psychic states. Counter-creativewise, we thus complete the circuit and arrive back at the cultural imagery with an enriched understanding of its nature and significance.

Regarding Diagram 8 as our summary formulation of the psycho-historical theory of cultural dynamics, let us follow the sequence of its component terms and relations, discussing each of them as far as may be needed to add further range or depth to our conception. In the course of this discussion, it will be convenient to refer retrospectively to cultures we have already studied and also to introduce new examples, chosen from various periods, as further illustrations of the principles involved.

The formulation of our major premise in terms of three main correlates — cultural imagery, collective psychic states, and historical circumstances — would seem to indicate that historical circumstances provide the ultimate foundation for cultural superstructures. Practically speaking this is true. For working purposes in most instances, the complex covered by the phrase "historical circumstances" is sufficiently broad to comprehend all the forces at work in the initial stage of cultural motivation. The student can return from a study of history to the interpretation of cultural phenomena without special attention to the subforces that underlie history itself.

Nevertheless, in principle, historical circumstances are not to be regarded in any absolute sense as the ultimate foundation of cultural dynamics. Indeed there is no ultimate foundation. Cultures are emanations of the living universe, the universe at work. They are products of forces within which the whole of existence — all time, all space — converges. The presence in the vicinity of Amiens of rock deposits that could provide building stone, the constitution of the soil that favored the growth of *waide*, project the conditioning of Amiens Cathedral back through the whole course of geological history. The stage of technological development that enabled thirteenth-century society in Amiens to convert the rock into Gothic structure and the *waide* into dye, involve the whole evolution of Western culture and, more generally behind it, the whole evolution of life. There is no force at work in the universe which does not in some manner and degree, directly or indirectly, exert its conditioning influence upon the formation of a human culture.

But we must set limits to a usable instrument of thought, even though there are none to the realities of which it is a partial image. For most practical purposes in applying our theory, the concept of historical circumstances is sufficiently broad and at the same time sufficiently concrete to provide a satisfactory base of operations. For theoretical purposes, such as concern us in the present chapter, a somewhat more careful statement of principles is desirable. With this end in view we are establishing our point of departure, as Diagram 8 indicates, one stage behind what are ordinarily thought of as historical circumstances, beginning with human life urges and their interaction with environment.

History is an account of the experience of particular groups of human beings under particular conditions. If there is any logical starting point for a summary of psycho-historical principles, it would seem to lie in the human group with its motivating biological drives and its limiting biological potentials.

This first term in our sequence, human life, though it exceeds all others in its power of cultural determination, usually requires little attention at the subhistorical level because it is constant for practically all cultural situations.

Had man lacked even so minor a physical attribute as hands, most of the major achievements of human culture would have been impossible, but since all men have hands, we gain little understanding of individual cultures by stressing the fact. The same can be said of other common aptitudes and faculties upon which cultural activity depends. They can be assumed as a universal base for cultural developments and require little specific attention in approaching particular cultural problems.

Occasionally there may be reasons for a more careful consideration of the conditions imposed upon culture by its human foundations. Thus in early Paleolithic cultures, life was a conditioning factor in an exceptional manner because it was still evolving through its subhuman phases. The full potentials of the human race, as first realized in Cromagnon man and as retained by subsequent human groups to date, were not at the disposal of earlier submen. In the cultures of the latter, relative stages of biological evolution thus became an important factor in setting limits to cultural achievement. Once we reach the later Paleolithic epochs, human potentials, biologically speaking, are complete. Thence forward through the Neolithic and the various historic periods they remain constant, or at least so constant that any developments they may have undergone do not appear to be measurable.

Normally speaking, therefore, we can accept human nature as a relatively unchanging factor in cultural studies. We can assume the universal activity of drives that are biological in origin, drives involved with the perpetuation of the species and the survival of the individual within the species. We can assume that these drives will operate largely through instinctive instrumentalities such as sex and hunger; also that man's comparatively sensitive physical organism will need protection against physical agencies that might destroy it through freezing, burning, or other severe forms of exposure. We can assume a general confluence of all these impulses and needs toward the pursuit of positive experiences such as comfort, pleasure, happiness, and fulfillment; and a converse avoidance, as far as possible, of negative experiences such as discomfort, pain, unhappiness, and frustration. And we can assume that in pursuing these positive ends and seeking to avoid the negative ones, men will employ to their utmost the capacities offered by their biological inheritance: among others the keenness of human sight and hearing, the adroitness of the human hand and, above all, the extraordinary powers of the human intelligence.

Such traits and activities as hunger and the need for shelter, the search for fulfillment and the use of intelligence, are immediately vested in the individual.

Our assumptions regarding the human base of culture would be one-sided, however, if we did not recognize one final fact of importance: namely that man is, in essence, a social, not a solitary, animal. The human individual in his native state falls comparatively easy prey to the stronger and swifter individuals of many species of animals and to the collective invasions of many microorganisms. Man has triumphed or is triumphing over such enemies, has attained his present mastery of the earth, chiefly because of his greater capacity for cumulative collective effort. His basic problems — the means of subsistence, the fight against disease, and so forth — are important, not to one alone, but to all. The recognition of such problems and the effort to solve them are collective. They are attacked by many minds, often selected and trained for that special purpose and materially supported during their studies and experiments by other coöperating agencies of society. Solutions and discoveries, when attained, can be transmitted to the species as a whole through collective mediums of communication such as language and perpetuated for permanent reference through writing and other forms of record.

Thus it happens that while the capacities of the human individual have apparently not improved during the twenty-five thousand years since the appearance of Cromagnon man, social or cultural growth during that same period has been enormous. Man to man, a twentieth-century individual and his Cromagnon predecessor would be more or less evenly matched, with the odds probably in favor of Cromagnon hardihood. Society to society, a twentieth-century group would be infinitely more powerful. And its increased power would be proportionate to its success in accumulating, socializing, and perpetuating human experience through culture.

This fundamental human trait of collectivity, while it has limited applications on a physical level, is primarily psychological. Men acted as a social body, in the literal sense, when large numbers of them strained together to drag a Neolithic menhir, an Egyptian obelisk, or a load of stone for a cathedral. But this merging of human physical energy has little more frequency or importance in history than has a tug of war among the activities of society today. Mankind has risen to its eminent position primarily through the merging of its *mental* power. And while at most a few hundred contemporaries can join their forces to pull at a cable, there is no limit either of space or time to mental coöperation. To say that we today can contemplate Paleolithic cave paintings, read the thoughts of Confucius and Aristotle, meditate upon the aspirations of Christ and Buddha, recapitulate the experiments of Galileo and Faraday, is to recognize human cultural mentality as a psychic entity which encompasses the entire earth, which endures from generation to generation with an eternity limited only by the life span of the human race, and which unites in one pervasive rhythm the mind pulsations of all the billions of human beings who have ever lived.

Among the many impulses, needs, and capacities that play their part in establishing the human basis of culture, none has greater importance than this capacity for collective mentality. The social development of intelligence which we may regard as collective consciousness, and the social sharing of intuitive experience which seems to imply some form of collective unconscious, are human attributes of paramount significance for cultural dynamics. We meet their pervasive influence in every phase of the psycho-historical process and shall return to them as later sections of this summary bring us to more advanced stages of their cultural operation and results.

II

To satisfy their needs, to realize their possibilities, human groups must act within and upon the world around them. Their environment, geographical and human, thus becomes a second factor in psycho-historical dynamics. And since geographical environments differ markedly in various parts of the world, and human environments show equally wide variations according to both place and period, environment is a factor some phase of which plays an important determining and differentiating part in nearly every cultural situation.

The cultural influence of the material or geographical environment is obvious and has long been recognized, has indeed sometimes been overemphasized at the expense of other considerations. Through climate and available natural resources, it conditions culture in many ways, both directly and indirectly. We can frequently observe its direct influence in the forms and structural systems of architecture. Climatic conditions ranging from the tropical to the northern temperate are reflected in the flat roofs of ancient Egyptian and Mesopotamian buildings, the low pitch used on Greek temples, and the steep pitch characteristic of the Gothic roof. Other results of the same climatic conditioning are the heavy walls, limited openings, shadowy interiors, and patios of the south, as compared with the more open structure, larger windows, luminous interiors, and comparative absence of courtyards in the temperate zones. The window walls of fully developed Gothic cathedrals like Amiens were organically related to a climate neither too extreme in its changes of temperature, too intense in its light, nor too violent in its wind velocities. The cathedrals of northern France could not have come into being in their present form had any of these factors differed in a marked degree.

The influence of natural resources rather than of climate is seen at work in the adoption of column and lintel construction by the Egyptians and of arch construction by the Mesopotamians. Egypt possessed rock deposits capable of providing the monumental stone needed for columns and lintels. Mestopotamia, lacking stone and even hard wood, was forced to depend upon sun-baked brick for structural purposes. A single brick can neither be made large enough nor strong enough to span the spaces required in architectural interiors. The covering of buildings in Mesopotamia therefore required some type of structure that could produce a wide and strong span from comparatively small and weak units. Such a type of structure was developed in the arch and its extensions, the barrel vault and the dome.

Indirectly, geographical environment influences culture in subtler ways: by conditioning the energy and temperament of men; by effecting their sense of color and their habitual perceptions of sharper or softer detail; by imposing upon them harder or more kindly conditions of existence and so influencing their accumulation of negative or positive tensions. As noted in an earlier chapter, the more severe climate of Scandinavian and Icelandic Europe, as compared to that of countries like France and England, was undoubtedly a factor in retarding the northern communities in their development of agriculture and of the psycho-technic changes related to it.

Whether direct or indirect, geographical influence is so generally recognized that we need not elaborate upon it. How great is its relative importance in any given cultural situation will depend in part upon its own inherent character — the more severe extremes tending to have a more pronounced conditioning effect — and in part upon the nature of the other factors interplaying with it. More or less advanced stages of life or of technology will enormously modify the potentials of men in dealing with any particular set of geographical conditions. Azilian man languished in approximately the same geographical environment where Gothic man thrived, because Azilian man was largely dependent upon a hunting economy depressed by the depletion of game, while Gothic man, with his agricultural techniques, could exploit entirely different potentials of the environment. The twentieth-century French architect can use flat roofs under the same climatic conditions that produced the steep Gothic pitch, because twentieth-century technology has produced impermeable roofing materials unknown in the Middle Ages.

Human or social, as distinct from greographical environment becomes one of the factors in a psycho-historical situation through the effect exerted upon the destinies of any community by its contacts with other communities. Human environment determines the nature and the number of the enemies against whom a given group may be called upon to defend itself; also of the neighbors from whom it may garner new ideas and with whom it may trade to the enrichment of its economic life. The extreme negative circumstances that brought the Huron Indians to the point of extinction were mainly due to their proximity and consequent exposure to the growing power of the Iroquois. Conversely, the Iroquois were attaining their superior power at least in part because, in a loosely organized human environment of small tribes, they were the first to advance through intertribal federation toward more "powerful kingdoms." Had the Iroquois inhabited a territory adjacent to the still more advanced and more powerful states of Central or South America, such as those of the Aztecs or the Incas, the situation would presumably have been reversed. Iroquois society would then have been the one threatened by stronger human powers.

On the positive side, a community exposed to a human environment more advanced than itself may profit by cultural stimulus. Such stimulus played an important part in helping the Pueblo Indians of the Southwest to attain their high position among the cultures of aboriginal North America. The Southwest area, largely desert, was not in itself a particularly favorable geographical environment, but geographical factors interplayed with human ones to give it a double advantage. Its inaccessible canyons and high mesas commanding wide areas of plain, offered the unique opportunities for military defense exploited in its early cliff dwellings. Its adjacency to the great centers of Central America, agricultural in particular and advanced in general, helped to promote Southwestern developments in irrigation, pottery, weaving, architectural construction, and other aspects of culture.

The California Indians, also inhabiting a land then largely desert, were far less advanced in cultural evolution. One of the major reasons for their relatively retarded state seems to have been their location between two great natural barriers — the Rocky Mountains and the Pacific Ocean. These barriers practically deprived the California tribes of an external human envrionment, leaving them in extreme cultural isolation. Here we have another of the many ways in which the geographical and the human aspects of environment interplay with, and modify, each other, geographical factors in this case exerting a decisive influence upon human ones.

At more advanced stages of cultural evolution, like those found in the Europe of the Dark and Middle Ages, human environment becomes correspondingly more complex. During the earlier Dark-Age centuries and those preceding them, adjacency to the Roman power in the south and to Asiatic power in the northeast, subjected central Europe to invasion and conquest from both directions. The original central populations underwent both the negative and the positive effects of these human inundations. Negatively, they were forced either to accept subjection or to flee their one-time territories; positively, they assimilated from their conquerors ideas and techniques which accelerated their own cultural evolution.

On the Roman side, by the time of the Dark Ages the human situation had been reversed. Contiguity between the declining south and the rising north resulted in the barbarian conquest of the Roman world, facilitating the further rise of the Teutonic peoples and accelerating the disintegration of a Roman society which otherwise might have persisted through a long terminal period as did its counterpart in the Byzantine east.

These scattered illustrations of the nature and effects of human environment may be concluded with a reference to some of the ways in which such environment affected Gothic culture. One was the relative equality of the newly developed city-states that constituted the most typical social unit of Gothic Europe. Hundreds, perhaps one should say thousands, of these communities were so nearly equal in size, power, and well-being that any one had a reasonable chance of self-defense if attacked, and therefore could enjoy a human environment relatively free from an overpowering menace to its existence. Correspondingly, comparative equality in vital and technological advance gave to large numbers of these communities an adequate share in the economic benefits of their time, a stimulating sense of rivalry with competitors against whom they were well-matched, and common advantages to be gained by the extension of trade between state and state over Europe as a whole.

Thus within Europe itself, human environment functioned positively in the life of the average Gothic city-state. On its external horizons, the expanding intra-European cultural organism met three main types of environing conditions, one primarily geographical, the other two primarily human. Westward, the unexplored Atlantic presented a natural barrier both to expansion and to human contacts. Human environment was confined to the north, east, and south, and was of two strikingly different kinds destined to exert correspondingly different influences on Gothic culture.

To the north and northeast the established populations were less advanced than were those of Europe itself, offering little competition to European economy and little resistance to European domination. Geographically, the northeastern territory presented many attractions and advantages. Such a combination of a weak human environment with a favorable geographical one provides an expansive society with a natural avenue for expansion. As we have already noted in our chapter on Gothic history, the colonization of the northeastern frontier became a major fact of Gothic history, contributing to the release of Gothic energies, the growth of Gothic population and resources, and the positive enhancement of Gothic life and culture.

To the south and southeast, the human environment was of a very different character. There lay the powerful empire of the Saracens. Encircling the southern and eastern shores of the Mediterranean and largely controlling Mediterranean commerce, possessing a foothold on European territory in Spain, and wielding the power accruing from an advanced culture and technology, this empire presented the only serious human barrier to Western expansion and the only serious threat to Western self-determination. Conflict between the Western and the Saracen powers, if not inevitable, was certainly natural in view of the insatiable and irrational nature of human will to power. Such conflict materialized in the crusades.

Incidentally, the mythical self-justification which the powers so often give themselves in historical conflicts, is well-illustrated by the religious imagery in terms of which the West conceived the motives for its crusading spirit. Actually, the East seems to have had the major ethical principles on its side. It was defending territories that already belonged to it. The West, despite its religious declarations, was assuming the role of the foreign invader and would-be conqueror.

In any event, human environment determined for Gothic Europe the nature, direction, and extent of its major external conflict. And as in most human conflicts, the results of this one upon the West were both positive and negative. They were positive in stimulating native energies and industries, in temporary psychic exhilaration and release, in extending the sphere of Western commerce, and in furthering an infusion of the West by new ideas borrowed from the culture of the enemy. They were negative in the dissipation of immense amounts of human energy and economic wealth, in suffering and loss of life, and in contributing to a subsequent disillusionment that was one of the first rifts in the confident world view attained by European society on the basis of its Gothic flowering.

III

From the interaction between the life force of a particular community and the responsiveness or resistance of a particular geographical-human environment arises the third phase of our dynamic process: a particular set of "historical circumstances." As already suggested, this third concept is so broad that, for most practical purposes, it can be accepted as embracing the other two — life force being assumed and ordinarily needing little special study, environment being considered as part of the background of the given historical conditions. We can confine our observations of the historical concept to a reminder, important for our general theory, that while all kinds of circumstances play their part in the governing historical complex, traditional history has tended to overemphasize certain ones like the military and political, and to underemphasize others like the technological and social. At least until this lack of balance is corrected, relatively less attention needs to be given to the one type of circumstance and relatively more to the other.

To men undergoing its immediate effects, a war or a revolution may seem to be the most convulsive upheaval of history. Culturally considered, it appears as a surface ripple rather than an activating dynamic surge; as an accompaniment and symptom of a historical state rather than a motivating force. The French Revolution dislocated European politics and shook the entire surface of European life, but had only superficial and ephemeral effects upon European culture. It could inspire the patriotic ardor of the "Marseillaise," but it could modify neither the literary nor the musical traditions drawn upon by Rouget de Lisle in composing that anthem. It left its mark upon French art, if anywhere, only in the stoic subject matter and stylistic mannerism of Davidian neoclassicism. Some such "ism" would doubtless have had its little hour in any case, for the age of isms in European culture had begun as early as the seventeenth century. Furthermore, the dominance of classicism in post-revolutionary France was short-lived. The nineteenth century returned to what the seventeenth and eighteenth centuries had inaugurated: an increasing divergence and mutual opposition between a pack of isms — classicism, romanticism, realism, eclecticism.

If, on the other hand, we turn from a political revolution to a technological one such as the Industrial Revolution, the relationship to cultural dynamics is reversed. Surface disruptions are minor and for a century or more may pass almost unnoticed. Profound changes are nevertheless taking place in the metabolism of society: changes which will effect the means by which humanity sustains itself and the relative meagreness or abundance of its sustenance; changes which, in due course, are destined to modify its own organic nature and its entire adjustment to the universe.

The revolutionary changes undergone by European culture during the first half of the twentieth century can be more fully understood in terms of techno-economic-scientific developments and resulting social dislocations than in those of political systems or even of such momentous military events as the world wars. This does not imply that the world wars and all the other circumstances of the age have not had their measure of influence. We are not *excluding* political and military developments from our conception of historical circumstances. We are merely asserting that to us they appear, not as the sole or even the main propellants of cultural expression, but rather as contributory factors dependent in their turn upon the force drawn from deeper and more pervasive techno-social roots.

Although there are probably no simple master keys to a given context of historical circumstances, the nearest thing to such keys would seem to lie in the nature of underlying economic foundation, the relative degree of technological advancement attained in realizing the potentials of that foundation, and the relative extent to which the resulting benefits circulate freely for the enrichment of community life.

Upon the first of these considerations — that of the sustaining economic foundation — depends the first and probably most basic subdivision of all history: the three-fold subdivision of cultures according to their respective dependence upon hunting, upon agriculture, or upon industry. If, in approaching a given culture, one first determines which of these three economic platforms supports it and how far the environment favors support on that platform, one can, broadly speaking, preconceive the relative amplitude of cultural development potential to the given society. A hunting base can support only limited tribal cultures. An agricultural base introduces vastly enriched cultural potentials, permitting the expansion of societies to national and international scale and the corresponding elaboration of their cultural activity. An industrial base presumably makes possible another great surge forward in cultural expansion, though this type of economic foundation is so recent a development that its cultural possibilities are still in large part visionary conjectures.

Having ascertained the economic base and corresponding potentials of a culture, the investigator may then consider the degree of technological advancement reached by the given community in exploiting these potentials. If the base is agricultural, for instance, he may ask himself, "Is the community's agricultural technology at a primitive, an archaic, or at some later stage of devolopment?" The answer to this question will indicate how far the potentials of the given platform are actually being realized in life benefits and cultural sustenance. We have seen, for example, the enormous difference in well-being which distinguished Gothic from Neolithic communities as a result of a more mature stage of agricultural development.

But there is still a third question to be considered in investigating the master circumstances behind a culture, and that is the manner and ratio in which the available goods of life, when produced, are distributed. It seems safe to say that in all societies post-dating a reasonable degree of agricultural maturity in a reasonably fertile environment, the economic potentials have been available for a satisfying measure of community well-being. Yet squalor and misery have been the recurrent lot of considerable portions of most, if not all, such societies because their economic production has been controlled in the interest of certain groups or individuals rather than diffused throughout the body social as a whole.

The narrower the range of such limited control, the more acute, in any society, becomes the contrast between riches and destitution. The fabulous wealth of many Indian potentates and the abject poverty of large sections of the populations ruled by them — to take an example reassuringly remote from our own social problems — is a case in point. The psychic state or states to which the historical circumstances give rise will be conditioned by the social results of the distribution ratio as well as by the actual amount of life-sustaining goods produced or producible.

With all this economic and social information in hand concerning any given society, the investigator should be able roughly to gauge the nature of the accompanying forms of cultural expression even if he had never seen examples of them. Thus in periods or areas of continued insecurity, whether due to intractable environments, undeveloped technology, transitions from one economic platform to another, or gross maladjustment in social distribution, one may expect to find a trend toward abstract rather than realistic art, monster fantasy or other negative imagery, the absence of a high religion, and other characteristics we have considered in connection with Neolithic cultures and to a lesser extent with modern ones.

In archaic periods of vigorous but still immature technological and social growth, the expectancy is for the rise of heroes to combat the monsters, conventionalized representation, experimental gropings in architecture — forms of cultural expression, in other words, which are parallel to those of the European Dark Ages. Periods long established on their given platform, advanced in the technology requisite for exploiting it, and socially organic in distributing its benefits, may be expected to provide cultural analogies to Gothic Europe: retreat of the monsters, advancing realism, great projects in temple building or similar community undertakings, and so forth.

These three types of historical and cultural situation, which may be roughly classed as primitive, archaic, and early mature, are by no means the only possible ones, but they are the only ones which have received careful attention in this book. Other possible phases of historical development, which will call for consideration in future studies, will be mentioned at the end of this chapter. For the present, and in special relation to cultural dynamics, the point of importance to us is that *whatever* the type of historical complex, acquaintance with its governing economic and social circumstances should provide important keys to the understanding of its culture and even permit a forecast on the general nature of that culture.

Confirmation of this point of view sometimes comes to hand from unexpected sources. In a book on recent conditions in China, for instance, the author came upon a description of life in the barren Taiyueh Mountains of the Shansi province. He had had no previous knowledge of conditions in that part of the world and had framed the psycho-historical theory entirely without reference to them. Yet here was a clear example of the relations assumed in the theory between a given set of economic and social circumstances and given forms of cultural expression.

"The land in this region is rocky, bare of forest and grudging in its fertility so that the hard-pressed farmers have been forced to build terraces and cultivate the hill slopes nearly to the top of every peak. For many centuries the peasants have been struggling not only against the parsimonious nature of these mountains, but against brutal exactions and dark superstitions . . . These people . . . believed in no Supreme God, but rather knew many gods, including the God of Fate who made them poor, and ghosts, devils and evil spirits whom they believed lurked in the rocks, trees and the bodies of the animals which roamed their hills." [1]

So extreme was the struggle for existence in this area that many of the peasants were prevented by destitution from ever marrying; others were forced to practice infanticide upon girl babies. Such economic conditions and the religious conceptions described above make a logical psycho-technic equation.

What level do the visual arts reach under these conditions? This question is not discussed as such, but some indications of the answer to it are given in connection with Stone Wall Village, a typical Shansi hamlet of 500 inhabitants. Here many of the people live "in caves hollowed out of the mountain at the base of which the village is situated." Some of their possessions are described in the following traditional verse:

> "Harvest every year; but yearly — nothing.
> Borrow money yearly; yearly still in debt.
> Broken huts, small basins, cracked pots;
> Half an acre of land; five graves." [2]

Evidently the people of Stone Wall Village know nothing of the splendor that we are likely to associate with the concept of Oriental art.

The interplay of social with economic factors is well-illustrated in this cultural situation by the fact that the negative circumstances endured by the community are only in part due to the difficult geographical factors. They are, or were, partially a result of the exactions of a domineering overlord who kept for himself the best land, taxed the people for the worst, and in general treated the population as his cattle. This social aspect of the situation has recently been changed and the people of the Shansi province face the future with two basic modifications of their economic-historical circumstances. New technological methods are increasing the productivity of their environment; new social regulations are making possible a wider distribution of the products.

According to our theory, these new circumstances should positivise the mentality of the community and correspondingly modify its cultural manifestations. It would be interesting to know, some decades hence, whether changes in this direction are actually discernible. According to Beldon's account, the recent economic and social changes and the educational activities that accompanied them were followed almost immediately by changes of religious outlook. "The people began to cast aside their superstitions, no longer believed in ghosts, fox goddesses or fate unalterable." [3]

Obviously, to conclude our general summary of historical conditioning, a community like Stone Wall Village would possess neither the technical skill, the economic resources, nor the overmastering positive psychic impulse to erect a great religious edifice of the type found in the Gothic cathedrals or the larger Buddhist temples. Conversely, when we find such edifices, as in the major temple-building epochs and communities, let us say, of China and India, we may assume an agricultural platform — since a hunting platform would not have sufficed for this degree of cultural amplitude — a favorable environment, a relatively mature stage of agricultural technology, and a relatively integrated social structure. And so, in principle, with any other techno-economic complex as a conditioning factor in a given psycho-historical situation.

IV

Neither a barren field nor a fertile one, neither a just nor an unjust social system, can convert itself directly into a work of art. It can only affect the spirits of the men who create works of art. Historical circumstances, in other words, do not in themselves produce accompanying forms of cultural expression. Between the circumstances and their expression lies a transformer that converts the cultural potentials of the one into the cultural actualities of the other. That transformer is the human psyche with all its flexible interplay of perception and thought, impulse, intuition, and emotion.

Other species of life may have one faculty or another more highly developed than man; some of man's own inventions surpass his native capacities in one respect or another. But no being or instrument known to us — except the one assumed in the conception of an omnipotent and omniscient God — equals human sensitivity in the range, variety, and subtlety of the existential data to which it can respond and which it can bring to the net balance of a total experienced correlation. Factors as disparate as the storm that brings rain, the manual skill that shapes an arrowhead, the mother's impulse to protect her child, and a thousand other intricacies of existence, major and minor, conscious and unconscious — factors as multiple and disparate as these can all exert their influence upon the human psyche, interact with each other like the terms of a complex mathematical equation, and emerge in one composite result as a quality of human experience. Such is the marvelous delicacy and precision of the psychic transformer through which circumstances affect some higher cultural manifestations.

In the attempt to fathom the depths of this psychic instrumentality, we reach the most elusive and perhaps the most distinctive aspect of our whole frame of reference. It is the subtleties and complexities of tensional dynamics that, on the one hand, make possible the transformation of historical experiences into forms of cultural imagery and, on the other hand, make *im*possible the comprehension of the process through any simple formula. Without assuming that we have penetrated all the secrets of the subject — and with reference to psychoanalysis for continued study of it — our presentation calls attention to five aspects of tensional dynamics as minimum considerations for psycho-historical analysis.

First, there is the possible range of emotional character as between positive, negative, and neutral tensions and their expressions (here Diagram 3 becomes relevant to the present summary). Second, there is the possible variation of tension imagery from the literal to the fantastic. Third, there is the interplay between tension imagery and rational discrimination which, in different combinations, leads to the distinction between the true myth and what we called the "near-myth." All three of these subjects were discussed at some length in our earlier chapters [4] and will be dismissed from the present review with no more than the above mention.

The two remaining aspects of tensional dynamics call for more careful attention than we have yet given them. They involve the possible variation in scope from minor individually centered tension to the master tensions of a whole epoch; and the differing modes of tensional expression that we may call direct or rational as contrasted with indirect or symbolical.

The range and depth of psychic life involved in any given tensional charge, the degree to which it emanates from or combines individual and social psychology, can vary greatly. The personal emotion of love may be cited as one of the most private and, from the cultural point of view, most restricted forms of tensional energy. Its typical cultural expression is the lyric verse which, however beautiful, is one of the more limited forms of cultural imagery. If the personal emotion assumes a larger meaning, as did Dante's love for Beatrice, it does so by merging with some form of suprapersonal imagery like the religious and historical cosmology of the *Divine Comedy*. In entering this broader context, the personal background is largely transformed into cultural symbolism.

The portrait, Fig. 85, like the lyric poem, is a form of art that might arise exclusively from personal impulse. In point of fact, however, it usually involves wider and more enduring tensional fields, one of which is power and pride of family. This played a large part in motivating traditions of ancestor portraiture in England, China, and elsewhere. Without the European emphasis on the aristocratic family, much of the art of painters like Clouet, Holbein, and Gains-borough would perforce have had to deal with other subjects than it did. One of its major sources of patronage would have been lacking. The effects of family impulse can also be seen in much of the heraldic pomp of medieval Europe, and in the equally heraldic totem poles that were the culminating monuments of the North Pacific Indians.

Civic impulse provides another and still more inclusive subdivision of the tensional field. It helped to motivate the exuberance of Gothic town halls like those of Brussels and Rouen, Fig. 86, and indeed contributed to the inspiration of many Gothic cathedrals, for the most characteristic of the latter were civic as well as religious undertakings. Civic feeling also inspired a considerable portion of Western European sculpture and mural painting. One thinks here of our greatest equestrian monuments: Donatello's *Gattamelata* and Verrocchio's *Colleoni* (Fig. 87). One thinks also of Lorenzetti's mural allegories for the *Palazzo Pubblico* in Siena, of the pictorial paeans to Venetian glory painted by Titian, Tintoretto, and Veronese for the Ducal Palace in Venice (Fig. 88). And in the literary field, some of the most moving passages of some of our greatest literature spring from patriotic impulse. Such impulse underlies most epics, as in the *Iliad* and the *Chanson de Roland*; it permeates the *Divine Comedy* through Dante's attachment to Florence, and inspires Shakespeare to alternate rhapsody and grief as he contemplates the shifting fortunes of state within his.

. . . other Eden, demi-paradise;
This blessed plot, this earth, this realm, this England.

Transcending even civic and patriotic limitations are the tensional complexes inherent in a given way and stage of social life; complexes common to all of that portion of humanity which, at any given time or successively at different times, depends for its survival and well-being upon similar resources and similar technologies for exploiting them and which therefore, whatever its mutual bickerings, shares a common destiny. These most pervasive and profound of tensional charges — the nearest thing we have to a "universal" basis of cultural motivation — may be least consciously experienced by the average individual most of the time, but they are the most powerful of all cultural energizers. From their deep-stirring, slow-working, irresistible pressure emerge the world's great mythologies and religions, its philosophies, its styles of art rising and falling with the slow motion of cyclic wave lengths extending over thousands of years.

The suggested subdivision of the tensional field into more or less inclusive dynamisms, personal or collective, is not a firm or complete one, but rather a fluid and partial differentiation akin to that which enables us to remark ripples, waves, and tides within the homogeneous sea. There is always the engulfing totality of some considerable section of mankind at some general phases of its psycho-historical development, however distinctive at any moment its component manifestations may appear. The personal impulse of love cannot be expressed in lyric poetry without the prior development of a language through which to express it, and the development of language is a social achievement. Furthermore, even with a language, the individual will have little impulse toward lyric expression if cultural circumstances embitter his emotional life with squalidness and misery. The lyric poets have not come from primitive societies in which the fruits of love had to be destroyed by infanticide. Neither have they come from industrial slums in which a miserable childhood is succeeded by a miserable effort to support another generation of miserable children.

Nor are the cultural factors conditioning individual impulse solely economic. The individual is not likely to seek lyric expression if he lives under circumstances that impose no sexual restraints, hence develop no tensions of delayed fulfillment or frustrated desire. In Western Europe love became a characteristic literary concern during the Gothic period and primarily among the courtly classes, as in the lyrics of the troubadours and the epics of chivalry. We can hardly doubt that the emergence of this theme under these circumstances was related both to the material well-being of courtly classes during the thirteenth century and to the restraints imposed upon them by the medieval ideal of Christian chastity. Thus even the seemingly personal impulse behind the love lyric is conditioned by an embracing cultural fabric and is the expression of collective as well as personal tensions. In short the most individualistic expressions of the ages of greatest individualism are in their own way social phenomena.

Considered in this light, all psychic tensions involve collective correlatives, all are mutually interrelated, and all are ultimately linked with the economic-technological-social foundation that sustains society as a whole. The relationship of the more limited to the more inclusive tensional dynamisms might best be stated by returning to an image already used and comparing tensional experience to a wave of the sea. Those who have watched the rhythm of the passing waves in mid-ocean will recall that what we ordinarily regard as a wave is a compound of a main form and at least two types of subform. First, there is the main lift of the wave as a whole: the force and form which gives it total identity. Second, this main wave is often subdivided into two or more subwaves which vary, while at the same time following, the major form. Finally the surface of wave and subwaves alike is flicked — at least under certain weather conditions — with a thousand wavelets or ripples. Thus the single great wave, as it rolls past, is at once a unity and an intricate interplay of shifting subdivisions of different amplitudes.

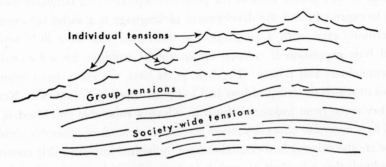

Diagram 9. Wave image of tensional dynamics suggesting relationship between individual, group, and society-wide tensions.

Analogous to the wave in these respects, as suggested in Diagram 9, are the tensional dynamics of a human society. Corresponding to the basic form force of the wave as a whole, underlying and impelling the whole dynamic phenomenon, are the tensions connected with the survival and well-being of society as a whole; tensions in the generation of which economic, technological, and sociological activities play a large and probably a determining part. To the subwaves correspond the various subdivisions of society, communities within the total human community, such as families and classes, municipalities and nations. Each of these social subdivisions may develop tensional, and corresponding cultural variations of the total tension-culture pattern. Last and least, but none the less a part of the dynamic whole, the wavelets correspond to the myriad individuals within society. Each has his own personal tensions but these at best are only partly emergent from the tensions of one or more social subdivisions, which in turn are only partly emergent from the master tensions of the engulfing collective totality.

A wave or even a wavelet may, at a given moment, form the crest of a wave. Equally, a subcommunity or even an individual may become the tensional focus of a society and for the time being serve as the immediate transformer of its tensions into its culture. But it would be an illusion — an illusion all too often entertained — to assume that the cresting wavelet is powering the wave or that the conducting class or individual is powering the culture. Subtensions and their accompanying subcultures are all fluid phases of the master tensions and the master culture, which may lift them temporarily to positions of eminence but which will also eventually draw them back into the depths.

The master tensions underlying culture are inevitably complex; so complex that any attempt to define them must be subject to modification in the light of future findings. According to the writer's present grasp of them, they seem to be the psychic index of some relative state of collective security and well-being, measured on a scale between annihilation at one extreme and complete mastery of the known world at the other. We have observed examples of such major cultural determinants in the persistent terrors of many Neolithic communities, the stress and redress that divided Dark Age experience, and the exaltation so characteristic of Gothic mentality.

It will be observed that what we are here regarding as the master tensions of a psycho-historical situation are closely related to what we earlier judged to be the major keys to historical circumstances. That is to say the master tensions will inevitably vary with the relationship between the economic potential and the distribution ratio current in a given society. The economic potential, by determining the relative availability of food and other necessities for social survival and well-being, sets the first brood limits within which the collective experience of security must develop and beyond which it cannot pass.

The distribution ratio, by affecting the relative circulation or congestion of life sustenance within the social body becomes in its turn an important factor in the generation of psychic tensions. A low potential with a high distribution ratio may result in a stronger and more cohesive sense of community well-being than a high potential with poor distribution. Under the latter circumstances, however high the potential, negative tensions inevitably accumulate. They accumulate in the depressed classes through malnutrition and other effects of actual deprivation, and more intangibly through the sense of social inequality and injustice. Less strongly and less consciously they may also accumulate in the possessing classes through conflict with their own sense of social justice and through fear of social resistance or revolt. Thus, however high the potential, the final positive sense of community well-being can be high only if the distribution ration is an adequately general one. And it is the final sum of experienced well-being, as consciously and unconsciously apprehended by the preponderant mass of a given society, that becomes the master tension of that society and its most powerful cultural dynamic.

If there is any single word for a community's sense of this experienced relationship between potential and realization it is probably the word "faith." Without an economic potential no faith can develop because there is no material support for it. Without a realization satisfying both to the actual needs and to the sense of justice of at least a large majority of the population involved, no vital faith can endure because, for different reasons, there is again no actual fulfilling experience to support it. This statement would appear to be true of religious faith in the narrower sense, as well as the more diffuse social faith of the individual or class in the fulfilling power of the social structure of which he or it is a part. And the former type of faith, it would seem, is closely related to and partly dependent upon the latter. The one may be conceived as a symbolical expression of the experiences, observations, and intuitions underlying the other.

Thus the religious exaltation of the Gothic Middle Ages synchronized with, and seemingly depended in no small part upon, a widely shared faith in the sustaining virtue of a way of life based upon a high potential combined with a relatively wide diffusion. The Renaissance, Baroque, and subsequent periods saw no diminution of European economic potential, but they witnessed a progressive loss of faith, both religious and social. The most convulsive religious demonstration of this loss was the revolution and counter-revolution involved in the Reformation. This great religious upheaval, which broke the homogeneity of Western Chirstianity, connected on a deeper level with growing economic and social inequalities in which institutionalized religion, by and large, had greedily participated on the side of the few against the many. Nothing contributed more to the dissatisfaction of the West with its religious institutions than the economic rapacity of monasteries degenerate from surfeit of material wealth, supposed ministers of the gospel selling spiritual salvation for material gain, popes playing in world politics to support and extend a life of worldly luxury and power. In the end, it would seem, all faith rests upon good faith, upon trust in the social integrity of one's compatriots, and that trust can be solid and enduring only if underwritten by a sharing of life benefits adequate to the health and fulfillment, and therefore satisfying to the conscience, of society as a whole.

All the tensions at work within a collective mentality — minor and master, more personally or more communally centered — will have their influence upon the culture within which and upon which they operate, but the master tensions — the state and stage of collective faith in the adequacy of a given way of life to fulfill the needs and aspirations of man as a social being — underlie, color, and eventually absorb all the others. These master tensions, which are usually so complex that they can only be gropingly and intuitively sensed, so inexorable and impartial that, when negative, they are likely to be repressed from consciousness, become the basic determinant of the higher forms of cultural expression. So deeply is the culture of an epoch permeated by their influence that almost thence its

> . . . nature is subdued
> To what it works in, like the dyer's hand,

and shows some tinge of the prevailing tensional hue even in the most marginal and vagrant of its manifestations.

V

In the preceding sections of the present summary, we have noted that human communities react with their environments under certain technological and social conditions to produce particular sets of historical circumstances, which in turn distill a quality of experience fraught with tensional energy. In the transmission of this energy to the creative agencies of cultural expression, we reach the final phase of the psycho-historical process. Here we can observe the effects upon art and other cultural activities of the preconditions previously considered.

We have already anticipated this concluding phase of the process by a number of references to the arts in the course of the foregoing discussion. As these examples have implied, cultural outcomes will vary in different respects with the nature of the tensions inspiring them. According to the relative amplitude of the tensions as between individual, subgroup, or community-wide focus, there will be corresponding amplitudes of product ranging from the more intimate and limited lyric or portrait through the family or civic monument to the comprehensive epic or cathedral and the even more comprehensive styles of expression that underlie both major and minor manifestations.

According as the tensions are dominantly positive or negative, the expressions of them will tend toward positive or negative imagery in subject matter and will undergo related modifications in style. The same positive or negative motivation — and here we once more anticipate cyclic studies — will tend to promote what may be called "convergent" or "divergent" types of culture.

When the master tensions of an epoch are increasingly positive, society appears to welcome their expression with increasing unanimity and to crystallize it in increasingly homogeneous and integrated forms. We have observed an example of such "convergence" in Gothic culture. All the different arts and crafts of the Gothic epoch are permeated by a common style impulse which precludes the development of conflicting artistic "isms" and unites the various mediums in a pervading atmosphere of spiritual and esthetic harmony.

Coupled with this stylistic unity is the actual reënforcement of art by art to achieve cumulative power in a master expression of the master tensions. Decorative art, painting, sculpture, architecture, music, drama were not, in their highest thirteenth-century forms, independent fields of endeavor producing detached results. They were all outlets for the master passion of the age and were all brought to the single register of the Gothic-cathedral-in-use, the cathedral in which the Mass, felt as a sublime and beneficent drama — as a *Divina Commedia* — was chanted as living poetry and music in a setting of lofty architecture, saintly imagery, radiant stained glass, resplendent needlework and jewelled metal craft. The Mass, thus celebrated, was not merely music drama of the character which Wagner sought to achieve by integrating two of the arts; it was culture drama spontaneously integrating all the arts.

Contrasting with such "convergent" cultures are the "divergent" ones in which unity of style gives way to an increasing number of conflicting artistic creeds — to a "battle of the styles" — and in which the several arts increasingly detach themselves one from the other to become self-determining and self-absorbed preoccupations. Western European culture in the seventeenth, eighteenth, nineteenth and early twentieth centuries presents this phenomenon of divergence. We observe its effects in the wide variety of cultural "isms," whether artistic as in realism, classicism, romanticism, surrealism and the others, religious as in Catholicism and the scores of Protestantisms, or correspondingly divergent points of view in other fields of activity.

And we observe at the same time the detachment of the arts from each other and from civic and religious concerns. A typical nineteenth-century statue had no coöperative tie with architecture, painting, or decorative art, no tie with the music or drama of its day; in most cases no relevance to current religious or social concerns. It stood by itself on a pedestal which isolated it from its surroundings, usually in a museum which isolated it from life. In many cases it never got beyond the confines of the sculptor's studio, remaining, so far as society was concerned, in complete oblivion. From whatever angle we consider it, it was a detached cultural fragment — so to speak, an unwanted and ne-glected cultural child — rather than an integral part of an embracing cultural totality.

In the general terms of our theory this difference between convergent and divergent cultures would inevitably imply some corresponding difference in the character of the tensions animating the cultures. As already suggested, the convergent type appears to be an expression of dominantly positive tensions and the divergent type of increasingly negative ones, with corresponding differ-ences back through respective sets of circumstances to basic fulfillments or frustrations of collective human impulse. The questions involved here are complex and deserving of more thorough analysis than can be afforded them in the present context. They have been given passing reference only because convergent and divergent cultures have their place among the differences of cultural outcome that may follow from different tensional motivations.

Thus far, we have noted that cultural products will vary according to the relatively individual or collective focus of the tensions inspiring them, and according to the relatively positive or negative character of those tensions. They will also vary according to the complexity of the tensions. Certain underlying needs can be satisfied, and the tensions resulting from them relieved, by what may be called direct cultural action. In such cases the cultural outcome will be utilitarian or factual and will be intelligible to the observer on rational grounds. In other cases, due presumably to more intricate tensional demands, direct utilitarian or factual expression is apparently impossible. The tensions then seek indirect, imaginative, or *symbolical* expression. The difference between the direct and the indirect cultural outcome, and especially the character and im-portance of the symbolical cultural outcome, is the last main topic to which we must give attention in this summary of the psycho-historical theory.

Direct cultural action is particularly efficacious in the more utilitarian arts like architecture, at least in their more utilitarian aspects like the provision of shelter. We have noticed how the human need for protection from the elements, interacting with varied climates under pre-industrial technological conditions, produced the flat roof terraces of Egypt and Mesopotamia, roofs of medium pitch in southern temperate regions like Greece, and roofs of steep pitch in northern temperate regions like medieval France. Creative effort could arrive at such utilitarian solutions to human needs largely through the exercise of intelligence and manual skill, and would therefore not be forced to seek ex-pression through more intricate and devious byways.

There is an equally direct relationship of a different type between the gratitude felt by the Venetian republic to General Colleoni, the decision to erect a monument in his honor, and the conception of that monument in terms of his equestrian image. Here the tension of relief and rejoicing, focused upon the patent fact of an individual's services to the community, could find direct expression in a monument dedicated to, and representing, that individual.

In the economy of mental life, that which can be accomplished as a utility or stated as a fact is likely to be so accomplished or stated. Objective and subjective reality connect in terms of a practical adjustment or a direct image with a minimum of mental transformation. But there can be tensional charges so complex that neither utilitarian nor factual disposal of them is possible. The underlying interplay of circumstance may be so involved that direct control of it, and consequent rational solution of the problems presented by it, is beyond human power. The facts involved in a given situation may be so many and disparate that the mind is incapable of grasping them as an intelligible unity. The facts, as such, may be partly or wholly unknown, though their effects are known in human experience. Or the facts, though known or knowable, may be distasteful to particular groups of men or to humanity in general and so may be subjected to conscious or unconscious repression or distortion.

For such reasons the more intricate and culturally more significant tensional dynamisms can rarely find complete expression through direct channels. Even the lover, animated by culturally minor personal tensions, cannot satisfyingly dispense them into practical or factual outcomes. Immediate utilitarian release through the sexual consummation of his impulse may be denied to him or, if obtainable, will be accompanied, in the earlier stages of its attainment, by an afflux of libido so powerful that only a portion of it can be practically utilized.

The possibility that the lover could reduce his tensions by factual means is so obviously remote that it will not even occur to him. If he knew and stated all the facts, describing among other things the complex glandular activities indispensable to his emotional condition, his statement would loose all relevancy to his emotional experience and probably all possibility of literary appeal. Confronted by these barriers to direct expression, his impulse seeks release through indirect imaginative channels. He exclaims,

> Shall I compare thee to a summer's day?
> Thou art more lovely and more temperate.

By the analogy of half-perceived associations, and by the easy flow of rhythmic measure, he expresses and conveys the psychic essence of his experience. The resulting sonnet or other verse is neither a practical fulfillment of the poet's needs, biologically speaking, nor a factual description of them. It is a symbol irrationally and intuitively reflecting his emotional state.

When the motivating psychic dynamism is as complex as the master tensions of an epoch, the difficulties in the way of its direct expression are multiplied many times over. The practical problems underlying the tensions are so intricate and many-sided that thus far humanity has at best achieved only a partial understanding and control of them. The facts involved are all the facts of all categories apprehended by all the minds of an epoch. Even if it were possible — which it is not — to hold them simultaneously in human consciousness, the result would be an image of the unresolved complexity of life, not the resolved essence of life in art. In short the master tensions of an age are probably the supreme example in all human experience of a psychic dynamism for which direct expression, in any complete sense, is impossible and for which symbolical expression is therefore inevitable.

Thus the powerful energies inherent in the master tensions, channeled as it were between dykes of utilitarian and factual resistance — or in positive cases, partially released by fortunate circumstances from utilitarian demands and factual concerns — arrive at the point of contact with the tension imagery process. Here they enter and animate a mental agency which, as we have seen in our study of myth, commands the full genius of the creative imagination in matching states of psychic tension with symbolically equivalent mental imagery. Like the vast calculating machines that perform almost inconceivable mathematical operations for atomic physicists, but in even subtler and more inconceivable ways, the tension-imagery powers of the mind transpose the unfathomable mental and emotional totalities of collective life into symbolical terms. From this discharge of master tensions into tension imagery emerges the grand symbolism of humanity's loftiest cultural achievements: the exalted visions and denunciations of the religious prophets, the epics and dramas of the poets, the tone worlds of the musicians, the thought worlds of the philosophers, the style worlds of the artists and architects. Thus master circumstances lead to master tensions and these in turn to the master imagery that constitutes the highest manifestation of a culture and the most unique expression of its character and genius.

The higher a tree rises above the ground, the deeper must its sustaining roots penetrate below the ground. Similarly these highest manifestations of culture are such because the forces preconditioning them emerge from, and retain a vital contact with, the most profound forces of human life. They penetrate back through consciousness into the unconscious, and within the unconscious extend their rootlets, their nerve endings, through the instinctual processes and all the other obscure activities in which life has its floating base. Spanning the arc from the *élan vital* at one extreme to the cultural image at the other, arriving at the latter through intricate transformations that involve all the circumstances of collective existence and all the power of psychic life, the process of higher cultural formation may indeed be regarded as the dream life of society. What an individual's most significant and revealing dreams are to him personally, the symbolism of a culture is collectively to the society that produces it.

The process of dream formation, collectively as well as individually, is remarkable in many ways, but in no ways more so than in its genius for synthesis and condensation. It distills the essence from situations which have all the complexity of collective existence in this complex universe. It condenses that essence into forms which, if they are visual, can in a certain sense be perceived at a glance, and which in all artistic mediums are extraordinarily summary as compared either with objective reality or with an intellectual analysis of it. To step inside the portals of Chartres Cathedral is to apprehend, as an immediate experience, the essence of what Aquinas attempted to demonstrate in a thousand pages — the essence of what hundreds of thousands of men felt about the way they lived in the world they lived in.

And it is, no doubt, because the individual object of art and the connecting cultural system are so deeply implicated in the whole adventure and challenge of existence that they exert such a persistent spell over humanity. If they were esthetic objects alone they would be significant, but in a less comprehensive way. If they were historical records alone, the same would be true of them. That they are measures and modes of existence itself, synthesizing esthetic, historical, and other phases of experience, gives them their haunting inescapableness and their power to be all things to all men and to all ages of men.

Physical science affords us understanding and mastery of one phase of existence but omits others. Life sciences provide the reverse illumination and involve the reverse obscurity. Only in philosophy, religion, and the arts do we approach a unified grasp of the totality of existence. And since the totality of existence cannot be grasped by the intellect alone, the intellect being an instrument for the apprehension of only one phase of existence, even philosophy may here be suspected of handicap. It would seem to be religion and the arts, which transcend intellectual formulations, taking the measure of subjective as well as objective factors, that come nearest to a full statement of being as it exists in and at the creative moment. More recent science has shown the inaccuracy of certain aspects of the thought of Thomas Aquinas. It can show nothing inaccurate or inadequate in the conception of a Gothic cathedral because the cathedral was not an effort to understand the conditions of existence but an organic product *of* the conditions of existence.

Thus, however fanciful or lacking in scientific objectivity the cultural symbols of a past epoch may appear to us, however arbitrary and "meaningless" the emerging symbols of our own epoch may at first seem, such symbols are actually the superstatements of reality. He who would understand life, though he may well seek facts about it, must above all be perceptive of the implications of its symbols. What can be told is important, but even more important, because more complete, is what cannot be told. What cannot be told can only be revealed, and the symbol is its revelation. "Legend," said one of the sages of India, "is the chalice of truth."

Before we leave the subject of cultural symbolism, two secondary points should be added to our conception of it. These are the immediacy of the true symbol, and the combination in most cultural products of effects resulting from both the direct and symbolical modes of expression.

It should be evident from the examples cited that the symbolism of the cultural image is, in its creative inception, spontaneous, dynamic, and immediately experienced. When we go to a lexicon to find out which of the evangelists is "symbolized" by the winged bull, we are not dealing with symbolism in the fundamental psychic sense of the term. We are dealing with a convention which had a psychic origin but which has lost all relevancy to contemporary psychology and become a cultural fossil. No one ever needs to look up the meaning of a vital symbol to which he is culturally related; that is to say, an imaginative expression of a living psychic state in which he shares. The "meaning," the psychic reality, existed before the form in which it found symbolical expression, necessitating and illuminating that expression. Men singing of love or of victory could not be conceived as looking up what they are singing about.

The psychological basis of a symbol may not be rationally clear to its creator, but its expressive fitness and inevitability, its cultural significance, will be self-evident to him and to any community out of which he speaks. Under certain historical circumstances, the community's grasp of the symbol may show itself in the negative form of resistance rather than the positive one of acceptance, as will be more fully suggested in later chapters, but even this resistance appears to be an unconscious form of comprehension.

The second point to be noted is that most cultural manifestations are an outcome, not of direct or indirect expression alone, but of some combination of the two. As a result they possess what may be considered a compound character, merging certain utilitarian or factual aspects with others of a symbolical nature. Thus the cathedral involves direct utility in its provision for shelter, ingress and exist, and other necessities of material functionalism; it also involves symbolical expressiveness in the soaring height of its spires, the radiance of its stained glass, and other effects inspired by the community's impulse to embody religious feeling.

Relatively obvious in the arts involving physical utility, this compound character is not so readily discerned in the representational arts of painting and sculpture or in the more immaterial phases of culture like literature and religion. Nevertheless, in varying measures and degrees, it is to be assumed in these cases as well. The monument to Colleoni, Fig. 87 as already noted, involves a direct recognition of historical facts in its use of an equestrian portrait. As a civic monument it also subserved social utilities, helping to unify and crystallize collective consciousness around the functions of state. These outcomes of direct expression did not prevent it from simultaneously giving symbolical expression to more involved tensional forces through its realistic style and in other ways.

Correspondingly, a religious system will normally combine both direct and indirect elements. Efforts to promote psychic and social utility will produce magical rites, ethical codes, charitable activities, exercises to relieve psychic tension or to strengthen the spiritual aspects of man's psychic endowment. Factual material of a historical nature will also play its part in the tradition. Interwoven with these direct aspects of the system, and usually regarded as their source and sanction, will be the symbolical conception of a supernatural world with its divine powers, personages, and events.

In short the direct and the symbolical modes of cultural expression are to be regarded, not as operating independently of each other, but as interplaying with each other in the formation of the cultural product. Proportions may vary from the mainly functional or factual at one extreme to the mainly symbolical at the other, but it is doubtful whether any important cultural manifestation emanates entirely from one of these types of motivation alone.

VI

We have now completed our summary of the psycho-historical theory developed in the preceding chapters, but this theory alone — or at any rate the present statement of it — does not complete the entire framework of psycho-historical thought. As a link between our present findings and studies that remain for the future, it will be useful to make a concluding distinction between two factors in cultural life which we have thus far accepted conjointly, and which in fact operate conjointly, but which nevertheless involve their separate problems and require individual as well as joint consideration. These factors may be described as the motivating forces or dynamics of culture, and the course or orbit of culture history. Similarly related factors, it would seem, appear in the analysis of every sphere of existence. Thus, the physicist distinguishes between force and motion and this basic distinction is applied by specialists to various aspects of the physical universe: by the astronomer to the momentum and the orbits of the heavenly bodies; by the student of military science to the propellant energy and the trajectory involved in the use of projectiles. Biologists make a corresponding differentiation between life force and the cycle of birth, growth, and decline followed both by individual organisms and by species.

Cultural phenomena have their equivalent dynamic drive and cyclic progression — a force which animates them and a course which they follow. In our studies thus far, the correlation we have found between forms of cultural expression, collective psychic states, and attendant historical circumstances lies in the sphere of cultural dynamics. The evolutionary development of Western European culture — which we followed in some detail from Neolithic to Gothic times, and more briefly and incidentally from Paleolithic times to the twentieth century — involves cultural orbits.

The complete pattern of culture history within any given society will involve the concept of an orbit as well as that of a dynamic. Such a pattern might be graphed as a spiral sequence of dynamic circuits following each other in a progressive direction (Diagram 10). Each of the successive rounds of the spiral comprises one of those dynamic circuits which we have already observed at closer range in Diagram 8; one of those circuits, that is, which begins in life force, extends through circumstance and tension to cultural imagery and returns again to life force. Successive circuits of this kind connect with each other, as the spiral implies, and the spiral as a whole follows a consistent historical progression through time; a progression suggested by the axial arrow of the diagram.

If one takes a progressive series of cultural objects and concerns oneself with the stylistic or other developments revealed by it, the axial movement appears to be continuous from one object to the other. But if one is concerned with the forces that produced the objects, and their interplay with the life of which they were an expression, then the spiral, ever revolving between life and its expressions, is the truer line of development.

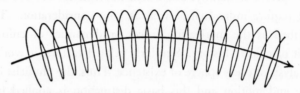

Diagram 10. Psycho-historical concept of the relations between dynamic and orbit in culture history.

Actually, a dynamic cannot operate without establishing some path or orbit, and an orbit cannot exist except in relation to some motivating dynamic, nor can the one be studied in complete independence of the other. We have found it necessary to introduce some consideration of both into the preceding chapters. Nevertheless, since our minds cannot concentrate full attention upon both these factors at the same time, a thorough study of culture requires at least a temporary emphasis, now upon the one, now upon the other. The necessity for such a selective emphasis has molded the form taken by the present studies and resulted in their division into two main parts which it is proposed to issue as separate volumes.

In the present volume our main effort has been to understand the dynamic which motivates artistic production in particular and cultural expression in general. Considerations of orbit have been introduced only incidentally and insofar as they have been necessary for a study of the underlying dynamic. Hence no complete analysis of the question of cultural orbits has been attempted, and none of the orbits from which we have used segments has been followed throughout its entire course or considered in all its significance and implications.

Fortune favoring, a sequel will be issued later under the title *Cycle and Psyche*. It will reverse the present emphasis, taking the psycho-historical dynamic for granted and giving it only incidental consideration. Chief attention will be concentrated on questions concerning cultural orbits. In dealing with these questions, it will be necessary to make a comparative study of the art of a number of different civilizations throughout the evolutionary sequence of their life spans. It will be necessary to interpret in some manner the similarities of cultural product that occur in different civilizations — similarities such as we have already noted between the abstraction of late Paleolithic times and that of the twentieth century, and between the archaic Western art of the tenth century A.D. and the archaic Greek art of the sixth century B.C. Are such recurrences of type due to chance or are they the similar results of similar conditioning circumstances? If the latter, is the possible similarity of circumstance limited to component phases of a culture or is there a similarity between the entire life cycle of one civilization and that of another? In other words, does every civilization pass successively through a number of consecutive phases which have many times recurred in the past, which are presumably destined to go on recurring in the future, and which constitute a cultural orbit in terms of which we can chart the position, and explain the nature, of any given form of cultural expression?

The study of cultural orbits is an important one both from the purely intellectual and from the practical point of view. Most of our present critical studies in the humanities deal with their subjects in terms of individual artists, writers, or philosophers, or in terms of component periods such as the Middle Ages or the Renaissance. They take little account of the possibility of an embracing cultural cycle which may play a large part in determining the nature of component periods and of their individual exponents. If such cycles do operate, then the study of periods and individuals without reference to them is somewhat comparable to the study of the planets in times before astronomers knew what orbits they were following. All the phases and component positions of an evolutionary sequence fall into place in a larger whole, once its orbit is discovered.

Practically, the study of cultural orbits is one of the most vital of all subjects because it involves, potentially at least, the future of all existing human groups. In general, human affairs have been conducted as if history had only a past — or at least as if only the past were knowable. The future has been a blank to which no appreciable amount of scientific study has been devoted. Yet if there are indeed cultural orbits, every nation, every civilization, is at some position in such an orbit and is moving toward future positions which, in their general nature, can be known. To proceed without knowledge toward a future which might in any degree be known, is to proceed blindly where one could proceed with foresight; to advance unprepared toward that for which one could prepare. If we today have any chance of avoiding the rocks on which previous civilizations foundered, it would seem to lie in the direction of a clearer vision of what those rocks are and where they are situated.

These issues are not new to the history of thought. They had their exponents in late classical antiquity; they have had others in Western culture from Machiavelli's day to our own. They have assumed major importance to some of our most influential recent writers like Spengler, Sorokin, and Toynbee, presumably because of widespread anxiety concerning the historical destiny in store for us.

We cannot here enter deeply into a subject which has already been discussed in many volumes, and to the psycho-historical analysis of which we propose to devote a separate volume of our own. We must leave this subject for future consideration after two concluding remarks. One is that none of the existing studies of cultural cycles has made systematic use of the history of art, or the history of any of the arts, as a major source of evidence for or against the existence of cyclic orbits. Yet in the changing forms of the arts as they emanate from the various stages of a civilization, we have one of the most tangible records of its historical evolution and one of the most profound and immediate revelations of its psychic and cultural experience. A careful study of the successive forms of art in different cultures, such as we propose to make in *Cycle and Psyche*, should therefore be one of the most reliable means of determining the extent to which cultural cycles exist and the number and characteristics of their component phases.

With regard to the ominous question as to whether our own civilization is in, or is approaching, its period of decline — as Spengler and others have maintained — the present author cannot resist anticipating future studies with a brief comment. From the psycho-historical point of view there does indeed seem to be considerable evidence that we are in the late stages of a Western European cycle that began in Neolithic times, rose to its "golden age" during the High Middle Ages and the Renaissance, and has been sinking to its decline during our most recent centuries. Decline, be it remembered, is not only one of the great realities; it is also one of the great sources of beauty and character — as we see in the radiance of autumn foliage; as we see again in the spiritual depth that Rembrandt found, not as a youth looking at youth, but as an old man looking at old men and women.

If the historical circumstances of our assumed Western decline were similar in essential respects to those of late Classical antiquity, then we might presumably look forward to a similar fate — to interception by younger and more vigorous cultural forces, as happened in the Roman west, or to a long terminal dusk of increasingly rigid convention, as happened in the Byzantine east. Such a parallelism between the Western and the Classical worlds has generally been assumed by the writers who have attempted to gain "universal" prespective on human affairs.

But there is one important — perhaps all-important — difference between present circumstances and those of late Classical times which most recent writers have overlooked. They have overlooked it because, in the main, they have limited their observation to surface history and have at best given only secondary attention to economic factors. They have overlooked it also because they have largely restricted their field to the historic civilizations of the past few thousand years, taking no account of the longer and more varied perspectives obtainable from the hundreds of thousands of years of prehistoric life.

The difference in question is one of economic platform. Late Classical antiquity involved no economic revolution that could project its future upon a new economic base and thus release the psycho-historical dynamism for new cultural developments. It rose and fell upon an agricultural base and when it had run the course potential to that base, its psycho-historical resources were exhausted.

Our own Western culture, on the other hand, *has* recently undergone an economic revolution, the Industrial Revolution; our future seems to depend, not upon the agricultural foundation that maintained it from Neolithic times to the eighteenth century, but upon the industrial one that has been articulating itself during the nineteenth and twentieth centuries. Such a situation has occurred only once in previous human experience and that was in prehistoric, not historic, times. It occurred in the agricultural revolution that followed the decline of hunting culture and that led humanity up the difficult but rewarding incline to a new economic platform — the agrarian one from which all the world's historic civilizations were to arise.

Late Classical times would therefore seem to parallel our present historical position in its negative aspects, but not in its positive potentials. The only complete parallel to our position would seem to be that of Neolithic man, who suffered from the decline of hunting cultures and from the immaturity of his groping agricultural techniques, but who nevertheless had a cluster of emergent cycles ahead of him as well as a declining one behind him. If this is true we can accept the historical insights of Spengler without being overcome by his pessimism, and those of Toynbee without resorting to his religious fire escape from the implications of history. With a mingling of historical nostalgia and historical hope we can exclaim, as do the British when one monarch passes and another takes the throne, "The King is dead! Long live the King! "

For the moment we must return from these anticipations to conclude our present survey of the psycho-historical theory as thus far stated and as further to be developed. When we have, in our proposed future volume, completed a full-length study of the problems involved in the study of cultural orbits, it will be necessary to combine the conclusions then reached with those at which we have already arrived concerning cultural dynamics. We can then formulate a complete statement of the psycho-historical approach to culture in its combined dynamic and cyclic totality.

PART III

SOME IMPLICATIONS FOR THE
HISTORY OF ART

In earlier chapters, we used the image of a mountain climb toward the great divide between a number of intellectual disciplines to illustrate our effort to correlate them. Insofar as the psycho-historical theory involves dynamic relationships between psychological factors, historical ones, and the cultural products of the humanities, we can view these areas of knowledge and experience as aspects of a single panorama. It frequently happens in actual mountain climbing, however, that what appeared from below to be a summit turns out, when reached, to be the shoulder of some higher peak. So with our intellectual efforts: the attainment of an inclusive concept of cultural dynamics finds us with unclimbed heights still above us. Our study of cultural orbits still remains to be made. If made successfully, it should raise us to a higher vantage point from which we can trace the effects of our dynamics around the entire horizon of the presumed cycles of successive civilizations.

But since our present effort was to reach a divide and as divides are never the highest summits of their ranges; and as each stage of an ascent, real or figurative, presents its own distinctive vistas, we shall pause at our present midway station and survey some of the prospects which it offers us. Relaxing for the moment from further efforts toward theoretical construction or detailed historical analysis, we shall consider in the remaining chapters some of the implications of our present findings for various intellectual pursuits and for various aspects of our cultural life. This and the chapter to follow will deal with some of the possible relations of our theory to current studies in the history and criticism of art. Our last two chapters will be devoted to observations on the artist and on the relations of art to society; in the latter special attention will be given to contemporary cultural conflicts. As usual, our illustrations will be drawn mainly from the field of visual art, but will have their parallels in other branches of culture.

II

Since the rise of Western historico-critical consciousness in the eighteenth century, the history, the criticism, and the philosophy of art, and the more generalized study of esthetics, have all proceeded as distinct but intertwined pursuits. Historical studies have concerned themselves primarily with the facts of artistic existence; the other disciplines just mentioned, with the quality and the meaning of art and with its significance for life.

The factual side of this development has made steady progress through two centuries of cumulative effort. From the rudimentary knowledge of ancient Classical art which comprised eighteenth-century horizons in art history, the historical telescope has swept backward and forward in time until its range of vision extends from the dawn of human life to the present day. From its early restriction to the tiny world of the Mediterranean, it has swept eastward over the vast art-laden territories of the Orient, westward across the Americas, north and south of the farthest margins of human culture in the arctic wastes and the Australian bush.

These progressive extensions seem to have carried historical vision close to the artistic limits both of time and of space. As a result, twentieth-century encyclopedists have been able to compile the first more or less universal histories of art. They have made the most of this opportunity in works ranging from single-volume summaries like Helen Gardner's *Art Through the Ages* to sets of such monumental proportions as the *Propylaean Kunst Geschicte* with its twenty volumes. What is equally significant, there is among art historians a general unity of agreement upon essentials of their subject. Conjecture and opinion have, in the main, given way to a structure of organized knowledge which promises to be definitive within its field.

The psycho-historical theory has little either to question or to contribute with regard to this strictly historical study of art. Since it is primarily a philosophy of art, its parallels are to be sought in the realm of interpretive theory rather than of factual knowledge. Its relationship to the latter is one of dependence, not of competition. It accepts the information provided by art historians, like that provided by psychologists and by social scientists, as being among the foundations prerequisite to the broader equation which it is seeking to establish. While accepting this general dependence of our approach upon the facts of art history, we can still make certain reservations.

Not infrequently it happens that the art historian accompanies his factual determinations with theoretical or critical interpretations. In this case the situation is different. He is no longer strictly speaking an historian, but has turned critic or philosopher. In this aspect of his work, he is to be considered among the theorists to whom we shall turn our attention in the next chapter.

Of more immediate bearing is the fact that while psycho-historical study attempts to make no direct contribution to the data of art history, it does indirectly suggest the possibility of certain modifications or extensions of historical perspective. Three of the potential reactions of psycho-historical, upon art-historical thinking are: the importance of cultural dynamics for the grasp of a historical period and its arts; the need for increased attention to long-range historical sequences; and the relation of what are commonly called historical "influences" to the internal dynamics of the culture being influenced.

Readers who were previously familiar with the art of any of the periods studied in our earlier chapters, may have felt that our analysis added little to the wealth of detailed information already in existence concerning the chronology, the iconography, and the other aspects of the art involved. This is true. But the major purpose of a correlational system is less to provide new information than to reveal new connections between bodies of existing information. If these connections are valid ones, however, they will inevitably react to some extent upon the attitude toward the given information in the minds of those who work with it. Although such considerations of attitude carry us to the border of the critical concerns of the next chapter, they do seem to involve historical assumptions to which some attention should be given here.

When we have marshaled all the facts concerning the art and the other higher cultural manifestations of a period, does this information provide us with a sufficient basis for understanding the given art and the given artistic period? Psycho-historical thinking replies that it does not: that the cultural products of the period and the information that can be assembled concerning them lie on the manifest surface of the culture, and that they can be fully understood only in relation to its motivating depths. In other words, from our point of view, art history, great as are its intrinsic achievements, is nevertheless not a self-contained nor a self-explanatory subject. It is an aspect of a larger whole and receives its full meaning only when conceived as part of that whole.

The point can be illustrated by reference to the Gothic period and its art. We have noted before that some of the more comprehensive interpretations of medieval culture have drawn parallelisms between various of its aspects. Henry Adams indicated similarities between its architecture, its religion, literature, and social structure; Erwin Panofsky, with the striking detail of a magnification, elaborated the similarities between its architecture and its scholastic philosophy. But where do we find studies of the relation between Gothic imagery and the imagery dynamics of the psyche? Or where do we find studies of the relation between Gothic architecture and Gothic agriculture? Yet if our approach is sound, these are ultimately the most revealing types of relationship and the only ones in terms of which Gothic art can be explained as opposed to being merely described.

Let us recall for a moment the bearing of agriculture upon the situation. Had not the progress of agricultural technology underpinned an expansive state of collective vitality, neither the material resources, the specialized human skills, nor the triumphant spirit necessary to the Gothic culmination would have existed. Suppose that at the opening of the twelfth century all the fields in Europe had been rendered sterile by some cosmic influence; or that all the peasants, husbandmen, and other agricultural workers had been completely wiped out by a plague, leaving only the small minority of theologians, artists, and craftsmen. Could there then have been the sublime cathedrals and *Summae*, or even an active development of the smaller forms of art like the manuscript illuminations? It seems improbable; indeed impossible.

The surviving intellectual minority would have had to descend to the menial level of struggling to find the means of physical subsistence. Europe would have returned to some position along the line of its earlier ascent from the insecurities and negative attitudes of Neolithic times. Vast constructional projects would have been economically and physically impossible; its vision would have shrunk in corresponding fashion. The culmination to which the twelfth century was to lead would, under our imagined conditions, have withered and died like the buds of a tree cut down in spring.

If on the other hand all the theologians, artists, and craftsmen had been wiped out at the opening of the twelfth century, but the economy had remained intact, the effect on Gothic culture would presumably have been much less radical and disastrous. Higher cultural production would have been temporarily checked, but the underlying resources and vitalities impelling cultural expression would have continued to exist. Men would have felt the continuing urge of these dynamic forces. Less quickly and no doubt less well, they would have redeveloped the skills necessary to give those forces expression.

Our point regarding these considerations is that since the higher culture of a period cannot come into existence without the psycho-social vitalities that lie beneath its manifest surface, its manifestations cannot be fully understood exclusively in their own terms without reference to those vitalities. It may not be the art historian's task to study these wider and more diffuse connections. At least in his more specialized undertakings, he is rightly concerned with maximum sharpness of surface detail. Our only warning is: insofar as his work is a specialty, that it be so recognized and that it avoid philosophical or interpretive projections made on a specialized and therefore insufficient basis.

If and when interpretive assumptions slip in without consideration of the motivating vitalities, they can hardly avoid falling short of their mark. This may happen in a number of ways. In what might be called the fallacious use of cultural parallelisms (which also have their more limited appropriate use), different sets of cultural symbols, all on the surface, will be accepted as if one were a sufficient explanation of the other. The cathedral will then be explained in terms of the power of the Virgin over medieval thought or the prevalent state of religious fervor or, more broadly, in terms of a derivation of medieval art from medieval religion. The power of the Virgin, the religious fervor, the concepts of the given religion, will be accepted axiomatically, as if they were first causes susceptible to no explanation.

This is hardly more satisfactory, from the point of view of cultural dynamics, than if we were to advance the opposite and in some ways equally plausible assumption that medieval religion owed its nature to art. Without the cathedral, the embroidered vestments, the music of chanting choirs, medieval religion could not have been what it was. The artist gave as much to the religion by clothing it in visual and aural splendor as the churchman gave to art by formulating its liturgical themes. The two were partners in realizing a dream which both derived from common tensional sources. Hence any assumed basis of interpretation which fails to take account of those sources must appear inadequate from our point of view.

Equally inadequate would be the assumption that the nature of given works of art has been sufficiently understood when their evolutionary lineage has been traced, as the rise of Gothic from Romanesque architecture can be traced through a series of structural and other developments. This might be a sufficient explanation if buildings had biological powers of reproduction and could engender their own offspring. In point of fact, of course, they do not. Every new building is conceived, not by preceding buildings, but by men whose building potential ultimately depends upon the state of the society in which they live. The given state of technical advancement within the art itself will certainly be *a* factor in determining what men create at any given time, but it will not be the only factor. Probably we should say it will not be the decisive factor. The logical next step in any evolutionary development of the arts will be taken only if social vitalities provide the motivation for it. Indeed the evolution as a whole is not a self-determined one; it floats upon, and outwardly helps to reveal, the underlying current of evolving social destinies.

Another tendency of thought which our theory would raise for question is the assumption that the character of works of art has been explained if it has been found that they were subject to historical "influences." Some scholarly readers may have felt considerable reserve in noting that our earlier discussion of medieval art included little if any reference to this subject. We omitted consideration of the fact, so frequently emphasized, that Romanesque architecture was influenced by Roman and Byzantine prototypes; that medieval iconography was influenced by Near Eastern prototypes, particularly Byzantine ones. We omitted these considerations because, here again, from our point of view, they are of the surface rather than the depths. Without questioning the facts of influence, our point of view suggests that to regard one form of art as an explanation of another is to ignore the dynamics by which both are controlled. Influences have been given so large a part in recent historical studies, and present such interesting problems for psycho-historical analysis, that we shall deal with them at greater length in the final section of this chapter.

All three of the subjects just touched upon — those of cultural parallelisms, of the evolutionary history of particular forms of art, and of the influence of one form of art upon another — reduce themselves to the single principle of divers relations between elements on the manifest cultural surface. All three have their intrinsic value in sharpening our vision of that surface; all three appear to us inadequate if regarded as explanations of it.

III

A different bearing of our point of view upon the study of art history relates to length of historical range or time span. Traditional studies have rarely devoted their attention to more than a single "period"; sometimes to no more than a single school within a period or a single artist within a school. Or, cutting the cultural continuum geographically instead of historically, they have concentrated on the art of a particular region or country (again usually within a fairly limited, though in this case not specifically indicated, time span).

Under these conditions scholars have tended to become specialists in medi-eval art or in Renaissance art, in Italian painting or in Flemish painting, in the work of Michelangelo or of Rembrandt. More extended domains of thought have been regarded as little more than backgrounds for such specialization. They have received critical attention, if at all, only in surveys compiled by piecing together the findings of the respective specialists. Surveys of this kind are broad, to be sure, but have made little effort to deal with the basic problems of comprehensiveness; indeed they rarely show an awareness that comprehen-sive problems, as such, exist.

Needless to say the various forms of short-range specialization have all made important contributions to our knowledge of their subjects. They have placed us in possession of precious data without which no accurate grasp of historical relations in art would be possible. At the same time, by their very success in filling in the details concerning periods, schools, and artists, they have carried historical vision to a point at which it can envisage the broader horizons of the long-range time span. These horizons call for more serious study of the rela-tions of period to period in evolutionary sequences; for the determination of the total span of any given sequence; for comparative study of different se-quences to discover the degree to which they prove or disprove the existence of a recurrent cyclic pattern; and, if cycles appear to exist, for an effort to clarify our understanding of them by more accurately determining their phases and, if possible, their causes.

Such concerns have played only a secondary part in the present volume, their main application lying in the study of cultural orbits which we have still to make. We did make some incidental use of long-range spans, particu-larly in using as our main cultural specimen a sequence that extended from Neolithic to Gothic times. If the results have justified the effort, they may at least permit us to affirm that there are some considerations regarding every cultural period which cannot be discovered within the limits of the period itself.

We have, as a minor instance, had occasion to observe that a medievalist who attempted to interpret the Gothic grotesque purely in terms of Gothic data, attributed it to mere fancy or to inadequate technique.[1] It is true that the writer in question also cited persistent Roman influence as a further causative factor, in this respect introducing long-range considerations. Both the im-portance and the present undeveloped state of such considerations are indicated by the fact that the connection with Rome appears actually to have been in-significant as compared to the connection extending back through Western life itself. By integrating the grotesque with an evolutionary sequence of monster fantasies stretching through the Dark Ages to Neolithic cultural horizons, we have been able to see it in a different and, it is hoped, truer light as a manifestation of profound and far-reaching cultural forces.

To summarize, many of the most complex, the least explored, and presumably the most fertile historical and critical problems of the present day would seem to lie within the supraperiod cyclic range. Consequently that range, far from being left to popular surveys, deserves its own special studies as an important phase of higher learning.

IV

Under the heading of "influences," we are concerned with the modifying effect exerted, or assumed to have been exerted, by the work of one artist, period, or civilization upon that of another. Familiar examples include the influence of the Near East upon archaic Greek art during its "Orientalizing" period, and Byzantine influence upon Western medieval art; also the influence of ancient Classical culture upon the artists of the Renaissance, of Japanese prints upon the Impressionists, and the Negro sculpture upon the Post-Impressionists.

In the more recent instances it has been possible to observe the influences at work. One knows that Whistler, Manet, and Degas were attracted to Japanese prints, collected them, introduced them as part of the subject matter of some of their paintings, and modified their own artistic styles in directions exemplified by Japanese prototypes. One knows that Picasso, Braque, and their compères experienced a similar fascination for primitive art and showed results of that fascination in their work. In such cases the correlation between the art exerting the influence and the art being influenced need not be deduced from resemblances between the two; it is established by biographical information on the creative activity of the artists involved.

When the material under consideration dates from the more distant past, influences must be rediscovered through historical research. The scholar recognizes resemblances between the art of one civilization or epoch and that of another. He then searches for documentary evidence of contact between the two civilizations or epochs. A vast amount of intellectual energy has been given, detective-like, to reëstablishing these vanished relations. Their importance for learning has appeared the greater, the higher the level of scholarly specialization. Advanced iconography, for instance, has devoted much of its energy to intricate problems of influence. The triumph of scholarship so oriented is to confront one work of art with another from a different culture which so exactly resembles it that the creator of the later work must have used the earlier one as a model — and best of all to clinch the case by finding literary evidence of such interrelationship.

Influences have normally been accepted as historical facts without becoming a subject of theoretical analysis. Little effort has been made to develop a *philosophy* of influences, but if such a philosophy were formulated on the basis of the assumptions commonly held with regard to the subject, it would prove to be at once mechanistic and what, for want of a better word, we might call "magical." It would be mechanistic in that contact between the two cultures is assumed to be the primary requisite for influence and that, such contact established, the influence is assumed to operate as an external pressure, forcing modifications upon an art which would otherwise have been different — perhaps radically different.

At the same time such a philosophy would be "magical" in that it envisages no governing laws by which influences are determined. Influences have in fact not been conceived as following any regular pattern or order. They have been assumed to result from the workings of chance: the chance of geographical adjacency between two cultures, the chance of historical voyages of exploration or commercial interchange through which the members of one culture discovered the products of others that were previously unknown to them.

Still a third common premise with regard to influences is that once they have been shown to exist, they provide the chief key to an understanding of the art that has been influenced. This premise, especially dear to the iconographer, may be illustrated by one of the statements with which Emile Mâle introduces his *Religious Art of the Twelfth Century in France*. "Born in the Orient, Christian iconography came to us already complete. It was not our artists who, meditating upon the sacred texts, conceived the scenes of the Gospel: they received them from a distant world. The historian of art who confined himself to the France of the twelfth century would condemn himself to understand nothing of the works he wished to explain. He must continually return to the origins, seek in Egypt, in Syria, in Cappadocia, the models of which our churches often contain only the copy.[2] Here we have both an assertion and an implication. The assertion is that without reference to Eastern influence we can understand nothing of twelfth-century Romanesque art in France; the implication, that once informed with regard to Eastern influence, we understand everything.

To summarize the philosophy implicit in the traditional attitude toward influences we may say, then, that it is mechanistic, uncontrolled by laws, and that it regards influences as basic for any effort to comprehend artistic forms.

If we confront such a point of view with our psycho-historical theory, it becomes evident that the two are in opposition to each other. Our theory maintains that the forms of art produced by a culture are determined by the internal dynamics of its own psycho-historical development. These dynamics, rooted in all the complex circumstances of historical existence, could hardly turn about in one direction or another as an influence happened to be exerted upon them by a neighboring culture or by the discoveries of an explorer voyaging abroad. Furthermore, if we believe internal forces to be the main determinants of art, we shall have to depend upon them for any fundamental interpretation of art forms and can allow influences only a secondary usefulness in this connection.

The conflict between these opposing points of view might be resolved in either of two ways. We could modify our theory to make allowance for deviations, conceivably even reversals, of development due to external pressures working at random. Or we could modify the traditional concept of influences by recognizing that they, like all the other aspects of culture, are subject to the laws of internal psycho-historical motivation.

While there may be exceptional cases to be explained by the first of these alternatives, the basic relationship between influences and psycho-history is, I believe, more accurately stated in the second. That is to say that we must recognize influences as an organic aspect of culture, subject to the same laws as other aspects, and occurring — if and when they occur — as ordered developments within the total pattern of cultural evolution.

The traditional concept of influence as externally imposed has so long seemed tenable because it developed on the basis of studies of this or that influence in isolation. The specialists involved were usually concerned in each case with only one historical relationship: the relationship of archaic Greek to Near Eastern art, or of medieval Western to Byzantine art. They gave relatively little thought to the total frame of reference within which their specialty was a detail; relatively little thought, let us say, to the place of medieval art in the evolution of Western art as a whole, to the series of diverse influences undergone by Western art during the entire course of its development, to the pattern established by these successive influences and its relationship to the patterns established by other phases of historical development. Once we coördinate influences with this broader field of historical reference, it becomes evident that they fulfill the same expectancies as other phases of culture.

As historical verification of these assertions, let us consider the influences that are commonly recognized as having affected Greek art and Western European art, and the relationship of those influences to the general pattern expected in the historical development of a civilization. In so doing we shall have again to trespass upon the domain of cyclic studies at least to the extent of recognizing that an all-over historical pattern normally involves successive phases described by such terms as primitive, archaic, mature, and decadent, and that one of the strands in the response of art to this pattern is a change from an initial abstraction to a medial realism and a later tendency to return through conventionalization toward abstraction. Given this general framework, it becomes evident that both Greek and Western European art followed the normal course of development and that the influences which have been noted in connection with them, far from modifying the course, were controlled by it.

Either the history of Greek art is singularly free from influence in its more literal forms or scholars have not laid bare the interconnections. Only two specific instances of influence are commonly mentioned in comprehensive surveys of Greek art. These are Oriental influence during the archaic phase and archaistic influence during the decadent phase.

The representational form typical of archaic culture is a conventionalized one stressing the decorative appeal of pattern, yet delighted with the vitalistic expressiveness resulting from an emergent observation of nature. Archaic Greek art exemplifies the type. It borrows elements from the Near East — Egyptian lotuses, Assyrian rosettes and tiers of winged beasts — but it does so in conformity with the expected archaic impulse. That impulse would undoubtedly have found expression regardless of whether Greece was in contact with the Near East or not, and regardless of whether Near Eastern art offered models congenial to it. But since the archaic artists of Greece were acquainted with Near Eastern art and since that art included aspects suggestive for the development of their own stylistic impulse, they accepted its influence.

Phrases like "Near Eastern art" are actually too sweeping to correspond to historical realities. During the Greek Orientalizing period, the seventh century B.C., the arts of Egypt and Mesopotamia were already so old that they presented, not a single style, but many of the varied styles that correspond to successive phases of a cycle. Egyptian sculpture, for instance, had passed through stages of realism in portraiture such as Greece was to reach only in Hellenistic times. It is not unlikely that the existence of such work was known to the archaic Greeks along with the more decorative forms of Near Eastern art. As archaic artists they responded to the decorative and ignored the realistic because the one harmonized with their own impulse and the other did not.

During the mature periods of Greek art, direct influence from the arts of other cultures seems to be conspicuous by its absence. It might be assumed that the Greeks were now pursuing artistic aims which, in their day, had no precedents and which, therefore, had to be independently developed. In point of total conception this is undoubtedly true but in that respect it is equally true everywhere and in cases where historical influence is recognized. So far as concerns underlying points of view and contributary effects, the older civilizations offered many fertile analogies for goals which the Greeks were pursuing. The "impersonal grandeur" that was to infuse the work of the Golden Age had had its manifestations in Old Kingdom Egypt and elsewhere; so had the impulse toward realism and individualization that succeeded it. The Greek realism of the third and second centuries B.C. was more broadly applied, but its observation of nature was no keener than the Assyrians had shown in their animal reliefs of the seventh century B.C. or the Egyptians in their portraits of the eighteenth and nineteenth centuries B.C.

Greek artists may or may not have received intangible stimulus from the accomplishments of such predecessors. For our present purpose, the mature phases of Greek art serve chiefly to emphasize, by their freedom from apparent influence, how little the latter is necessary and how little it contributes to the internally motivated course of cultural development. All the general characteristics which, in the Western Renaissance, we have so often attributed to the influence of ancient classical culture, have their original classical equivalents as aspects of a natural growth, without recourse to influence and hence without the association of any concept of rebirth. And this despite the fact, already suggested, that they had earlier parallels to which they might have related themselves as "renaissances."

When the time for the recession of realism arrived in Greek art, we meet the second patent example of influence: archaism. Any of the preëxisting types of conventionalized art could have offered "inspiration" at this point. The artist of so late a phase in a cycle can find precedents not only in the work of other cultures but also in the earlier stages of his own, and he is likely to be attracted to the latter by historical nostalgia. As a result we find the late Greek artists, or at least one coterie of them, reviving as a mannerism the conventions through which their archaic precursors had created a style. But the archaic influence manifest in the revival synchronizes with, and reflects, an expected decadent impulse toward returning conventionality.

If, as seems cyclically inevitable, we link Byzantine art with the last phases of the declining Greek culture, the further return to decorative norms, the eventual solidification of convention to the verge of abstraction, are recognized in their turn as expected tendencies. The reopening of Greek consciousness to decorative precedents from the East is correspondingly recognized as one of the results which these internal tendencies could produce if and when they were projected into the sphere of influences.

The Greek examples of influence are hardly numerous enough to offer a convincing demonstration of the principle with which we are concerned, nor can any one historical context substantiate such a principle. When we turn to a consideration of the influences undergone by the art of Western Europe, we find that they are at once more numerous, more varied, and more accurately documented, and that they strongly reinforce the psycho-historical interpretation of influence as a dynamic reflection of internal necessities.

Archaic Western Europe responded to Byzantine influence (Fig. 89) under psychic circumstances similar to those which had sensitized archaic Greece to Near Eastern influence. The period was motivated toward a conventionalized art and was accordingly open to the appeal of conventionalized models. But we can say that Western archaic artists produced many of their finest achievements where their own internal dynamism was most independent and least conscious of Byzantine precedents, as in the case of Norse and Celtic ornament.

We can also say that the receptiveness of Western Europe to Byzantine influence during the Dark and Early Middle Ages must have had its obverse in a more or less conscious rejection of realistic types of classical art. There was a great deal more high classical art to be seen in Rome and its dependencies during the fourth and fifth centuries than there was in the fifteenth. Western barbarians had conquered the Roman world and looked upon that art, but they remained aloof from its influence because, at that time, they were motivated by creative impulses with which advanced realism had no affinity. In short, Byzantine influence on early medieval Europe was not indispensable nor was it inevitable as the only influence historically possible. It was a utilization of a reference selected and enjoyed for its congeniality.

The passage of the West from the archaic to the mature phases of its culture, accomplished during the later Middle Ages and the Renaissance, was inevitably attended by an impulse away from decorative toward realistic forms of art. Byzantine art ceased to influence the West at that time because it offered no assistance to the emergent movement. What had been congenial to Western development and consequently welcome to Western consciousness, now appeared repressive and was censured as "rude" and "lifeless."

In the late Gothic art of the north this emergence from Byzantine influence takes place on a self-reliant basis, with relatively little substitution of any new external model for the outgrown one. The Latin south, finding around it evidences of a past which synchronized with its own future, assimilated its new realism to that of corresponding phases of antique art (Fig. 90). To the influence which the barbarians had resisted, their descendents of a thousand years later abandoned themselves with passion, labeling their own career a "rebirth" of what they were selecting to encourage it. Thus the south discarded one influence to assume another, reflecting by its choice in both cases a stage of its own development.

The particular use of classical models made by the Renaissance is one of our clearest examples of the selectivity of influence. The Renaissance saw in antiquity a golden age of high classical achievement. Actually, high classical culture was only one phase of a complete cyclic sequence. This sequence included artistic beginnings as primitive as Negro sculpture; it included archaic conventionality and, after the passage of its realistic phase, a return to convention in archaistic and Byzantine formality. Each of these varied manifestations was as antique, as genuinely Greek or Roman, as was high Classical realism, but to all but the latter the supposedly antique-minded Renaissance was insensitive. As late as the eighteenth century, Winckelmann could still dismiss primitive Greek art as a crude forerunner to Classical achievement. It was not the influence of ancient Classical art in general to which the Renaissance responded, though it judged itself to be so doing. Practically speaking that would have been impossible, for it would have meant responding to all types of influence at once and the various types are mutually opposed to each other. What the Renaissance responded to was a single selected phase of the Classical heritage. The selection was its own and was motivated by contemporary Western predilections.

But there was destined to come a time, as had been the case in earlier civilizations, when the creative will of the West was no longer toward realism but away from it. Inevitably then, high classical models paled of inspiration for Western artists. The Renaissance gave place to a counter-Renaissance; whatever had been reborn must now be unborn again. If influences were to be associated with this new phase of our cultural evolution, they must come from forms of art that subjected natural appearance to one degree or another of conventionalization. Accordingly, Western artists began to rediscover charm in the decorative arts of the Orient. The new Oriental influence revealed itself ornamentally in the eighteenth century in such manifestations as Chippendale's Chinese manner, probably reached its climax in the impact of the Japanese print (Fig. 91) on the Impressionists, and has recently been extended by Matisse to Persian miniatures (Fig. 92) and other Eastern forms of colorful pictorial convention.

Time early joined with space to augment the archives from which the West could support its growing anti-realism. The nineteenth century was resensitized, archaistically, to the conventions of its own Gothic and Romanesque past — precisely that past which the Renaissance had repudiated. Western eyes also opened to a beauty which they had not previously been able to see in the arts of archaic Greece, Chaldea, and Egypt. Western artists accordingly added these arts to the repertory of models now deemed worthy of emulation.

It becomes evident upon reflection that all these varied influences of the eighteenth, nineteenth and early twentieth centuries — Oriental, medieval, ancient archaic — that all these influences, so heterogenous in their sources, are nevertheless homogeneous in their creative utility. They all subserve an impulse to replace realism by increasing artistic formality and so reflect the inherent drive of Western art.

Eventually, the midway stage of conventionalized natural forms was not enough for our creative pioneers. As abstract and fantastic art became imminent forms of Western expression, influence turned to the source from which we have most conspicuously derived it during the first half of the twentieth century: the primitive arts of the world. The tribal arts of Africa (Fig. 93), aboriginal America, and the South Pacific, originally collected by ethnologists for scientific purposes and regarded by others as mere curiosities, now revealed an unforeseen creative import for our artists. Pictograph and fetish, elevated to the sanctity of art, are currently admired for their wealth of design and for the fantasy of their demonic and totemic monsters, and are considered indispensable aids to creative research. Under the spell of this primitivizing impulse, we are moved today to seek the primitive even in our converse with historic civilizations. Geometric "fiddle figures" from the Cyclades (Fig. 94) are more revealing to our advanced sculptors than the Elgin marbles from the Parthenon.

Such has been the succession of influences — Byzantine, late Classical, Orien-

tal and medieval, early Classical, primitive — undergone by Western art from
the early Middle Ages to the present day. When viewed as a whole this succession reveals a definite order. The influencing forms of art change from the
conventionalized to the realistic and back to the conventionalized with the
smooth rhythm of a rising and falling wave. The two influences which we can
clearly detect in the history of Greek art adhere to a similar curve, adjusting
themselves to its earlier and to its later period of conventionalization. Finally it
appears that the curve thus followed by influences in both cases synchronizes with
the development of style internal to the arts of the two civilizations and normal to
a cultural cycle.

These historical instances reinforce the psycho-historical implication with
regard to influences: the implication that under normal conditions influences
are due, not to mere familiarity or external pressure, but to a selection controlled
by internal cultural dynamics. We seem to be safe in concluding that influences
are subject to the same laws and reflect the same tendencies as other aspects of
culture. A culture is not an amorphism passively subject to whatever impressions impinge upon it. It is a dynamic organism, subject indeed to many impressions, but rejecting some and accepting others according to its own inherent
needs. It involves an active though perhaps unconscious will to be influenced
or *not* to be influenced, and its will to be influenced is an aspect of its will to
express itself.

The forms of art known to members of a given culture through geographical
interchange or historical acquaintance will determine the idioms in terms of
which influences might be felt, but their effect will be the negative one of al-
lowing certain choices, not the positive one of forcing creative adherence. Many
and varied forms of art have been known at most times in history, but those
which did not accord with the internal creative impulse exerted no widespread
influence. If they had not recently synchronized with internal movements they
were ignored or disparaged: the barbarian attitude toward Roman realism, the
attitude of the eighteenth and nineteenth centuries toward primitivism. If they
had recently synchronized with the internal development but were being left
behind it, they were repudiated with considerable vehemence: the revulsion of
the Renaissance from Byzantine influence and of the twentieth century from
Renaissance influence.

Stated in positive terms, the artists of a culture can be influenced only by
types of art that correspond to their own emergent creative necessity. If the
art known to them includes forms which previously lacked, but which are now

acquiring, relevancy to the internal development, those forms will come to be seen in a new light. The inner veil of psychic nonassimilation having been withdrawn from them, they will be "discovered" and irradiated with the energy of contemporary creative experience. They may then serve as sources of influence.

In a sense a culture can thus be said to create the forms of art by which it is influenced as well as those which it produces; that is to say it *re*creates the influencing forms *as art*. To put this another way, a culture can be influenced only by itself; only by its own emergent future. Its advancing cultural dynamics demand expression in certain types of art. It creates those types of art and, if it recognizes similar types in its cultural environment, it may adopt them, so to speak, as guardian spirits and totemic ancestors. If it does *not* recognize similar types in its environment, it will proceed on its course without benefit of influence.

From the point of view of traditional concepts, what we have been saying amounts to a denial of influence. In the sense of external pressure forcing a change of direction upon internal impulse, influence does not seem to exist. At any rate it does not seem to exist under normal conditions. If and when it might be found to operate, it would do so under abnormal circumstances such as interference with the internal development through military conquest or dictatorial control. And even in most cases of conquest or dictatorship the internal cultural laws appear to continue on their own basic course. The conquest of the Roman world by the barbarians had relatively little influence either on the receding realism of Roman Christian art or on the archaic conventionality of barbarian art. And the Nazi imposition of academic realism in no way changed the creative impulses of experimental German artists; that is to say, in no way changed the internal creative motivation of the contemporary Western world.

In epochs impelled by positive psycho-historical determinants, influences are likely to be of secondary importance to the artist because the internal relations of art to society are such as to inspire creative confidence. When the internal determinants are being negativized, influences may acquire a new function in the creative life of the artist. Gravitating irresistibly in directions from which he himself often recoils in doubt, uncertain whether he should proceed in such directions yet unable to do otherwise, he discovers that others have already followed a similar course. Their work becomes significant for him not only as a formal prototype but also as a source of guidance in his cultural dilemma. Through that work they say to him, "Proceed, my son. We have been here before you. You may advance with confidence." And with relief he advances, submitting to their influence because it frees him from his own inhibitions, fortifies his hesitant creative impulse, and provides the encouragement denied to him by his contemporary public.

If we accept the views proposed above, the study of influences may or may not continue to deserve the scholarly emphasis which it has received during recent generations. That question archaeologists, iconologists, and others interested can decide for themselves. But it appears that from the psycho-historical point of view we can make one affirmation. After all the influences have been determined and catalogued, it will still remain to seek a basic understanding of art in other directions. Influences as such are a matter of surface relationships. The depth question is not *what* influences the art of a given culture reveals, but *why* the artists of that culture submitted to those particular influences rather than to others. In dynamic terms, the question becomes one of deciding why the artists selected and energized those particular influences — which is identical with the question why they created the art of their own period.

In Freudian terms, influences may sometimes help to explain the manifest imagery of art, as day residues may help to explain the manifest imagery of dreams, but the symbolical significance of the manifest imagery in either case can be realized only in terms of an underlying and often unconscious latent content. In the case of art, understanding of the latent content must be sought through an analysis, not of similarities between objects, but of psycho-historical states of collective consciousness.

The personal influence of one artist upon another might be described as a minor complication within the cultural process we have been considering. Here influence, in the sense of external and possibly deflective pressure, is possible. A strong individual may influence a weaker one in ways opposed to the latter's natural bent. This happens most frequently in situations where one individual has matured a creative conviction and the other has not, as in the relationship of pupil to teacher, or of beginner to masters already venerated in the cultural tradition.

But only an artist incapable of personal development will remain permanently under an influence alien to his own impulse. A creative nature will soon reduce the influences playing upon it to an order determined by their affinities or antipathies with itself. Henceforth, it will accept some influences and reject others, exercising a will to be influenced or not to be influenced similar to that which we have discussed for cultures as a whole.

And since all creative individuals, influencing or influenced, are ultimately guided through their sensitivity by cultural directives, successive personal influences in successive generations fall back into the general pattern of cultural evolution. The respective influences exerted upon contemporaries or successors by Courbet, Manet, Cézanne, and Picasso are so many personal soundings of the social current responsible for the course of Western art. The same progression, telescoped in time, is evident in the successive influences to which single artists have submitted. Cézanne beginning under the influence of realists like Courbet, then responding to the Impressionists, then gravitating toward formal preoccupations that foretell abstraction; Picasso turning in order from his realistic father to Toulouse-Lautrec, then to Cézanne, and then to Negro sculpture — such personal sequences of influence are reflections on an individual scale of the tidal drift of culture as a whole. Again we come back to psychohistorical directives as the ultimate determinants of all cultural phenomena. Effective personal influences, we might say, are lighthouses through which one sensitive individual flashes to other sensitive individuals an intuition of the course being motivated by the cultural current.

TOWARD A UNIFIED FIELD
IN CRITICAL STUDIES

The approach to universality and definitiveness achieved by the historical side of our historico-critical development, has by no means characterized its critical side. Here our knowledge is still in a formative and fermentive state. Any effort to grasp the field as a whole confronts us with a bewildering intricacy of schools and counter-schools, of oppositions and conflicts, of multiple problems rather than unifying solutions.

An iconographer like Mâle will tell us that medieval art is a "closed world" to us unless we learn to decipher the obscure "hieroglyphics of its subject-matter." [1] Exactly opposite assertions come to us from critics imbued with the concept of "pure visibility." They insist that subject matter is "irrelevant" to artistic significance and that we should concentrate our attention on the "plastic form" inherent to visual creations as such. One recurrent point of view urges that to understand art and artist we must, in Taine's words, "comprehend the general social and intellectual condition of the time to which they belong. Herein is to be found the final explanation; herein resides the primitive cause determining all that follows it." [2] We have had earlier occasion to quote Lionello Venturi as a spokesman of the opposite view that "the consideration of art as a document in the life of peoples" is to be classed among the "deviations from the criticism of art," and that "the only reality of art is the personality of the artist, as it is manifested in his works of art." [3]

Other mutually conflicting points of view could be indicated. The reader desiring a comprehensive survey of the intricacies of recent critical thought can turn to the later chapters in such summaries as Bernard Bosanquet's *History of Aesthetic* (1892), Lionello Venturi's *History of Art Criticism* (1936), and Gilbert and Kuhn's *History of Aesthetics* (1939).

It is doubtful whether the ferment of ideas just suggested can be reduced to any single systematic framework which would be satisfactory to everybody. After considerable effort to obtain perspective on the field as a whole, however, the author has concluded that it can fairly well be charted under six headings: six approaches or points of view, six directions of attention and emphasis, each of which may be said to constitute a tradition within the totality of recent efforts to interpret art. These six main critical traditions, together with some outstanding representatives of each of them are as follows:

(1) *Iconography*. Emphasis on subject matter and its natural or literary sources as a basis for understanding art. Active during the Middle Ages in a preoccupation with sacred texts, the iconographical approach expanded during the Renaissance to include the direct imitation of nature among the objectives of art and keys to its subject matter. It has since reverted mainly to concern with literary sources, especially the forgotten ones associated with past forms of art. Characteristic recent contributions to this tradition have been made by Emile Mâle, Erwin Panofsky, and Edgar Wind.

(2) *Biographical Criticism*. Emphasis on the creative personality as the chief basis for understanding art. Exponents of this point of view have been chiefly concerned with the life and work of individual artists. The tradition extends from the Renaissance, when Vasari and others wrote their *Lives*, to the present day. Under the influence of psychoanalysis, its sphere of inquiry has been extended in the twentieth century to include the unconscious depths of the creative personality — an extension illustrated by Freud's *Leonardo Da Vinci*.

(3) *Historical Determinism*. Emphasis on civilization and environment as the conditioning sources of art forms. This point of view was presented by John Winckelmann in the eighteenth century, by Hippolyte Taine in the nineteenth. E. Viollet-Le-Duc, Henry Adams, and others have thought in more restricted ranges of historical reference. A marginal, ethically centered variation of the tradition occurs in the work of Ruskin, Tolstoy, and others who stress the moral effect which art should have on society, as distinguished from the historical effect which society has upon art.

(4) *"Esthetic materialism."* Emphasis on material, technique, and function as the chief factors determining art forms. Most frequently applied to architecture and the useful crafts, but has been proposed for all the arts. Lessing advanced the thesis in his *Laocoon* (1766). A century later Gottfried Semper formulated it into a system in *Der Stil in den Technischen und Tektonischen Kunsten* (Style in the Crafts and Structural Arts; 1863). Viollet-Le-Duc em-

ployed this point of view as well as the preceding one. One of the earlier statements of it by an American was Charles Herbert Moore's *Gothic Architecture*
(1899).

(5) *"Esthetic teleology."* Art forms explained as the outcome of a psychological "will to art" associated with epochs or races. Enunciated at the beginning of the twentieth century by Alois Riegl as an incidental critical aspect of
a historical work: *Spatromische Kunstindustrie* (Late Roman Industrial Arts).
Adopted as the basis for a "psychology of style" by Wilhelm Worringer in his
Abstraction and Empathy and *Form Problems of Gothic.*

(6) *Pure Visibility.* Works of art explained in terms of the formal significance resulting from the organization of lines, colors, and other plastic elements.
Employed as a means of descriptive classification by Heinrich Wolfflin in his
Principles of Art History. Indicated as the chief basis of esthetic values by many
recent critics, among others Roger Fry, Clive Bell, and Albert C. Barnes.

In the foregoing outline we have listed the six approaches chronologically,
following the approximate order of their historical emergence in works which
still play an active part in our critical literature. In this order they seem indis-
tinctly to reveal the same sequence which we discussed earlier in connection
with the evolution of artistic styles and of related influences during the same
centuries. One of the earliest concepts of creative motivation is the medieval
one of divine inspiration, which corresponds with the religious emphasis in
medieval life and art; one of the latest of such concepts is that of pure visibility,
which corresponds with recent abstraction. Between these temporal extremes
we can find other correspondences, such as that between the individualism of
the Renaissance, its artistic expression in such forms as portraiture, and its critical
expression in emphasizing individual genius as the source of what is artistically
important.

From our point of view it is not surprising that theories about art should
reveal evolutionary directions corresponding to those followed by art itself.
Not only are the theorists dependent upon the work of the artists; the artists
are influenced by an intellectual climate which includes the work of the theorists
and both, in the measure of their creative capacity, are responding to common
cultural directives.

Dialectically, the six traditions have tended to group themselves into three
pairs of thesis and antithesis. Iconographical interpretations have been opposed
by formal ones, individualistic by social ones, mechanistic by teleological ones.
In the heat of debate, which is usually intensified by the clash of personalities,

it has frequently seemed to the champions of each point of view that the difference between their position and that of their opponents was one of truth as opposed to error. Reflective wisdom suggests that any point of view maintained by a number of serious thinkers over a period of time has *something* to recommend it; that each of the six traditions, therefore, may be accepted as embodying *a* truth, or *an aspect* of truth, and that if *the* truth can be reached at all, it presumably lies in the direction of a synthesis capable of resolving the oppositions between the various traditions into a larger unity.

If we turn our attention to possible bases for such a unity, organic relations between the six traditions begin to suggest themselves. In the first place, as indicated by Diagram 11, they would seem to fall into two groups: one concerned with the inherent attributes of art, the other with forces which motivate the creation of art. In the first group are the traditions devoted primarily to the subject matter, the form, the material, the technique, and the physical functions of works of art. In the second group are those devoted to creative motivation as ascribed respectively to the individual artist, to races, and to historical states of civilization.

ASPECTS OF ART INVOLVED	CRITICAL TRADITIONS
Intrinsic attributes of art	Iconography and other studies in subject matter
	Pure visibility emphasizing form
	Esthetic materialism emphasizing material, technique, and function
Motivation of art	Biographical studies emphasizing personality of the artist
	Esthetic teleology emphasizing will to art resident in races
	Historical determinism emphasizing influence of civilization and environment

Diagram 11. An organic classification of recent critical traditions.

The three approaches gathered in our first group, though they have occasioned more than one internecine feud, are in no sense incompatible with each other. Each deals with, and illuminates, certain aspects of the work of art. In studying a fully integrated work of art like a Gothic cathedral, where all aspects are merged, we might follow each approach in turn to our enlightenment. Through the iconographic approach we could penetrate the mysterious world of religious imagery presented by the sculpture and stained glass of the building itself, and by the painting of its altarpieces and other accessories. The visibility approach would quicken our perceptions of design, focusing our attention upon the proportions of mass and space, the rhythmic flow of lines, the harmonies of color, the repetition and endless variation of motifs such as that presented by the pointed arch. The material approach would show us the dependence of the whole fabric upon the physical properties of stone and glass, upon the physical forces of weight and thrust, and the marvelous adaptation of pier, arch, and buttress to their functions as members of the structural organism. From this same material approach we could also, if we wished (thinking back to Lessing), learn some of the reasons why the same religious subject receives different formations in the portals, the windows, and the altarpieces; differences due in part to the respective natures of carved stone, of stained glass, and of painted surfaces.

It is obvious that each of these approaches contributes something to the observer's understanding of, and responsiveness to, the work of art; obvious, therefore, that all have their value for the study of art. The limitations that may be ascribed to them are not those of insignificance or error but of partiality. If and when any of them has revealed such limitations, it has done so either in regarding itself as a self-sufficient basis for the interpretation of art, or in opposing other approaches. Truth for each would seem to lie in recognizing itself as a component aspect of a larger whole, and in maintaining positive relationships toward other approaches in the interests of that larger whole. Such an attitude would promote integration on two levels. It would liberate the three approaches of our first group from their respective limitations and their mutual conflicts, harmonizing them within the balanced totality of the group. And it would open the way for recognition of organic connections between the first group as a whole and the factors comprising our second group.

The author's earlier work, *Representation and Form*, was an effort in the first of these directions. Its point of departure was the recent opposition between the pure-visibility tradition and that which has ascribed significance to subject matter. Its outcome was the proposal of a basis of synthesis within which, from the esthetic point of view, the two could be integrated with each other. This was a step toward a unitary conception of the work of art, but the unity which it conceived was one of surface factors, or what we are here calling the "intrinsic attributes" of art objects. It did not extend the inquiry to the forces of motivation or inspiration upon which both the formal and the representational characteristics of works of art are ultimately dependent. Hence it might be compared to a study of the manifest imagery of dreams that did not raise the question of what latent motivation had inspired the manifest imagery. Its depth limitation in this respect is shared by all studies that confine their fields of reference to the factors dealt with by the traditions of our first group. This brings us to the second and wider basis of integration suggested above: the relationship between the traditions listed in our first and our second groups which is, in principle, the relationship between resulting effects and their motivating causes.

Iconographical, formal, and functional studies, when pursued in isolation, have not concerned themselves directly with questions of creative motivation, but each approach has tended to assume motives reflecting its own preoccupations. Iconography has attached so much importance to "influences" that it might seem to imply that the historic works of art were created for the purpose of being influenced — an idea so preposterous that no one seriously entertains it. More reasonable, as a motive related to iconography, would be the assumption that the creative purpose lay in representing the subject matter of the work studied. Functionalism, for its part, has tacitly assumed that the aim of art was to achieve fitness to material and structural demands; formalism, that its aim was to achieve finely organized perceptual relationships.

In each case we may accept the statement as involving a partial motivation: the immediate motivation for a component aspect of the total work. But reflection should make clear that in no case alone, nor in all together, do these statements involve an adequate motivation for art as a whole. If we say in so many words that the purpose of building the Gothic cathedrals was to allow architects to pose and solve problems of thrust and counter-thrust, the proposition joins the ranks of the preposterous. That the purpose was to represent subject matter for its own sake is hardly less so. The subjects were considered important for their power to express something external to themselves — religion — and if we extend our frame of reference to include religion, then we have left our first group of concerns, strictly speaking, and connected the subject matter intrinsic to the first group with one of the forces of civilization included in the second.

The remaining alternative, that the artist creates in order to achieve esthetic form, corresponds so well with the conscious aspect of his own creative experience, and also with our enjoyment of formal beauty, that we might seem justified in accepting it as an ultimate motivation. That it can hardly be so, however, is suggested by various considerations. In the case of artistic undertakings as vast as those of the cathedrals, the pleasures of perceiving harmony and proportion would hardly seem a sufficient incentive to inspire whole communities to spend immense sums of wealth and effort over generations of time. And even in the case of small individually executed works such as easel paintings, for which esthetic form may seem a sufficient justification, the student of depth psychology can hardly accept the conscious formal experience as independent of presumed unconscious motivants.

Subject, form, and structure, it appears, are means to more inclusive and elusive ends, not ends in themselves. They are agencies for fulfilling motivation, not types of motivation. The realization of this fact has led various thinkers to proceed upon the assumptions, or to formulate the theories comprising our second group of traditions: those ascribing the motivation of art to the impulse and capacity of the individual artist, to a racial will to art, and to the historical energies of a state of civilization. Before scanning these traditions, we might note that the Middle Ages had previously proposed a motivation for art which has faded out of more recent thought but which, like all things past, is no doubt destined to reappear in modified and perhaps more analytical form in the future.

There was in medieval consciousness no realization that art had a history, no sense of it as a reflection of human cultures, no emphasis upon individuals as its creators. Like the rest of the universe it was explained and justified as a revelation of the glory of God. A monk, Theophilus, wrote a treatise on art in the twelfth century. He discusses techniques and formal concerns, but presents them as recipes serving a purpose, not as purposes in themselves. The purpose was to manifest divinity through the adornment of places of worship. In accomplishing that purpose, Theophilus tells the artist, "you have in some way exposed to the eyes of the faithful the Paradise of God. . . You have succeeded in letting the Creator be praised in creation and in showing God to be admirable in his work." [4]

The Renaissance, still unaware of historical and cultural determinism, but highly aware of a new individualistic detachment from the body social, proposed the first of our extant ideas of motive: the genius of the individual artist. At the time of its Renaissance inception, this individualistic motivation was "still trailing clouds of glory." As we read one of its early literary embodiments, Vasari's *Lives*, we are continually made aware of genius as the special gift of God. Giotto accomplishes his artistic revolution "by the favour of Heaven." Leonardo's superiority is such as "manifestly to prove that he has been specially endowed by the hand of God himself, and has not obtained his pre-eminence by human teaching, or the power of man."[5] Vasari seems but to paraphrase himself in ascribing the genius of Raphael, of Michelangelo, and other great artists to the same divine source. There was in this conception a recognition that genius, though embodied in individuals, is not individually self-contained or self-explanatory, but the external source here ascribed to it was not destined to remain convincing for subsequent Western thought. The greatness of the great man was gradually detached from religious affiliations and was explained in terms of superior intellectual and esthetic endowment or, with the advent of psychoanalysis, in terms of impulse generated by the individual unconscious.

Biographical criticism had special value for the development of the philosophy of art in that it was an instrument of correlation and synthesis. Instead of confining attention exclusively to objects of art, it called for observation of the relations between certain objects of art and a human being. In thus recognizing a tie between art and life, it introduced a correlative approach which, if pursued to its logical conclusion, was bound eventually to lead beyond the individual. Although the purely biographical approach was long considered, and by biographers is sometimes still accepted, as a sufficient basis for the discussion of an artist's work, it contains ingredients for its own dissolution into larger circles of human experience.

The individual, as we have more than once had occasion to observe, does not exist alone but in society. The study of his life and art inevitably leads to some degree of consideration for the given society in general and for the particular members of it with whom the individual was most closely associated. Leonardo da Vinci may, in Vasari's eyes, have derived his genius from God and have owed nothing "to the power of man," but he did not study with God; he studied with Verrochio. Accordingly, having explained the divine source of the artist's genius on the first page of his *Life* of Leonardo, Vasari arrives on the second page at the youthful aspirant's apprenticeship to the older master, and by page three is relating Leonardo to social enterprises full of the techno-economic concerns of the epoch such as "the formation of a canal from Pisa to Florence."[6]

Thus, while the theoretical assumption as to the motivating source of art might remain centered in the psychology of the individual, the practice of biographical criticism inevitably demanded a larger frame of reference. Recognition of this fact led many writers subsequent to the Renaissance to entitle their works, not the "Life," but the "Life and Times" of the given artist. Through the "times," the way was open for a consideration of historical and social factors in their relationship to art.

In the biographical tradition, historical factors remained a background against which the individual stood out in vigorous highlight. By the eighteenth century another tradition was arising to reverse the emphasis. Synchronizing with the emergence of Western historical consciousness, aware for the first time of such inclusive entities as the whole rise and fall of Greek civilization, this tradition gave its chief thought to the saga of societies, the epic march of civilizations. Seen in such panoramic perspective the individual shrank to the role of a participant, albeit perhaps a leading participant, in the historical destiny of his epoch, and even his epoch receded into place as one of the phases of a cycle of civilization. This point of view in general we are calling historical determinism (the biographical one might be called personal determinism). Actually historical and social factors are so numerous and complex that they permit of many intellectual analyses, with the result that the tradition concerned with them is a complex of several different formulations or subtraditions.

The two most important of these in the literature of art are listed last in our table of traditions (Diagram 11). They are historical determinism proper and what, for purposes of distinction, may be called racial determinism. We have noted in an earlier and more general context that a third variant, economic determinism, can be considered as a restricted form of historical determinism. Historical determinism proper received its first major exposition in *The History of Ancient Art* by John Winckelmann (1764). Winckelmann ascribed the progress and superiority of art among the Greeks "partly to the influence of climate, partly to their constitution and government, and the habits of thinking which originated therefrom, and, in equal degree also, to respect for the artist, and the use and application of art." [7] "Being consecrated to the gods, and devoted only to the holiest and best purposes of the land," the artist's "work was made to conform to the lofty ideas of the whole nation." All these conditioning factors — geographical, political, religious, and others — are elaborated in Winckelmann's discussion.

What the eighteenth century thus conceived with reference to its absorption in Classical antiquity, the nineteenth applied to its new enthusiasm for the Western Middle Ages. Writers like Viollet-le-Duc and, later and within narrower limits, Henry Adams, studied medieval art in relation to its historical background. Supported by an intervening century of growth in both historical and critical consciousness, Viollet-le-Duc related Gothic art to a remarkably extensive and remarkably solid frame of reference. His exposition of the functional aspects of Gothic architecture, such as the evolution of its structural organism, remains basic today, and his conception of the conditioning forces to which architectural structure must adapt itself extends from "the nature of the materials" to "the climate" and "the historical conditions of an epoch." [8] His discussion of the historical background of Gothic art refers to the new expansive force of Western life after the eleventh century, the emergence of the free cities, and many of the other historical circumstances adduced in our chapter on Gothic history.

Winckelmann and Viollet-Le-Duc had both related their concepts of historical determinism to the study of one selected type of art: in the first case, primarily Greek art, with marginal references to other ancient national styles; in the second case, French medieval art. The first writer to separate historical determinism from a single context and propose it as a theory having the validity of a general principle, applicable to all historical contexts, appears to have been Hippolyte Taine (1828–1893). Relating his observations to the art of Greece, of medieval Europe, of Renaissance Italy, and of the seventeenth-century Low Countries, with references to other areas and periods, and also in the light of extensive studies in English, Spanish, and other literatures, Taine proposed a motivation sequence in four principal terms. These terms, elaborated in their author's *Philosophy of Art*,[9] are as follows.

(1) A "general situation" involving such realities as a "state of wealth or poverty, a particular form of society, a certain species of religious faith," gives rise (2) to "corresponding needs, aptitudes, and sentiments." This reigning mentality finds its most complete embodiment in (3) a "representative man" — the youthful Greek athlete, the medieval monk — who becomes the culture hero of the period and the primary subject of its art. The artists then strive to express the character of this representative man in (4) "sounds, forms, colors, or language giving this character sensuous form, or which comport with the tendencies and faculties comprising it."

It will be observed that the first, second, and fourth terms of the above sequence — general situation, resulting sentiments, and their artistic expressions — closely parallel the psycho-historical sequence of historical circumstances, psychic state, and cultural expressions. Taine's theory, much more solid and penetrating in his development than it may sound in our summary, is probably the most complete formulation of the principle of historical determinism to be found in the literature specifically devoted to art.

The last of our six main critical traditions, which we have referred to as "racial determinism," emerged somewhat obliquely from the esthetic teleology of Riegl. The latter had enunciated a "will to art" — *kunstwollen* — as the basic factor in the motivation of works of art. The principle was important not only because it related art to obscure psychological impulse, but because it provided a corrective to the widespread tendency to judge one form of art in terms of another. Riegl was himself chiefly occupied with the decorative arts of the declining Roman world; arts which, in relation to the High Classical standards of preceding periods, had frequently been condemned as decadent. Riegl maintained that these arts owed their nature, not to negative inability to fulfill the artistic aims of previous periods, but to a positive fulfillment of the intent, the artistic will, of their own period. Every period, he said, has its own will impulse or "will" as a motivation for its art. Consequently, that art can be judged only by the degree to which it fulfills its own will. To judge it by comparison with other types of art that owed their nature to other intentions is to misjudge and to fail to understand it.[10]

The will to art as Riegl conceives it has much in common with the second term in Taine's motivating sequence: the "needs, aptitudes, and sentiments" corresponding to a particular historical situation. Riegl himself leaves the nature of the artistic will vague and its source largely undetermined. As Gilbert and Kuhn have put it, "Riegl's 'will to art' leaves us in doubt as to whether we have to do with a psychological hypothesis or a rudimentary metaphysics." [11] Riegl's most direct successor, Wilhelm Worringer, ostensibly decided for the psychological alternative by making the "will" concept the basis of a "psychology of style." In Worringer's general statements of theory, both psychological and historical determinants are given due consideration. The changes in the will to art as it passes from period to period are recognized as standing in orderly relationship to "the variations that take place in the constitution of the mind and soul of mankind," and these variations in turn are governed by the "fundamental process of the whole historical evolution of mankind: the checkered, fateful process of man's adjustment to the outer world." [12]

In practice, Worringer abandons both psychology and history. He makes no use of the findings of scientific psychology of any school, and little if any reference to the political, economic, or other circumstances of historical epochs.

His "psychical categories" turn out, in Spenglerian fashion, to be "timeless racial phenomena" associated with the supposedly unchanging natures of primitive man, of Classical man, of Oriental man, and of Gothic man. We are thus left with race as the ultimate determinant of art in Worringer's system. Teutonic racial stock becomes "the *conditio sine qua non* of the Gothic." [13] Its artistic expression is not limited to Gothic proper of the high Middle Ages "but through the centuries manifests itself continually in ever new disguises" as a "latent Gothic." This "latent Gothic" characterizes all Western European art from the bronze age to the present day.

Such a theory provides no means of explaining the differences which Western European or other art undergoes in its passage through successive phases of its history, but it does call attention to a certain continuing element which, in Worringer's terms, is conceived as the result of racial determinism. The precarious equilibrium of the concept of race is amusingly illustrated by the fact that to the German, Worringer, Teutonic stock is the indispensable racial source of Gothic art, whereas the Frenchman, Viollet-Le-Duc, attributes Gothic achievements to the genius of the Gallo-Roman peoples occupying the basins of the Seine, the Loire, and the Somme.[14]

In summary, our second group of traditions may be said to indicate the personality of the individual artist, the genius of the race to which he belongs, and the historical and environmental conditions which that race is experiencing, as three alternative bases for the motivation of art. Here again the three proposals are in no sense incompatible with each other. An individual artist emerges from some racial stock and the stock to which he belongs undergoes the conditioning circumstances of historical evolution. Each of these levels of life and experience might well be expected to play some part in the motivation of art.

We have now briefly reviewed all six of the traditions in terms of which I have been attempting to analyze our inheritance of critical thought within the field of art. Although these traditions have by no means existed in ideal harmony with each other, we can see from the foregoing discussion that they are capable of ideal interrelationships. They mutually complete, rather than contradict, each other. The traditions of historical and racial determinism emphasize the ultimate sources of collective human experience. The biographical tradition emphasizes the individual artist who emerges from this collective background and becomes an organ of expression for it. The traditions of subject, form, and function emphasize characteristic instrumentalities employed by the artist, or submitted to by him, in fashioning specific works of art. Thus grouped, our six traditions may be conceived as component aspects of an organic totality, providing together our most comprehensive perspective on the interpretation of art. It is no doubt because each contributes knowledge and insight essential to the completeness of the totality that all have survived as living critical traditions.

But if each tradition envisages some aspect of the artistic totality, and if all are capable of organic interconnections, we should also observe that the several traditions differ greatly in their relative inclusiveness. The iconographic, formal, and functional ones, when pursued within the limits of their own disciplines, are relatively narrow, each confining itself to one component aspect of works of art. The biographical tradition provides a beginning of synthesis by bringing all the aspects of the work of an artist into relationship with his creative personality. The racial tradition offers a broader synthesis, for theoretically at least, it can consider all the factors just indicated plus their relationship to the race to which the artist belongs. The historical tradition reaches a maximum synthesis, including all the foregoing factors as seen in relationship to the environment and the historical condition of the race or society involved.

With the foregoing summary in mind, we are now in position to compare the psycho-historical theory with the background of art studies against which it must take its place. Three observations emerge from such a comparison. First, our theory is most nearly identified with the specific tradition which we have called historical determinism. Its direct critical antecedents are to be found in the work of writers like Winckelmann, Viollet-Le-Duc, and Taine. In varying lesser degrees it overlaps with the theories of all thinkers who have stressed connections between art and society: with those of Ruskin and Tolstoy, though it does not involve their ethical emphasis; with those of Coomaraswamy, though it does not involve his metaphysical emphasis.

Second, like its predecessors in the tradition of historical determinism, it involves the maximum range of analytical and interpretive interrelationships. Its concern extends from the specific characteristics of works of art through states of individual and cultural mentality to historical and geographical preconditions. Within this extended range of observation, it includes elements equivalent to all those emphasized by the several other traditions. It therefore provides a medium of synthesis within which these other traditions can be unified with each other or, since they will presumably persist as specializations, can at least be seen in relationship to an encompassing whole. The basis of equivalence between the specialities and our psycho-historical frame of reference may be indicated in another table.

CRITICAL TRADITIONS	PSYCHO-HISTORICAL EQUIVALENTS
Iconographical concern with religious and other subject matter Pure visibility concern with form Materialist concern with material, technique, function	Varied aspects of cultural tension imagery
Biographical emphasis on individual creative personality	Individual artist as immediate formulator of cultural tension imagery
Teleological emphasis on will to art in Riegl's original general sense	Creative potential of a collective psychic state
Racial determinants Historical and environmental determinants	Historical circumstances emerging from the interplay of human groups and their environments

Diagram 12. Correlation of factors emphasized by six critical traditions with equivalent elements of psycho-historical theory.

In their more philosophical moments, when detached from the narrower problems of their specific disciplines, the representatives of the several traditions are usually aware of extensions which connect their field with others in a larger whole. As an example, we may cite the essay in which Erwin Panofsky has summarized his views on the aims and methods of iconography. Beginning with a definition of iconography as "that branch of the history of art which concerns itself with the subject matter or meaning of works of art, as opposed to their form," [15] Dr. Panofsky subdivides the realm of meaning into three strata. First, and largely "pre-iconographical," is the meaning of natural subject matter which can be interpreted in terms of practical experience with everyday objects and events. Second, and constituting the main field for "iconographical analysis in the narrower sense of the word," is the "conventional

subject matter constituting the world of images, stories, and allegories"
which can be interpreted only through a "knowledge of literary sources."
Third, calling for "iconographical interpretation in a deeper sense," is the
world of " 'symbolical' values" "conditioned by personal psychology and 'Welt-
anschauung.' " On this third and deepest level, the interpretation of the meaning of a work of art must envisage the "History of cultural symptoms or
'symbols' in general (insight into the manner in which, under varying historical conditions, essential tendencies of the human mind were expressed by
specific themes and concepts)."

It is evident that on Panofsky's third stratum, where iconography extends
its borders to encompass the "essential tendencies of the human mind" as affected by "varying historical conditions," the iconographer recognizes connections between the subject matter of art and the entire frame of reference
involved in the psycho-historical theory. But this third stratum is more in the
nature of an ideal horizon for iconography than a territory which it has occupied and developed. In practice iconographers have rarely turned to psychologists for any accurate analysis of mental tendencies, and have seldom related
their material to the intricacies of historical circumstance. Their efforts have
largely been confined to "iconographical analysis in the narrower sense of
the word"; in short, to a study of possible connections between artistic subject
matter and literary sources. Hence the need for the correlation of iconography
with other traditions in a more extended frame of reference such as that provided by the psycho-historical theory. In varying degrees, the same can be
said of the other traditions we have been reviewing.

A third relationship between the psycho-historical theory and its background of critical traditions remains to be mentioned. If we synthesize those
traditions in the manner suggested by our last table, we obtain a frame of
reference sufficiently inclusive for a full interpretation of art but in certain
respects not sufficiently intensive. Of the total range from historical backgrounds through psychological states to their artistic manifestations, only the
latter have been exhaustively studied by our critical writers. All that can be
known about the structure, function, and representational significance of objects of art has been, or is being, made available to us by these writers in ample
measure. When they deal with the biographies of artists, that subject also
is likely to be well covered. But their broader allusions to general history and
to psychology rarely if ever possess an equivalent depth.

History, it is true, received serious attention from the more penetrating historical determinists like Winckelmann and Viollet-Le-Duc. In emphasizing the importance of a study of general history for an understanding of art, we are following in their footsteps, but we can do so with the hope of progress in a number of respects. Funds of historical knowledge and gains in historical perspective that were not available in the eighteenth and nineteenth centuries are at our disposition today. The recent interplay between history and other social sciences like anthropology has helped to close the mental gap between conceptions of the dead past and the living present. The increasing diffusion of depth concepts permits us to recognize as historical effects what earlier determinists often mistook for historical causes. Consequently we can pursue the search for causes on a deeper level.

A greater deficiency of our critical heritage as a basis for interpreting art lies in its relation to psychology. Although the spokesmen of more than one critical tradition have acknowledged the importance of this subject, pointing in its direction with such gracious phrases as "the essential tendencies of the human mind" and "the variations that take place in the constitution of the mind and soul of mankind"; and although Worringer has described his findings as a "psychology of style," the fact remains none of our major critical writers has attempted to come to grips with the intricacies of detailed study of psychology and the further intricacies of an attempt to apply the results of that study to an understanding of art.

In view of the limitations — or let us say in view of the need for further development — of our critical heritage with regard to history and to psychology, our final observation concerning the relation of the psycho-historical theory to its critical antecedents carries us back full circle to the general correlational studies with which this volume began. To achieve a frame of reference fully adequate for the interpretation of art, we need not only to synthesize our critical inheritance as such, but also to bring it into more active interplay with the growing volumes of historico-social knowledge and of psychological knowledge. This, as our earlier chapters have emphasized, the psycho-historical theory attempts to do. What we have been saying about critical studies is, so to speak, an enlarged detail of our more general reference to the humanities in Part I. By reintegrating this detail with the discussion of psychological studies and of historical studies that was there advanced, we return to the total psycho-historical concept on which the present volume is based.

II

It would be tempting, perhaps desirable, to extend our discussion of implications to the more remote realms of the philosophy of art and of esthetics. The psycho-historical theory is itself a philosophy of culture and therefore invites comparison with other such philosophies. Since the humanities in general comprise one of its component terms, it must also carry implications with regard both to esthetic experience and to the formulation of esthetic theories. These subjects, however, are so complex, sometimes so remote from artistic actuality, and in part so dependent upon long-range cyclic considerations, that only passing reference to them will be made at the present time.

Without attempting any extensive comparison of the various efforts that have been made to arrive at a philosophy of the arts, we may note that one of the systems most recently proposed by a philosopher seems to be essentially in harmony with our own. This is the system presented by Suzanne Langer in her books, *Philosophy in a New Key* and *Feeling and Form: a Theory of Art*. In emphasizing the importance of "symbolic transformation," in defining art as "the creation of forms symbolic of human feelings," [16] Dr. Langer worked her way from philosophic sources to a position which we in turn have reached on the basis of quite different sources.

What our sources can perhaps assist us in contributing is a greater integration of the concept of symbolic transformation with the actualities of cultural life. It is not clear to the present writer that *Feeling and Form* offers very concrete indication as to *what*, beyond the vague concept of "feeling," is being transformed or *by what process* it is being transformed. And the results of the transformation appear to be rather distantly viewed as types, without detailed study of any art as found in any specific cultural epoch or of the historical developments undergone by any art during a considerable span of its cultural evolution.

The psycho-historical point of view, while following the same general line of thought with regard to the principle of symbolic transformation, attempts to graft that principle as fully as possible with actuality at each of the three main levels in our conception of it. In our view it is, in the last analysis, the social pressures of history that are being transformed, they being the ultimate determinants of human feeling at any given time and place. It is the obscure working of the tension-imagery process within the psyche by which the transformation is affected. And it is in the arts, philosophy, and religion, ob-

served in the organic order of their historic unfolding, that the results of the
transformation appear to us. Hence a continuing and deepening study of the
subject cannot remain within the scope of the principle, but must pursue the
intensive studies at the foundation level of depth history, at the transforma-
tional level of depth psychology, and at the manifest level of the history and
criticism of the varied forms of cultural expression.

Turning now to cast a glance in the direction of esthetics, we should
give the estheticians credit for one accomplishment that has been lacking in
most of the disciplines previously considered: that is a serious study of psychology as a means of increasing our understanding of the arts. The progress
recently made in this direction can probably best be followed by referring
to the files of the *Journal of Aesthetics and Art Criticism*.[17] But if the estheti-
cian has frequently been strong with respect to psychology, he has not infrequently been weak with respect to artistic and historical actuality. His
studies, like those in the philosophy of art, have usually been conducted on a
plane of such generality that works of art are seen as conceptual types rather
than as concrete specimens related to each other in sequences of historical
change. Esthetics would gain much if it could achieve an integration with
the history of the arts comparable to its present close relations with psychology.

With regard to specific esthetic points of view, it is obvious that the
psycho-historical theory aligns itself with relativistic rather than with absolute conceptions of the subject. Neither esthetic experience nor the intellectual
analysis of it can be exceptions to principles which, in our view, affect culture
as a whole. They must therefore be conditioned by, and subject to change with,
the changing interrelationships between mediums of expression, collective
psychic states, and historical circumstances. Their orientation will shift from
period to period as part of the same drift of cultural symbolism that modifies
the forms of art.

Within the mobile of conditioning relationships, there will be a number
of inner systems: the powerful dynamism of the passing period, the slow movement of cultural tradition through the whole cycle of a given civilization, and
the general range of responses that operates — or can be assumed to operate —
for humanity as a whole. This last relativism to human constitution would
seem to be the nearest we can come to any absolute determination of beauty,
but it would also seem to be the least effective in determining the artist's ideals
for, or the observer's reactions to, specific forms of art or specific aspects of
nature.

In fact we might go so far as to assert that the permanence of the human constitution, if assumed to imply a corresponding permanence of esthetic reactions, involves an illusion. We might call it the "illusion of esthetic fixity" and compare it to the illusion of cosmic fixity which makes us feel that the earth is standing still, when in fact it is spinning on its axis and rotating around a sun that is itself in motion — all at terrific velocities.

The illusion of esthetic fixity results from a failure to discriminate between our biological potentials and their actualization through culture. If, because all men have eyes, we are led to the assumption that therefore they see alike, we are forgetting the indications of the social sciences that what they see is largely a result of their socialization. To an anatomist the eyes of our grandfathers and of ourselves would be of the same type, but most of our grandfathers could not "see" the beauty in the paintings of Cézanne and most of us can see it. The difference of seeing is cultural, not constitutional. Correspondingly, every change of cultural context will produce some equivalent change of perception and of esthetic response.

The conception of esthetic experience as a focus of changing relationships involves implications for all the aspects of the subject. Some of these implications can be suggested by a brief reference to "esthetic types" — the beautiful, the sublime, the humorous, the grotesque, and others. Traditional studies of these types are largely confined to what we may call the "descriptive" level: that is to say their main concern is to describe the characteristics of each type as observable in certain examples from nature and from art.[18] Accepting the description as accurate, psycho-historical thinking identifies it with the manifest cultural surface and, here as elsewhere, calls for a study of the motivating depths.

If we search the classic discussions of the esthetic types for motivations, only one is likely to appear. That consists in the perceptions, responses, and impulses of the individual artist or observer. Thus in contrasting different effects produced by different artists in treating the theme of the Laocoön, Louis Flaccus asks why "tragedy and pathos are so arrestingly present" in some of the examples and yet "are all but absent in El Greco's painting. If Michelangelo had painted the picture they would have been there. The reason must lie in personal preferences and attitudes." [19]

The esthetic types are in fact identified by Flaccus with "a personal bent . . . Sublimity marks the genius of Aeschylus; Sappho, Catullus, and Keats are voices of beauty; Whitman's poetry naturally falls within the characteristic; Tennyson is idyllic; and Byron is picturesque. There is sensuous beauty in Titian, tragedy in Michelangelo, grace in Praxiteles, pathos in Scopas, rough strength in Van Gogh, idyllic charm in Watteau, decorative appeal in Botticelli and in Gauguin." [20]

Our whole frame of reference would indicate that while the personal bent of the artist or observer will play a part in any esthetic situation it will, so to speak, float upon the double current of a cultural context which is in historical motion. Our earlier study of the grotesque can here be recalled as an indication that this esthetic type owed its vitality in Gothic times to forces which, far from stopping with individual aptitude, involved the whole destiny of Gothic society. Our study also indicated that the grotesque, which may appear static as a descriptive type, was in constant change from the largely terrible to the largely humorous when it was observed as a cultural actuality.

If we extend our study of the types in evolutionary directions, integrating the description of them with their history as an aspect of the history of the arts, a further relation appears. The various types do not all occur miscellaneously with equal force at the same time, and they do not occur in haphazard order. The historical relationship between the sublime in Masaccio and the beautiful in Raphael appears to be the same as that between the sublime in Phidias and the beautiful in Praxiteles. In other words, the emergence of esthetic dispositions and their maximum expressions in art, as well as their maximum effulgence upon nature, appears to be controlled by historical laws. There is in every historical situation a high potential for certain types, a low potential for others, and the changing sequence of potentials apparently follows an equivalent cyclic pattern in different civilizations.

To summarize the general attitude toward esthetic problems that would accord with psycho-historical thinking, we might say that this attitude would not only be relativistic, but would also be dynamic, socially conscious, and historically conscious. It would be dynamic in relating all esthetic considerations to motivating forces that must be explored within the realm of cultural dynamics. It would be socially conscious in conceiving individual motivations as emergent from collective ones. It would be historically conscious in recognizing that collective motivations follow evolutionary courses and that therefore esthetic sensitivities, like works of art, present problems of historical order.

III

In concluding the attempt of the last two chapters to review the present state of studies in the history and criticism of art, and in the philosophy of art and esthetics, one is tempted to make a comparison which would have been appropriate at a number of points along the way. It is a comparison that has a bearing upon our conception of cultural orbits and was in fact implied by an earlier allusion to planetary orbits; a comparison that bears also upon the relation of short-range to long-range studies in the history of art, and upon the relation of the factual data of art history to the theoretical constructions of the philosophy of art and of esthetics. It is the comparison that can be drawn between our recent studies in the arts and the condition of astronomy at the end of the sixteenth century. To make clear the interest of this comparison, let us recall the situation that had developed in the astronomical studies of that time.

Earlier developments culminating in the assiduous observations of Tycho Brahe on the changing positions of the planets, had resulted in the accumulation of larger and larger funds of astronomical data. Most of these data, however, had not as yet been integrated and illuminated by the discovery of the general laws of which they were particular outcomes.

Meanwhile, in Kepler, the age had produced an astronomer gifted with unusual powers of generalization but one who was not himself an exhaustive observer. Much of Kepler's earlier effort was wasted in developing hypothetical systems that were inadequate because not based on sufficiently detailed data. Some of these systems were published in the *Prodromus of Cosmographical Dissertations* (1596). When Kepler asked his older colleagues, Galileo and Brahe, for an opinion of this volume, "The former praised the ingenuity and good faith which it displayed; and Tycho, though he requested him to try to adapt something of the same nature to the Tychonic system, saw the speculative character of his mind, and advised him 'to lay a solid foundation for his views by actual observation, and then, by ascending from these, to strive to reach the cause of things.' " [21]

The highest results of the whole scientific development could, in fact, only be achieved if speculative genius was brought to bear upon a large accumulation of accurate data. Kepler eventually realized this and thenceforth burned with eagerness to gain possession of Brahe's observations and to use them as a basis for higher calculations of a general order. This fruitful union of opposites became possible in 1601 when, as assistant to Brahe, Kepler was given access to the latter's observations on the movements of Mars. With these observations to guide and correct his speculations, Kepler was eventually able to work out his epoch-making laws of planetary motion. Fact and concept merged as two aspects of a single statement of observed reality. "The great performance in the sky" became more wonderful, not less so, because man had found the key to "the artful structure of the movements," and was able to recognize organized relations behind what had previously appeared as unrelated facts or discrepancies.

In our field of the study of the arts, we seem to have reached a stage of development much like that which prevailed in astronomy before Kepler's culminating discoveries. The vast funds of detail accumulated by our art historians, like Brahe's observations, are still largely on a factual plane, but their extent and variety suggest that it should be possible to achieve broader generalizations on the basis of them.

Generalizing effort is not lacking on the part of our philosophers and estheticians, but all too often it suffers from the same limitation as Kepler's early efforts: the dominance of conceptual or speculative principles over observation. One feels that the theorist in these fields might well heed Brahe's advice "to lay a solid foundation for his views by actual observation" before attempting to formulate general principles.

But with such a wealth of accurate historical observation available to us, and with a large amount of speculative talent being exercised, it seems that if the latter could be brought squarely into line with the former, the time should be ripe for discoveries of a higher order. Perhaps we could reach the position in which speculation and fact would coalesce with each other to emerge as demonstrable laws. Who knows, for instance, but that long-range historical studies pursued into the realm of cultural orbits may not one day culminate in the discovery of laws of cultural motion more momentous in their bearing on human life than are the laws of planetary motion?

Chapter X V I I I

THE VOCATION OF THE ARTIST

The personality and creative activity of the artist have been a subject for discussion in Western culture ever since the Renaissance. Within our own time, psychoanalysis has reopened this subject on an extensive scale, bringing into the account a newly acquired preoccupation with unconscious impulse, infantile conditioning, sublimation, and similar matters. The psycho-historical theory in its turn implies a distinctive approach to the question of creative personality; an approach overlapping with that of psychoanalysis, but also differing from it in a number of respects.

According to our central conception, art is a symbolical projection of collective psychic tensions. It follows that the basic task of the artist — or speaking subjectively, the basic impulse of the artist — is first to apprehend the tensional condition of the world in which he lives and, second, to find the means by which that condition can be revealed. Within the organism of a culture, the artist functions as a kind of preconsciousness, providing a zone of infiltration through which the obscure stirrings of collective intuition can emerge into collective consciousness. The artist is the personal transformer within whose sensitivity a collective psychic charge, latent in society, condenses into a cultural image. He is in short the dreamer, at least the immediate dreamer, of the collective dream.

To be accurate, we should say, of course, that the artist is *one* of the dreamers of the collective dream. His activity in this respect is shared by cultural agents of many other kinds. Individual dispositions and circumstances make one man outstandingly sensitive to visual impressions and materials, another to those of musical tone, another to those of language. Still others are conditioned to sensitivity in philosophical thought or religious experience. Each is a specialized channel within a broad composite channel. Each may participate in the activity of cultural transformation according to his own sensitivity. But all are dependent for their creative motivation upon a common reservoir of collective tensional energy with the result, historically familiar to us, that their varied products, at any given time and place, are permeated by a common character.

In "divergent" periods like our own, this common character may not be apparent to surface observation, for the manifestations of such periods oppose each other in all manner of isms and counter-isms. But if these isms are subjected to analysis they are found to have lower common denominators in terms of which they merge as divers expressions of common tensional depths. Indeed what we may call their "ismatic" character is in itself a general nature which they share in common.

From the artist's basic vocation as the formulator of cultural tension imagery, and from the varied historical conditions under which it is called upon to operate, we can derive all our other observations concerning the present subject. One of them is our own particular conception of artistic ability and, with regard to the highest levels of such ability, our own particular definition of genius.

Current popular thought judges artistic ability in terms of two supposed requisites: skill in representing nature and proficiency in handling technical processes. Critical perspective soon convinces us that both these considerations are secondary. Historically, as we have seen, there are periods during which the artist is impelled to reproduce nature ever more faithfully, others during which he is impelled to disregard nature ever more completely. Whether he does the one or the other is not a question of ability but of creative intention as motivated by psycho-historical forces. Basically, therefore, skill in representation cannot be taken as a criterion of artistic talent. It becomes a temporary accessory to such talent only when called for by more fundamental directives.

Technical skill is a more constant ingredient of creative activity. Without a considerable measure of it no artist can adequately embody his conceptions. Criticism has long recognized, however, that technical skill, in and of itself, is one of the least fundamental constituents of artistic genius. Even in the field of musical performance, where such skill finds one of its maximal uses, discerning listeners recognize the virtuosity of mere "finger twiddlers" as a shallow form of musical expression. More important is depth of interpretive insight which can comprehend and reveal the essentials of the composition being played.

In such arts as painting and sculpture, where the artist combines the twin functions of composer and performer, skill as such ranks even less high among the constituents of genius than is the case with musicians. One of the recent confirmations of this statement may be found in the high value ascribed by our culture to the work of the so-called "modern primitives." Most of these artists have had no technical training in art. The more significant of them do possess innate visual sensitivity and have developed a technique of their own suited to express their individual vision, but their deep and widespread appeal lies elsewhere than in technical dexterity and can even make itself felt despite technical crudity. Indeed there are types of art, of which theirs is sometimes one, in which technical crudity becomes an intrinsic and necessary aspect of the governing creative conception. We might say, then, that although under most circumstances technical skill does contribute to the proficiency of an artist, it is not always called for and can never, of itself, make an artist significant.

If reproductive and technical skill are thus secondary considerations — and no doubt there are others equally secondary which we shall not attempt to enumerate — what provides the basic test of artistic ability? What constant unites the significant artists of all types and periods: the realistic Leonardo with the abstract Picasso, the technically brilliant Rubens with the technically elementary painter of Romanesque murals? What, in short, is the quality the lack of which causes a painter inevitably to fall short of greatness, and the possession of which in the highest degree raises him to genius?

Obviously from our point of view it is the double faculty of responding to collective tensions and of translating them into visual form. The greatest painters of any age are those with the deepest apprehension of the gathering psychic atmosphere of their time and the highest imaginative capacity to condense that atmosphere into visual form. Genius, for us, is outstanding ability to translate collective mentality into cultural imagery.

The seeming narrowness of the last statement causes one to hesitate. Instead of saying genius *is* the outstanding ability to translate collective tensions into cultural imagery, it would be more circumspect to say that genius must *include* such ability. Undoubtedly there are other necessary components such as outstanding visual or aural sensitivity, superior perceptiveness of relationships, a unique ability to organize them, and the "staying power" required for sustained creative effort. Genius, the highest manifestation of life, like life itself is too complex to be reduced to any single element. Nevertheless it still appears that a supernormal sensitivity to collective tensions is the key and core of genius. Given that, a way will open: all else will automatically unfold under the fertilizing and intoxicating stimulus of the collective emanations, or can be added through the personal effort of the individual. Failing that, the highest talents in other respects and the most heroic personal efforts would seem to fail of enduring greatness.

"Fill your mind with the ideas of your century," said Goethe to the young poets of his time, "and the work will come." That is the essential creative principle of psycho-historical thought, except that it is stated rationally and therefore, if taken literally, would be superficial. An artist can fill his mind with ideas, if by them we mean intellectual concepts, and still produce only artificial formulations — 'machines' as the French sometimes call them. What the creative artist needs is intuitive access to the accumulating pool of collective feeling which as yet has not been channeled, or has been only partly channeled, into either intellectual or artistic conceptions. Having that, what he further needs is a creative alchemy capable of transforming the intangible essence of the feeling into the tangible form of the cultural image. His task is not so much to reflect the ideas of his century as to help find and formulate them; not so much to fill his mind with the ideas of his time as to help fill his time with the ideas implicit in its cultural destiny. His work when achieved *is* among the great ideas of his century.

Creative activity thus conceived extends the energies of the artist in two directions: one inward, the other outward. Inwardly he must in some sense be a mystic, seeking to establish communication with the obscure depths of the conscious and unconscious psyche; groping his way, as it were, through the dark waters under the firmament, sinking his consciousness into the collective unconsciousness in order that the accumulating collective charges may reach him and use him as a conductor. Like Dante, he must have experiences which will enable him to give a firsthand account of heaven and hell; that is, of the negative and positive reaches of psychic reality during his epoch. Otherwise his work cannot participate in the destiny of his epoch.

When the artist has something to report from the nether world — when he has received from the depths a creative conception, or at least feels the stirring of a creative impulse or intuition — then he must reverse his orientation and, so to speak, return to earth. There, using tools and materials, he must seek to embody his conception in objective form. He must show us what he has found in the world below and above rational consciousness. For this purpose he must possess or develop whatever technical skill is necessary, and master any other aspects of experience, such as the observation of nature, which may be called for by the particular psychic directive impelling his effort. Only in relation to the demands of that directive can these secondary requirements be determined by the artist or evaluated by the observer.

Going one step further in the same line of thought, we might add our particular definition of artistic inspiration. Inspiration for us is primarily the reception of a collective psychic charge. In the moment of inspiration the artist is functioning as conductor. The collective force is entering and animating his creative system, stimulating his imagination to symbolic vision and energizing his impulse to give the vision objective embodiment. Loss of inspiration would be the expenditure of this energy before the embodiment is complete, attended by loss of contact with the psychic source from which further charges could be obtained.

It is true that the artist will often feel his inspiration as coming from an external stimulus rather than from within. A face, a landscape, or other object may be the source of the impression which affects him as an inspiration. This is simply stating the case without reference to the unconscious. The manifest imagery of a dream may be inspired by day residues of objective origin, but the selection and psychic animation of certain residues rather than others is the work of unconscious motives and impulses. Similarly, the circumstance that a particular face or landscape inspires an artist may be understood as due, not to its own nature as such, but to the fact that by means of it unconscious energy, previously unsuccessful in finding its symbolic equivalent, has now done so. The inspiration consists in the release of the accumulated psychic impulse through the establishment of an appropriate connection between its subjective source and an objective outlet.

It goes without saying that in emphasizing collective tensions as the source of creative energy and inspiration, we have been thinking of the more comprehensive aspects of artistic activity. Individual rather than collective consciousness can, of course, be the immediate source of creative motivation, as suggested in our earlier discussion of the tensional range from personal through group to master tensions. The creative process of tension-imagery formation, with its searching of inward depths and its construction of outward forms, is the same anywhere along the tensional scale. But the more exclusively personal the artist's motivation, the more minor will be his production. Major artists *are* such, precisely because responsiveness to collective motivation charges their creative activity with the full force of the master tensions of their epoch.

This view of the relation between individual genius and collective inspiration carries with it a particular conception of originality. The latter cannot be, as it is often thought to be and as it may actually seem to be when experienced, a purely personal capacity for invention. Neither can it be measured primarily in the degrees of difference that distinguish the work of one artist from that of another within any group of contemporaries. The collective tensions motivating creative activity are essentially the same for all the artists of a given culture and they are determined by historical forces, not by the personalities of individuals. The kinds of art which the given tensional dynamism can generate are, in their general but fundamental nature, predetermined before the artist creates them.

If, then, the essence of originality consists neither in being unexpected, historically speaking, nor in being individually distinctive, in what does it consist? For us primarily in a great and, in point of time, advanced sensitivity to cultural determinants. An artist is original insofar as his responsiveness and imagination enable him to assist in formulating the symbols demanded by his culture. To put it another way, he is original insofar as he becomes a personal exponent of an emergent social necessity. Giotto, Leonardo, Picasso displayed their originality, not in changing the essential directions of cultural evolution, and not in the individual aspects of their respective styles, but in manifesting sooner and more completely the artistic implications of the psycho-historical situations in which they lived.

It will be observed that originality, thus conceived, liberates creative spirits from personal competition with each other and unites them in a common creative quest. On the market, perhaps, they may be competitors; in the epoch, they are fellow seekers after cultural reality. Giorgioni and Titian are both highly original in our sense though at times the work of one is barely distinguishable from that of the other. The same can be said of Braque, Picasso, Gris, and related artists of the early twentieth century. The basic measure of originality, in either of these historical instances, is not the degree to which the work of one artist differs from that of the others, but the degree to which it resembles that of the others. Through their similarities these artists reveal their age; through their differences they reveal only themselves. Both these aspects of their work are important, but culturally speaking the former is more important.

Thus originality tends to unite one with one's more sensitive contemporaries, and separates one only from one's predecessors — that is to say from the exponents of cultural situations that no longer exist. Pseudo-originality has the opposite effect. It emphasized contemporary oppositions and historical similarities. Ingres and Delacroix magnified the conflict between Classicism and Romanticism, a conflict which in the perspective of history seems minor and which tended to subordinate Ingres to Poussin and Raphael, Delacroix to precursors like Rubens and the Venetians. Braque and Picasso sought common ends and helped to inaugurate an epoch.

The conception of originality set forth above may perhaps throw some light upon one of the puzzling problems of criticism: the problem of evaluating the work of the so-called "followers" of any movement in relation to that of its "leaders." The followers, to practice their art with conviction, must naturally regard themselves as creative and original artists in their own right. The leaders, it appears, may be prone to regard the followers as insignificant imitators. Picasso has been quoted as expressing disdain for those whom he considered his imitators by referring to them as "the lice that feed on my head." The critic, for his part, may well be at a loss to decide whether the widening host of exponents of the given movement — whether it be Renaissance realism or twentieth-century abstraction — must be discounted as mere imitators of the few great pioneers, or whether their activity in its turn is vital to the significance of the movement as a whole.

Mere imitators there will always be, but the personnel of a movement, psycho-historically considered, is by no means so simple as to be divisible into the two categories of innovators and imitators. There can be a creative as well as an imitative following and the former, it would seem, is essential to the very existence of the movement as such. A leader does not constitute a movement; indeed without a creative following he is not a leader. Those who deviate from the channels of cultural destiny into byways where they remain alone are eccentrics, not cultural pioneers. The rise of the creative following is the indispensable confirmation that an experiment has cultural validity and that the experimenter can be recognized as a cultural leader. Without confirming movements like that of recent abstraction, Picasso would be a freak and not a genius. Even the basic originality of the leader, that is to say his responsiveness to the determinants of his age, can be recognized only when the movement supplies evidence that such are indeed the determinants of the age.

The difference between the imitative followers and the creative participants in a movement is that the first group will emulate the leaders while the second, perhaps receiving the clue from the leaders, will succeed in establishing personal contact with the underlying tensional reservoir from which the leaders received their motivation. The imitator will be such, not because of inability to be dif-

ferent, but because of inability to be the same; that is to say inability to respond
at first hand to the prevailing psycho-cultural directives. And the creative participant, responding to those directives, will inevitably and rightly do things
which are in some measure similar to the work of the leaders because they are
motivated by the same directives.

The point of fundamental importance for the creative artist, it would seem,
is not whether his work is like or unlike that of some one else, but whether it
is true to himself. If it represents the most complete expression of the creative
intuitions available to his own sensitivity as conditioned by the cultural atmosphere in which he lives, it will be the right work for him. Its historical importance, like that of any other work, will depend upon the relative priority and
the relative intensity of its transmutation of the culture-wide creative potentials.

And since the animating cultural dynamism is a vast ocean of psychic force,
the possible transmutations of it can be exhausted neither by its first nor even
by its greatest expressions. They will offer reserves of creative stimulus which
large numbers of individuals can conduct into art according to their personal
temperaments and capacities and according to their local, national, or racial conditionings. The complex of psycho-historical energy that we call the Renaissance no doubt received its highest pictorial embodiment in the work of a
score of Italian painters, but there were hundreds of other Italian artists who
caught some measure of its vibration, and there was destined to be a French, a
German, an English, and many another regional Renaissance. For each of the
thousands of artists involved there was some coöperative part in formulating
the cultural epoch. For each of the communities involved there was the evolutionary experience of passing from one stage of its existence to another and of
giving expression to the new stage in a new artistic vision. For history there is
the total panorama which, if it owes its highlights to the leaders of the age,
derives its breadth and convincing reality from its range as a cultural
phenomenon.

The aspects of creative experience discussed above form the constants of the
artist's vocation, operating at all times and places. They are not, however, the
only factors involved in setting the problems and moulding the professional
personality of the individual artist. Interplaying with them in specific cases
are the variables of cultural evolution. These variables change from period to
period, now integrating the artist with his community, now rendering him a
bohemian outcast; now encouraging his creative intuitions, now subjecting
them to the ordeal of rejection and consequently testing the artist's creative

integrity. Since the variables involve evolutionary and therefore cyclic consider-ations, we shall not attempt a detailed analysis of them at the present time.

II

What, so far as we can define it, is the exact relationship between the indi-viduality of the artist and his cultural milieu? This question, emergent a num-ber of times in our earlier discussions, deserves more careful attention than we have yet given it.

As we have many times stressed, cultural conditioning superimposes itself upon the narrower conditionings of parentage and family in the formation of the artist's personality. For analytical purposes, the one must receive as full consideration as the other. The creative dynamics of an artist's life are to be understood as emanating not from personal complexes alone, nor even from personal and cultural impulses in isolation from each other, but from their coexistence and from the tensional interplay between them. What seems likely as the key to their interrelationship is that while culture determines the tasks to which the artists of any generation are destined to devote their energies, individual conditioning will play a part in determining which individuals are best suited to accomplish those tasks. Private and cultural impulse can rein-force each other, gaining combined power, or they can oppose and neutralize each other.

In discussing Leonardo da Vinci, we noted that Freud had found evidence of a mother fixation in this artist's life and in his work. Such a fixation, like any other personal attribute, would facilitate some artistic undertakings and impede others. It would synchronize with the style-and-subject trends of some periods and meet with resistance from those of other periods. The High Renais-sance stage of Christian culture, when the humanized madonna was emergent as a focal symbol of the age, was perhaps the most favorable moment in our entire cultural history for the artistic expression of the personalized image of the tender and loving mother. At such a moment the repressed energies of a mother fixation could respond, as it were, to the call of cultural duty, like prisoners amnestied to join a line of battle. In this respect and also with regard to the uninhibited growth of his investigation impulse, Leonardo benefited by a fortunate coalescence of his personal with his cultural destiny. Personal dy-namics helped him to accomplish certain aspects of his cultural mission, while collective approval of the mission must have helped to relieve and to justify otherwise frustrating personal complexes. We have noted, however, that in some other respects Leonardo's personal conditioning hampered his cultural effectiveness as an artist.

An instance from later times is brought to our attention in a stimulating essay on Henry Moore by Frederick Wight.[1] It is impossible to do justice to this engaging study by a passing reference, but we can partially summarize its import as follows. Moore's father was a miner. His imprisonment during working hours in the depths of the earth facilitated the desire of the infant sculptor for possession of the mother; the cavernous mine in turn became unconsciously identified with the grave as a means of permanently removing the competitive father. Childhood conditioning of this nature has subsequently motivated Moore to avoid the representation of the male figure, to specialize in the image of the mother and child and a related reclining female figure, to penetrate his figures with cavernous voids, and through such evisceration to reflect a preoccupation with death and to lift his sculptural forms into symbols of eternity.

Here again, in our view, personal energies may well have worked as Wight indicates. But, extending the sphere of the inquiry, we should then add that if negative volumes are important aspects of many forms of modern art, this is not because a personally inspired impulse has gained a cultural following, but rather the reverse. Picasso, whose father was a painter, preceded Moore in preoccupation with sculpturesque voids, as may be seen in some of his early "bone" paintings. Neither case would be of great significance unless psycho-historical forces were attuning men's sensitivities to symbols of a perishing cultural order and of the imperishable foundations of new orders to come. Moore's personal background may have helped to make him a man of the hour in sculpture, but it has not made the hour. The hour, giving value and currency to the personal background, has been made by such forces and events as the culturally disruptive impact of the Industrial Revolution, social conflicts within society, and death struggles between societies. The personal fantasy of the father in the mine could become artistically potent because it sychronized with such collective realities as London in the bomb shelter.

The psycho-historical conception of the relations of the individual artist to society, as those relations affect creative activity, may be summarized in the following general terms. The individual artist, like any other individual, is a member of an embracing socio-cultural organism that transcends and conditions him in a double way. As compared to the span of his individual life, it possesses a relative immortality extending through centuries and perhaps millenniums. Its historical development during this long suprapersonal life span is accompanied by long-range cultural developments. Each individual artist, born into some particular phase of such a cultural development, receives its accumulated skills and processes, its heritage of earlier forms of art, and other aspects of its traditions as a first conditioning mold to his own development.

Second the artist is affected, not only by the evolutionary current pressing upon him from the past of his society, but also by the vast suprapersonal complexities of its present. He is one among thousands of other artists, writers, philosophers, and scientists whose varied efforts react upon each other. And all such cultural workers in turn comprise only a handful of specialists within the vast mass of millions of other human beings; millions from whom the specialists have emerged biologically, and to whom they are bound by ties of common humanity, by common cultural aspirations and potentials, by a common dependence upon the economic and social structure of their society and therefore, in the last analysis, by a common social fate.

The total cultural situation in which an artist thus finds himself is hardly less intricate than the stellar universe. At every moment its millions of living components throb and interweave while, from moment to moment, the whole vast system moves through its orbit of historical change. That any individual could personally create such a cultural universe-in-motion is unthinkable. That he could even deflect it in any appreciable degree from its socially determined course comes to seem improbable, if not impossible, after one has considered the facts involved. The main influence is inevitably the other way around. By the concentration of its powerful gravities and magnetisms upon the individual, culture transforms the "human animal" into an individuality capable of creative activity — that is to say, activity which will continue, reflect, and further enrich the culture.

Once an individual has acquired a creative formation from his cultural environment, what he can then do is to function in relation to that environment as an instrument of selection, detection, and creative expression. From the heritage of his cultural tradition, which may include the imported products and influences of other traditions, he can select the elements that seem to him to possess continuing, or perhaps newly emergent, validity. From the pulsation of collective life in his own historical moment he can absorb current tensional energies, receiving creative direction from their magnetic force and inspiration from their inexhaustible power. And by his own creative effort he can seek to weld inherited elements, original tension imagery, or some fusion of the two, into expressions of existing reality — "reality" being perceptible to him only through his culture and therefore being, in the last analysis, cultural reality.

Thus, culture establishes the potentials of any given creative situation, sets the primary tasks, and indicates the general course of development. The individual brings greater or lesser sensitivity to a grasp of the potentials, greater or lesser ability to accomplish the tasks, greater or lesser power of advancing along the course. Mediocre practitioners trail behind in all these respects; able ones keep abreast. We honor as geniuses those who, by their high individual capacities, are able to grasp the potentials profoundly, to accomplish the tasks superbly, and to accelerate the movement by anticipating its emergent trends.

The interaction between cultural demands and personal capacities will be influenced by childhood conditioning and all other aspects of the individual's private life, but these private factors are to be thought of, not as the root of creative ability, but as complications which may affect it. Personal conditioning will contribute to major work only insofar as it coincides with, and reinforces, cultural demands.

The cultural demands, though they emanate from external or social sources, are not to be thought of as entirely external to the artist's individuality. Since mature individuality is itself largely a cultural product, cultural awareness tends with growth to become an integral phase of personality and thenceforth to operate as a force within, and a capacity of, the individual. To put this in another way, the human individuality, which we are likely to regard as an indivisible unit, is actually a compound of two individualities: a cultural one and a private one. The cultural individuality develops through the socializing action of the enveloping cultural environment. The private one, though not detachable from cultural influences, remains more largely centered in the biological sphere of birth, sustenance, mating, and death. In the creative achievement of an artist, the stature of his cultural individuality counts for far more than that of his private individuality and may sometimes set the latter in strange disproportion. Indeed to judge from the biographies of some, though not all, of our great artists, the dwarfing of private individuality by the imperative demands and monumental growth of cultural individuality, is a not-infrequent complication of genius.

So far as concerns critical principles, we can only repeat the conclusion already reached in Part I: that studies in artistic individuality must be regarded, not as complete in themselves, but as contributions to more complex analyses of the relations between individuality and the forces of cultural dynamics. And so far as concerns the dignity and freedom of life, there should be no cause for alarm in our admission of the preponderance of cultural factors over private ones. Without a culture to confer them, dignity and freedom can hardly exist. Men acquire dignity in proportion to their power of fulfilling social needs; they achieve freedom in the degree to which they coördinate personal impulse with social opportunity.

The mythical inclinations of the ego may be deflated by a recognition of the true relations between the individual and society, but the realities of individual stature and personal accomplishment suffer no loss. Genius will be as rare and precious a phenomenon however we are led to explain it. It will, in Lionello Venturi's words, continue to "open the eyes of the world, so that men realize that they were blind before then." If we conceive it psycho-historically, we shall only be recognizing that what men are blind to, above all else, is themselves and that the revelations of genius exert their magical power — and sometimes meet with stubborn resistance — precisely because they confront society with its own emergent image.

ART AND SOCIETY: CONTEM-
PORARY CULTURAL CONFLICTS

In Western experience for at least a century and a half, the relations
between art and society have been a source of constant conflict. The general
public, that is to say practically the entire community, has looked and still looks
with bewilderment upon the productions of its own more advanced artists. The
man in the street was at a loss to understand Blake's mysticism, Monet's impressionism, and Cézanne's post-impressionism. He is at a similar loss today. Abstract art appears to him distorted or denatured, surrealist art nonsensical. And
the general attitude represented by the man in the street, we do well to remember, is not the exception to a social norm established by advanced artists and
critics, but the social norm to which advanced artists and critics are
exceptions.

At some time during the course of our development, even the most sympathetic of us have presumably undergone the negative reactions to new art that
characterize our culture. The author can well remember passing through such
experiences himself. They are frustrating, dismaying, experiences, in which
we look for beauty and find ugliness; in which we look for pleasure and find
pain. Thrown off our balance, we spontaneously seek to maintain our self-
esteem by charging the artists with crudity, incompetence, and charlatanism.

Feeling thus within ourselves, we are grateful that critics are not lacking to
confirm us in these indignant opinions. The records abound in critical attacks
on creative innovators. We need cite but one example: Ruskin's scathing denunciation of some works exhibited by Whistler (Fig. 95). "For Mr. Whistler's
own sake," wrote Ruskin in his monthly pronouncement, *Fors Clavigera*, "no
less than for the protection of the purchaser, Sir Coutts Lindsay ought not to
have admitted works into the gallery in which the ill-educated conceit of the

artist so nearly approached the aspect of wilful imposture. I have seen and heard much cockney impudence before now, but never expected to hear a coxcomb ask two hundred guineas for flinging a pot of paint in the public's face." [1] That Ruskin was in many respects one of our greatest critics, that Whistler today soothes rather than offends most observers, indicates in rational perspective how violent and irrational our immediate negative responses to new art can be.

It is not the least sign of our cultural confusion that innovators who have had to resist public misunderstanding in their own field, have sometimes joined the public in attacking their creative contemporaries in other fields. A good designer, Robsjohn-Gibbings, who defended twentieth-century furniture in his book *Goodbye, Mr. Chippendale*, wrote another book, *Mona Lisa's Moustache*, to denounce twentieth-century painting. And one of the greatest of the twentieth-century architects, Frank Lloyd Wright, joined Mr. Robsjohn-Gibbings in depreciating modern art and approvingly distributed copies of *Mona Lisa's Moustache* to some of his artist friends.

Official agencies early added their authority to the cultural defense reaction of the community. Usually they did so, like the French *Salon* and the equivalent academies in other countries, by the indirect method of excluding experimental work from their exhibitions. Museums long followed a parallel course, building their collections of old masters purchased at high cost and ignoring new masters available to them at low cost. Sometimes — here Nazi Germany provided the most pronounced example to date — official disapproval went beyond polite rejection to open repression. The official cultural program of the National Socialists branded experimental art as "degenerate," barred it from public display, and condemned its exponents to the renunciation of their creative faith and integrity or, keeping faith and integrity, to such extremes as underground creative practice, suicide, or exile. Plate 36 (Figs. 98, 99, 100) reproduces three paintings by three of the well-known artists then working in Germany whose work was typical of the many distinguished modern paintings which were repudiated by the Nazis and suffered such indignities at their hands; examples which, in these three cases, have since happily found their way into Amercian public-museum collections.

A few individuals and agencies in each generation have taken up the cause of creative expression and have sought to withstand the tide of what we may call counter-expression. Probably most effective of these have been the organizations that circumvented the will to repress experimental art by keeping such art on public or semi-public view. Programs of this kind sometimes resulted from the coöperative effort of rejected artists, as in the case of the *Salon des Refusés* in Paris and the Armory Show of 1913 in New York; sometimes from pioneering convictions on the part of dealers like Vollard in Paris, and sometimes from regularly established institutions. Among the latter, the Museum of Modern Art in New York has held a notable place during the past two decades. Most of the general art museums are now aiding the cause, with varying degrees of alacrity or reluctance, by giving a portion of their permanent or temporary exhibition space to contemporary developments.

Meanwhile a certain number of favorably disposed critics have sought to increase public understanding of the artist and his work by interpreting the difficult new forms of art in print and from the lecture platform. As for the artist, the whole situation has affected him as "outrageous fortune" of the worst sort. Under "normal" circumstances it has subjected him to public disapproval and neglect, left him without any secure or effective patronage, and rendered his calling an ordeal of sacrificial and often despairing love. Under abnormal circumstances, as noted in our mention of Nazi Germany, the negative pressure upon the artist could increase to the point of imposing complete collapse of creative effort and even of life itself.

As already suggested, the artists who suffered these difficulties were those in each recent generation who might be characterized — depending upon the observer's point of view — as the more "advanced" and "creative" or the more "extreme" and "degenerate." There has been another category of artist variously known as "conservative," "traditional," or "academic." This type, adhering to familiar conceptions of art, has in general met with public acceptance and received official honors, though still usually without sustained patronage. Bougereau (Fig. 96) dominating the *Salon* which consistently rejected Cézanne (Fig. 97) is one of the classic examples of the contrast between academic success and creative rejection. Inevitably, the conservative and the experimental artists have opposed each other's points of view and fought each other for the cultural honors of their day — usually with immediate success going to the former and ultimate fame to the latter. The antagonism between the two groups has added another skirmish to the "battle of the styles" and another conflict to the recent Western relations of art to society.

This tangled cultural situation has more often been described than analyzed. Allusions to the decline of patronage by the Church and the aristocracy indicate a vague sense that things are not as they have been of yore. Responsibility for the situation is sometimes placed upon the shoulders of the industrial *nouveaux riches* who, according to their critics, lack the tradition and taste necessary for the maintenance of art patronage. As to the failure of the general public to comprehend contemporary creative art, this is most often assumed to result from a kind of culture lag. Less preoccupied than the artist with esthetics, the layman is described as clinging to the familiar concepts of art by which his taste has been conditioned. But give him a generation or two, the right kind of critical guidance, and (we are told) he catches up, decorating his mantlepiece with reproductions of the work of the artists whom his grandfathers rejected — and incidentally paying for the reproductions a price for which his grandfathers could have secured the originals.

II

What light does psycho-historical thinking throw, either upon our recent cultural conflicts themselves or upon the explanations of them just suggested?

In the first place, it reveals an unconscious inconsistency in the mental attitude of those who condemn experimental art. According to our theory, forms of art are not primarily the willed creation of individuals but the expression of collective tensions generated by existent historical circumstances. At least this is so of all those forms of art that become sufficiently widespread to constitute styles and movements, as have the twentieth-century developments to which the public objects. Hence any criticism of such forms of art as bad or degenerate cannot be restricted to the art itself or to the artist who created it. The artist is only acting as a mouthpiece for his world. His art is one of symbolical reflections of that world. If, therefore, we condemn the art and artist, what we are unwittingly doing is to condemn the society that made them what they are and, in the last analysis, to condemn ourselves as members of that society and participating units in its cultural dynamism. To condemn the art and artist and to defend ourselves and our world, to assume a disparity and opposition between the two, does not make psycho-historical sense.

Unfortunately for the reasonable conduct of life, failure to make sense has never been a barrier to human action. When instinctive or unconscious forces seek expression, they all too easily override the barriers of reason. What is more, by the subterfuge of rationalization, they hide the fact from themselves, setting up a puppet reason to justify them. But in so doing they reveal, to an observer capable of analyzing the situation, some lack of integration between the rational and irrational forces of the mentality involved; some inner conflict which has resulted in the repression of real motives and the substitution of fabricated ones. Mental aberrations of this kind are presumably involved in the condemnation of creative art by those who fail to see their own intimate connection with it. What can be the cause and nature of this deflection in our cultural mentality?

Before answering this question, but in order to assist us in answering it more adequately, let us seek some historical perspective on the whole matter of the relations of art to society. So widespread and persistent has been the recent distaste for new developments in art that we might be tempted to regard it as a universal phenomenon —perhaps a kind of cultural growing pains inherent to the nature of life and of art. Such is by no means the case. There have been epochs in Western European and other cultures marked by entirely different relations of art to society than those with which we are currently familiar. During such periods, each creative experiment of the artists, each replacement of traditional forms by new ones, was regarded as an *improvement* upon the past, not as a destruction of something from the past that had been more precious. The community rewarded its most advanced — that is to say its most "extreme" — artists with enthusiastic response, financial security, and honorable station in society. The paint could scarcely dry on their work before the latter was withdrawn from the artist's hands for public or private enjoyment, sometimes with elaborate ceremonies of civic rejoicing.

When Duccio completed his *Majesta* in 1311 (Fig. 101), a municipal procession carried it from the artist's studio to its appointed place in the cathedral of Siena. An account of this procession has gone down to us and, though oft quoted, is worth rereading in the present connection.

"At this time the altarpiece for the high altar was finished, and the picture which was called the 'Madonna with the large eyes,' or Our Lady of Grace, that now hangs over the altar of St. Boniface, was taken down. Now this Our Lady was she who had hearkened to the people of Siena when the Florentines were routed at Monte Aperto, and her place was changed because the new one was made, which is far more beautiful and devout and larger, and is painted on the back with the stories of the Old and New Testament. And on the day that it was carried to the Duomo the shops were shut, and the bishop conducted a great and devout company of priests and friars in solemn procession, accompanied by the nine signiors, and all the officers of the commune, and all the people, and one after another the worthiest with lighted candles in their hands took places near the picture, and behind came the women and children with great devotion. And they accompanied the said picture up to the Duomo, making the procession around the Campo, as is the custom, all the bells ringing joyously out of reverence for so noble a picture as this . . . . And all that day they stood in prayer with great almsgiving for poor persons, praying God and His Mother, who is our advocate, to defend us by their infinite mercy from every adversity and all evil, and keep us from the hands of traitors and of the enemies of Siena." [2]

It would be impossible to imagine a sharper contrast in the relations of art to society than exists between the above scene and the fate endured by so many outstanding artists of the nineteenth and twentieth centuries. Imagine Paris declaring a holiday in order to transport to the Louvre in triumph a new crea- tion by Van Gogh or Cézanne! Most of the time it would not even allow their works the brief recognition of the *Salon* — and this despite the fact that a generation or two later many of those same works were to be welcomed by the Louvre for the national collections and posthumously recognized as tri- umphs of recent art.

This difference of cultural situation can hardly be due to a superiority in Duccio's work as compared to that of recent artists like Cézanne. The con- sensus of critical opinion would undoubtedly deny such superiority; if anything it would probably accord Cézannea higher rank as a creative genius. Neither would there seem to be grounds for ascribing to fourteenth-century Siena a greater esthetic sensitivity and discernment than existed in nineteenth-century Paris. As the account of the Sienese procession indicates, a work of art in Duccio's time was not considered exclusively or primarily as an object of esthetic or critical attention. Siena acclaimed the *Majesta* first and foremost as an embodiment of socially conceived religious imagery that symbolized the community's intuition of its security and well-being. Size, nobility, and beauty, though enjoyable to the Sienese and mentioned in our quotation, were not enjoyed in and for themselves. They were enhancements, amplifications, vivi- fications of the even more profound and poignant sense of collective aspiration. This suggests that the fundamental difference between the two cultural situa- tions lay rather in the social than in the esthetic spheres — a suggestion which we can substantiate by further inquiry.

As a basis of investigation, let us follow the usual psycho-historical pro- cedure of correlating the given cultural phenomenon with its particular span and context of historical circumstances and then considering the psychological relations that might connect the two. In the present instance this will first involve determining which periods of Western European culture have experienced a positive bond between art and society, and which periods a negative one.

Leaving aside the uncertainties of the situation in Neolithic times, we can say with assurance that positive relations between art and society existed during the Dark Ages, the Middle Ages, and the Renaissance. Approval and renown were enjoyed by the successive generations of artists who carved the Viking prows and illuminated the Celtic manuscripts, who built the Gothic cathedrals and enriched them with altarpieces like the *Majesta*; who fulfilled the pictorial ideals of Renaissance Florence and Venice. When da Vinci completed his cartoon of the *Madonna with Saint Anne*, "the chamber wherein it stood was crowded for two days by men and women, old and young; a concourse, in short, such as one sees flock to the most solemn festivals, all hastening to behold the wonders produced by Leonardo . . ." [3] Titian sometimes kept his patrons waiting for years because the demands for his work far exceeded his powers of production.

Signs of the reverse situation begin to appear in the sixteenth and seventeenth centuries. Differences of attitude between Michelangelo and his papal patrons did much to frustrate that unhappy artist and contributed, along with other premonitions of the times, to the unrest and foreboding of his work. Veronese was called before the Inquisition on the charge of making light of sacred subjects and was so called, if his inquisitors were typical churchmen of their times, by prelates some of whom stopped at no political or personal corruption.

It would probably be safe to say, however, that the earliest case on Western record of actual public rejection of a major creative artist occurred about the middle of the seventeenth century in the career of Rembrandt. The Dutch master began his work in an aura of renown and emolument. He ended it in neglect and poverty, though his later work is now universally recognized as greater than his earlier. Differences of outlook between the artist and his public were not the only causes of Rembrandt's later ordeal. Nevertheless they were important ones, as indicated by the crisis over the *Night Watch* and its rejection by the organization that had commissioned it.

Thus Rembrandt stood, as it were, on the divide between an earlier positive and a later negative slope in the relations of art to society in Western Europe. Up to his time, for a least a thousand years, the recognition of the creative artist by the community had been high. From his day to our own, an increasing number of the artists ultimately recognized as great were to experience rejection and frustration.

So much for the relations of art to society as a specific cultural phenomenon. What, now, about the general context of historical circumstances of which this phenomenon was or is a part? We have seen earlier in this book that historical circumstances improved during the Dark and Middle Ages as Western humanity emerged from the insecurities of earlier Neolithic life and developed the powers and resources of vigorous young agricultural civilization. Increasingly positive circumstances thus synchronized with positive relations between art and society during these periods. We have made no detailed historical study of subsequent periods, but in discussing recent changes of artistic style, we did have occasion to note that there has been considerable evidence of increasing negative stress in recent Western history. Although a complete analysis of these later historical circumstances cannot be attempted in the present connection, the reader is no doubt acquainted with their salient features. Here are a few reminders.

The same centuries that witnessed the growth of our recent conflicts between art and society either included, or were immediately preceded by, the religious conflicts of the Reformation and the Counter-Reformation and widespread disillusionment as to the power of organized religion to solve the basic problems of human security; social and political dissatisfactions so intense as to precipitate revolutions in America, France, Russia, and elsewhere; economic tensions manifestating themselves in depressions, strikes, antagonism between capital and labor, and even more acute antagonism between conflicting economic philosophies such as capitalism, socialism, and communism; the devastating spiritual effects and irreplaceable losses of two world wars; the collapse of great Western nations like Germany, and the weakening of Western power extensions like the Dutch, the French, and the British empires. As these lines are written in 1955, the world is tense with the fear of a third world war — a war which, if it comes, is expected to be monstrously intensified by the use of atom and hydrogen bombs.

If one wished to cite opinions of others in support of the view that there has been a multiplication of problems in recent Western life, such opinions would not be difficult to find. H. G. Wells, whose *Outline of History* was one of our pioneer efforts to gain universal historical perspective, saw the period beginning with the seventeenth century as "an interregnum . . . in the consolidation of human affairs, a phase of the type the Chinese analists would call an 'Age of Confusion.' This interregnum has lasted as long as that between the fall of the Western Empire and the crowning of Charlemagne in Rome. We are living in it today. It may be drawing to its close; we cannot tell yet. The old leading ideas had broken down, a medley of new and untried projects and suggestions perplexed men's minds and actions . . ."[4] Oswald Spengler based his hypothesis of "the decline of the west" on what he regarded as the law of cyclic old age. In the interval between the first two world wars Salvador Dali could write in his autobiography, with retrospect and prophecy equally poignant: "The Europe that we loved was sinking amid the ruins of contemporary history — ruins without memory and without glory, the enemy of all of us . . ."[5]

Some two decades later Bertrand Russell — and it is significant of the westward march of empire that he wrote in America — gave the theme of our tensions one of its most startling expressions to date. In an article entitled *If We Are to Survive This Dark Time*, he writes, "There is only too much reason to fear that Western civilization, if not the whole world, is likely in the near future to go through a period of immense sorrow and suffering and pain — a period during which if we are not careful to remember them, the things we are attempting to preserve may be forgotten in bitterness and poverty and disorder."[6]

It is true that recent centuries have witnessed enormous scientific and technological progress, with corresponding positive contributions to, or potentials for, human welfare. But, as our quotation from Wells suggested, the very rapidity of positive advance in these respects was fraught with negative repercussions: immensely increased powers of destruction, conflicts between persistent older systems and emergent new ones, a general undermining of traditional cultural patterns before new ones have adequately developed to replace them.

If at least it be granted that there was evolutionary improvement of Western circumstances during the Dark and Middle Ages, followed by some centuries of confidence and expansion, but more recently subject to increasing difficulties and insecurities, then our general course of historical circumstance has followed a path very similar in its main inclinations to that noted above with regard to the relations between art and our society. Both developments involve an earlier rise, a plateau of persistent elevation, and a later tendency to deteriorate.

The approximate correspondence between these two developments suggests what our whole psycho-historical conception would lead us to assume: namely that the relationships between art and society are neither an independent nor a haphazard phenomenon. Like all the other aspects of culture, they would seem to be a law-controlled manifestation of psycho-historical dynamics. They take their place, along with the style and subject matter of art, as another result of the energies and frictions involved in the interplay between circumstance, tension, and tensional expression. And like all the other aspects of culture, they obey opposite impulses at different stages of a cycle according to whether the cultural determinants active at the time are relatively positive or relatively negative.

The psychological principle underlying the changing attitude of a community toward its art may be accepted as the same which we invoked in connection with changes of style in the art itself: the tendency to welcome pleasure and the counter-tendency to resist pain. Just as increasing realism appears to accompany increasingly positive states of consciousness, so does an increasing alacrity on the part of the public to receive, encourage, and support the creations of its artists. Society, in other words, opens its heart to the manifestations of its faith in itself; welcomes the expressions and reminders of its own confidence and exaltation. At such times social assurance strains ahead so far and so fast that creative art has difficulty in keeping up with it. Public expectation is always there in advance, so to speak, eagerly waiting for the artist to confirm it in his work.

But when, for evolutionary or other reasons, a point is reached at which negative begin to overbalance positive determinants, then the conscious or unconscious counter-tendency emerges. Cultures, however ready to behold motes in the eyes of others, are strongly averse to perceiving beams in their own. When their own internal negative tensions begin to reach the surface in negative symbolism, they will to perceive no longer. They resist. A poet may cry, "Lest we forget! " but the unconscious will of society is determined to forget — determined to forget present cultural reality, determined, without realizing it, thenceforth to feed upon one degree or another of cultural illusion.

The social institutions of church and state withdraw their support from the further development of collective-dream imagery because they are unwilling to recognize their own implication in a negative cultural situation, and because they are afraid to attack difficult and unfamiliar cultural problems. Such minor patronage as they continue to offer, they shift from the ever-changing, reality-conscious creative art to a conventional art which is a wistful echo of a vanished past.

Thus there develops a growing rift between the type of art in which the community desires to see itself reflected and that which it actually motivates, and a consequent rift between the desiring public and the most sensitively motivated of its artists. The result is a period of conflict between art and society such as we have known during recent generations, and such as provided the point of departure for the present discussion.

The contrast between the attitude of recent communities toward artists like Van Gogh and Cézanne and that of earlier communities toward artists like Duccio, is fundamentally a contrast in cultural faith. Siena exalted Duccio because it received from his work a reflection of its own sense of collective fulfillment. In the age of Cézanne there remained no universally felt symbols of collective fulfillment because, as we have seen, circumstances were generating increasingly negative tensions in Western mentality.

Not being able to incorporate a social faith that did not exist, our art from the seventeenth century onward was increasingly forced into one or the other of two paths. It could detach itself from social concerns, which it did in turning to landscape and still life and to the more distinctively formal and esthetic preoccupations of movements like Impressionism and much of Post-Impressionism. Or it could express negative social reactions, which it did in its social-consciousness aspects from Goya, Hogarth, and Daumier to Kollowitz, Dix, Grosz and Gropper. In either case, knowingly or unknowingly, it reflected society's loss of faith, if not in itself, then certainly in the traditions and institutions to which it had been entrusting its destiny. Unwilling to face this cultural recession, unable to rise with the creative artist to the plane and the pain of negative self-realization, society justified itself by an indirect defense reaction. It rejected its creative artists, offering esthetic distaste as an excuse for its rejection.

Our findings up to this point can be summarized as follows. The relationship of art to society, like the nature of art itself, is determined by existing psycho-historical conditions. When those conditions tend to be positive, the relationship between artist and public will tend to be harmonious and mutually rewarding. Creative art will be understood and enjoyed without culture lag. Patronage for the artist will be assured. When the underlying psycho-historical conditions tend to become negative, the relations between artist and public will deteriorate into misunderstanding and conflict, patronage will wane, and creative art will meet with opposition and rejection.

III

If we accept the general principle summarized above, the problems of contemporary culture become at once more serious and more complicated than has commonly been recognized. Far from being mere questions of likes and dislikes, they are linked with social pressures involving the very foundations of community life. Our whole collective future will be determined, is being determined, by the way in which we deal, not with our cultural problems alone, but with the total psycho-historical situation of which they are an important and symptomatic part. Hence we cannot take our cultural conflicts too seriously nor devote to them too large a measure of our concern and effort. For what they may be worth, our remaining pages will be devoted to reflections on some practical aspects of the problem as related to programs of artistic and educational activity.

Favorably disposed critics, as we have noted, usually assume that public misunderstanding of contemporary creative art involves no more than an innocent unfamiliarity. Understanding has been lacking; there is a sort of esthetic or intellectual emptiness awaiting it, and the critic has only to fill the gap with the necessary information or insight. According to our analysis, the difficulty is more profound and less easily overcome. The public, we assume, intuitively understands the symbolical import of contemporary art but dislikes that import because of its negative implications. As a result it wills not to allow its intuitions to become conscious, represses them, and so finds expressions of the repressed material distasteful to it.

If this analysis is accurate, what we are confronted by is not a mental vacuum waiting to be filled, but a force of dynamic resistance. The records of psychoanalysis offer abundant proof that resistance of this kind can be diabolically cunning in its activities, and so powerful as to involve the whole structure of individual — and in our case, we may assume, of collective — personality. Hence, the educator concerned with the defense of contemporary art will hardly be dealing with reality if he conceives himself merely as the sage offering to fill a gap in public understanding. He might better — to speak in archetypes — consider himself a hero taking issue with a powerful monster; a monster which, if completely unleashed as it was in Germany, does not hesitate to inflict denunciation, imprisonment, and exile upon those who oppose it.

But like the bee which is said to kill itself in stinging others, the cultural monster can inflict penalties upon creative individuals only by exposing itself and its entire society to destruction. Creative expression reveals realities of community life. Creative repression does not change those realities; it merely refuses to recognize them. In doing so it builds up social illusion, and the result of illusion is eventual collapse under the impact of the reality that was refused recognition.

This relationship between social illusion and cultural repression, and the dangers to which it exposes any community, were dramatically illustrated for us by the Nazi regime in Germany. So vital for all of us is the issue at stake that we may well review the German situation in the present connection.

If excuses had any meaning for history, Germany might have been spared a great deal of punishment. Pre-Nazi Germany certainly had all the excuses necessary to make her subsequent actions, not justifiable, but comprehensible. She was faced with acute, indeed seemingly insoluble, problems of overpopulation, industrial overproduction, strife between capital and labor, and a defeated nation's handicaps in the field of international finance.

The republican government that followed the first World War labored at these problems with intelligence and good will but, as is likely to be the case in such complex social situations, its progress was painfully slow. The Nazis undertook to throw off the strain of these persistent tensions. Instead of continuing the effort to solve the basic problems, they sought to efface them arbitrarily by such social and military expedients as eliminating part of the population, forcing labor into a position of servility, and providing industry with the immense demands of a twentieth-century war machine.

The Nazi attitude toward culture was an integral and internally logical aspect of this flight-from-tension program. Experimental art has its existence in the search for symbols of existing cultural reality. Any force that determines to suppress the reality cannot do other than repress the symbols of it. Conversely, the impulse to create a political *personna* — a façade of arbitrarily willed order hiding the suppressed conflicts — will seek its reflection in a *personna art*: an art that obscures the features of cultural actuality behind a mask of cultural pretense. The more conventional forms of academic art provide a medium admirably suited to this purpose. They withhold from consciousness the effects of centuries of cultural change. They evade the symbols of perplexity; the requirements of effort and understanding. They make the world seem comprehensible, reassuring; in due measure wholesome, heroic, or seductive. Such was the art the Nazis substituted for the "degenerate" creative art which they banished from German culture (compare Plates 38 and 36).

Given Hitler's social premises, he was only proceeding to their logical cultural conclusions in this double program of suppressing experimental art and exalting academic art. The illusory nature of his premises and consequent deceptiveness of his conclusions has been demonstrated to the world by subsequent history. The war to which many Germans had looked forward as an escape from intolerable tensions, turned out in the end to be the *Götterdämmerung* of their escape mythology.

It would be an oversimplification to attribute the defeat of the Nazis and the downfall of the German people solely to their political and cultural substitution of illusion for reality. But certainly the second World War and its aftermath for Germany present us with a clear example of the fact that comforting illusion helps nothing permanently or fundamentally. If — perhaps an impossible "if" in Germany or anywhere else in our emotion-driven world — if Germany could have taken the difficult beauty of its experimental art as glimmers of a spirit that would promote the difficult solution of its underlying social problems; if it could have watched and waited for the insights which that beauty had to offer, sensitively preparing itself for self-revelation; and if — no doubt the biggest "if" of all — rival forces in the sphere of international commerce and finance had been willing and able to relieve Germany of their pressures, then it is conceivable that the German nation could have spared itself the devastation which was to follow. The flight from pain, in the sense with which we are here concerned, can lead to only one outcome: more acute and prolonged pain.

The importance of Germany's example for the rest of the world lies in the fact that the Nazi program was merely an intensificaton of tendencies observable in the recent cultures of practically all other nations, including our own. *Everywhere* for the past century and a half, as we have noted above, there has been a general preference for academic art, a general distaste for experimental art. *Anywhere* the subterranean pressures of difficult collective experience can generate a new intensification of illusion and repression. If, when, and where this comes about, history would doubtless repeat itself as to the ultimate consequences.

Apart from their immediate relationship to art and artists, contemporary conflicts between art and society are thus symptomatic of social dangers to which no man of good will would wish to have his community, or any other community, exposed. How can we combat and if possible overcome these dangers?

In principle, by opposing creative repression and supporting creative expression. In practice, by taking issue with repressive activity whenever and wherever it appears, by encouraging the creative artist, and by exhibiting and interpreting his work. So long as the artist is free to pursue his quest, the attitude of the community to which he belongs is at least open to the recognition of social truth and capable of continued contact with reality. If and when creative freedom is taken from the artist, freedom in general may be expected to collapse. Hence the experimental artist deserves double support: first for his creative achievements, second as a test individual with whose cultural fate is linked the fate of us all.

Almost as important as continued activity on the part of the artist is the public exhibition, reproduction, and discussion of his work. However "misunderstood" or ridiculed the work may be, it serves a valuable function which might be called cultural *confrontation*. It forces collective mentality to retain consciousness of the contemporary creative vision. So long as this remains true, the symbols incorporated in that vision can never be entirely ignored nor the interpretive effort to penetrate their significance entirely abandoned. There is thus a saving thread of connection between collective conduct and the collective dream; that is to say between collective conduct and the realities within which and upon which it must operate. If and when society loses all consciousness of contemporary cultural experiment, this last link between social and cultural reality is severed. Psychotically dangerous illusions like those of the Nazis then have no further opposition.

In discussing the difficulties faced by contemporary civilization, Jung wrote, "Such problems are never solved by legislation or tricks. They are only solved by a general change of attitude. And the change does not begin with propaganda and mass meetings or with violence. It begins with a change in individuals. It will continue as a transformation of their personal likes and dislikes, of their outlook on life and of their values, and only the accumulation of such individual changes will produce a collective solution." [7] Among the forces that can help to accomplish the "transformation of personal likes and dislikes," with accompanying changes of "attitude," "outlook," and "values," few are stronger than the demand for reorientation forced upon public consciousness by contemporary culture. Hence the social importance of creative cultural activity.

In addition to the creation and exhibition of experimental art, constructive cultural activity includes educational and critical efforts to interpret such art to the community. All efforts of this kind are beneficial, since all promote the work of confrontation. If psycho-technic assumptions are correct, however, the more formal esthetic and critical approaches can have at best only a slight impact upon public consciousness in general. Perception and the pleasures attendant upon its sensitive exercise, considerations of artistic form and technique, are too conscious and rational to exert a profound influence upon the unconscious and irrational aspects of collective mentality. And as we have seen, it is these unconscious and irrational forces which are largely responsible, both for the art created at any given time and for the community's reaction to it.

Whether any educational or critical activity can have an appreciable effect upon the dynamics of cultural consciousness is by no means certain. Psycho-historical thinking does, however, suggest a possibility that might be worthy of experiment: the possibility of an approach to contemporary art that would seek to reach through and beyond the forms of art to the cultural depths from which they are emerging; and correspondingly through and beyond the perceptions of the observer to the personal depths which are, so to speak, a particular sounding of the collective ones. If deep could be opened unto deep in this manner, it seems likely that the same kind of reconciliation would take place culturally as takes place personally when psychoanalysis has revealed the roots of neurotic symptoms. Resistance to the new art would presumably cease and all related mental and emotional adjustments change accordingly from negative to positive inclinations. That which had been misunderstood and disliked would be understood and would have correspondingly improved chances of being liked.

In the terms of two contrasting psychic orientations described by Freud, the program here suggested might be said to replace the "pleasure principle" by the more inclusive "reality principle" as the basis for our cultural outlook. "It is quite plain," writes Freud in defining these two types of adjustment, "that the sexual instincts pursue the aim of gratification from the beginning to the end of their development; throughout they keep up this primary function without alteration. At first the other group, the ego-instincts do the same; but under the influence of necessity, their mistress, they soon learn to replace the pleasure-principle by a modification of it. The task of avoiding pain becomes for them almost equal in importance to that of gaining pleasure; the ego learns that it must inevitably go without immediate satisfaction, postpone gratification, learn to endure a degree of pain, and altogether renounce certain sources of pleasure. Thus trained, the ego becomes 'reasonable,' is no longer controlled by the pleasure-principle, but follows the *reality-principle*, which at bottom also seeks pleasure — although a delayed and diminished pleasure, one which is assured by its realization of fact, its relation to reality.

"The transition from the pleasure-principle to the reality principle is one of the more important advances in the development of the ego. . ." [8]

Is it not true that our customary approach to art is an extension of the pleasure-principle? A work of art, we assume, should please us by affording us experiences of beauty. If it does so, we like it and call it good. If it fails to do so, we dislike it and call it bad, opening the way for all those condemnations and conflicts which we have been considering.

Most of the controversies concerning experimental art have resulted from this point of view — which both sides share. "This work is distorted and ugly," say its opponents. "It displeases us and therefore it is bad art." "This work may in a sense be distorted," say its defenders, "but that does not make it ugly. On the contrary, its distortions are esthetically purposeful. They contribute to beauty of color and design, of form and expression. Once you grasp these esthetic effects, this art will seem beautiful to you and give you pleasure. Therefore it is really good art."

On the esthetic level there is truth of experience in both these statements. The second one, defending experimental art, offers the more comprehensive truth since it takes account of ultimate as well as immediate reactions, and of the fact that the one may be quite the opposite of the other. Historically, however, no purely esthetic program seems to have been able to resist the forces of cultural repression when they become extreme. The most that conventional esthetics can hold forth to a public bewildered by experimental art is the promise of modified responses which will ultimately afford pleasure. This is apparently too remote and ethereal a possibility to overcome, or even to withstand, cultural resistances and the social illusions with which they may be linked. Hence it seems possible that more significant results might be obtained by transferring the basis of approach from the esthetic pleasure principle to a cultural reality principle.

If this were done, esthetic considerations would cease to be the sole or even the primary concern of those who were attempting to understand or interpret experimental art. Naturally, the artist and critic would retain their interest in esthetic effects; naturally every observer would have some immediate esthetic reaction to the work which he viewed and would undergo some course of esthetic development as a result of his observations. But the question whether an individual observer, or the public in general, considered the work to be beautiful or ugly — whether, in other words, it gave the given observers pleasure or displeasure — would no longer be regarded as the ultimate basis either for justifying or condemning contemporary art. Whether we like or dislike a given type of art is irrelevant to the psycho-historical fact that art is a symbol and symptom of collective realities involving the fate of society. These realities, as art helps us to apprehend them, would become the matter of primary concern in the approach that we are suggesting.

An observer approaching difficult new forms of art in this spirit would not ask himself first and foremost, "Is this work beautiful? " or "How is it organized? " or "How does it fit into the traditions of art? " Instead his first observations might be, "Though at present incomprehensible to me, this work is presumably an expression of something significant about my world, my time, my own unconscious experience as a member of society. What can it be expressing in these respects? What kind of collective tensions, what kind of historical forces, could have given rise to it? What can be the destiny of an age that inspires art of such a nature? What spiritual attitudes, what types of adaptation does it suggest in preparation for the future to which history is leading us? "

Such an approach, even when rewarded by no illumined responses, would be realistic and receptive. It would at least liberate us from the evil of condemning what we do not understand. In so doing, it would help to protect us against the danger of cultural repression and the attendant dangers of social illusion and later collision with unrecognized reality.

When rewarded by illumined responses, as this approach would sometimes certainly be, it might well surpass all others in its possibilities of esthetic emotion and critical insight. Once we touch the symbolized psychic depths, the symbol is transfigured. Its form and expression are grasped, its beauty felt, not as independent and therefore limited entities, but as aspects of an unlimited totality within which and upon which all experience converges. The esthetic experience of a work of art expands into an esthetic recognition of the universe as we today are destined to know it. The critical interpretation of a work of art correspondingly becomes an interpretation of our position in that universe. Our esthetic sensitivity and critical perceptiveness are reintegrated with, and reinforced by, the dynamic pulsation of our whole existence.

An approach of this kind would make the experience of art what one suspects it basically should be, and in certain respects always is: a religious experience; an experience not of pleasure alone but of pleasure felt, or when necessity compels, pain accepted, as a phase of human destiny in a universe which includes but transcends both. It is perhaps not an accident — it seems to be a possible forecast of a new cultural integration lying beyond our present conflicts — that creative artists of the sensitivity of Rouault and Rattner have lately returned to religious themes not touched by most experimental artists for three centuries.

It is equally, perhaps socially an even more hopeful sign, that an increasing number of our religious institutions are turning from conventional to experimental artists for their architecture and its decorations (Plate 39). The church at Assy in the French Alps (Fig. 105) may be cited as one of the pioneer examples of this trend. The apsidal tapestry by Lurçat (Fig. 106) mosaics, stained glass, and altarpieces by Rouault (Fig. 107), Braque, Leger, Matisse (Fig. 108), and other artists, sculpture by Lipschitz, have made this modest village edifice a center of pilgrimage alike for the lover of contemporary art, for the faithful within the Church and, above all, for those who have been concerned about our crying need for cultural integration.

The voice of God, if it speaks in the twentieth century, does not do so in familiar phrases from the records of the past, but in mysteries from the creative depths of contemporary life. Experimental art is one of those mysterious writings on the wall which are in some sense divine revelations because they truly represent the forces controlling the destiny of society. If many of our religious leaders are prepared to face these current mysteries instead of limiting themselves to Biblical records of mysteries; if they are prepared to orient the mind and spirit of the community toward reality through contemporary mystery, then there is indeed hope for our cultural future. However hazardous our universe may sometimes be, it seems always to sustain the forms of life that succeed in sensing and adapting themselves to its changing reality.

The project at Assy is the more significant because, although a Catholic church, it has called upon the services of artists some of whom are anti-Catholic and some Communist. To this, sectarian minds have objected. But the promoters of the project, Canon Jean Devemy and Father Pierre Couturier, have insisted that insofar as concerned their use of art, only one thing was important: that it rank with the most significant art of its time. "The Church," said Father Couturier, "must lay priority on the creative genius of the artists, not on their beliefs." [9]

To recognize that reality is greater than belief or opinion; to realize that those who seek reality in a living religion must be receptive to reality in living art and, by implication, in all other fields of creative growth — that is a spirit rare and sorely needed in the world today. It is, as Devemy and Couturier rightly suggest, the true spirit of those Middle Ages which the Catholic Church professes to revere: the spirit of cultural integration and therefore of cultural health. In such a spirit there is a basis for the removal of illusion, the reconciliation of conflict, the cumulative growth of social unity through the progressive recognition of cultural reality. Churches like that at Assy — and their number is increasing both in Europe and America — offer us some of our most reassuring evidence that in the midst of our reeling, negatively threatened world, there may be seeds capable of germinating a positive future.

NOTES

I. Introduction

1. Sigmund Freud, *New Introductory Lectures on Psycho-Analysis*, translated by W. J. H. Sprott (New York: W. W. Norton, 1933), p. 208.

II. Psychoanalysis and the Interpretation of Culture

1. Sigmund Freud, *Leonardo da Vinci: A Study in Psychosexuality*, authorized translation by A. A. Brill (New York: Random House, 1947). Our brief quotations, in the order in which they occur, are taken from pp. 52, 113–114, 57, 114, 114, 116, 117, 111, 93, 92.

2. The reader who desires to refresh his visual impressions of all Leonardo's major works will find them excellently reproduced in the Phaidon Press volume, *Leonardo da Vinci*, with foreword and notes on the plates by Ludwig Goldscheider (New York: Oxford University Press, 1944).

3. *Ibid.*, p. 36.

4. Giorgio Vasari, *Lives of Seventy of the Most Eminent Painters, Sculptors and Architects*, edited and annotated by E. H. and E. W. Blashfield and A. A. Hopkins (New York: Charles Scribner's Sons, 1926), I, 48–50.

5. Lionello Venturi, *History of Art Criticism*, translated with notes by C. Marriott (New York: E. P. Dutton, 1936), p. 309.

6. *Ibid.*, p. 280.

7. *Ibid.*, p. 301.

8. Kingsley Davis, *Human Society* (New York: The Macmillan Company, 1949), p. 195.

9. *Ibid.*, pp. 205–206.

10. Otto Rank, *Art and Artist*, translated by C. F. Atkinson (New York: Alfred A. Knopf, 1932). My several quotations, in the order of their occurrence, are from pp. 139, 153, 138, 137, 354, 163, 177–179.

11. "Id" is the term used by Freud to denote the unconscious psychic reservoir of instinctual impulse. In one passage he describes it as "the obscure inaccessible part of our personality . . . Instinctual cathexes seeking discharge — that, in our view, is all that the id contains . . . In popular language, we may say that the ego stands for reason and circumspection, while the id stands for the untamed passions." Freud, *New Introductory Lectures on Psycho-Analysis* (W. J. H. Sprott), pp. 103–107.

12. *Ibid.*, p. 106.

13. *Ibid.*, p. 120.

14. *Ibid.*, p. 151.

15. Freud, *Leonardo da Vinci* (Brill), pp. 54–55.

III. Historical and Materialist Interpretations of Culture

1. Henry Adams, *Mont-Saint-Michel and Chartres* (Boston: Houghton Mifflin, 1913). The sentences quoted are taken respectively from pp. 12, 380, 73, and 29.

2. Reference will be made later to another example which, like Adams' book, is distinguished at its own level but limited to surface parallelisms: Erwin Panofsky's *Gothic Architecture and Scholasticism* (Latrobe, Pa: Archabbey Press, 1951).

3. Freud, *New Introductory Lectures on Psycho-Analysis* (Sprott), p. 198.

4. For an integral reprint of Buckle's text with valuable recent annotations, see H. T. Buckle, *Introduction to the History of Civilization in England*, New and Revised Edition with annotations and an introduction by John M. Robertson (London: Routledge, n.d.).

5. *Ibid.*, p. 902.

6. *Encyclopedia Britannica*, 14th Edition, XIV, 996.

7. Karl Marx, *A Contribution to the Critique of Political Economy*, translated by N. I. Stone (Chicago: Kerr, 1904). The quotations are taken respectively from pp. 15, 11, 11–12.

8. M. M. Bober, *Karl Marx's Interpretation of History* (Cambridge: Harvard University Press, 1948), p. 427.

9. Quoted in Lucy M. Salmon, *Why is History Rewritten?* (New York: Oxford University Press, 1929), p. 213.

10. Quoted in Harry Elmer Barnes, *A History of Historical Writing* (Norman: University of Oklahoma Press, 1938), p. 3.

11. G. V. Plekhanov, *Art, and Society*, translated from the Russian, introduction by Granville Hicks (New York: Critics Group, 1936), p. 48.

12. Bober, *Karl Marx's Interpretation of History*, p. 427.

13. F. Antal, *Florentine Painting and Its Social Background* (London: Kegan and Paul, 1947), p. 1.

14. A. Hauser, *The Social History of Art* (New York: Alfred A. Knopf, 1951), I, 65.

15. *Ibid.*, p. 287.

16. *Ibid.*, p. 294.

17. *Ibid.*, p. 64.

18. *Ibid.*, p. 70.

19. Freud, *New Introductory Lectures on Psycho-Analysis* (Sprott). This and the two following quotations are taken from pp. 241–245.

IV. THE THEORY OF THE COLLECTIVE UNCONSCIOUS

1. C. G. Jung, *Psychological Types*, translated by H. G. and C. F. Baynes (New York: Harcourt, Brace & Co., 1926), p. 211.

2. C. G. Jung, *Contributions to Analytical Psychology*, translated by H. G. Baynes (New York: Harcourt, Brace, 1928), p. 246.

3. Jung, *Psychological Types*, p. 211.

4. *The Basic Writings of Sigmund Freud*, translated and edited, with an introduction by A. A. Brill (New York: Modern Library, 1938), p. 497.

5. Sigmund Freud, *Collected Papers*, edited by James Strachey (London: The Hogarth Press and The Institute of Psychoanalysis, 1933), V, 116.

6. Sigmund Freud, *A General Introduction to Psychoanalysis*, authorized translation by Joan Riviere, preface by G. Stanley Hall (New York: Liveright, 1935), p. 324.

7. Karl Abraham, *Dreams and Myths: A Study in Race Psychology* (New York: Journal of Nervous and Mental Disease Publishing Co., 1913), p. 36

8. Lines from Herman Melville quoted as a prelude to Selden Rodman, *Portrait of the Artist as an American; Ben Shahn: a Biography with Pictures* (New York: Harper & Brothers, 1951).

9. Marius Barbeau, *Maîtres Artisans de Chez Nous* (Montreal: Editions du Zodiaque, 1942), pp. 218–219. This passage has been translated for present use by W. Abell.

10. C. G. Jung, *Psychology of the Unconscious*, translated by B. M. Hinkle (New York: Dodd, Mead, 1949), p. 402.

11. Jung, *Contributions to Analytical Psychology* (Baynes), p. 265. This passage is from an essay entitled "Psychological Foundations of Belief in Spirits."

12. Jung, *Psychology of the Unconscious*, pp. 79–80.

13. *Ibid.*, p. 497 n.36.

14. Pp. 319–320.

V. The Tension Imagery Process in Psycho-Historical Integration

1. Freud, *New Introductory Lectures on Psycho-Analysis* (Sprott), p. 131.
2. Freud, *Collected Papers*, V, 95.
3. *Ibid.*, p. 293. (Italics mine.)
4. Freud, *Leonardo da Vinci* (Brill), p. 117.
5. Jung, "On Psychical Energy" in *Contributions to Analytical Psychology* (Baynes), p. 15.
6. Freud, *General Introduction to Psychoanalysis*, p. 258.
7. *The Basic Writings of Sigmund Freud*, p. 195. The statement occurs in the introductory section of *The Interpretation of Dreams*. Freud is explaining why he includes many dreams of his own in demonstrating his method of interpretation.
8. *Collected Papers*, V, 115.
9. Throughout the present section the term "historical" will be used in the special restricted sense applicable to individual case histories. The purpose of the term in this connection is to emphasize the fact that actual events of the objective waking world have a necessary casual relation to the dream situation.
10. See *A General Introduction to Psychoanalysis*, pp. 322–323.
11. Freud, *A General Introduction to Psychoanalysis*, p. 321. (Italics mine.)
12. *Ibid.*, p. 106.
13. *Ibid.*, p. 110. (The italics in the quotations are Freud's.)
14. *Ibid.*
15. *Ibid.*, p. 111.
16. Sexual gazing impulse.
17. Freud, *A General Introduction to Psychoanalysis*, pp. 196–197.
18. *Ibid.*, pp. 119–120.

VI. Tension Imagery and Culture in Psycho-Historical Integration

1. See p. 51.
2. Abram Kardiner and Ralph Linton, *The Individual and his Society; the Psychodynamics of Primitive Social Organization* (New York: Columbia University Press, Fourth Printing 1947). The same material is summarized on a reduced scale in Abram Kardiner, with the collaboration of Ralph Linton, Cora du Bois, and James West, *The Psychological Frontiers of Society* (New York: Columbia University Press, Fourth Printing 1948), pp. 418–421.
3. Kardiner and Linton, *The Individual and His Society*, pp. 335–336.
4. Kardiner and associates, *The Psychological Frontiers of Society*, pp. 420–421.
5. Juan Larrea, *Guernica; Pablo Picasso*, introduction by Alfred H. Barr, Jr. (New York: Curt Valentin, 1947), p. 27.
6. P. 20.
7. Otto Klineberg, *Social Psychology* (New York: Henry Holt revised edition, 1954), p. 4.
8. *Ibid.*, p. 211.
9. Kardiner and associates, *The Psychological Frontiers of Society*, pp. vii–viii.
10. Ralph Linton, *The Cultural Background of Personality* (New York: Appleton-Century-Crofts, 1945), pp. 4–5.
11. Sigmund Freud, *Group Psychology and the Analysis of the Ego*, authorized translation by James Strachey (London: The Hogarth Press and the Institute of Psychoanalysis, Fifth Impression 1949), pp. 1–2.
12. *Ibid.*, p. 92.

13. Jackson Steward Lincoln, *The Dream in Primitive Cultures* (London: Crescent Press, 1935).

14. *Ibid.*, p. 50. He is quoting B. Laufer, "Inspirational Dreams in Eastern Asia," *Journal of American Folk Lore*, 44: 208–216, 1931.

VII. Myth and Near Myth in Psycho-Historical Integration

1. P. 70.

2. Ruth Landes, "The Abnormal among the Ojibwa Indians," *Journal of Abnormal and Social Psychology*, vol. 33, no. 1, January 1938, pp. 24–26.

3. Vilhjalmur Stefansson, *My Life with the Eskimo* (New York: Macmillan, 1919), pp. 170–172.

4. My former friend and colleague, the late Dr. Hans Leonhardt, reminded me that a parallel and more momentous instance occurred when the Spaniards under Cortez first came into contact with the Aztecs and were regarded by the latter as supernatural beings. Unlike Stefansson's party, the Spanish were motivated by quite other than friendly intentions. The protection and favors which they received from the Aztecs enabled them, while still considered supernatural, to entrench themselves for military conquest and overthrow the Aztec state. Had the Aztecs not originally been confused by their own mythological mentality, had they recognized the Spanish from the first as human enemies, the outcome of the war between the two groups, and indeed the vicissitudes of white conquest in the Americas, might have been different.

5. *Ibid.*, pp. 183–184.

6. *Ibid.*, pp. 184–185.

7. For a carefully documented statement of this point of view see Acton Griscom, *The Historia Regum Britanniae of Geoffrey of Monmouth with Contributions to the Study of its Place in Early British History* (London, New York: Longmans, Green, 1929). Some relevant passages will be found on pp. 99–101, 195, 211–216.

8. Quoted by Carl Zigrosser, *Six Centuries of Fine Prints* (New York: Garden City, 1937), p. 30.

VIII. Tensional Transformation

1. *The Basic Writings of Sigmund Freud*, p. 181.

2. J. S. Slotkin, "Social Psychology of a Menomini Community," *Journal of Abnormal and Social Psychology*, vol. 48, no. 1, January 1953, pp. 10, 16.

3. Freud, *Collected Papers*, V, 114–116. The italics, brackets, and other details of the quotation are exactly those used by Freud himself. The original German version of the article quoted was written for Max Marcuse's *Handwörterbuch für Sexualwissenschaft*.

4. Sigmund Freud, *Remarks upon the Theory and Practice of Dream-Interpretation* (1923). *The Yearbook of Psychoanalysis* (New York: International Universities Press, 1945), I, 20.

5. Wilhelm Steckel, *The Interpretation of Dreams*, authorized translation by E. and C. Paul (New York: Liveright, 1943), p. 5.

6. Pp. 247–284.

IX. Correlation Summary

1. Klineberg, *Social Psychology*, p. 5.

X. Art and Myth in Medieval Western Europe — with Suggested Equivalents for Lost Predecessors

1. Louis Flaccus, *The Spirit and Substance of Art* (New York: Crofts, 1926), p. 253.

2. George Lansing Raymond, *The Representative Significance of Form; a Study in Comparative Aesthetics* (New York: Putnam, 1909), p. 309.

3. Joseph Pijoan, *History of Art*, translated by Ralph L. Roys (New York: Harper Brothers, 1927), II, 378.

4. Helen Gardner, *Art Through the Ages* (New York: Harcourt Brace, revised edition 1936), p. 323. In response, no doubt, to changing attitudes toward fantasy, the statement quoted has been dropped from the subsequent third edition of Gardner's work, issued in 1948.

5. Arthur Kingsley Porter, *Lombard Architecture* (New Haven: Yale University Press, 1917), I, 217.

6. Emile Mâle, *Religious Art in France, XIII Century*, translated by Dora Nussey (New York: E. P. Dutton, 1913), pp. 58–59.

7. Freud, *A General Introduction to Psychoanalysis*, p. 213.

8. *Le Morte D'Arthur; Sir Thomas Malory's Book of King Arthur and his Noble Knights of the Round Table*, with bibliographical note by A. W. Pollard and preface by William Caxton, two vols. (London: Macmillan & Company, Ltd., 1900). The passage quoted here and those immediately following are from vol. II, pp. 265–272.

9. G. G. Coulton, *Life in the Middle Ages*, four vols. in one, (New York: The Macmillan Company, 1930), IV, 110–111.

10. *Ibid.*, I, 157–159.

11. *The Romance of Tristan and Iseult*, retold by Joseph Bedier, translated by Hilaire Belloc and Paul Rosenfeld (New York: Pantheon Books, 1945), pp. 42–44.

12. *Beowulf and the Finnesburg Fragment*, translated from the Old English by C. G. Child (Boston: Houghton Mifflin, 1904). Our several brief quotations, in the order of their occurrence, are from pp. 37, 20–21, 22, 62, 63–64, 73.

13. Statens Historiska Museum, *Tiotusen Ar I Swerige*, I, 179. The passage was translated for the author by Miss Marta Larson.

14. See page 164 for quotations describing Gunnar's death. Identification of the carving with this subject is based on *Osebergfundet, Utgit av dem Norske Stat*, III, 349. The versions of the incident represented in the carving and saga differ from each other in some details.

15. Tacitus, *Dialogus, Agricola, Germania*, translated by W. Peterson and M. Hutton (New York: Putnam, 1932), p. 321.

16. *The Works of Samuel de Champlain* (Toronto: Edition of the Champlain Society, 1922–1936), I, 186–188.

17. See pp. 86–87.

18. André Gide, *Le Retour du Tchad*, vol. XIV in *Oeuvres Complètes*, edited by L. Martin-Chauflier (Paris: N.R.F., 1932–1939), p. 102. The passage was translated for present use by W. Abell.

XI. Myth and History in Some Neolithic Cultures

1. Freud, *A General Introduction to Psychoanalysis*, p. 213.

2. Champlain, *Works*, II, 46.

3. *Ibid.*, I, 110.

4. *Ibid.*, II, 53–55.

5. *Ibid.*, p. 56.

6. Edna Kenton, editor, *The Indians of North America from 'The Jesuit Relations and Allied Documents'* (New York: Harcourt Brace, 1925), I, 171–172.

7. *Ibid.*, II, 25.

8. *Ibid.*, II, 26.

9. Champlain, *Works*, II, 50–51.

10. *Ibid.*, II, 105.

11. Kenton, *The Indians of North America*, II, 277.

12. "The Interpretation of Dreams," in *The Basic Writings of Sigmund Freud*, p. 527.

13. Kenton, *The Indians of North America*, I, 16. The passage is taken from "The History of the Society of Jesus," book IV, part V, published in 1710.

14. *Ibid.*, I, 57. From a letter written by Father Charles l'Allemant in 1626.

15. Champlain, *Works*, I, 112.

16. Kenton, *The Indians of North America*, I, 110–111. From the *Relation* of 1634.

17. Gide, *Le Retour du Tchad*, pp. 102–104. Passage translated by W. Abell.

18. Champlain, *Works*, I, 114–115.

19. *Ibid.*, p. 115.

20. Kenton, *The Indians of North America*, I, 185.

21. A. C. Howland, editor, Caesar, "Extract from the Gallic War," in *Translations and Reprints from The Original Sources of European History* (Philadelphia: University of Pennsylvania, 1900), vol. VI, no. 3, p. 2.

22. Tacitus, *Dialogus, Agricola, Germania*, pp. 231–232.

23. Caesar's *The Gallic War*, pp. 2–3.

24. Tacitus, *Dialogus, Agricola, Germania*, pp. 285 and 329.

XII. Myth and History in the Dark Ages

1. Margaret Schlauch, translator, *The Saga of the Volsungs; the Saga of Ragnar Lodbrok, together with the Lay of Kraka* (Scandinavian-American Foundation, New York: W. W. Norton, 1930), pp. 169–170.

2. Schlauch, *The Saga of the Volunsungs*, p. xxv.

3. As our chief references on early Teutonic religion, we shall use four articles in the *Encyclopedia of Religion and Ethics*, edited by James Hasting, and others (Edinburgh: Clark; New York: Scribner's, 1917–1929). Unless otherwise indicated, quotations in the remainder of the present section are from one or another of these articles. As the sources are condensed and systematic, individual page references will be omitted unless a given quotation is of some length. The authors and articles, with the encyclopedia volume and page numbers are as follows: J. A. MacCulloch, "Abode of the Blest (Teutonic)," II, 707–710; K. Sudhoff, "Diseases and Medicine (Teutonic)," IV, 759–762; E. Mogk, "God (Teutonic)," VI, 302–306; B. S. Phillpotts, "Soul (Teutonic)," XI, 707–710.

4. J. von Pflugk-Harttung, *The Early Middle Ages*, from *A History of All Nations* translated by J. H. Wright (Philadelphia and New York: Lea Brothers, 1902), VII, 299.

5. F. A. Ogg, *A Source Book of Medieval History* (New York: American Book Co., 1908), p. 32.

6. Gregory, Bishop of Tours, *History of the Franks* selections, translated with notes by Ernest Brehaut (New York: Columbia University Press, 1916). The passages quoted above are taken respectively from pp. 165, 172, and 160.

7. Coulton, *Life in the Middle Ages*, II, 106.

8. Ogg, *A Source Book of Medieval History*, pp. 169–170.

9. Gregory, *History of the Franks*, p. 184.

10. Gregory, *History of the Franks*, pp. 236, 238. The complete account of the rebellion occupies pp. 236–243.

11. Gregory, *History of the Franks*, p. 186.

12. Bede, *Historical Works*, translated by J. E. King (Loeb Classical Library), II, 75.

13. Gregory, *History of the Franks*, p. 92.

14. Pflugk-Harttung, *The Early Middle Ages*, VII, 283.

15. H. St. L. B. Moss, *The Birth of the Middle Ages* (Oxford: Clarendon Press, 1935), p. 67.

16. J. W. Thompson, *An Economic and Social History of the Middle Ages, 300–1300* (New York: Century, 1928), p. 211.

17. The phrases from *Beowulf* quoted above, as well as those dealing with textiles, ships, and buildings to be quoted below, are from the edition translated by G. G. Child. Individual page references seem unnecessary in these cases.

18. W. L. Langer, *An Encyclopedia of World History*, revised edition (Boston: Houghton Mifflin Co., 1948), p. 166.

19. Langer, *An Encyclopedia of World History*, 143.

20. O. Thatcher and E. McNeal, *A Source Book for Mediaeval History* (New York: Scribner's, 1905), p. 48.

21. Langer, *An Encyclopedia of World History*, pp. 144, 145.

22. The *solidus* was a golden coin adapted by the Franks from the Romans and equalling 1/12 of a pound of gold. The *denarius* was a silver coin, forty of which equalled a solidus.

23. Thatcher and McNeal, *A Source Book for Mediaeval History*, pp. 15–18.

24. C. Delisle Burn, *The First Europe* (New York: W. W. Norton, 1948), p. 18.

25. To be quoted on pp. 190–191.

26. Langer, *An Encyclopedia of World History*, p. 144.

27. Thatcher and McNeal, *A Source Book for Mediaeval History*, pp. 44–45.

28. *Ibid.*, pp. 49–51.

29. Julius Pokorny, "The Origin of Druidism," in the *Annual Report of the Smithsonian Institution* (1910), pp. 585–586.

30. Thatcher and McNeal, *A Source Book for Mediaeval History*, pp. 438–440.

31. Thatcher and McNeal, *A Source Book of Mediaeval History*, pp. 49–50.

32. See R. W. Chambers, *Beowulf; an Introduction to the Study of the Poem and a Discussion of the Stories of Offa and Finn*, second edition (Cambridge: The University Press, 1932), p. 87.

33. K. Sudhoff, "Diseases and Medicine (Teutonic)" in the *Encyclopedia of Religion and Ethics*, IV, 760.

XIII. Myth and History in the Middle Ages

1. See *The Divine Comedy, Hell*, Canto XXXIV, verses 37–59, Charles Eliot Norton's prose translation (Boston: Houghton Mifflin Co., 1920), pp. 234–235.

2. Thompson, *An Economic and Social History of the Middle Ages*, p. 799.

3. G. G. Coulton, *From St. Francis to Dante* (London: Nutt, 1906), p. 150.

4. H. Pirenne, *Economic and Social History of Medieval Europe*, translated by I. E. Clegg (New York: Harcourt Brace, 1937), p. 196.

5. H. Pirenne, *Medieval Cities*, translated by F. D. Halsey (Princeton: Princeton University Press, 1925), pp. 80–81.

6. Thompson, *An Economic and Social History of the Middle Ages*, pp. 774–775 and 670.

7. E. B. Osborn, *The Middle Ages* (Garden City: Doubleday, Doran, 1928), p. 3.

8. H. O. Taylor, *The Mediaeval Mind* (New York: The Macmillan Co., second edition 1925), II, 502.

9. Pirenne, *Economic and Social History of Medieval Europe*, pp. 67–68.

10. See Lefebvre des Noëttes, *La Force Animale à travers les Ages* (1924) and the revised and extended *L'Attelage, Le Cheval de Selle à travers les Ages*, two vols. (Paris: Picard, 1931).

11. Lefebvre des Noëttes, *L'Attelage, Le Cheval de Selle à travers les Ages,* vol. I. See especially pp. 121–125 and 144–147.

12. E. Parmalee Prentice, *Hunger and History* (New York: Harper Brothers, 1939), p. 50.

13. Thompson, *An Economic and Social History of the Middle Ages,* p. 734.

14. N. S. B. Gras, *A History of Agriculture in Europe and America* (New York: Crofts, 1940), p. 48.

15. E. Lamond, editor, *Walter of Henley's Husbandry together with an anonymous Husbandry, Seneschaucie, and Robert Grosseteste's Rules* (London and New York: Longmans, Green, 1890), pp. 29–115.

16. *Ibid.,* pp. 99–100.

17. *Ibid.,* p. 117.

18. *Ibid.,* p. 89.

19. *Ibid.,* p. 107.

20. For translations of these poems see C. H. Bell, *Peasant Life in Old German Epics* (New York: Columbia University Press, 1931).

21. Pirenne, *Medieval Cities,* pp. 81–82 and 224.

22. Thompson, *An Economic and Social History of the Middle Ages,* p. 758.

23. Cattle pastures.

24. Pirenne, *Economic and Social History of Medieval Europe,* p. 76.

25. Thompson, *An Economic and Social History of the Middle Ages,* p. 518.

26. *Ibid.,* pp. 523, 526.

27. See Pirenne's *Medieval Cities,* pp. 117–119.

28. *Libellus de vita et miraculis S. Drodici, heremitae de Finchale, auctore Regil Reginaldo monacho dunelmensi,* editor, Stevenson (London, 1847). Discussed in Pirenne, *Medieval Cities,* pp. 119–121.

29. Pirenne, *Medieval Cities,* pp. 216–219.

30. Coulton, *From St. Francis to Dante,* p. 29.

31. E. G. Holt, editor, *Literary Sources of Art History* (Princeton: Princeton University Press, 1947), pp. 43–44.

32. *Ibid.,* pp. 45–46. This compilation also includes the other accounts of church building referred to above. See pp. 5, 34, 45–47.

33. A. C. Pegis, *Basic Writings of Saint Thomas Aquinas,* two vols. (New York: Random House, 1945), I, 19.

34. Coulton, *Life in the Middle Ages,* II, 35–37.

35. Thompson, *An Economic and Social History of the Middle Ages,* pp. 780–781.

36. *Ibid.,* p. 786.

37. Thompson, *An Economic and Social History of the Middle Ages,* p. 472.

38. *Ibid.,* p. 491.

XIV. Realism, Abstraction, and Psycho-History

1. A. J. Schardt, "Style," in the *Encyclopedia of the Arts,* edited by D. D. Runes and H. G. Schrickel (New York: Philosophical Library, 1946), p. 974.

2. Freud, *A General Introduction to Psychoanalysis,* p. 67.

3. Jung, *Contributions to Analytical Psychology,* p. 43.

XV. The Psycho-Historical Theory: Recapitulation and Expansion

1. J. Beldon, *China Shakes the World* (New York: Harper & Brothers, 1949), pp. 174–175.

2. *Ibid.*

3. *Ibid.*

4. Respectively, pp. 84–88, 107–111, 88–98.

XVI. SOME IMPLICATIONS FOR THE HISTORY OF ART

1. Pp. 120–121.

2. Emile Mâle, *L'Art Religieux du XIIe Siècle en France,* third edition (Paris: A. Colin, 1928), p. i.

XVII. TOWARD A UNIFIED FIELD IN CRITICAL STUDIES

1. See his *Religious Art in France, XIII Century,* pp. vii–viii.

2. Hippolyte Taine, *Lectures on Art, First Series,* translated by J. Durand (New York: Henry Holt, 1875), p. 30.

3. Venturi, *History of Art Criticism,* pp. 309 and 301.

4. Venturi, *History of Art Criticism,* p. 70.

5. Giorgio Vasari, *Lives.* My two quotations are taken respectively from I, 48, and II, 370.

6. Vasari, *Lives,* II, 372.

7. John Winckelmann, *The History of Ancient Art,* translated by G. H. Lodge (Boston: Osgood, 1872). Our two consecutive quotations are taken respectively from II, 4 and 21.

8. E. Viollet-Le-Duc, *Dictionnaire Raisonné de l'Architecture Française du XIe au XVIe Siècle* (Paris: Morel, 1882), I, 116.

9. Included in Taine, *Lectures on Art, First Series.* My quoted references are taken from the summary which Taine gives in chapter IX, pp. 157–161.

10. Riegl gives a general statement of his will-to-art theory on pp. 8–11 in *Spätromische Kunstindustrie,* Vienna edition (Wien. Osterr: Staatstruckerei, 1927).

11. Gilbert and Kuhn, *History of Aesthetics* (Bloomington: Indiana University Press, 1953), p. 547.

12. Wilhelm Worringer, *Form Problems of Gothic* (New York: Steckert, 1920), pp. 25–26.

13. Worringer, *Form Problems of Gothic,* p. 45 and again p. 146.

14. Viollet-Le-Duc, *Dictionnaire Raisonné,* I, 144–145.

15. Erwin Panofsky, *Studies in Iconology* (New York: Oxford University Press, 1939), p. 3. My remaining quotations are taken from the synoptic table, pp. 14–15.

16. Suzanne K. Langer, *Feeling and Form: a Theory of Art* (New York: Charles Scribner's Sons, 1953), p. 40.

17. Published by the American Society for Aesthetics, under the editorship of Thomas Munro. This journal is issuing its thirteenth volume during 1955–56.

18. See Flaccus, *The Spirit and Substance of Art,* part IV, "The Aesthetic Types" (New York: Crofts, 1926), pp. 225–337.

19. *Ibid.,* p. 226.

20. *Ibid.*

21. David Brewster, *Martyrs of Science* (London: Chatto and Windus, 1895), p. 196.

XVIII. THE VOCATION OF THE ARTIST

1. Frederick S. Wight, "Henry Moore: the Reclining Figure," *Journal of Aesthetics and Art Criticism* (December, 1947), pp. 95–105.

XIX. ART AND SOCIETY: CONTEMPORARY CULTURAL CONFLICTS

1. James Laver, *Whistler* (New York: Cosmopolitan, 1930), p. 187.

2. Holt, editor, *Literary Sources of Art History*, p. 69. The account of the procession was translated by Charles Eliot Norton from a medieval chronicle.

3. Vasari, *Lives*, II, 393–394.

4. H. G. Wells, *The Outline of History* (New York: The Macmillan Co., 1921), pp. 767–768.

5. Salvador Dali, *The Secret Life of Salvador Dali* (New York: Dial Press, 1942), p. 343.

6. Bertrand Russell, "If We Are to Survive This Dark Time," *The New York Times Magazine*, September 3, 1950, p. 5.

7. C. G. Jung, *Psychology and Religion* (New Haven: Yale University Press, 1938), p. 95.

8. Freud, *A General Introduction to Psychoanalysis*, p. 312.

9. Father M. A. Couturier, "The Assy Church; Famous Artists Decorate Chapel in Alps," *Life Magazine*, June 19, 1950, p. 72. For a more complete statement of this point of view, see Father M. A. Couturier, "Religious Art and the Modern Artists" in the *Magazine of Art*, vol. 44, no. 7, November 1951, pp. 268–272.

INDEX

PLATES

Fig. 1. Leonardo da Vinci. Madonna and Child with St. Anne.

PLATE 1

Fig. 4. Gentile da Fabriano. Madonna and Child.

Fig. 7. Correggio. Marriage of St. Catherine.

Fig. 3. Giotto. Madonna Enthroned.

Fig. 6. Leonardo da Vinci. Madonna and Child with St. Anne.

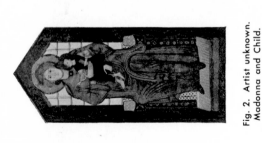

Fig. 2. Artist unknown. Madonna and Child.

Fig. 5. Fra Filippo Lippi. Madonna and Child with Angels.

PLATE 2

Fig. 8. Gnawing-Squirrel Totem.
Detail of Eagle's Nest Totem Pole.

Fig. 9. Akstakhl, a Haida Indian. Eagle's Nest Totem Pole.

PLATE 3

Fig. 10. Picasso. Guernica. (Collection Museum of Modern Art.)

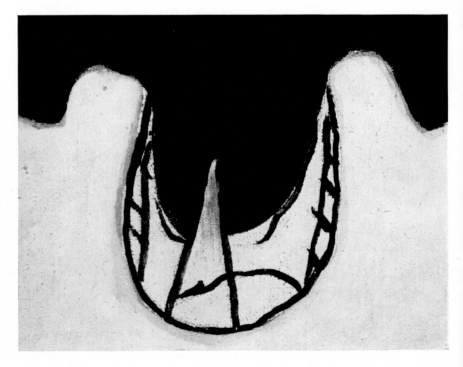

Fig. 11. Picasso. Woman's Mouth. Detail of **Guernica.** (Collection Museum of Modern Art.)

PLATE 4

Fig. 13. Fra Angelico. Coronation of the Virgin.

Fig. 12. Vermeer. The Little Street.

PLATE 5

Fig. 15. Perceval slays a Dragon. French School.

Fig. 17. Gargoyle.

Fig. 14. Dragon on Apsidal Parapet.

Fig. 16. Gargoyles above Apsidal Chapels.

PLATE 6

Fig. 18. Demon Carrying off a Woman.

Fig. 19. Potiphar's Wife and Demon in Dragon Form.

Fig. 20. Lion and Dragon under Feet of Christ
(le **Beau Dieu**).

Fig. 21. Nicola d'Apulia. Lion: Base of Column
Supporting Pulpit.

PLATE 7

Fig. 22. Giotto. Inferno.

PLATE 8

Fig. 23. Griffins Used as Ornamental Motif.

Fig. 24. Monkey Riding a Griffin. Misericorde.

Fig. 25. Demons Boiling in a Pot. Misericorde.

PLATE 9

Fig. 27. Demons Attacking a Man.

Fig. 26. Monsters and Demons on Voussoir of Portal.

PLATE 10

Fig. 28. Samson and the Lion. Lombard Relief.

Fig. 29. St. George and the Dragon. Tympanum.

PLATE 11

Fig. 30. Combat between Hero and Griffin. Relief in Facade.

Fig. 31. Dragon Swallowing a Knight. Tympanum.

Fig. 32. Men Attacked by a Dragon. Carving in Portal.

PLATE 12

Fig. 33. Man between Lionlike Monsters. Tympanum.

Fig. 34. Lion with Human Victim. Carving in a Portal.

PLATE 13

Fig. 35. Struggle of Chimerical Birds, Beasts, and Men.

Fig. 36. Man Attacked by a Bear. Capital.

Fig. 37. Combat of Monstrous Beasts. Relief in Portal.

PLATE 14

Fig. 38. Vestiges of Monster Combat.

Fig. 39. Lion from a Dismantled Church Portal.

PLATE 15

Fig. 40. Heroes and Monsters. Bronze Plate from the Vendel Period.

Fig. 41. Heroes and Monsters. Bronze Plate from the Vendel Period.

PLATE 16

Fig. 48. Gunnar in the Snake Pit.

Fig. 49. Temptation of Adam and Eve.

PLATE 19

Fig. 51. St. John. Page from the Book of Kells.

Fig. 52. Ornamental Carving on Yoke
of a Ceremonial Sledge.

Fig. 50. Tassilo Chalice.

PLATE 20

Fig. 53. Gateway ("Torhalle").

Fig. 54. Nave toward East. Church of Germigny-des-Prés.

PLATE 21

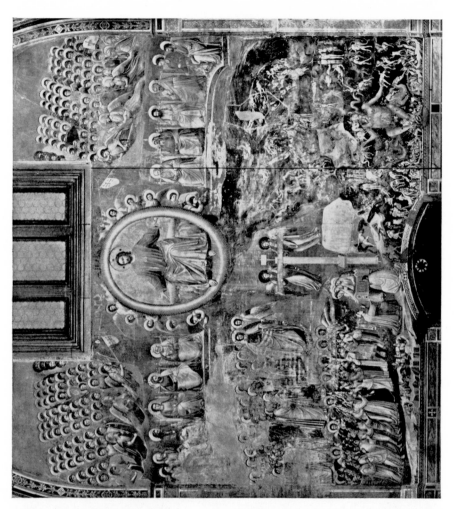

Fig. 56. Giotto. Last Judgement.

Fig. 55. Christ (le Beau Dieu). Trumecu.

PLATE 22

Fig. 57. West Front. Cathedral of Amiens.

PLATE 23

Fig. 58. Nave toward East. Cathedral of Amiens.

PLATE 24

Fig. 59. Heads, possibly King David
and the Queen of Sheba.

Fig. 60. Head of Angel. Detail of Annunciation.

Fig. 61. Abraham's Bosom.

Fig. 62. Giotto. Sts. Joachim and Anna.

PLATE 25

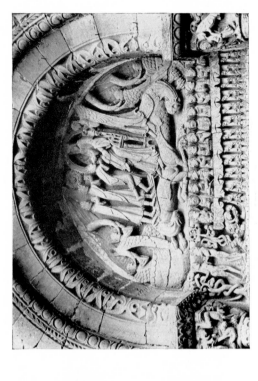

Fig. 64. Last Judgement with Chimerical Beasts. Tympanum.

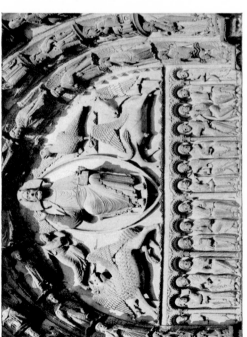

Fig. 66. Last Judgement. Tympanum.

Fig. 63. Samson and the Lion.

Fig. 65. Apocalyptic Vision. Tympanum.

PLATE 26

Fig. 67. City Gate. Aigues Mortes.

Fig. 68. Medieval Houses in Frankfurt am Main.

PLATE 27

Fig. 69. Choir and Apse looking upward toward Vault. Cathedral of Amiens.

PLATE 28

Fig. 70. Oxen on West Towers. Cathedral of Laon.

Fig. 71. Reaper, or Month of July.

Fig. 72. **Les Waidiers.** Carving on Facade.

PLATE 29

Fig. 73. Menhir du Champ
Dolent.

Fig. 74. Female Figure.

Fig. 75. Crucifix from Athlone.

Fig 76. Prophet.
In Main Portal.

Fig. 77. St. Firmin.
Trumeau.

PLATE 30

Fig. 78. Reindeer. Magdalenian Period.

Fig. 81. Raphael. Head of Madonna.
Detail of **La Belle Jardinière**.

Fig. 79. Animals and Human Figures.

Fig. 82. Picasso. Female Figure & Detail
of **Les Demoiselles d' Avignon.** (Collection
Museum of Modern Art.)

Fig. 80. Abstract Designs Painted on Pebbles.
Azillian Period.

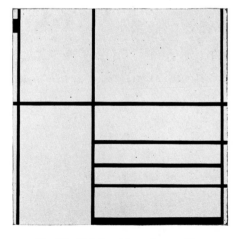

Fig. 83. Piet Mondrian. Composition
in White, Black, and Red.
(Collection Museum of Modern Art.)

PLATE 31

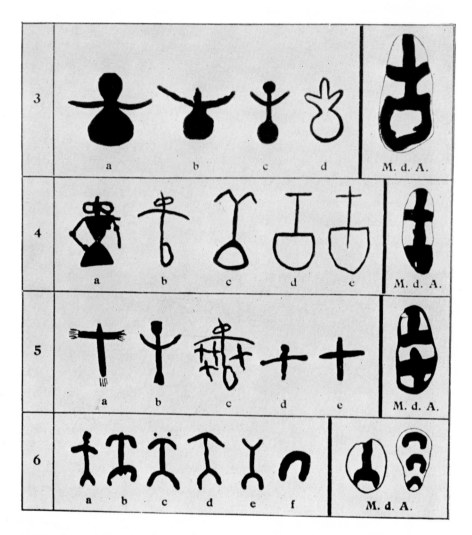

Fig. 84. Transformation from Representation to Abstraction in Terminal Paleolithic Art.

PLATE 32

Fig. 85. Sir Thomas Lawrence.
The Calmady Children.

Fig. 86. Verocchio. Colleoni.

Fig. 87. Palais de Justice. Rouen, France.

Fig. 88. D. Tintoretto. Battle of Salvore.

PLATE 33

Fig. 89. St. Matthew. Illumination
from a Byzantine Gospel Book.

Fig. 90. Venus
of Cirene.

Fig. 91. Toyonubo.
Ciran in Night Attire.

Fig. 92. Mirak. Laila and
Majnun.

Fig. 93. Mask from Ivory Coast,
Africa.

Fig. 94. Pre-Greek Idol
from Cyclades Islands.

PLATE 34

Fig. 95. Whistler. Nocturne in Black and Gold.

Fig. 96. Bougereau. The Bathers.

Fig. 97. Cézanne. Landscape with the Bathers.
(Louise and Walter Arensberg Collection,
Philadelphia Museum of Art.)

PLATE 35

Fig. 98. Max Beckmann. Departure. (Collection Museum of Modern Art.)

Fig. 99. Carl Schmidt-Rottluff. Rain Clouds, Lago di Garda.

Fig. 100. Paul Klee. Nearly Hit.

PLATE 36

Fig. 101. Duccio. Madonna with Child.

PLATE 37

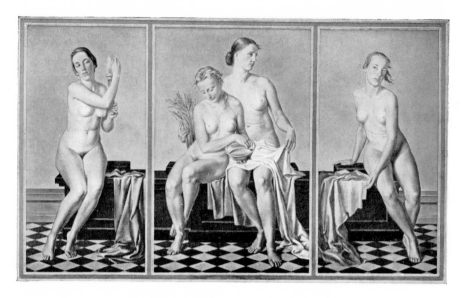

Fig. 102. Adolph Ziegler. The Four Elements.

Fig. 103. Leo Frank. The Hochter and
Reichstein Mountains with Approaching Storm.

Fig. 104. Raffael Schuster-Wolan.
Frau Emmy Göring.

PLATE 38

Fig. 105. Fernand Léger.
Mosaic of the Litany of the Virgin.

Fig. 106. Jean Lurcat. Apocalyptic Vision
of Life and Death.

Fig. 107. Georges Rouault.
Christ as Man of Sorrows.

Fig. 108. Henri Matisse. Saint Dominique.

PLATE 39